Triangulating Peace

Triangulating Peace

*Democracy, Interdependence, and
International Organizations*

Bruce Russett

John R. Oneal

W. W. Norton & Company · New York · London

Library of Congress Cataloging-in-Publication Data
Russett, Bruce M.
    Triangulating peace : democracy, interdependence, and
international organizations / Bruce Russett, John R. Oneal.
        p. cm.
    Includes bibliographical references and index.
    ISBN 0-393-97684-X (pbk.)
    1. International relations. 2. International organization.
3. Democracy. I. Oneal, John R. II. Title.

JZ1320 .R87 2000
327.1'7'01—dc21
                                                00-063794

W. W. Norton & Company, Inc., 500 Fifth Avenue, New York, N.Y. 10110
www.wwnorton.com

W. W. Norton & Company Ltd., Castle House, 75/76 Wells Street, London W1T 3QT

2 3 4 5 6 7 8 9 0

Contents

Preface   9

1 International Systems: Vicious Circles and Virtuous Circles   15

The Modern State System   16

Anarchy as a Potentially Vicious Circle   22

The Creation of Virtuous Circles   24

Background and Legacy of the European Achievement   29

A Complex System of Interactions Supporting Peace   33

The Kantian Triangle   35

2 From Democratic Peace to Kantian Peace   43

Democracy as the Focus   44

Two Dimensions: Pairs of States and Individual States   47

Theories of the Dyadic Democratic Peace: Culture or Structure?   53
The Convergence and Expansion of Theories   58
Common Interests   59
Interventions   62
Conflict Management   64
Why Do Democracies Win the Wars They Fight?   66
The Domestic Conflict–Foreign Conflict Puzzle   68
Civil Wars   70
Beyond the "Democratic" Peace   71
Democracy and Political Integration   74
Legitimacy, Liberalism, and Society   76

3   Democracy Reduces Conflict   81
The Epidemiology of War and Peace   82
What Causes or Constrains States' Use of Force?   85
A Database for Epidemiological Studies of Interstate Conflict   91
Militarized Disputes   94
Influences and Constraints: Democracy   97
Realist Constraints   100
Analyzing the Global Experience of a Century   104
Was the Effect of Democracy Different in Different Periods?   111
Peaceful Autocracies?   114
Are Political Transitions Dangerous?   116
More Democracy and More Peace   122

4   Both Democracy and Economic Interdependence
    Reduce Conflict   125
The Liberal Peace: Classical Perspectives and Recent Research   127
Analytical Problems   133
Testing the Effects of Trade   138
Trade Does Reduce Conflict   145
Are Open Economies More Pacific?   148
Economic Growth and Conflict   151
Economic Interdependence and Peace   154

5 International Organizations Also Reduce Conflict 157
Networks of Intergovernmental Organizations 159
Why and How IGOs Might Matter 161
Indirect Effects and Reverse Causality 167
The Analysis of Dense Networks 169
International Organizations Also Reduce Disputes 171
World War I as an Example 174
Systemic Changes over Time 177
Or Is It Hegemony That Reduces Violence? 184
Coercion or Persuasion? 191
The Three Kantian Legs 193

6 Virtuous Circles and Indirect Influences 197
Two Questions We Cannot Settle Here 198
United Nations Peace-Building through Democracy 200
The Effort in Mozambique 206
Do IGOs Promote Peace, or Vice Versa? 212
Who Trades with Whom? 218
Interests, Preferences, and Alliances 228

7 Clash of Civilizations, or Realism and Liberalism
Déjà Vu? 239
Civilizations and Identity 242
Exploring the Effects of Civilizational Differences 246
Designing a Simple Test 250
Civilizational, Realist, and Liberal Influences on Conflict 253
*What Are the Patterns of Conflict within and between Particular
Civilizations?* 255
Do Regional Hegemonies Reduce the Likelihood of Conflict? 260
Does the Clash of Civilizations Grow over Time? 262
Are Civilizations the Prime Mover? 264
The Insignificance of Civilizational Differences 267

8 The Kantian Peace in the Twenty-First Century   271

 The Evidence for a Kantian Peace   273

 Incorporating Russia and China into the Kantian System 282

 Russia's Options   285

 How to Avoid the Dangers of a Russia-China Alliance 286

 Why Not Bring Russia into NATO?   288

 How Would the Chinese React?   292

 The False Hope of Hegemony   297

 Appendix: Methods and Tables   307

 References   331

 Index   371

Preface

Triangulation is a surveyor's term for a means to establish one's location. It is employed in the Global Positioning System: a GPS unit held by someone in the field picks up signals from three NAVSTAR satellites in different orbits. Since the position of each satellite is known, the GPS unit at the point of intersection of the three signals can establish its own location. Triangulation in social science is far less precise than in the world of global positioning. Nevertheless, an assumption of this book is that the political situation of countries in international relations can be plotted with some confidence if one knows three pieces of information. More precisely, through careful statistical analysis, the chance that any two countries will get into a serious military dispute can be estimated if one knows what kinds of governments they have, how economically interdependent they are, and how well connected they are by a web of international organizations. Additional information can make that estimation better, but nothing can approach the precision of the GPS system. In world politics we get, at best, a rough estimate of the likelihood of conflict, analogous to locating us somewhere in the state of Montana. Yet we believe that's better than an estimate that can only say we are somewhere in North America.

The title is also an indirect allusion to Immanuel Kant's three-cornered intellectual construct of the structure of a peaceful world, which he believed was dependent on democracy, economic interdependence, and international law and institutions. This construct provides the basic inspiration for the book—not because Kant said it, but because we believe contemporary as well as classical theory, and much empirical research, support Kant's understanding. Intellectually, therefore, we also stand at yet another three-way intersection, that of contemporary thought, classical theory, and systematic empirical investigation.

This project has been a decade in creation and execution, with many journal articles and book chapters produced along the way. Both the theory and the empirical analyses, in interaction with each other, required extensive refinement. The book could not have been written without the work for the articles, as its empirical underpinnings slowly emerged. As J. Robert Oppenheimer once said about research, you put your two bits into the one-armed bandit and pull the handle. You never know what will turn up, and it is often lemons. We knew more or less what we hoped to find, as informed by our theory and our intuitions. But hopes cannot be allowed to produce self-deception; actually, we often felt we were pushing the envelope too hard and expected the results to disappoint us. In the end, however, we were not disappointed.

We hope the book will be intellectually credible to readers who are technically proficient in statistical analysis yet accessible to those who are not. That is a hard balance to strike, particularly when many methodological points are still in development and in dispute among specialists. Our solution has been to present our results in the text in as nontechnical a fashion as possible, with technical points largely relegated to footnotes. The appendix presents some of the estimations in a form more familiar to technically proficient readers, along with some discussion of the methodological issues and how we resolved them. Readers who wish to evaluate our technical decisions further should consult the various articles in which we have dealt with the issues of data creation and analysis in more depth. Because our work has already been extensively subjected to the peer-review process of professional journals and several articles are in print, we are able to skip some details here. Those who wish to explore these matters further using our new data set can get it from our Web sites: http://www.yale.edu/unsy/democ/democ1.htm or http://bama.ua.edu/~joneal/triangle_data.

Earlier versions of three chapters were initially written in collaboration with other authors: Harvey Starr (Russett and Starr 2000) for Chapter 2, Michaelene Cox (Russett, Oneal, and Cox 2000) for Chapter 7, and Allan C. Stam (Russett and Stam 1998) for Chapter 8. All, however, have been very substantially cut and added to, so while we deeply thank the initial coauthors, they are not responsible for the present form of the work. Chapters 5 and 6 incorporate a lot of material from other efforts (Bliss and Russett 1998; Oneal and Russett 1999a, 1999b, 1999c; Russett, Oneal, and Davis 1998), including those with coauthors Harry Bliss and David Davis, whom we thank; but this material has been thoroughly revised, condensed, extended, chopped up, and scattered throughout the middle of the book. We have redone all the empirical analyses with a common data set and a common theoretical model, bringing unity to the presentation and the substance. The revision differs in detail as well as organization, but the central conclusions of the original work remain intact.

The project required an immense effort of data collection, refinement, and analysis. Much of the data on militarized disputes, alliances, national capabilities, and international organizations originated with the Correlates of War Project, founded by J. David Singer; we, like so many social scientists of international relations, owe a great debt to those who have labored in that project. We owe a similar debt to the Polity III project of Ted Robert Gurr and Keith Jaggers for information on types of national political systems. Much other data-related work, as well as editorial tasks and management of various parts of the project, depended on the devoted and intelligent help of our assistants—Jennifer Beam, Margit Bussmann, Michaelene Cox, Karen Ellis, David Hennigan, Susan Hennigan, Soo Yeon Kim, Chris Lee, Viara Nedeva, Yuri Omelchenko, Brian Radigan, Jacob Sullivan, and David Yoon. Without them we would have lost the project and perhaps our sanity.

Many friends and colleagues have given us their comments and advice at various stages. While we risk forgetting some, we know they include Katherine Barbieri, Nathaniel Beck, Michael Berbaum, Stephen Brooks, David Davis, William Dixon, Michael Doyle, Bruno Frey, Nils Petter Gleditsch, Birger Heldt, Charles Hill, Paul Kennedy, Mark Lawrence, James Lindsay, David Lumsdaine, John McCormick, Zeev Maoz, Bruce

Moon, William Odom, Frances Oneal, Barry O'Neill, James Lee Ray, Gerald Schneider, J. Lew Silver, Allan Stam, Richard Tucker, Peter van den Dungen, Celeste Wallander, Peter Wallensteen, H. Bradford Westerfield, and William Wohlforth. And while we did not accept all their advice, the book is certainly much better for the critiques and comments of our tough but excellent editors: Roby Harrington, Jack Snyder, Rob Whiteside, and Ann Tappert.

Finally, the project was expensive and would have been impossible without financial support. We therefore have the need, and the opportunity, to thank those who shared our vision—at the Carnegie Corporation of New York, the Ford Foundation, the Norwegian Nobel Institute, the Korea Foundation, the John D. and Catherine T. MacArthur Foundation, the National Science Foundation, the U.S.-Norway Fulbright Foundation, and the World Society Foundation of Switzerland. We alone, of course, are responsible for the views presented here.

B.R.
J.R.O.
April 2000

Triangulating Peace

1

International Systems: Vicious Circles and

Virtuous Circles

We hoped to build our relations with Russia, Ukraine, and the other new independent states on the basis of democracy and free markets. . . . These nations had little in the way of democratic traditions, and we were far from certain that democracy would take root. But we did not want to create a self-fulfilling prophecy by pursuing a pure balance-of-power policy that assumed from the outset that these states would eventually return to authoritarianism. (Baker 1995, 654)

In this statement, James Baker, secretary of state under President George Bush, tried to address some of the central questions of international relations. They come down to these: Why can some states live at peace with their neighbors, neither fighting nor threatening them, while others seem to be constantly enmeshed in acts of violence and intermittent war? And why do some states, after a long history of conflict, change their basic relations and embark upon peaceful coexistence and cooperative relations? How are we to understand the dramatic turnaround in Soviet-American relations that ended the cold war, the harmonious cooperation between the United States and Canada, or the increasingly important relations between a growing China and the West? Certainly basic military and economic factors affect countries' relations with each other. But, as we will see, so does the character of their domestic politics, whether they share economic interests, and the extent to which they cooperate in international governmental and nongovernmental organizations. To comprehend these influences on national decisions for war or peace requires understanding the complex international system in which those decisions are made. This book is about seeking that understanding.

People who talk about world politics often refer to an international or global system. When they use the word "system," they imply that states, the units of the system, interact in a variety of ways within an environment of relatively stable conditions. Geography, the distribution of power, alliances and other international organizations, etc. constitute the environment of interstate relations and constrain national decision makers in important ways.

The Modern State System

In world politics, the actors most commonly considered are countries, often referred to as states. They are certainly not the only actors, nor always the most important ones. Other actors include international organizations, both intergovernmental organizations (IGOs) and international nongovernmental organizations (INGOs). IGOs are those whose constituent members are states. They are formed by treaties or other formal agreements and have some form of long-term organization. The United Nations, NATO, the North American Free Trade Agreement (NAFTA), the Association of South East Asian States (ASEAN), the African Telecommunications Union, and the Inter American Children's Institute are examples. INGOs are organizations whose members are either other nonstate organizations or individuals. INGOs are far more common than IGOs and include transnational organizations devoted to professional (the International Political Science Association), political (Amnesty International), religious (the Catholic Church), economic (trade and industry associations), and cultural (the English-Speaking Union) matters. Whether their purpose is overtly political or not, they may affect national and international politics profoundly. Even many nongovernmental organizations located wholly within a single state can have important effects. So, too, sometimes can private individuals.

The global system is comprised of all these actors. To some degree, they interact, affecting one another. A system consists of institutions, patterns of interaction, and causal relations linking its component units. Of course, many of the components do not seriously affect the system most of the time on many issues. For example, states may be the most important actors, but some states are more important than others. We start with states as the principal actors in the global system, but throughout the book we give considerable attention to how states are governed internally, to the economic linkages among them, and to international organizations. A narrow focus on states alone would give a very deceptive picture of how international relations work.

States are the institutions that govern the people within their territorial boundaries. The interstate system developed most deeply and extensively in Europe, beginning in the late medieval era and extending to the present. Although this process was gradual as well as uneven, many observers regard the Treaty of Westphalia, which ended the horrendously destructive Thirty Years War in 1648, as a key moment in the emergence of the European international system. In this treaty, the principle of sovereignty was central. The king (or queen, prince, or other royalty) was declared sovereign; legitimate rule within the realm's boundaries stemmed from him and this legitimacy extended to the ruler's offspring according to the principle of dynastic succession. As a means of managing the religious conflict between Catholics and Protestants that had inspired the bitter Thirty Years War, the treaty recognized a general right of the ruler to decide the religion of his people, although in many cases there was toleration and more than one faith was practiced within a country. Even then, however, the ruler had the right to make such decisions on behalf of those he governed, and other states had no right to interfere in this "internal" matter. Nor was there any superior authority over states and kings that could interfere. The power of both the Holy Roman Emperor and the pope was a thing of the past. States, at least in principle, were sovereign. They had "internal sovereignty," authority over their subjects and others living within their territories, and "external sovereignty," which gave them autonomy and independence of action vis-à-vis other sovereigns and powers. In theory, no external power had the right to tell a sovereign state what to do (Bull 1977).

Of course, not all states were of equal size or power, and weak states often had to accept a great deal of interference from more powerful neighbors. They might even, as a result of losing a war, lose their sovereign independence entirely, such as happened to Poland at the end of the eighteenth century. Nevertheless, the normative principle of sovereignty provided a guide to behavior that was considered both right and prudent. As such, it offered some protection to weaker states, which jealously guarded their rights. Strong states frequently did act with restraint, if only to prevent a breakdown of the new system and a reversion to the old—which would have meant a return to the intense competition among powerful states and frequent interventions in the affairs of the weak, just the situation that had led to the Thirty Years War. Restraint was strengthened by the common interest sovereign rulers had in reinforcing one another's claims to legitimate rule over their own peoples. Interference had the potential to undermine that general claim.

This system of competitive states has been called anarchic, but anarchy should not be equated with chaos. Derived from Greek, anarchy means "without a ruler." Certainly the Westphalian international system had no overarching authority, but even in anarchy there may be a good deal of order and predictability. Even antagonistic states could collaborate, coordinate, and cooperate in diplomacy, trade, and a host of other mutually beneficial activities. Yet because there was no superior power above the state to enforce the principle of sovereignty and punish rule-breakers, all rulers were dependent on the power they could muster, and their wits, to look after their own interests in the interstate system. It was a self-help system. This gave rise to the "security dilemma," whereby one state's actions, even if intended as defensive, nevertheless were likely to endanger the security of others. This aspect of the anarchic system meant there was always the risk of spiraling conflict and war.

The legitimacy of the system was thus reinforced when states followed the rules of the game; but when they violated them, the system threatened to break down into something nastier and more dangerous—either a free-for-all conflict or an effort by one state to become dominant and extinguish the independence of others. The French Revolution and the Napoleonic Wars posed this latter threat. The French republic proclaimed the doctrine of popular sovereignty: that the legitimacy of rule derived from the will of the people rather than from a dynastic ruler. This had wide appeal in Europe and so undercut the legitimacy of other states. In addition, Napoleon Bonaparte, drawing on popular enthusiasm, created a large nationalist army drawn from the mass of the French citizenry, rather than from professional soldiers and mercenaries. This nationalist army, combined with Napoleon's military genius, had the potential to overwhelm the old, more aristocracy-based armies of other states. Consequently, France threatened to become the dominant state, a hegemon, that could reduce all others on the continent to a more or less subservient status.

It took the other states of Europe, especially Great Britain, Prussia, Russia, and Austria-Hungary, nearly thirty years to bring the French challenge under control. Once they had succeeded, the victors recognized their close call. They learned from the near failure, and tried to revise the system even as they reinstituted it. Their formation of the Concert of Europe marked an effort, like the Treaty of Westphalia, to create an era of peace following a catastrophic period of Europewide warfare. The victorious allies tried to restore dynastic authority but in a form tempered to the republican spirit that could not be erased from Europe's consciousness. They also allowed France to recover and reenter the system as an equal partner in great-power politics. The Concert of Europe established certain normative principles: states have a right to security and independence, states should respect each other's legitimate interests and observe international law, and differences should be settled by diplomacy and negotiation. These rules were to be backed by military power: no state was again to aspire to dominance, nor be permitted to make the effort. Threatened by an expansionist state, other states would join together to "balance" (actually, overwhelm) the belligerent to guarantee their collective security (Watson 1992; Schroeder 1994).

This restored but modified Westphalian system worked reasonably well for a century. Since then, it has been repeatedly reaffirmed, and extended to the entire world. Two major challenges in world war, both led by Germany, threatened to establish a hegemon over Europe and perhaps the globe, but both challenges were beaten back by a large alliance created to preserve the system. Following each of these wars, the victors attempted to create a universal international organization whose purpose would be to prevent another great conflict while at the same time preserve the essential elements of the interstate system. The first of these, the League of Nations, foundered in part because the United States failed to join, despite the fact that President Woodrow Wilson was the league's most fervent advocate. It also failed because of institutional weaknesses, which left it unable to deal with the breakdown of the world economy during the Great Depression of the 1930s and the subsequent turn of many countries (Germany, Italy, Japan, and most of Central and Eastern Europe) to dictatorial rule. When those dictatorships waged war on their neighbors, the major powers in the league could not agree on whether or how to respond.

The United Nations, founded at the end of World War II, was also an organization that lacked, at the insistence of its member states, any substantial supranational authority. Perhaps there was the potential for it to develop over time into an institution with real power over matters of peace and security, but that potential was quickly lost as the cold war developed. In any case, the founders knew that the UN could not function as a powerful institution without agreement among the great powers. This understanding underlay the rule that any one of the five permanent members of the Security Council (the United States, the USSR, Britain, France, and China) could veto any action. The UN has always possessed some, limited means of modifying states' behavior so as to reduce the risk of war, but it has not been permitted to compromise its members' sovereignty in any fundamental way. Indeed, the organization has promoted the interests of sovereign states. As former colonial powers such as Britain, France, and Portugal yielded their overseas territories to independence movements, the UN become a principal instrument for expanding the state system throughout the globe and for protecting the principle of sovereignty as applied to newly independent states.

Since as early as the sixteenth century elements of a global economy had existed, tying together plantations, manufacturing industry, and consumers through the market. British, Dutch, Portuguese, and other traders, backed by their countries' naval power, were the principal creators of this system. The slowness and cost of transportation and communication, however, reduced the impact of these transactions. Although market towns and port cities across the globe were part of the system, millions of people were little affected. Hundreds of millions were not even organized politically into sovereign states. Beginning in the middle of the nineteenth century, however, modern technologies of transportation, communication, and weaponry extended the European state system, both its political and economic elements, into one that affected, directly and powerfully, the whole globe. The connections thus forged made the wars that began in 1914 and 1939 world wars. Even then, however, vast areas of the world, notably in Africa and Asia, were colonies of the great powers and were not yet organized as independent states.

After World War II, the role of international organizations in global politics began to catch up with economic and technological influences. The United Nations, under the influence of an ever-expanding majority of non-European states, helped delegitimize colonialism and assisted former colonies in securing their independence. Through this process, the global economic system, based on the rapidly evolving technologies of communication and transportation, was transformed into a global state system, one still organized according to the principles codified at Westphalia three centuries before. In particular the principle of sovereignty has been continually reaffirmed. A recent, notable example was the United Nations' approval of action by a large coalition to restore Kuwait's independence after Iraq's invasion in 1990. Quite a few states have seized pieces of others' territory since 1945, and a few have voluntarily surrendered their independence, as East Germany did in 1991. But it is important to note that in no case has a state's sovereignty been extinguished by force in the post–World War II period.

Leaders of the capitalist states who emerged victorious from World War II also laid plans to restore and stimulate the global economy. Delegates meeting in 1944 in Bretton Woods, New Hampshire, agreed to plans, put forth especially by the United States, to establish new global institutions loosely associated with the UN. One, the International Monetary Fund (IMF), was charged with stabilizing exchange rates for international currencies. A second, the International Bank for Reconstruction and Development, subsequently known more commonly as the World Bank, was initially devoted primarily to rebuilding the shattered economies of postwar Europe. As that task was accomplished, its attention shifted to supporting programs of economic development in the world's poorer countries. A third global institution, the General Agreement on Tariffs and Trade (GATT), was formed in 1948 to reduce tariffs and other barriers to international trade, on principles of reciprocity and nondiscrimination. Initially GATT dealt largely with trade in manufactured goods, but it ultimately expanded, as the World Trade Organization (WTO), to include all elements of international trade. Together these three institutions represented a compromise between national autonomy and international norms (Ruggie 1982). Although during the cold war most of the Communist states stayed outside of them, these global institutions deserve much credit for the enormous growth in international commerce and interdependence in the second half of the twentieth century.

Anarchy as a Potentially Vicious Circle

The anarchic system of sovereign states has maintained itself for centuries—though sometimes precariously. "Realist" theories of world politics emphasize that because there is no supranational government, the international system has the characteristics Thomas Hobbes attributed, in the seventeenth century, to a country undergoing civil war. (Hobbes wrote his book *Leviathan* right after a bitter civil war between royalists and republicans in Britain.) To Hobbes, chaos was the greatest danger: a war of all against all. An additional danger is the potential for strong states to establish hegemony over others in the international system. According to realist theories, for these reasons, states must always be vigilant. They must be prepared to act vigorously to confront emerging powers controlled by ambitious, aggressive leaders. Preferably they must act preventively, before the emerging power becomes too great. Consequently, military strategy may have a hair trigger. And states may feel obliged to react against emerging powers regardless of the others' intentions; for if the power of a potential adversary becomes too great and what seemed originally to be (or in fact was) limited ambition turns out to be something more, a challenge to a state's sovereignty could only be beaten back at great cost, or possibly not at all. The necessity for vigilance is especially great in periods when military technology and organizational doctrine are evolving rapidly or seem to favor the offense over the defense. If by quick and powerful invasion (like Hitler's blitzkrieg early in World War II) an attacker can overwhelm defenders, then even a defensive-minded state may feel obliged to strike first just to protect itself. It may not feel able to afford the luxury of waiting to figure out whether its opponent's intentions are, like its own, merely defensive.

Here then is an example of a potentially vicious circle, a series of strategic interactions within a Hobbesian system that magnify hostility and end in war—even though neither state originally intended it. The danger in international politics is that reasonable, defensive behavior can lead to a self-perpetuating downward spiral of action and reaction that produces an outcome no one desired. One state's military capabilities are seen to threaten another state, whether or not that is the intention. Indeed military leaders are trained to focus on the capabilities, not the intentions, of other states and to plan for the worst case because intentions can change. Frequently states regard their own intentions as clear and defensive and, to be prudent, regard their capabilities as relatively weak. But at the same time, they fear their adversaries are strong and expansionist. This was so in the crisis that produced World War I (Holsti 1972). The security dilemma may merely drive an escalating arms race or the competition for spheres of influence, but growing military capabilities, reduced diplomatic and economic contacts, and increasing distrust can end in a catastrophic war (Choucri and North 1975). Indeed, those who counsel a "realistic" strategy of military preparedness and constant vigilance because of the dangers of international politics may create a self-fulfilling prophecy (Smith 1986, 48). Of course, realists do not believe that war is equally probable with everyone, and states do not always assume the worst is likely to happen (Brooks 1997); but the Westphalian system is vulnerable to vicious circles.

The extreme form of an anarchic system is Hobbesian; a less severe form can be termed Lockean, after John Locke, another great seventeenth-century English thinker. In his *Second Treatise on Government*, Locke emphasized the need for a civil society to moderate the exercise of power. This need applies to international relations as well as to national governments. A sense of respect by states for one another's right to a sovereign existence is key to a Lockean international system, and over time that recognition has become more generally accepted. Respect for other states' sovereignty in itself does not abolish war, aggression, or seizures of territory, but it can help prevent them. Because all states wish to exercise the prerogatives of sovereignty, they may be reluctant to violate the sovereignty of others, especially by absorbing or eliminating them (Bull 1977; Wendt 1999; Doyle 1997). The experience of turning back Axis occupation of many states during World War II and then the liberation of many colonial territories strengthened adherence to that principle even more. By the late twentieth century, most of the world had accepted Lockean principles. The Middle East seems the biggest exception, although the eviction of Iraq from Kuwait in 1991 and recent developments in the Arab-Israeli peace talks show some progress even there.

The Creation of Virtuous Circles

There are also virtuous circles in world politics. Much of international relations involves peaceful interactions that are not seen as threatening but rather as mutually beneficial. These benefits can increase over time and expand in scope. What began as a vicious circle can sometimes be broken by deliberate policy and turned into a virtuous circle. Perhaps the most prominent case of such a reversal occurred in Western Europe after World War II. With tens of millions dead, their economies in shambles, and cities in ashes, the new European leaders consciously decided to break the old pattern of hostility and war. Those leaders, including Konrad Adenauer, Alcide de Gasperi, Jean Monnet, and Robert Schuman, did not make the change all at once simply by an act of will. Rather, they set up an intricate system of political, economic, and social institutions designed to reinforce one another, creating a set of virtuous circles that would both directly and indirectly promote peaceful relations. This system depended upon three elements that are key to "liberal" theories of international relations.

First was the *promotion of democracy*. The post–World War II European leaders believed that the breakdown of democracy had played a key role in destroying peace. Dictators had been aggressively expansionist, and World War II could readily be blamed on authoritarian or totalitarian states, especially Germany, Japan, and Italy. Even World War I could plausibly be blamed on the ambitions or incompetence of authoritarian rulers in Austria-Hungary, Germany, and Russia. The initial task, therefore, was to establish stable democratic institutions throughout Europe and to root out old nationalist and authoritarian ideologies. In this the victors were aided by the total defeat and discrediting of the old authoritarian leaders (some of whom were executed for war crimes) and by institutional changes put in place by the Allied occupation of western Germany.

The second element in establishing a virtuous circle was the *bolstering of national economies*. European leaders realized that authoritarian governments had arisen in large part because of the breakdown of the world economy in the 1930s and the poverty induced by depression. During the course of the depression, most governments tried to protect their own citizens' income by restricting trade; it seemed better to preserve jobs at home than to import goods produced by foreign workers. In its extreme form, this kind of economic policy leads to economic isolation, or autarky. Autarky has a basis in eighteenth-century doctrines and practices of mercantilism, which were intended to strengthen a state's security by promoting exports, controlling and discouraging imports, and producing an inflow of gold and foreign currency that the state could tap to build its power. The Soviet Union practiced a modern version of this extreme policy in its quest to construct an independent military and industrial base, and in various periods, so, too, did China and some other poor countries.

Even less extreme mercantilistic practices can turn into the kind of competitive imposition of tariffs and other trade barriers characteristic of the "beggar my neighbor" policies of the Great Depression (Kindleberger 1973). One of the countries hardest hit by this vicious circle of economic policies was Germany. The Weimar Republic, established in 1918 after the forced abdication of Kaiser Wilhelm, was distrusted by supporters of the old autocratic system. Only slowly recovering from World War I, Germany was especially damaged by the drop in global prosperity and trade of the early 1930s. Millions of Germans, impoverished by unemployment and inflation, turned away from democracy. They became ready to accept drastic action by Hitler, who promised to restore prosperity and their country's glory. After World War II, Europe's new leaders understood that real prosperity, and an approach toward American living standards, would require the efficiencies and economies of scale made possible by a market bigger than that of any one European country. The economies of Europe were relatively small, at least as compared with the United States, especially after the destructiveness of the war. Adenauer, de Gasperi, Monnet, and Schuman believed that democracy must rest on a foundation of prosperity and that the economic well-being of each of their countries depended on stable, cooperative economic relations among themselves and with others.

To this the leaders of the new Europe added a further insight. A complex network of economic interdependence would not only underpin democracy, thereby indirectly contributing to peace, it would also strengthen peace directly. Businessmen, companies, and workers with strong economic interests in other countries would naturally oppose war with those countries. If they were dependent on other countries for markets, for vital raw materials and other supplies, they would resist any policy or movement that threatened to break those economic ties. If international investment could be encouraged, capitalists would resist war, because to permit their country to attack another would risk the destruction of factories they owned in that other country. War would be economically irrational: those with important economic interests would suffer from war, and so they would use their political power to oppose policies that might lead to it. Consequently, European leaders in the late 1940s planned to open their markets to trade and investment with one another. They expected this to lead to stable economic relations, prosperity, and peace.

These efforts at economic integration began with the industries—coal and steel—then considered most important to an industrialized economy and especially to its war potential. In 1951, European leaders formed a new institution, the European Coal and Steel Community, designed to create a common market in these vital commodities, to facilitate investment across national borders and to insure that Germany could not again turn its heavy industries into a war machine. This was followed by a similar plan for the nuclear industry (Euratom) and others. Despite some concerns that a united Europe might become an economic and political rival to the United States, American policy makers encouraged this program of economic integration. Indeed, the United States insisted that its aid for European recovery from World War II, provided through the Marshall Plan, be coordinated by a new organization, the Organization for European Economic Cooperation. This ultimately became a global organization, the Organization for Economic Cooperation and Development (OECD), with members around the world, including a number of newly industrialized countries.

Thus emerged the third element in establishing a virtuous circle in Europe after World War II: the *construction of a thick web of international institutions*, based on the belief that trade and other forms of economic interchange would not develop unless there were organizations empowered to promote cooperation and to make rules that encouraged and protected that cooperation. European leaders therefore created international institutions that would promote freer trade in goods and services. As they did so, it became apparent that all the benefits of a free trade area could not be achieved if member states had radically different labor or social policies. True economic interdependence meant dismantling the regulatory barriers to free movement not just of goods but of services, capital, and workers, too. Travel and even immigration, for example, had to be freed of old restrictions. With the old regulations eliminated, then the legal gaps had to be filled by writing new regulations based on common principles. Common environmental policies and health standards were necessary if producers in countries with lax standards were not to have a market advantage over those in countries with strict controls. Economic policies had to be coordinated, and fluctuations in the relative value of national currencies brought under control. Therefore, one form of economic liberalization led almost inevitably to others in related areas of activity. This process is called "spillover": institutions built to fulfill particular needs or functions create the necessity for cooperation in other, related areas of society. Theorists of economic integration had foreseen that this would occur (Mitrany 1966; Haas 1958; Lindberg 1963): the European Common Market, once established, became the European Community and ultimately the European Union. At each stage of development the institutions assumed much broader functions. The process and institutionalization of integration was so successful that other countries wanted to join, bringing the EU to a total of fifteen members with more likely to join in the near future.

The EU clearly has elements of supranationality in its powers. It can collect taxes (called "fees") from its member states. The European Commission, one of the EU's principal institutions, can produce and enforce common regulations covering a wide range of activities. The Council of Ministers acts as an executive body in which important decisions concerning the internal market must be approved by a 70 percent vote in a weighted-voting scheme, meaning that a small minority of Europe's population cannot block action. The European Parliament is directly elected by the citizens of member states (though its powers are limited). The European Court of Justice settles conflicts between the separate institutions of the EU and takes referrals from states for the interpretation of EU regulations, and EU laws prevail over national ones. A non-EU institution, the European Court of Human Rights, has elaborated a bill of rights to which citizens may appeal against their national governments. For example, court rulings have required Britain to change its policies in order to permit gays to serve in its military and to restrict the use of corporal punishment in its schools. With the achievement of the Economic and Monetary Union among some of the EU members on January 1, 1999, the European Central Bank took over greater supranational authority than had been achieved by any institution since the founding of the European Coal and Steel Community, in this case, in the vital area of fiscal and monetary policy.

At the same time, much of what the EU does is as an intergovernmental body, and the member states preserve important elements of their traditional sovereignty. An attempt to form a European army through the European Defense Community failed in 1954. Recently, the Maastricht Treaty of 1991 declared that the EU "shall define a common foreign and security policy." Despite some steps in that direction, including strengthening of the Western European Union, the creation of a limited European military force for crisis intervention, and steps toward some kind of joint command, the member states still do not have a common foreign policy nor, in significant form, common defense institutions.[1] The breadth and success of the move toward full economic and monetary union is still uncertain. Most of the EU's citizens still direct their primary political loyalties to their particular states. Although elements of supranationality have developed much further in Europe than elsewhere in the world and citizens feel multiple loyalties, to Europe and to local units (such as Scotland or Catalonia) as well as to states, the system of separate states has not been abolished. But it has been made to work in ways far more productive of stable peace among those states and in line with the visions of the late 1940s.

This move toward European integration was begun during the cold war, when the security of Europe depended to a substantial degree upon the strategic protection of the United States and the United States was eager to see its allies more integrated and therefore stronger. Thus Western concerns regarding the global balance of power surely helped propel this process. It is also true, however, that this integration has expanded beyond the initial cold war allies, has become deeper than originally envisioned by most, and has outlasted the cold war. European economic interdependence and its political and economic integration did not depend on cold war imperatives. The European experience of the late twentieth century shows that it is possible to establish virtuous circles that solidify peaceful relations even while states retain many of their traditional Westphalian characteristics. And, as we shall see in subsequent

---

[1]On the EU's foreign policy, see Nuttall 1992. Other good discussions of the European experience with integration include Keohane, Nye, and Hoffmann 1993; Archer 1994; Urwin 1995. Armstrong and Bulmer (1998) stress the role of institutions, while Moravcsik (1998) emphasizes the importance of economic interests. A useful collection of documents is Nelsen and Stubb 1998.

chapters, peaceful relations can often be achieved even without such extensive institutional structures as the Europeans have now built.

Background and Legacy of the European Achievement

The post–World War II leaders of Europe were not the first to recognize that these three key elements—democracy, economic interdependence, and international institutions—had great potential to create a system of virtuous circles supporting each other and, together, underpinning peace between states. A number of eighteenth-century writers had theorized about the conditions that would produce a stable long-term peace. The most famous of these writers was Immanuel Kant, whose 1795 essay, *Perpetual Peace*, is still widely cited. Kant thought peace could be rooted in relations between states governed by three principles of conflict resolution. One is what he called "republican constitutions," which in the present era we interpret as *representative democracy*, with freedom, legal equality of subjects, and the separation of governmental powers. An understanding of the legitimate rights of all citizens and republics in turn creates, in Kant's view, a moral foundation upon which a "pacific union" can be established by treaty in *international law and organization*. Finally, what he called "cosmopolitan law," embodied in *commerce and free trade*, creates transnational ties of material incentives that encourage accommodation rather than conflict. Kant's vision was remarkably perspicacious for a time when he could have little practical experience with key parts of it. There were very few democracies in the world in the late 1700s and no international organizations as we now know them. Kant's vision was complex and subtle, and we will refer to it throughout the book. Our theoretical analyses and empirical tests build explicitly on his insights and those of the founders of the European Union.

Other classical writers stressed various elements of the same vision. There have been advocates of free trade for several centuries and from many countries. Their position came to be expressed most powerfully in the eighteenth and nineteenth century in Britain. Adam Smith linked free trade to both prosperity and peace in his famous book *The Wealth of Nations*, which was published in 1776. Later, Richard Cobden, a manufacturer and parliamentary leader, further developed this argument, suggesting that trade would both strengthen economic interests with a stake in avoiding the disruptions caused by war and serve as an instrument of communication to promote understanding between countries. We will consider the development of these arguments and their implications in Chapter 4. Hugo Grotius, a Dutch contemporary of Hobbes, was an early advocate of the pacific benefits of international law, which he believed could ameliorate conflict not only directly but also by providing a basis for the promotion of trade and a sense of community among states.

In the modern era, Woodrow Wilson expressed Kant's three principles in the Fourteen Points he laid out as the basis for a more peaceful world after World War I. Wilson did not explicitly invoke the need for universal democracy, since not all of America's wartime allies were democratic. But his meaning is clear if one considers the domestic political conditions necessary for his first point: "Open covenants of peace, openly arrived at, after which there shall be no private international understandings of any kind but diplomacy shall proceed always frankly and in the public view." Point three echoed Kant's notion of "cosmopolitan law" in demanding "removal, so far as possible, of all economic barriers and the establishment of an equality of trade conditions among all the nations consenting to the peace and associating themselves for its maintenance." The fourteenth point expressed his vision of a "pacific union": "A general association of nations must be formed under specific covenants for the purpose of affording mutual guarantees of political independence and territorial integrity to great and small states alike." He made this last the basis for the League of Nations.

In 1945, the founders of the United Nations were certainly realistic about the necessity of pursuing power politics in a dangerous world, but many also shared a commitment to incorporating Wilson's principles into their plans (Ikenberry 1996). These principles are clearly evident in the structure of the UN, with major units devoted to peace and security (notably the Security Council and the mediation activities of the secretary general), economic development and interdependence (especially the UN Development Programme, the Economic and Social Council, and UN-associated institutions such as the International Monetary Fund, the World Bank, and the World Trade Organization), and, following the Universal Declaration of Human Rights in 1948, human rights (UN High Commissioners for Human Rights and for Refugees, the Council on Human Rights, and the new International Criminal Court). Many of these institutions have developed their powers over the years, but they are not nearly as extensive as those of the European Union.

Europeans had learned from their historical experience, particularly the world wars of the twentieth century, what needed to change. They were aided in their efforts to reshape the regional interstate system by having begun from a greater degree of cultural and political homogeneity and a higher level of economic development than those which characterize most other parts of the world. Nevertheless, while Europe has advanced furthest in establishing the three Kantian principles, other areas of the world have also achieved substantial success but with less development of intergovernmental organizations. The United States, Canada, and increasingly Mexico constitute one such area; cooperation among the Nordic states another; and Japan's relations with the United States and other industrialized democracies both in Europe and the Pacific yet another. (Like Germany, Japan drastically changed its domestic and international policies following its World War II debacle. Japan, again like Germany, had some precedent in its history for this transformation: its period of Taisho democracy in the 1920s was marked by parliamentary politics and a wide franchise, and cooperative economic and political engagement with the world.) States within these three areas abide by Kantian principles and refrain from power politics.

Others have made efforts to break out of the vicious circle of fear, hostility, and war. Mikhail Gorbachev, the last president of the Soviet Union, deserves significant credit for ending the period of East-West hostility. Gorbachev was certainly not alone in bringing an end to the cold war, and his reasons surely were rooted in his understanding of what was best for his country and his own ruling group. Nor did he understand the full impact his policies would have, leading as they did to the political and economic collapse of the Soviet Union and the end of power for himself and most of those around him. Yet his actions changed the destructive pattern of relations in which the Soviet Union had become mired. As important as anything else, Gorbachev and his advisers accepted the idea that there are "universal interests and values" (Brown 1996, chap. 7; Wohlforth 1993, chap. 9). In this, they may well have been inspired by the success of Western Europe in establishing peace and prosperity based on the three principles discussed above.

Understanding the implications of democracy, economic interdependence, and international organizations may help us understand the end of the cold war: not simply why it ended, but why it ended prior to the drastic change in the bipolar distribution of power, and why it ended peacefully. In November 1988, British prime minister Margaret Thatcher proclaimed, "The cold war is over." By the spring of 1989 the U.S. State Department stopped referring to the Soviet Union as an enemy of the United States. The fundamental patterns of East-West behavior had changed, on both sides, beginning even before the razing of the Berlin Wall in November 1989, the unification of Germany in October 1990, and the dissolution of the Warsaw Pact in July 1991. Even after these events, the military power of the Soviet Union remained largely intact until the dissolution of the USSR on the last day of December 1991. None of these events was resisted violently by Soviet leaders.

Some of the actions that led to the end of the cold war were initiated by the West, and the West in time also reciprocated Soviet initiatives. Nevertheless, Gorbachev's policies of glasnost (openness) and perestroika (restructuring) were key to the unfolding of events. He instituted substantial political liberalization and movement toward democracy in the Soviet Union, with consequent improvements in free expression and the treatment of dissidents. Though his reforms fell short of full democracy, they were the beginning of a process of democratization, a major step in the journey away from authoritarianism. Notably, Gorbachev also permitted the process of liberalization to develop in the East European satellites, not just at home.

The Soviet and East European economies were in dire shape; they had been stagnant or in decline for a decade. In the early Stalinist years of the cold war they had been very autarkic, with most trade limited to the Communist bloc. Slowly they opened to the West, but the reform was insufficient. Gorbachev decided that imminent collapse of these economies could only be avoided by seeking economic interdependence with the West. This would allow the Soviet bloc access to Western markets, goods, technology, and capital. To get these, Soviet military and diplomatic behavior toward the West had to become markedly less antagonistic.

Gorbachev and the "new thinkers" around him also showed greatly increased interest in international organizations. In the late 1980s, perhaps anticipating political instability in parts of the empire they could no longer afford to maintain (outposts in Africa, Asia, Latin America, and even Eastern Europe), Soviet foreign policy leaders took a number of initiatives to revitalize the United Nations and considered innovative ways, including greater use of the International Court of Justice (Rosenne 1995, 258), by which it might be strengthened. When, after Iraq's aggression against Kuwait in 1990, the United States chose to work with and through the UN to legitimate American military actions, Gorbachev was supportive. Some other experiences of the Soviet Union's involvement with international organizations were unanticipated. The Conference on Security and Cooperation in Europe (CSCE, later the Organization for Security and Cooperation in Europe) and the human rights accords of the Helsinki agreements of 1975 were important for legitimating dissent in the Soviet Union and Eastern Europe. The Soviet Union did not repudiate these agreements and even came to see the CSCE as a potential bulwark for a new kind of political stability (Adler 1998).

One other world leader who has appreciated the importance of the Kantian principles and their interrelatedness should be acknowledged. Boutros Boutros-Ghali (1993, paragraphs 10–12), who was secretary general of the United Nations from 1992 to 1996, declared that the United Nations needed to support three interlinked efforts:

> The real development of a State must be based on the participation of its population; that requires human rights and democracy. . . . Without peace, there can be no development and there can be no democracy. Without development, the basis for democracy will be lacking and societies will tend to fall into conflict. And without democracy, no sustainable development can occur; without such development peace cannot long be maintained. And so it has become evident that three great concepts and priorities are interlinked, and they must be addressed at every level of human society.

A Complex System of Interactions Supporting Peace

The view of international politics as potentially cooperative, at least among large numbers of states, is by no means universally held. The Westphalian system is a European construction, and key realist thinkers such as Machiavelli and Hobbes wrote around the time of its origin, in the sixteenth and seventeenth centuries. Not only were the states of that era ruled by autocrats, but most were fairly self-sufficient economically rather than interdependent, international law was little developed, and international organizations were virtually nonexistent. (Grotius and Kant are interesting exceptions; both lived in small trading states, and the

Dutch Republic where Grotius lived was relatively liberal.) These characteristics remained true of the international system up to the nineteenth
century. (Cobden and the British liberals lived in a trading state that was
democratic, but the popular control of government was still limited: only
men with property had the right to vote, for example.)

Even in the twentieth century, the spread of the Kantian principles was
limited. The colonial systems established by the European powers remained in place until after the end of World War II, and the colonies
were, of course, not democratically governed. Nor were they allowed to
develop interdependent economic relations or participate in international
organizations. Understandably, leaders of countries outside the West are
now vigorous defenders of the concepts of state sovereignty and noninter-
vention. Moreover, early Asian theorists who wrote in periods of political
independence—such as Kautilya in India and Sun Szu in China, both in
the fourth century B.C.—observed Asian interstate systems that were very
like the Westphalian system that later developed in Europe. Their rulers
were autocrats, controlling substantially self-sufficient states, essentially
unconstrained by concepts of international law. The Communist tradition of Marx, Lenin, and Mao Zedong—still represented in somewhat
weakened form in China, North Korea, Cuba, and Vietnam—constitutes
another overlay of beliefs about the inherently conflictual and dangerous
character of international relations. Even now, democracies live close to
autocracies in Asia, where economic interdependence has become significant only recently and the network of international organizations is less
dense than in Europe or even Latin America. It is therefore hardly surprising that, to this day, many Asian leaders adhere more to realist views
than to liberal ones. Still, we have seen how, in a variety of historical
times and circumstances, some political leaders have tried to reverse vicious circles with a new pattern of behavior drawing upon mutually reinforcing influences for peace. Contemporary Germany and Japan, for
instance, having experienced disastrous consequences from abiding by
the principles of realpolitik, now largely follow liberal policies (Maull
1990–91).

We have reached a point in our discussion where we can think explicitly not just of an international system of states but of a multilevel system
that incorporates other important actors, such as IGOs and INGOs, that
influence states to behave in certain ways and constrain their actions in
others. We also include a wide variety of processes in our understanding

of a system: not just political processes but economic, cultural, and informational ones. Finally, our conception is of a dynamic system, one not simply maintaining itself in some unchanging equilibrium but able to evolve. We will argue that certain virtuous circles exist that are self-reinforcing. This means that the probabilistic generalizations we will make (democracy, economic interdependence, and international organizations make military conflict less likely; democracies are more likely to be interdependent; etc.) are apt to become stronger, and the system itself more stable over time. This evolutionary development is not inevitable, but there are good reasons to believe that it will continue, especially if leading states adopt sound policies.

The Kantian Triangle

A simple diagram helps in visualizing the three elements of the Kantian system and the virtuous circles connecting them that we will discuss in detail in this book.

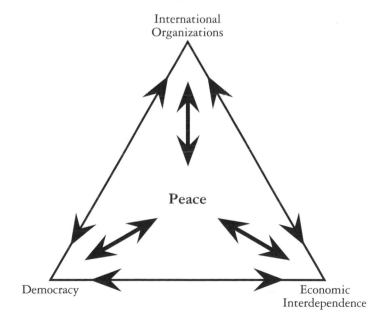

This schematic representation is a roadmap for the rest of the book. First, notice the arrows running toward peace from each of the three

points of the triangle. The one from the lower left (democracy) represents
the widespread understanding that democracies rarely fight each other. As
we will see, not only do democracies virtually never wage war on other
democracies, they are also much less likely than other kinds of states to
have serious military disputes or skirmishes with each other. Democracies
are also more peaceful in general than are authoritarian political systems,
although this proposition is more controversial and the evidence more
mixed.[2] We will look at the theories and some of the evidence for the
"democratic peace" in Chapters 2 and 3.

The arrow from the lower right (economic interdependence) represents the proposition that economically important trade and investment
limit the likelihood that a state will use force against its commercial partner. It draws on the theoretical tradition in support of free trade strongly
advanced by Smith, Cobden, and the other British liberals. It also finds
strong support in recent evidence. Critics of the argument that democracies are less likely to fight each other do not contend that democracies are
more likely to fight each other; at most, they maintain that democracies
act in the same ways autocracies do, that the character of a state's political
system is irrelevant in an anarchic international system. Critics of the argument that interdependence increases the chances for peace, on the
other hand, sometimes do take the stronger position that trade can increase military conflict. Others maintain that economic relations, like domestic politics, do not much influence the probability that military force
will be used. They claim that states fight over other issues, territory or access to resources, for example. In our view, the critical perspective on economic interdependence, in either its strong or weaker form, is not
supported by the evidence. We will take up these issues in Chapter 4.

Finally, the arrow from the top (international organizations) to the
center (peace) signifies that international organizations also make a direct

---

[2]A number of theoretical explanations have been offered to account for democracies' pacific relations with one another, and the evidence for the "democratic peace"
is substantial and diverse, though not undisputed. Chapter 2 discusses some of the
challenges, not so much to refute specific arguments as to illustrate the criteria for
evaluating a scientific research program. In the process of discovery, new generalizations are contested, in ways that are partly adversarial and partly "objective." New
claims are subject to modification as well as refutation. So far, however, the democratic peace proposition has held up well. Chapter 3 provides an illustrative empirical
analysis.

contribution to preventing and resolving conflicts between countries. This proposition implies that the more international organizations to which two states belong together, the less likely they will be to fight one another or even to threaten the use of military force. International organizations may reduce the likelihood of conflict in various ways. They may directly coerce and restrain those who break the peace, serve as agents of mediation and arbitration, or reduce uncertainty in negotiations by conveying information. They may encourage states to expand their conception of the interests at stake, promoting more inclusive and longer-term thinking; shape general norms and principles of appropriate behavior; or encourage empathy and mutual identification among peoples. Different organizations concentrate on different activities. We return to this topic in Chapter 5.

In addition to these three arrows, there are separate arrows returning to each of the corners from the center. The reciprocal effects represented by these arrows are important in understanding the international system. Democracy is easier to sustain in a peaceful environment. States involved in serious protracted conflict or militarized rivalries with other states are likely to have bigger military establishments, to restrict public information about key government activities, and to limit public criticism of those activities. In more extreme forms, external threats become reasons or justifications for suspending normal civil liberties, elections, and constitutional government. On the other hand, if the states relevant to democracies' security become themselves more democratic, the democracies will reduce their military expenditure and get involved in fewer conflicts, as the end of the cold war indicates (Maoz 1996). This factor, too, will require careful consideration later, principally in Chapter 6.

Trade is discouraged by international conflict and especially by war. States do not look kindly on their citizens who try to profit from commercial relations with a national adversary. Economic sanctions are a common tool of policy in dealing with hostile nations, either as an alternative or as a supplement to military means. During the cold war, the Soviet Union tried to maintain a high degree of autarky so as not to have its military capabilities dependent on the West. Western states, in turn, developed a system for restricting the sale of weapons and a wide range of military-related technology that could strengthen their adversary. Private traders are naturally reluctant to trade with, or invest in, countries with which political relations may at any time be violently disrupted.

International organizations sometimes are created to reduce or manage tensions between adversarial states. These organizations may seek to strengthen uncertain or ambivalent political relations, perhaps by encouraging arms control or by becoming involved in crisis management. The United Nations is an obvious example, organized with the full knowledge that peaceful relations among its members, especially the great powers, could not be taken for granted. Most IGOs, however, depend on reasonably peaceful relations among their members to be effective. They are devoted to promoting international cooperation in a wide range of activities, including diplomacy, trade and investment, health and education, and human rights, as well as mundane things such as postal services, the standardization of weights and measures, etc. They are most often formed when a certain level of peace seems probable.

These reverse arrows, or "feedback loops," create the potential for the virtuous circles we want to emphasize in this book. But there are also arrows along the sides of the triangle. Some of these links are speculative while others are quite well established, as we shall see in Chapter 6. We show, for example, that democracies are more likely to trade with one another, partly because, confident in peaceful relations, they do not feel that the economic benefits that accrue from trade will strengthen a state likely to become an adversary. They do not have such assurance with authoritarian states, as was the case during the cold war. Interdependence in turn may induce a certain externally supported pluralism that encourages democracy. Democracies are more likely than authoritarian states to form and to join many international organizations, and international organizations (such as organs of the EU and parts of the contemporary UN) may overtly support and strengthen democratic governments. For example, countries that hope to join the European Union in order to benefit from economic interdependence must first meet EU standards for political democracy. Finally, IGOs may be formed specifically for the purpose of promoting international trade and finance, embedding free trade in a structure of liberal international institutions to promote an integrated world market-based economy (Gardner 1980; Ruggie 1982; Murphy 1994). In turn, a high level of interdependence among states is likely to create a need for institutions to manage and stabilize their commercial relations; the World Trade Organization, for example, plays an important role in arbitrating disputes over fair trading practices.

We should also say something about the nongovernmental influences on world affairs that are not represented in our diagram or discussed in any substantial way in this book. Our focus here is on relations between states, and so we might risk overemphasizing the role of states or organizations formed by states as their agents. That would be a serious error. Peace between states is also a result of actions taken by transnational actors or international nongovernmental organizations, such as multinational corporations, churches, international labor unions, charitable organizations, and a wide variety of other groups, of which there are thousands in the contemporary world. These INGOs may promote democracy or attempt to influence the policies of democracies, foster cultural exchange, encourage interdependence, or support the activities of IGOs. Individuals, too, can make a difference. The Swedish industrialist Alfred Nobel did so by funding the peace prize that bears his name; so, too, have many of the winners of that prize over the years. But one need not do something so grand to affect international relations and promote peace. Studying abroad and culturally sensitive tourism count, too.

Not all of the arrows in our diagram are equally important. Some of our hypotheses may even prove to be unfounded. But if most or even many of them are true, as we attempt to show in the chapters that follow, there is a basis for a dynamic international system that is able to perpetuate and enhance itself. Peace between states, the special focus of this book, would comprise a key product of, but also an ingredient in, this Kantian system of virtuous circles. In such a complex, dynamic system, it is inherently difficult to identify one or two single "causes" and say that they are key. Particular relationships cannot readily be plucked out and considered in isolation from the others.[3] Nevertheless, we attempt to identify in the empirical analyses presented below those that affect most powerfully the prospects for peace.

It is also important to identify those processes most susceptible to human intervention and manipulation. Which influences can states, citizens, and private individuals most readily affect: the promotion of democracy, interdependence, or international organizations? The great

---

[3]In statistical analyses, which necessarily focus on only a few variables and relationships at any one time, the amount of variance explained by even the most significant variable may be relatively modest. The power of the hypothesized relations may only emerge from a set of analyses especially designed to pick up all the interactions and reciprocal relations.

forces of world politics may seem to influence and constrain us in ways over which we have little or no control. But human agents are not impotent against these great forces and structures. We hope to convince the reader in the following pages that there are sound grounds for optimism about the future of global interstate relations.

Different instruments will be available in different historical and regional contexts, so we need to consider when, where, and how they operate. In Europe after World War II, the most effective entry point in creating a virtuous circle may have been through promoting economic interdependence. In South America in the last decade or so, the effective entry point was probably the revival of democracy. Under military dictatorships, Argentina, Brazil, and Chile conducted an arms race in conventional weapons, especially in ships and aircraft. Argentina and Chile had serious border disputes that could readily have erupted into war, and the Argentine military actually seems to have wanted war in the 1970s and early 1980s. Argentina and Brazil were involved in a scarcely covert race to gain nuclear arms. All that changed, however, after the Argentine military regime was overthrown in 1983. This development was followed later in the decade by the restoration of civilian governments in Brazil and Chile. Between 1985 and 1994 Argentina's military budget fell from 3.8 percent of its gross national product to only 1.7 percent. Brazil decreased its military expenditures from 1.7 to 1.2 percent from 1990 to 1994. Argentina and Chile settled their border disputes with arbitration by the pope. Argentina and Brazil ratified the Nuclear Non-Proliferation Treaty and became fully compliant with the Treaty of Tlateloco, which established a regional nuclear nonproliferation regime in Latin America. They abandoned their nuclear weapons programs. In 1991, Argentina, Brazil, Paraguay, and Uruguay formed a regional trading market (Mercosur), and trade among the largest economies (including Chile) grew by 50 percent between 1991 and 1994. Thus the establishment of democratic governments in these countries was a sufficient condition for peace among them (Kacowicz 1998, chap. 3; also Hurrell 1998). Some of them had experienced peace for periods even under dictatorships. Yet conditions in the 1990s became much more cooperative, warmer than just a "negative peace" of no overt conflict, and a return to authoritarian government would put severe strains on their international relations. One means to prevent this is the provision of Mercosur that requires member governments to be democracies.

In contemporary East Asia, a region that is still far short of a generalized system of virtuous circles and where there are only a minority of stable democracies, the most effective entry point for the promotion of peace may again be through continuing growth in economic interdependence. North Korea, while holding tightly to its authoritarian political system, seems to be inching toward partially opening its closed economy. China, though hardly democratic, now has a ratio of foreign trade to GDP higher than Japan's and has come far toward a more open economy and better integration into global economic institutions. All the Kantian elements of change remain severely restricted in China, but major improvements have occurred. The strength of internal forces with an interest in maintaining and extending political and economic reforms and constructive engagement in world affairs suggests this is likely to continue. Still, it is possible to imagine circumstances—an economic slump, internal political unrest, or a deterioration of relations with the West—that could halt or even reverse this trend.

The downside is that, like vicious circles, virtuous circles can sometimes be interrupted or broken. Hobbesian thinking emphasizes the danger of vicious circles of military threats and the impossibility of breaking out of them. The first efforts to build a global system of peace based on Wilson's version of Kant's vision failed. They were imperfectly instituted, as the United States refused to join the League of Nations. International trade took a dive in the Great Depression, spreading misery rather than prosperity. A really deep and sustained economic downturn is probably the primary threat to a Kantian system. Newly established democracy proved fragile in much of Europe, Japan, and elsewhere. The Weimar Republic collapsed and gave way to Hitler, and Taisho democracy fell to Japanese militarism. The League of Nations collapsed, and the world was once again at war.

Another possible threat to a global Kantian system—a clash of civilizations—is addressed in Chapter 7. Our findings show this danger is greatly exaggerated. Chapter 8 considers the cost of failing to integrate Russia and China fully into the Kantian system and how that outcome might be prevented. The revived Kantian vision emphasizes the *possibility* of changing international politics, especially with the peaceful end of the cold war, from one dominated by vicious circles into something more constructive. The next century of world politics may build on the achievements of the past century, or it may see them reversed. A collapse of the world economy, a war triggered by an aggressive dictatorship, or a global environmental catastrophe could cause a collapse in the system that was so painfully constructed on the desolation of two world wars and a third, nuclear, near miss. Once broken, the same relationships in reverse could lead to a negative spiral: declining trade, failed democracies, further wars, and impotent international organizations. This would no longer be a Kantian system but would represent a return to a Hobbesian system of insecurity, economic decline, and war. Proponents of peace may be able to relax periodically, but they can never sleep. Every good thing must be re-won each day.

2

From Democratic Peace to Kantian Peace[1]

Truth has the property that it is not so deeply concealed as many have thought; indeed, its traces shine brightly in various places and there are many paths by which it is approached. (Galilei [1590] 1960, chap. 9)

We start from the observation that democracies very rarely, if ever, make war on each other. This statement, commonly known as the democratic peace proposition, should be considered a strong probabilistic observation (democracies rarely fight each other), rather than an absolute "law" (democracies never fight each other). In Chapter 3, we conduct statistical tests of the basic hypothesis that there is a separate peace among democracies. As in many analyses that we and others have reported before, we find strong support for this view. That democracies rarely fight each other is now generally, if not universally, accepted, so we do not

[1]Harvey Starr collaborated on an earlier version of this chapter (Russett and Starr 2000).

spend much time discussing it in this chapter.[2] Instead, we address a wide range of related issues to show the ways in which democracy, and other consequences of free choice, affect foreign policy. Doing so brings several benefits. It gives us a framework within which to place the empirical analysis of the next chapter, and it provides a springboard to the rest of the book, where we explore the full Kantian triangle for peace. The democratic peace thus becomes one of those phenomena that, as Galileo foresaw, shines unexpected light into many corners.

Democracy as the Focus

We begin by defining democracy. A democracy is a country where (1) most citizens can vote, (2) the government comes to power in a free and fair election contested by two or more parties, and (3) the executive is either popularly elected (a presidential system) or is held responsible to an elected legislature (a parliamentary system) (Dahl 1971). Democratic institutions appear most frequently in Western Europe and the states that once were part of the British Empire. Indeed, some critics call this definition culturally bound and ethnocentric, as not acknowledging systems where people may choose to vote for different individuals but political parties are not permitted or where there is little separation of powers between the executive and legislative branches of government. But systems sharing the characteristics of "Western" democracy now exist on every continent, and these characteristics have profound consequences for the way people govern themselves. For one, they insure that citizens will enjoy human rights and civil liberties, such as free speech and assembly. These characteristics—notably, control over the executive branch and the expectation that a leader who does not serve the interests of most of the people can be voted out of office—are key to theories about why democracies rarely fight each other.

[2] This conclusion is reached by three extensive review articles: Chan 1997; Ray 1997, 1998. Book-length studies supporting it include Bueno de Mesquita and Lalman 1992; Russett 1993; Singer and Wildavsky 1993; Ray 1995; Risse-Kappen 1995a; Maoz 1996; Weede 1996; Owen 1997; Rummel 1997; Weart 1998; and Gaubatz 1999.

Various scholars have rated the countries of the world over time according to how closely they approach the democratic ideal. They have used somewhat different specific criteria to identify democracies in an objective and comparable way. This is important because in social science and in this book we seek to make generalizations covering not only political systems in the contemporary world but also historical cases over an extended period of time. The practices and institutions expected of a true democracy have changed and evolved over time. It is not always easy to identify a democracy. Different rating systems, especially over long periods, produce somewhat different rankings of states.[3] This is to be expected when we consider democracy as a matter of degree rather than of kind. The world is not neatly divided into democracies and dictatorships, nor is any democracy in the real world a perfect one. Some, like those in Scandinavia, come closer to the theoretical ideal than do others. Others, like contemporary Russia, meet most elements of the definition formally but concentrate so much power in the executive branch that no one can call them fully democratic. Consequently, we need a continuous scale that ranges from very democratic states to very autocratic—even totalitarian— ones, with mixed systems in between.

Several features of these rating systems are important to note. First, none was produced by a scholar who was involved in research on the democratic peace or had staked out a prior position as to whether the democratic peace proposition was correct. In fact, they were produced before many analysts took the democratic peace proposition seriously, or even knew about it. Rather, scholars produced the rankings primarily to study the political conditions within countries, for example, to learn why some governments are more stable than others or what political or social characteristics make democracy stronger or weaker.

Second, most of the rating systems were created by American social scientists, but a scholar from Finland (Tatu Vanhanen) produced one of the earliest. Thus, whereas all adopt the perspective of Western democracies and use similar criteria consistent with this view, not all reflect what might be considered a North American bias.

Finally, these systems, though compiled independently, are in substan-

[3]For example, see the Freedom House annuals beginning with Gastil 1978; Vanhanen 1984, 1990; Jaggers and Gurr 1995.

tial agreement, with correlations among the most prominent ones ranging in recent decades from above .80 to more than .90 (Jaggers and Gurr 1995; Bollen 1993). Furthermore, Jaggers and Gurr, the source we prefer, concur with Vanhanen on the key cases of big countries participating in big wars; both agree, for example, that Germany in the years before World War I had some characteristics of both autocracy and democracy but that overall it was less democratic than was Great Britain. Most important, the basic conclusion that democracies rarely fight one another appears to be solid regardless of the rating scheme used. Support for the democratic peace is, then, "robust": the conclusion is basically the same despite different tests and measures.

It is also now generally accepted, as a corollary of the democratic peace proposition, that pairs of democracies are much less likely than other pairs of states to fight or to threaten each other in militarized disputes less violent than war. This extension has survived very sophisticated scrutiny (e.g., Beck, Katz, and Tucker 1998), providing greater confidence for the conclusion about war between democracies.[4] This is important, as wars are rather rare historical events, which makes it hard to establish strong generalizations about them. Thus, in this chapter (and in our tests in subsequent chapters), we consider the incidence of conflict between democracies across a broad range of intensity and destructiveness. We address a variety of issues raised about the democratic peace and, in the process, provide an overview of theory and research. We do not attempt, however,

---

[4]Moving to low-level disputes does not just increase the number of cases. It also permits asking whether pairs of democracies are less likely to initiate such disputes, and also whether they are less likely to escalate them once they have begun. Usually the answer to both questions is yes (Bremer 1993; Maoz 1993; Russett 1993; Hewitt and Wilkenfeld 1996; Rousseau et al. 1996; Hart and Reed 1999). The low frequency of democratic-democratic escalations is important, since some game-theoretic perspectives suggest that a strong and well-known aversion to initiating wars between democracies could lead them, for bargaining purposes, to initiate or escalate crises with one another, knowing that the process would stop short of war. Senese (1997, 1999) claims evidence for within-crisis escalation between democracies, but he uses a more problematic escalation scale than do Rousseau et al. The most recent analysis finds that democratic dyads are only minimally less likely than others to escalate their disputes, but that pairs of democracies avoid war chiefly by not getting into lower-level disputes (Reed 2000).

a complete review of all the work on the basic finding that democracies rarely fight each other.[5]

This chapter is more about theory than empirical results. It is especially a report on extensions of research on the democratic peace. We are particularly interested in the propositions that plausibly follow from the initial one—that democracies do not fight each other—and whether these extensions are supported by evidence. We look at these developments as part of a progressive research program, one that brings the pieces together and integrates them. Deductive logic has produced a range of auxiliary puzzles or hypotheses that lead to encouraging empirical findings.

Two Dimensions: Pairs of States and Individual States

The most widely accepted assertion of the democratic peace project concerns the behavior of pairs of states. (Pairs are sometimes called "dyads," a term used often in this book.) The democratic peace is sometimes defended as an absolute historical statement about democracies and war. James Lee Ray (1995, 125) claims, for example, that none of the several possible exceptions to the rule "is appropriately categorized as an international war between democratic states," either because the states were not both democratic or because the conflict was not serious enough to be considered a "war." Since Ray wrote, there has been just one war between democracies, despite the

---

[5]Russett (1995, 1996a) addresses some early critiques of the democratic peace. The most thorough response to the quantitative critiques is by Maoz (1997, 1998). An edited collection (Elman 1997) uses a comparative case-study method. It reaches a mixed conclusion and suggests some modifications to the democratic peace thesis; it is marred by conceptual inconsistencies and the absence of any clear research design to guide the selection of cases. A proper framework for case studies must address the mystery of the dogs that do not bark. Focusing just on crises between democracies to determine whether the character of their political regime was critical to avoiding war ignores, for example, the question of why militarized disputes between them are so rare. One might address this question by comparing the behavior in crises of states involved in enduring rivalries where both states were at some times democratic but not at others. One might also systematically compare cases of crisis bargaining and management between democracies to such behavior between otherwise comparable autocracies or democratic-autocratic pairs.

continued expansion of the international system and the spread of democracy within it. The India-Pakistan conflict of 1999 is the exception.[6] Most proponents of the democratic peace both expand the range of conflict considered and more cautiously express the proposition as a probabilistic statement: democracies rarely use military force against each other even at levels of violence below the threshold of war. For wars, however, and allowing for some ambiguity in the determination of which states are democratic, joint democracy does seem to be virtually a *sufficient* condition for peace between two countries (Russett 1996a; Starr 1997a, chap. 7; Chan 1997).

This does not, of course, mean that joint democracy is a *necessary* condition for peace. Many pairs of states, particularly small ones far from one another (such as Uganda and New Zealand), have neither the opportunity nor the willingness to fight each other. They lack the military means to threaten or attack at great distance, and they do not have issues in dispute. Many other dyads that have both the opportunity and the willingness to fight are dissuaded from doing so by well-understood realist influences, such as a great imbalance of power. The weak know better than to make war, the strong know they can get their way without it. Alliance configurations or even domestic constraints unrelated to democracy may also effectively prevent states from resorting to force. Even two democracies may be constrained from fighting each other by power or other considerations although some popular movements are clamoring for a fight.

Nonetheless, the general pattern is clear: the pairs of states, or dyads, most likely to be at peace, whether we speak of wars or lower-level mili-

[6]The Polity data by Jaggers and Gurr label both countries democratic (Pakistan at 7, just at the usual cutoff point for characterizing a state as democratic rather than having mixed characteristics). Battle deaths probably did exceed 1,000 (the Correlates of War Project's criterion for a war), but many of those were of Islamic guerrillas, not regular Pakistani troops; thus, the conflict may not qualify as a true interstate war. Ethiopia and Eritrea clearly fought a war from 1998 to 2000, but Polity scores both right in the middle of the twenty-one-point combined democracy-autocracy scale (Eritrea at -2 slightly on the autocratic side and Ethiopia at +1). The border conflict between Ecuador and Peru in 1995 probably fell short of 1,000 deaths, and in any case, Polity rates Peru under President Fujimori's emergency powers as just +2, in the anocratic (mixed) part of the scale. Yugoslavia/Serbia is consistently autocratic (-5 to -7) in the 1990s. The recent Polity codings are from www.bsos.umd.edu/cidcm/polity/polity98.htm; conflict information is from Wallensteen and Sollenberg 1998 and a communication from Professor Wallensteen.

tary disputes, are those composed of two democracies. Two autocracies are much more prone to wars and disputes, as are dyads containing a democracy and an autocracy. Because democracy is a continuous variable rather than an either/or condition, perceptions regarding another state can differ, and disputes are more likely when one state is only marginally democratic than when both are clearly so.[7]

Perhaps the most prominent puzzle about the democratic peace pivots on the distinction between pairs of states and individual states. If researchers focus on individual states, they ask how the political characteristics of a state affect its relations with *all* other states rather than just with particular kinds, such as other democratic states. The big question is whether democracies are more peaceful in general (that is, when considered individually) than nondemocracies? There has long been skepticism that they are. The authors of an early investigation (Small and Singer 1976) are well known for asserting that democracies in general are as warprone as other states. They were so convinced of this that they even dismissed their evidence that democracies rarely made war on one another. They believed that the relationship was spurious, perhaps merely a result of democracies' being physically far apart. Almost all scholars now reject Small and Singer's second conclusion regarding pairs of democracies, at least in the twentieth century (Bremer 1992, 1993; Henderson 1998; chaps. 3–5 of this book). But their other conclusion, that democracies are no more peaceful in general than are other states, is still widely accepted.[8]

---

[7]Peceny (1997) makes this point in regard to the Spanish-American War in the context of a "constructivist" argument about the importance of perceptions in shaping people's sense of who is like them and who is different. Oren (1995) and Bachteler (1997) carry the constructivist perspective further. It is probably more useful to recognize that perceptions will vary concerning political regimes that are on the margins of the standard categories. It is also important to note that the categories themselves will vary over long periods of time.

[8]Even one author of this book leaned toward acceptance of what then was nearly a consensus: "Though there are elements of plausibility in the argument that democracies are inherently peaceful, it contains too many holes, and is accompanied by too many exceptions, to be usable as a major theoretical building block" (Russett 1993, 30–31). There have always been those who have accepted that democracies are more peaceful generally. Rummel is conspicuously in this group, as his recent book (1997) reminds us. The position has subsequently been advanced by Ray (1995), Benoit (1996), and Oneal and Russett (1997).

If it were true that democracies rarely fought each other but were not more peaceful in general, we would need a good theoretical explanation for that. Many people have tried to produce one. But if democracies are generally more peaceful than autocracies are, the implications are much more profound. Indeed, the emerging view seems to be that democracies are more peaceful overall, especially if we consider which states initiate militarized disputes (Rousseau 1996; Rousseau et al. 1996; Rioux 1998). Crises are more often initiated by autocracies. That democracies are more often the victim of aggression than its instigator is masked when one looks only at states' involvement in conflict. The effect of democracy on the likelihood of conflict at the level of the individual state is not nearly as strong as the dyadic effect that emerges when the interactions of two states are considered. This is one reason why so many people at first missed it. Two other reasons may help explain why the state-level evidence was initially ignored or underappreciated.

The first reason is that in the early stages of research, too few analysts thought in terms of multiple influences. A simple count of political systems and the number of wars or militarized disputes in which they were involved ignores the other influences on conflict, notably the challenges states face in global and especially regional systems. Since geographical proximity makes conflict more likely, it is important to know what types of regimes democratic states have as neighbors: one would expect those with many autocratic neighbors to have more conflicts than those largely surrounded by democracies. Throughout the nineteenth century and much of the twentieth, democracies were rare. Democracies, therefore, usually had autocratic neighbors, and if autocracies are prone to conflict (as we contend they are), we would expect the few democracies to have been involved in many disputes with them. For example, France has long been a democracy, but until the end of World War II many of the states on its borders were autocracies (Germany, Italy, Spain), so France was involved in frequent wars. Now, as more and more countries become democratic, France and other democracies are increasingly peaceful (Gleditsch and Hegre 1997).

This means it is important to situate each country within its politically relevant environment, looking at the network of relations it has with its neighbors and with the great powers. We must also consider whether these states were allies or significant trading partners, and we must estimate the balance of power among them. As we would expect if they are generally more peaceful than other states, democracies have had lower military expenditures and have experienced far less international conflict when their political environments were predominantly made up of other democracies (Garfinkel 1994; Maoz 1996, 1998). On the other hand, when democracies were in the minority internationally, there were more disputes because of the aggressiveness of the autocracies (Maoz and Abdolali 1989).

Thinking about multiple influences can help us solve another puzzle, regarding the effect that the *process of democratization* has on the likelihood of conflict. Some have argued that the transition from autocracy to democracy might make a new government politically unstable and so lead it into greater conflict in the short term—even if it will be more peaceful once its democratic institutions are well established. Mansfield and Snyder (1995) agree that there is a separate peace among mature democracies, but they make a strong theoretical argument, with some empirical support, that democratizing regimes are more war-prone than stable political systems, whether autocratic or democratic. As old dictatorships fell, especially in Eastern Europe and the successor states of the old Soviet Union, this seemed a particularly important question (Kozhemiakin 1998). Would the new democracies find themselves at war with their neighbors over disputed boundaries or because of ethnic rivalries?

Efforts to reproduce Mansfield and Snyder's results, however, have not been very successful. Their findings are not robust when analysts employ different data sets, indicators, and analytical procedures. It is not at all clear, for one thing, that democratizing states are typically the initiators, rather than the victims, of interstate violence. Moreover, regime instability in general may be the problem, not democratization. A process of autocratization (moving from a democratic to authoritarian regime) may be as likely to induce conflict as democratization, or more so.[9] Also, a big shift to a high level of democracy produces more peaceful behavior than do halting, tentative moves toward liberalization (Ward and Gleditsch 1998). In addition, many investigations of this phenomenon stop at the level of the individual country. Public opinion surveys in Eastern Europe

[9]Mansfield and Snyder 1996, 1997; Enterline 1996, 1998a; Maoz 1998; Thompson and Tucker 1997a, 1997b.

and Russia (Braumoeller 1997) suggest that the more people in democratizing states *perceive* their neighbors as democratizing the less they expect to fight them. Analyses taking into account the characteristics of states' neighbors, with a good multivariate set of controls, find that democratization does not affect the likelihood of conflict (Oneal and Russett 1997; Rousseau 1997; Enterline 1998b). Gleditsch and Ward (2000) report that democratization generally reduces the risk of war, but that large swings back and forth between democracy and autocracy raise that risk.

It is important to resolve the debate regarding the effects of democratization because it has important implications for policy. If democratization encourages wars, even in the short term, we would have to be cautious about urging democratic reforms abroad, especially if a gradual approach to liberalization seemed necessary. If, however, new democracies are not particularly prone to conflict, the promotion of democracy, for its own sake and for its long-term pacific benefits, would clearly be warranted. We will return to this topic in the next chapter.

The failure early on to recognize that democracies are more peaceful in general than autocracies also arose from not thinking in strategic terms, that is, how two states interact when each must anticipate how the other will behave. This important perspective became prominent in investigations of international relations only after the initial empirical observation—that pairs of democracies are unusually peaceful—was established. Indeed, it was the need to explain this empirical generalization that prompted sophisticated efforts to think strategically. Among other things, it means asking whether democracies are threatened by autocracies. Perhaps autocratic leaders behave like bullies, trying to take advantage of democracies, which prefer peace but will fight rather than surrender too much. The run-up to World War II in Europe, between an aggressive Hitler and appeasing British and French leaders, is a prime historical example. A strategic perspective demands that we consider the sequence of events that leads to war, not just its end point: what kinds of states are likely to initiate disputes and war, and which are apt to be the targets of aggression? This theoretical innovation, which in turn prompted a fresh look at the evidence, shows how pieces of the puzzle regarding the democratic peace accumulated to produce a more nuanced and integrated understanding. We now consider some of these theoretical developments.

Theories of the Dyadic Democratic Peace: Culture or Structure?

A strong empirical relationship between democracy and peace alone is not enough. We also need to know *why* such a relationship exists; without a theoretical explanation, we do not understand the cause of the phenomenon and cannot be sure that the finding is not purely coincidental. Early efforts to explain the democratic peace fall into two categories (Maoz and Russett 1993; Starr 1992b). *Cultural explanations* emphasize the role of shared democratic principles, perceptions, and expectations of behavior. Democratic peoples, who solve their domestic political disputes without resorting to organized violence against their opponents, should be inclined to resolve problems arising in their relations with other democratic peoples in the same way. *Structural explanations*, on the other hand, stress the importance of the institutional constraints democracy characteristically imposes on decision makers. A separation of powers requires the executive to secure legislative approval and funding for war, and institutions that make democratic leaders accountable for bad decisions make democracies reluctant to go to war. The two explanations are really complementary: culture influences the creation and evolution of political institutions, and institutions shape culture. Kant, in *Perpetual Peace* ([1795] 1970), took an evolutionary view: a good constitution for representative government would, over time, generate a good moral culture.

There was an early notion that these explanations for the democratic peace must be mutually exclusive. They were treated as "contending" approaches, as though one were correct and the other incorrect. Rather than ask which theory is right and which is wrong, we should ask if and how they both could be true. One might be more important under some conditions and less important under others, and they might well reinforce one another (Most and Starr 1989). Treating them as contending approaches delayed investigation into how the two explanations are related and how they interact to generate peace between democracies.

It is more helpful to think of peace among democracies as "overdetermined," explainable by several related but conceptually distinct and reinforcing, perhaps sequential, causal mechanisms. The culture-structure debate obscured this. Just as there are multiple paths to war (Bremer 1996), there are multiple, "substitutable" paths to peace. Moreover, both the cultural and structural arguments are contextual theories, theories that consider how conditions existing within democracies constrain or enable certain behaviors in international politics (Goertz 1994; Most and Starr 1989). As such, the two approaches can be reconciled to show how they affect the opportunity and willingness of decision makers to choose between conflict and cooperation under particular conditions. This sort of effort is promising, though no single deductive structure may ever cover the diversity of countries' experiences or satisfy those who expect theories to explain everything by means of just a few variables.

One of the first theories using strategic choice to explain why democracies rarely fight each other was offered by Bueno de Mesquita and Lalman (1992). Their international interaction game situates domestic factors within a general structure of decision making at two levels: a nation's leaders interact with the leaders of another country and within their own domestic political system. From their game-theoretic approach, Bueno de Mesquita and Lalman deduce the conditions that are logically associated with various outcomes of the interactions of two states. They develop the important idea that the demands states make of one another do not reflect solely a desire for more power vis-à-vis potential rivals. Rather, internal political processes and norms of behavior influence states' goals in the international system and their choice of the means to these ends.

Internal politics affects the democratic peace because the domestic political costs associated with the use of force differ for democracies and nondemocracies. Leaders of democracies typically experience high political costs from fighting wars—always from losing them, and often despite winning them. These domestic costs of war make the use of force less attractive to democratic leaders. Decision makers in the real world can never be sure whether an opposing state is a "dove," averse to the use of force, but they generally can tell whether another state is a liberal democracy. This gives them valuable information about the likelihood that it will use force in pursuing its interests. Decision makers know that democratic leaders will bear heavier costs than the leaders of nondemocracies if they use force and so will be under greater constraints and be more inclined to adopt peaceful foreign policies. All of this comes from the free movement of information in liberal democracies, the existence of opposition groups, and the accountability of national leaders, which make democracies *transparent* to outsiders.

The strategic logic of the international interaction game can also account for the widely held belief that democracies are as inclined to violence as nondemocracies when considered individually. An autocratic bully, relatively unconstrained by domestic politics, may believe it can force a constrained democratic rival to capitulate, but even a democracy is apt to defend itself when attacked. Ironically, given reasonable assumptions about the cost of losing the military initiative versus the domestic costs of capitulating to a demand backed by force, a democratic leader may anticipate the consequences of delay and choose to preempt an attack it expects from its autocratic rival. In short, democratic constraints on the use of force can make democracies "vulnerable to threats of war or exploitation" and possibly liable to launch preemptive attacks against presumed aggressors (Bueno de Mesquita and Lalman 1992, 159).[10] In fact, preemptive attacks are rare (Reiter 1995a), but the international interaction game can provide one account of the peace between democracies and the belligerence between autocracies and democracies.

The assumption that the leaders of democracies have incentives to be doves is based on both cultural and structural arguments (Starr 1992a, 211). Separating opponents into hawks and doves affects the payoff a state expects from resorting to war and, hence, its choice of options. The political survival of decision makers is affected by both their participation in conflict and its outcome. Key to their survival is the nature of the constituencies to whom decision makers are responsible and the institutional context: "Leaders can anticipate that they will be held accountable for failed foreign policy adventures. Consequently, the choice of war-related behavior is likely to be dampened by the fear that the regime will be punished if things go awry" (Bueno de Mesquita, Siverson, and Woller 1992, 644). Leaders are punished for policy failures: they are forced from office. Democratic leaders are particularly subject to being forced out of office because of the electoral process, so they avoid wars, especially those they are likely to lose (Bueno de Mesquita and Siverson 1995).[11] (Authoritar-

---

[10]Schweller (1992) reports that dominant democracies, when declining in power relative to a challenger, do not initiate preventive wars. Preventive wars are deliberately planned and initiated to meet a growing threat, whereas preemptive wars arise out of crisis conditions favoring the side that makes a first strike.

[11]Bueno de Mesquita and Siverson (1997) and Bueno de Mesquita et al. (1999) expand and integrate these arguments. Such arguments assume that voters are "rational," stable in their opinions, and reasonably well informed on foreign policy. Almond (1950) contended they are not, but more recent work supports the affirmative. See Graham 1988; Nincic 1992; Russett 1990; Page and Shapiro 1992; Oneal, Lian, and Joyner 1996.

ian leaders are harder to dislodge but are more likely to lose their lives if they are, as Hitler and Mussolini discovered.) In addition, the citizens of democratic countries, accustomed to the peaceful resolution of political differences domestically, may expect their leaders to do the same internationally, at least in relations with other democracies. Thus, even successful uses of force may entail political costs for the leaders of democratic states.

Bueno de Mesquita and his colleagues assume that all national leaders are motivated by the desire to remain in power. To do this, leaders must satisfy a sufficiently large segment of those who influence the selection process (whether this is in formal elections or a "smoke-filled" room or through control of the nation's armed forces) so that they maintain a winning coalition in the game of domestic politics. To influence potential supporters, leaders distribute special benefits (private goods) to their supporters or pursue collective goods (public policies that benefit everyone). A combination of these strategies is most common, but democratic leaders have to satisfy a wide electorate, not just a small set of cronies or military officers. Consequently, they are driven less to pass along wealth to a small group and more to provide collective goods to large segments of the population (Olson 1993). They are expected to do so by democratic norms and held to account by democratic institutions. This gives them greater legitimacy and support from society (Lake 1992; Brawley 1993a).

A dictator like Saddam Hussein of Iraq, however, cannot easily be removed from office. It he takes the country into a war, the majority of the population may suffer, but there are no elections whereby voters can depose him. All he has to do to stay in power is buy off his clan and the army. However, in a state with a wide franchise, a leader cannot seek wealth for just a small group of supporters while spreading the costs of military action among the populace (Verdier 1994). Losing a war, or even winning a costly one, is a ticket to early retirement.

Another variant of the strategic perspective suggests that the democratic peace can be traced to democracies' historical satisfaction with the international status quo. Again, the argument addresses the utility of war and the use of force. Satisfied states make few demands to change the status quo; thus, they are less likely to generate disputes that could escalate to war (Organski and Kugler 1980; Gilpin 1981; Doran 1991). States that are satisfied with the status quo are deterred from challenging or attacking other states. The essence of deterrence is that one state, based on its calculation of costs and benefits, chooses not to undertake an action because of the behavior of another state. A state seeking to deter another may either raise the costs to its opponent of undertaking some activity (the threat of punishment, which is how analysts usually think of deterrence) or increase the benefits of abstaining. We shall see later in this book that trade reduces the likelihood of conflict because trading partners derive major benefits from the economic status quo, benefits that would be disrupted by military conflict.

Democracies may have been more satisfied historically with the status quo than autocracies due to their greater well-being. This is potentially the result of two factors. First, democratic societies receive greater political, social, and economic benefits because their governments are limited and there is competition for public office. As a result, the wealth extracted by a democratic state from its society, by corruption or by sheer force, is lower than in an autocracy, where national leaders may be little more than bandits. In a democracy with a wide franchise, the government must provide high levels of public goods in return for taxes, as noted above. The domestic satisfaction that comes from greater political freedom and economic prosperity may easily translate into satisfaction with the international status quo, including satisfaction with the state's existing territorial boundaries.[12]

The satisfaction of democracies with the status quo, and their resulting peacefulness, may also be historically contingent on the fact that the most powerful state in the system, the "hegemon," has, since the end of the Napoleonic Wars in 1815, been a democracy. If the hegemon was powerful enough to distribute private benefits to other states and if democracies were likely to support its hegemonic position, then democracies have been more satisfied (and more peaceful) because they have been privileged in a system run by powerful democracies. In the nineteenth and early twentieth centuries, Britain was the leading power, and it was satisfied with the status quo it had shaped. German leaders, on the other hand, seeing deep social tensions between workers, capitalists, and the landed aristocracy, wanted to revise the system by acquiring new colonies. Such a change would have come at Britain's expense and would have strengthened an autocratic state. Both reasons may explain Britain's resistance to

---

[12]Rousseau et al. (1996) find that democracies' satisfaction with the status quo helps reduce their willingness to initiate and escalate crises, both with other democracies and in general.

German initiatives. Britain had less to fear from America's rising power, which occurred at the same time. Later the United States did eclipse Great Britain, but the privileged position of democracies remained. Analysis of the territorial demands of democracies in the contemporary period supports the idea that democracies are still satisfied with the status quo (Kacowicz 1998).

In this theoretical argument, the peace among democracies is linked explicitly to their support for and the benefits they receive from the international status quo. If this is correct, the democratic peace could be subsumed under what is called "power transition theory" (Lemke and Reed 1996). According to this theory, the power of the hegemon to reward states with which it maintains good relations is the key to understanding the pattern of interstate conflict. The implication is that if by historical happenstance the hegemons of the last two centuries had been autocracies, we could now be discussing the autocratic peace proposition. We address this argument in Chapter 5.

The essence of the strategic viewpoint is probably this: for any country, a decision to expand, make demands, and fight must clear a threshold of costs and benefits. The costs of conquest and then of ruling conquered lands must be less than the benefits that accrue from peace and the status quo (Lake 1992, 29). The costs of resorting to force become almost insuperable when one democracy faces another. This hurdle is especially high because democracies expect, thanks to both cultural and structural incentives, to reconcile their conflicts peacefully. As we will discuss below, a degree of mutual responsiveness is required for the development of the zones of peace found within security communities. Thus, theories of strategic decision making can combine cultural and structural explanations of the democratic peace in a framework that considers national leaders agents of other political actors within a particular domestic political structure. This framework forces us to consider both the incentives for leaders to fight and the constraints that prevent them from doing so.

The Convergence and Expansion of Theories

Models of strategic decision making built upon previous accounts of the democratic peace, explained the same phenomenon, and then expanded the domain of explanation. Other research has integrated diverse findings regarding a broad range of interstate behavior and incorporated several explanatory models. As a result, we now have a more comprehensive and more persuasive theory. Indeed, rather than a simple descriptive statement—"pairs of democracies do not fight wars against each other"—we have a research program that embodies Imre Lakatos's (1970, 1978) notion of scientific progress. Thus, the basic descriptive proposition about peaceful relations among democracies served as the basis for developing theories to explain why that might be true. Generating theories and then comparing them to the evidence forced analysts to consider how well they explained not only this but other empirical phenomena. Some recent creative efforts (Bueno de Mesquita et al. 1999; Reiter and Stam 2000) are notable in this regard. Accounting for a new range of phenomena suggests a stronger theory. These exercises of expanding applicability and converging findings take two forms: looking either at alternative phenomena to explain or at different explanatory influences. We begin by exploring new phenomena that have been related to the democratic peace; that is, other cooperative or conflictual behaviors we should expect democracies to exhibit.

Common Interests

If democracies reap rewards from avoiding conflict with each other because they share common interests, we should expect those common interests to show up in a wide range of cooperative behavior. And they do. Democracies are more likely to collaborate with each other at the start of militarized disputes (Mousseau 1997), and perhaps to ally with one another.[13] Werner and Lemke (1997) show that, in deciding to join an ongoing war, democracies are more likely to align with other democracies, and autocracies with other autocracies. They also find that autocracies tend to bandwagon with stronger states whose power is growing but that democracies' decisions to form alliances are not very sensitive to changes

---

[13]Siverson and Emmons 1991; Raknerud and Hegre 1997. Democracies seem to have been more likely to ally with each other only during the cold war era, principally by forming defensive pacts, which are the strongest type of alliance, as contrasted with weaker ententes or neutrality pacts. See Simon and Gartzke 1996; Lai and Reiter 2000.

in power; ideological affinity is more important for democracies. Some of these empirical regularities may be due to the strong ideological differences central to the cold war. Nonetheless, alliances between democracies are more durable, apparently because democracies are able to make more credible long-term commitments. This is a result of the public way in which commitments are produced in their domestic political processes (Gaubatz 1996; Bennett 1997b).

Perhaps the most cogent realist critique of the democratic peace has been offered by Farber and Gowa (1995, 1997b). They argue that the empirical association between the character of political regimes and the likelihood of conflict is spurious. The peace among democracies, they suggest, is not primarily a result of these states' being democratic but rather a consequence of shared (and transient) strategic interests: during the cold war, democracies such as Britain, France, and the United States allied with one another in order to defend themselves against a common enemy, the Soviet bloc. If Farber and Gowa are right that alliances are just a consequence of the international balance of power and that allies rarely fight one another because they must remain united against their common enemy, then shared democracy would be irrelevant in explaining the pattern of conflict. Once the source of threat is eliminated, as with the end of the cold war, the peace among democracies would be expected to cease as well. Clearly this is an important issue, for both theoretical and practical reasons.

Yet the idea that alliances are formed against a common enemy ignores the deeper question of why the enemy is perceived as common. Certainly, some of the democracies' cold war allies, especially in Latin America and Asia, were dictatorships; but why were all the democracies that took a side in the cold war on one and the same side? Surely their wish to maintain democratic forms of government and extensive civil liberties shaped their conception of their vital interests. If democracies are particularly likely to trade with other democracies (and they are, as we shall see in Chapter 6), then the benefits of that trade, too, are part of the interests they seek to protect in becoming allied. Thus, their interests as liberal democratic states affect both their choice of alliance partners and the kinds of countries (expansive dictatorships, especially those with state-run economies) with whom they are likely to come into conflict. A broad conception of "national interest" can thus explain alliances as well as patterns of conflict.

It is certainly true, nevertheless, that the institutional bonds of military alliances make war among their members less likely. NATO, for instance, was formed by free-market democracies. Admittedly, Portugal and Spain were military dictatorships when they joined, and Greece and Turkey reverted to autocratic rule for a time after joining as democracies. But since 1983, NATO has been composed exclusively of democracies. It has defended democracy among its members and promoted democracy among its neighbors. Its members share the interests of democratic states in not fighting among themselves. To this the institutional benefits of the alliance have been added. Thus, when the possibility of war has arisen between Greece and Turkey, NATO has helped to mediate the conflict and discourage its escalation.

Similar relationships between democracy, common interests, and behavior emerge if we look at voting blocs in the United Nations. States that regularly vote together in the General Assembly are also unlikely to fight each other. Presumably, they vote together because they share common interests and policy preferences (Gartzke 1998). But the policy preferences themselves are derived to a substantial degree from the shared interests of liberal democratic states. Democracies often vote together in the UN, as do states that trade heavily with each other (Kim and Russett 1996). Democracy and the pattern of trade, therefore, affect the likelihood of military disputes both directly, for the reasons we have explored in discussing the Kantian peace, and indirectly, by shaping other shared preferences, as represented by UN voting. We explore this complex causal system in Chapter 6.

One response to the challenge posed by Farber and Gowa comes from changing the question: instead of asking who fights whom, let us ask who wins after a fight is begun. If both shared democracy and common security interests (as measured by alliances) have prompted democracies to settle disputes among themselves peacefully, we can sort out the relative importance of these two variables by asking which state in a dispute is likely to prevail under different conditions. The existence of an alliance offers no prediction about this, but a realist would surely predict that the more powerful state will usually win. The democratic peace perspective predicts, on the other hand, that in disputes between democracies, shared norms and institutional procedures for peaceful conflict resolution will temper the dominance of power. Gelpi and Griesdorf (1997), therefore, looked to see which side won or lost in all disputes over most of the twentieth century. The realist prediction that relative power matters holds true in most instances, but among democracies, relative power has no effect.

Interventions

If democracies rarely fight each other and share many common interests, why have democracies sometimes intervened in the internal affairs of other democracies? Several critiques of the democratic peace raise this question (Forsythe 1992; James and Mitchell 1995). One form of such intervention is covert action. The United States, for instance, conducted covert operations against left-leaning governments in Guatemala, in 1954, and in Chile, in 1973, both of which came to power through democratic elections.

Two questions about these operations need attention: First, why did the United States support the violent overthrow of these regimes if democracies share common interests and nonviolent modes of conflict resolution? This question is raised by critics of the democratic peace. But we should also ask why the United States intervened covertly and not openly, with its own troops? The answer is that the administrations that undertook these operations feared they would be widely denounced, so they hid their actions. Fear of criticism in a free press—a feature of democracies, of course—increases the incentives to keep an intervention covert (Van Belle 1997). Covert action by one democracy against another would usually be perceived as illegitimate by citizens of the intervening power. Citizens differentiate between democracies and autocracies as potential targets of military action (Mintz and Geva 1993; Geva, DeRouen, and Mintz 1993). Policy makers who do not share this sentiment have political incentives to keep their actions low-key in the hope that they will remain secret or at least not attract much public attention. Overt intervention with high levels of military force would invite political opposition because public norms do not support such inherently antidemocratic activity (Russett 1993, 122–24).

This is what happened when an initially covert intervention against the leftist revolutionary Sandinista government of Nicaragua became public and escalated in the 1980s. The U.S. Congress explicitly forbade the administration to support military action to overthrow the Nicaraguan government. To evade those constraints, the administration undertook illegal arms sales to finance its activities, but these were exposed in the Iran-contra scandal and led to the prosecution of some of the officials responsible. Thus, consideration of the political necessity of covert operations—in violation of democratic norms and institutions—ameliorates the challenge to the democratic peace raised by the cases when democracies have intervened in the internal affairs of other democracies. We may never know how many efforts at covert influence or even subversion are directed by democratic governments against officially friendly regimes, especially other democracies. These efforts—in defiance of democratic norms—are probably the least likely to emerge into the light of day.

With regard to overt interventions by military forces, the data more clearly support the existence of a separate peace among democracies. While powerful democratic states have sometimes intervened in weaker democratic or semidemocratic states, it has not been common;[14] and in most instances, the action was taken either to protect the intervenor's citizens or their property or to support the government. Only a minority of cases were hostile acts of coercive diplomacy. This finding is in keeping with the preferences of democratic citizens. The American public, for example, has supported presidents when they use force to resist aggression but not when they seek to engineer internal changes in other countries (Oneal, Lian, and Joyner 1996). Moreover, democracy helps inoculate a country against overt interventions. Democracies have been less likely than nondemocratic states to suffer such aggression, whether by democracies or by autocracies. This may be because the internal political strength of democracies (Hermann and Kegley 1996) discourages intervenors.

Although there are counterexamples (U.S. troops in Vietnam), states subjected to military intervention by the United States during the cold war generally became more democratic as a consequence, especially if the U.S. president declared this to be his goal (Meernik 1996; Hermann and Kegley 1998). The invasion of Grenada in 1989 is an example. An analysis of U.S. interventions over a century-long period concludes that although intervention itself did not generally promote democracy, when

---

[14]At first, Kegley and Hermann (1995) reported that democracies were more likely to intervene in other democratic or partly free states than in autocracies. When they analyzed different data, however, they found this was not true (Kegley and Hermann 1997).

the United States actively supported free and fair elections, the result was often profound (Peceny 1999). Open interventions, especially when the promotion of democracy was a goal, have not generally had antidemocratic consequences. Whether that makes them acceptable violations of traditional norms of sovereignty and noninterference in the internal affairs of another country is another matter.

Conflict Management

The public's ability to observe the making of public policy and its implementation means that democratic political systems are transparent, and the political competition characteristic of democracies contributes importantly to this. Transparency, in turn, helps democracies signal their interests more clearly and credibly and, if they are willing to use force, to communicate that resolve more effectively.[15] If a democracy is determined to achieve a certain objective and the political opposition supports the government, it can communicate this resolve and often prevail without war. But if the political opposition does not want to confront a foreign power, the government will be in a weak position. If it were to initiate a dispute under these circumstances, its adversary would likely interpret that initiation as a bluff. Consequently, democracies are more likely than autocracies to settle disputes peacefully, less likely to initiate disputes, and less likely to escalate a dispute when they do initiate it (Schultz 1998). Key to this process are the transparency of political decision making in democracies and the ability this gives them to communicate resolve internationally.

Numerous studies have extended the logic underlying the democratic peace to explain conflict management and cooperation among democracies. States engaged in long-term rivalries are more likely to end those rivalries at times when both states happen to be democratic (Bennett 1997a, 1998). Disputes between democracies are both shorter (nearly half lasted only a day) and less severe than those between other kinds of states (Mitchell and Prins 1999). Leeds and Davis (1999; also Leeds 1999) constructed a game-theoretic model to show that pairs of democracies engage

[15]See Fearon 1994a; Schultz 1999; Partell and Palmer 1999; Eyerman and Hart 1996.

more in cooperative behaviors than mixed democratic-autocratic pairs do. Democracies are much more likely to conclude preferential trade agreements (Mansfield, Milner, and Rosendorff 2000). Democracies use different conflict-management techniques and institutions than autocracies do. They are more likely to settle conflicts peacefully through mutual concession and compromise and to use third parties for mediation (Dixon 1993, 1994, 1998; Mousseau 1998). If, however, one focuses on the involvement of third parties with powers of arbitration or adjudication to impose binding settlements, the picture becomes murkier. Democracies are more likely to submit their disputes to arbitration, but the results of arbitration are not more durable than for nondemocratic pairs (Raymond 1994, 1996). This may result from the reluctance of nondemocratic states to use binding third-party mechanisms to resolve their disputes. When they do, it may be because they are ready to abide by the imposed solution, as when Libya accepted the International Court of Justice's finding in its border dispute with Chad in 1994.

What constitutes a legitimate cause for democracies to use military force against other democracies is limited by their cultural norms. People living in a democracy know that the citizens of other democracies share norms of limited self-government, civil liberties, and democratic transparency. They expect their government, consequently, to find appropriate modes of nonviolent conflict resolution in the event of an interstate dispute. Thus, the range of legitimate reasons to use force is greatly restricted between democracies. Moreover, the transparency of democracies, along with shared democratic norms and procedures, makes it very hard for democratic leaders to dehumanize people living in another democracy by manipulating images of the other to portray them as the "enemy." In contrast, authoritarian and totalitarian states are less transparent to others and limit their own people's access to information, encouraging the development of harsh images of the adversary on both sides. In the Gulf War of 1990–91, President Bush could characterize the Iraqi leader as another Hitler, and Saddam Hussein could equally demonize the American leadership. Such accusations would be unimaginable between the leaders of two democracies.

Experimental work on the political incentives for peace between democracies supports this argument. Mintz and Geva (1993) found that in laboratory settings their subjects interpreted the use of force by one democracy against another as incompetent leadership—incompetent because peaceful conflict resolution should be possible and, therefore, is expected. These results are consistent with Bueno de Mesquita and Lalman's arguments (1992) about pairs of international "doves." The leader of a democracy, after her political cost-benefit analysis of war against another democracy, sees no gain in it. Decision makers leading democracies can expect less support for the use of force against other democracies than for the use of force against dictatorships.

We began this discussion with the strong result of the dyadic democratic peace and considered a variety of related analyses that link democracy, both dyadically and individually, to less violence and more cooperation. We then considered the whole range of conflict: the onset of disputes, their escalation and de-escalation, and the dynamics of conflict management that move conflicts away from violent outcomes. Democracies are not pacifists; they do participate in violent conflict and even initiate it at times. Yet by analyzing how they interact strategically with other governments, we are better able to appreciate the peacefulness of democratic states and to understand the conditions (i.e., types of opponents and situations) that may prompt democracies to threaten and to use force.

Why Do Democracies Win the Wars They Fight?

It has been carefully documented that democracies win most of the wars they fight (Lake 1992; Bueno de Mesquita, Siverson, and Woller 1992; Stam 1996; Bennett and Stam 1996). But it is not obvious why this is so. One view is that the citizens in democratic societies are more motivated to support their state and that their participation in policy making produces better decisions (Russett 1993, 137). An alternative view is that democracies are better able to generate wealth and military capability, making them more powerful and more likely to prevail in wars (Lake 1992; Huntley 1996). By limiting the scope of government's involvement in the economy, for example, democracies make themselves more attractive to lenders of international capital; hence, they are more able to raise the resources needed to compete with authoritarian powers in international politics (Schultz and Weingast 1997). Other analysts (Reiter and Stam 1998b) doubt that democracies fare better because they mobilize greater material capabilities. Rather, they say that democracies choose to fight only wars they are likely to win because of the high costs that a democratic leader can expect to pay for losing a war. This argument is strengthened by the fact that, historically, democracies have been particularly likely to win only those wars they initiated, rather than those in which they were the target of an attack and did not actively choose war.

Democratic leaders not only fear losing wars; they also fear incurring casualties. There are severe political consequences of soldiers' not returning home alive. Recall President Clinton's insistence on using air power and not ground forces in the war in Kosovo—avoiding *any* American battle deaths in this case. Democracies generally suffer fewer casualties in war than autocracies do (Siverson 1995). If democracies continue wars for very long, civilian support and military morale drop because of mounting casualties.[16] The decline is faster in democracies than in autocracies, and the longer the war lasts, the less likely democracies are to triumph. The United States' experience in the Vietnam War illustrates this vividly. So democratic leaders must win their wars quickly (Bennett and Stam 1998). How can they do this? Again, part of the answer is in carefully choosing which wars to fight. Democratic leaders try to initiate wars they are likely not only to win but to win quickly. Once involved in war, democracies do exhibit superior organizational effectiveness and leadership, though the logistical competence and morale of democratic armies declines over time (Reiter and Stam 1998a). Democratic leaders are more likely to choose maneuver strategies in wartime, and those strategies can win with lower human costs. Such strategies, however, require granting considerable autonomy to field commanders, something autocratic governments are usually less willing to do (Reiter and Meek 1999).

The characteristics of democratic and autocratic governments affect operations on the battlefield in other ways, too. Remember that democracies' wars are virtually always with autocracies. Autocracies treat prisoners of war far more brutally than democracies do, regularly violating the Geneva Convention. Soldiers from democratic states know this and are motivated to fight harder to avoid that fate. In their wars with democracies, on the other hand, soldiers of autocratic states often vote with their feet to become POWs (Reiter and Stam 1997). This account of the motivations of individual soldiers helps explain why democracies usually win the wars they fight.

---

[16]Mueller 1973; Lian and Oneal 1993; Oneal and Bryan 1995; Gartner and Segura 1998.

Ultimately, for a variety of reasons, democracy is a source of security, not vulnerability, even in a Hobbesian world. Democracies win most of the wars they choose to fight and, in so far as possible, stay out of the wars they cannot win or can win only at great cost. In a major theoretical and empirical synthesis, Reiter and Stam (2000) account for these phenomena within a model of consent: democracies win wars because their citizens will withdraw their support from governments that make bad choices and because the armed forces of democratic states are better able to conduct successful operations when called upon to do so.

The Domestic Conflict–Foreign Conflict Puzzle

A long-standing hypothesis is that governmental leaders may pursue diversionary policies to promote their own political interests; that is, confronted with domestic political troubles a leader may try to invoke a "rally 'round the flag" by diverting his people's attentions toward foreign "enemies." Some Republican leaders accused Clinton of this tactic when he ordered the bombing of suspected terrorist sites in Sudan and Afghanistan during the Monica Lewinsky scandal in 1998. President Bush was accused of the same thing when new attacks against Iraq were made at the time of the Republican convention in 1992. Are such actions especially common in democracies, where public opinion affects the power of the president and his ability to promote his agenda and where the government must present itself periodically for elections? Is the use of force more likely to occur just before elections? And does a bad economy increase the chances that force will be used abroad? A government's popularity depends heavily on whether its people are suffering from inflation or recession, so the temptation to divert attention from economic troubles could be strong. If democratic governments are prone to use force for domestic political advantage, this would pose a major challenge to the belief that democracies are more peaceful than autocracies.

Recent inquiries into these questions have produced mixed results, with no preponderant evidence that democratic leaders are more inclined to pursue diversionary adventures than dictators are.[17] Several studies

---

[17]Heldt 1997a reviews the recent literature; Levy 1989b is the standard earlier survey.

(Lian and Oneal 1993; Oneal and Bryan 1995; James and Rioux 1998) find only modest support for the existence of a "rally" effect following a use of force by an American president. There is also little systematic evidence that American leaders have tried to invoke a rally at politically convenient times (Gowa 1999, p. 69),[18] or that other democracies experience international conflict according to internal political or economic cycles (Miller 1999; Leeds and Davis 1997; cf. Gaubatz 1999). International influences usually have greater impact on American decisions to use force than domestic conditions do, especially if one looks at situations in which the U.S. government might have used military force but did not (Meernik 1994; Meernik and Waterman 1996; cf. James and Oneal 1991). Wang (1996) finds that both internal and international influences operate but that force is invoked *less frequently* when elections are near (perhaps because the rally effect is too unreliable) and more often to avoid a foreign policy defeat that would be politically damaging than to achieve outright political gains.

We need to address these issues in a more theoretically sophisticated way. If the use or threat of force is associated primarily with international conditions, then one must consider the particularly dispute-prone relationships embodied in democracies' rivalries with authoritarian states. Democratic leaders who do not respond as "realists" to a dictator's challenge may be vulnerable at home (Huth 1996). Remember that many crises are provoked not by a democracy but by its autocratic adversary. If a dictator believes that a democratic government might respond forcefully as a way of diverting attention from its domestic political troubles, the dictator might be especially careful not to provoke democratic leaders during such times (Smith 1996; Leeds and Davis 1997; Miller 1999). Saddam Hussein, for instance, seems to have been careful not to challenge Clinton at the height of the impeachment hearings. Thinking about multiple influences and relations with particular countries and considering both countries as sophisticated strategic actors are the best ways to untangle this troublesome puzzle. This approach provides no reason to

---

[18]Gowa seems to consider this to be evidence against the democratic peace. But since the vast majority of U.S. militarized disputes have been with autocracies, it is hard to see how it bears on the dyadic democratic peace proposition. As for the individual state level, at most it suggests that domestic politics made the United States neither more nor less dispute-prone than its international situation would require.

believe that democracies are especially prone to violent foreign policy acts as a means to rally support for domestic political objectives.

Civil Wars

A consideration of politics within countries suggests another extension of the democratic peace: democracies should have fewer civil wars than non-democratic states. Indeed, they do. Perhaps this is because of higher levels of legitimacy in democracies. Effective governance in a democracy requires leaders to attend to a wide range of societal interests. States that are thoroughly democratic and those democracies that are effective experience the least amount of violence within their borders.[19] Actually, the relationship between the character of the political system and the incidence of civil wars is probably curvilinear. Partial democracies experience violent state failures more often than either full democracies or autocracies do. Countries with little international trade are also prone to domestic conflict.[20] The vast majority of civil wars in the twentieth century occurred neither in democracies nor in effective totalitarian states able to repress opposition vigorously. Rather, they occurred in regimes of mixed political characteristics or in decaying autocracies. Transitional regimes may evoke dissatisfaction and frustration just when their people are first able to vent it.

Democracies experience less domestic violence *in general*, especially what Rudolph Rummel has called "democide," the killing of people by their own government. Drawing on both cultural and institutional constraints (and linking economics and politics as well), Rummel (1985, 1994, 1995a, 1995b, 1997) shows that authoritarian governments are more likely to use force domestically and to engage in mass murder (also see Krain 1997). The obvious examples are, of course, Hitler, Stalin, and Mao. Rummel concludes that in addition to peacefulness abroad, democracy is a "method of non-violence" at home.

The American Civil War is often cited as an important exception to the domestic peacefulness of democracies. Undoubtedly it is. As with

[19]Hegre et al. 1997; Krain and Myers 1997; Benson and Kugler 1998; Gurr 2000.
[20]Muller and Weede 1990; Ellingsen and Gleditsch 1996; Ellingsen 2000; Henderson and Singer 2000; Esty et al. 1998.

military disputes between democracies, the number of civil wars in democracies is small, not zero. In understanding the American case, it is important to remember, however, that democracy is a matter of degree. In this case, though both the Union and the Confederacy had important elements of democratic government, there was considerable difference between them. While its voting franchise was limited to males, the North arguably represented the most democratic large political system in the world at the time. In the South, not only did females have no vote, one-third of the total population, in addition to lacking the franchise, was legally no more than property. Weart (1998) plausibly labels the South not as a democracy but as an oligarchic republic run by a slave-owning landed aristocracy. Thus while the difference in political systems between North and South was less than between, say, the North and tsarist Russia, it was so great that it is hardly surprising the two systems could not coexist within the same state.

Beyond the "Democratic" Peace

We have been asking what other phenomena, besides the democratic peace, democracy can explain. This has led to our discussions of why democracies win wars, intervene in other countries, and experience fewer civil wars. We now ask a different question: Of what is democracy an example? In other words, what broader phenomena are represented by democracy? The democratic peace, we might say, provides the base camp for the expedition undertaken in this book, not the summit.

Chapter 1 introduced the idea of a Kantian peace, that peace is the result of multiple and overlapping liberal behaviors (democracy, economic interdependence, and international law and organizations). In the rest of this book, we will look in detail at the full triangle of factors underlying Kant's prognosis for peace. In his view, the three elements are intricately interrelated; it is not simply that each is useful. Democracy may be the keystone, but trade and international organizations contribute importantly to the establishment of a stable peace (Doyle 1997; also see Cederman's learning model [2000]).

As we suggested earlier, the Kantian perspective is strengthened by considering the various relationships linking democracy, trade, and peace. Free trade was a central concern of the nineteenth-century liberals who contended that the economic interests of traders would promote not just prosperity but also peace between nations. This was necessary if trade and prosperity were to be maintained. Chapter 4 will look at this theoretical perspective in detail and consider the evidence for it. And Chapter 6 will consider whether the correlation between peace and trade is primarily the result of trade's reducing conflict or of conflict's reducing trade.[21] Chapter 6 will also show that, after allowing for the influences typically employed by economists to predict trade patterns (size of economy, distance, and relative costs), democracies trade more with one another than with autocracies. Because they share common interests and are able to employ nonviolent means of resolving disputes, democratic leaders need be less concerned that a democratic trading partner will use its gains from trade in ways that threaten their country's security. In addition, private actors prefer, where possible, to trade with enterprises located in states with which relations are stable. The democratic peace provides them with this assurance. They also can be more confident in the business practices and laws of another democracy than in those of an autocracy, where capricious acts such as expropriations might threaten their interests.

Another matter regarding the causal relationship between democracy and economic development is hotly contested and beyond full review here. The position that high levels of economic development facilitate democracy is generally accepted. Some of the most comprehensive work (Burkhart and Lewis-Beck 1994; Przeworski et al. 1996; Przeworski and Limongi 1997) confirms at least a strong correlation. Wealthy democracies survive: no state that has achieved both democracy and a moderately high level of prosperity (the level Argentina attained in 1975) has subsequently become undemocratic. In less affluent countries, democracy is more likely to survive if the economy is growing, inflation is moderate, and economic inequality is limited and narrowing. It is less clear whether democracy causes growth. Some recent work suggests that it does once it

---

[21]Weede (1996, chap. 7) contends that free trade increases prosperity (for evidence, see Frankel and Romer 1999), which in turn promotes democracy (and thus peace). The experience of industrialized countries (Volgy and Schwarz 1997) poses a long-term concern for Weede's argument, however. Free trade can magnify income inequality, which may ultimately endanger democracy. This perspective is part of the international debate about the consequences of free trade, globalization, and the creation of common markets.

has become institutionalized and stable (Feng 1997; Leblang 1997). This seems to have happened in contemporary Poland, the Czech Republic, and Hungary. Other countries in Eastern Europe, Asia (notably Indonesia), and Africa (including Nigeria) still have a long way to go to attain either stable democracy or steady economic growth.

The belief that international organizations and international law have a beneficial effect on interstate relations derives partly from arguments analogous to those made in norm-based explanations of the democratic peace. We have discussed some of the evidence that democracies extend their domestic processes of conflict management and resolution to their dealings with other democracies, that they employ "democratic" means in dealing with other democracies. These processes, we argue below, are manifestations of community, legitimacy, and responsiveness.

Organizations, rules, and norms are constructed within societies to reduce decision costs, to provide buffers against costly mistakes, and to make implementing policy more efficient. Democratic societies create not only laws but also procedures for how laws are to be written, interpreted, applied, appealed, and changed. Legislatures, courts, instruments of mediation or arbitration, as well as the whole range of political and social organizations serve these functions. Political and social organizations of a wide variety of types exist to facilitate the application of law in conflict management and resolution; they also facilitate societal responsiveness: the willingness of most citizens most of the time to comply voluntarily with the legitimate demands of the government and of other citizens. They socialize members to accept common norms and to generate narratives of mutual identity: to believe that "they" are part of "us." (This is how nations are built from a mix of ethnic and religious groups.) Within democratic societies, organizations and rules are core components of complex systems that ease interactions among individuals and groups, permit the recognition and pursuit of common interests, and manage conflict.

Consistent with both cultural explanations and with analyses of strategic behavior, democratic leaders expect to use international organizations and law—elements of international civil society—in a similar fashion when interacting with other states, especially other democracies. Democratic leaders use international organizations and law because these offer means to achieve their state's objectives and meet their people's expectations regarding the proper conduct of relations with other democratic states. As we argued above, leaders who do not do so will be considered incompetent.

International organizations are often regarded as weak and ineffectual, particularly on matters that critically affect states' security interests. It is true that in most circumstances international organizations lack the coercive power over states that states have over their citizens. But international organizations, whether global, regional, or organized to accomplish a particular functional objective, can and do fulfill many of the same functions among nation-states that domestic organizations do within them. Consequently, we will consider whether pairs of states that belong to many of the same international organizations are less likely to engage in militarized disputes with one another than are states that share few international institutional affiliations. We undertake this analysis in Chapter 5. We will also consider, in Chapter 6, whether militarized disputes reduce states' readiness to become involved in the same international organizations. Is there a virtuous circle whereby peace and IGOs strengthen each other? Finally, are democracies and economically interdependent states more likely to join international organizations with one another, bringing together the three elements of the Kantian peace? If so, this would provide powerful additional evidence that a Kantian system of feedback loops, or virtuous circles, operates within a big part of the international system.

Democracy and Political Integration

The democratic peace can be seen as a consequence of the processes of integration and social communication explored by Karl Deutsch et al. (1957).[22] Deutsch et al. argue that these processes are capable of producing a security community, composed of a population—whether within a

---

[22]Starr (1992a, 1997a, 1997b) argues that Bueno de Mesquita and Lalman's international interaction game (1992) can explain how Deutsch et al. (1957) got from a process of social communication and responsiveness (Russett 1963) to a security community. Deutsch et al.'s model has begun to attract renewed interest, as, for example, the collaborative enterprise stimulated by Adler and Barnett (1998); see also Wendt 1994.

single country or consisting of numerous sovereign states—that does not expect war to occur with other members of the community and so does not prepare for such an eventuality. A security community is the consequence of a wide array of transactions within civil society. The people involved in those political, economic, social, and cultural transactions learn that they bring mutual benefits. As interactions expand and become institutionalized, the people become more and more interdependent, and the costs of stopping such exchanges go up. Because these interactions are especially rich and varied for democracies, democracies may benefit most from the experience (Reiter 1995b).

As peaceful interactions increase, people develop greater responsiveness to one another; they develop the expectation that their wants and needs will be met. At some point, this produces the "we-feeling," trust, and mutual consideration, which Deutsch et al. (1957) call "community." The experience of the European Union exemplifies this process. It is a matter of mutual sympathy, trust, and loyalties that are found in greater identification of self-images and interests. It thrives on mutually successful predictions of behavior. It operates as a dynamic process of reciprocal attention, communication, perception of needs, and responsiveness. Responsiveness and community arise out of social transactions through which people learn to respect and trust others, and through which they receive respect and trust in return. Dense networks of social exchange are an essential form of social capital: the denser such networks are in a community, the more easily citizens can cooperate for mutual benefit (Putnam 1993). Community reduces uncertainty and so lowers the cost of collective problem solving (Taylor and Singleton 1993).

The security community represents one of the most tangible and significant outcomes of the process of integration. Countries within a security community have given up the military option in their mutual interactions and replaced it with "dependable expectations of 'peaceful change' " (Deutsch et al. 1957, 5). This need not involve the creation of a single supranational entity (amalgamation); states can retain their sovereign independence, forming a pluralistic security community with a high degree of shared identity (Risse-Kappen 1996). The European Union is not a "United States of Europe," as some originally envisioned, but it has, nevertheless, achieved a stable peace. If leaders are to incur the significant costs of breaking the bonds of interdependence, then they will have to present compelling reasons for doing so. Within a security community, this is effectively impossible. Bonds of mutually rewarding transactions and feelings of community make the costs of using force prohibitive.

Foreign-policy decision makers must distinguish between states that are potentially threatening and those with which mutually beneficial, peaceful relations are likely. The process of integration provides them with an abundance of relevant information, which gives them confidence in their ability to make this determination. If knowing that a state is a democracy raises the prospects of correctly identifying it as a dove, relationships of mutual responsiveness, interdependence, and community—the bonds that unite the members of a security community—create virtual certainty in identifying friendly states. A recent volume "thinks the unthinkable: that community exists at the international level, that security politics is profoundly shaped by it, and that those states dwelling within an international community might develop a pacific disposition" toward one another (Adler and Barnett 1998, 3).[23] This is why we carefully examine the role of international organizations in subsequent chapters.

Legitimacy, Liberalism, and Society

Many writers stress Kant's attention to republicanism as the core of liberalism; others stress the rational self-interest of economic actors in expanding markets and profits. Analyses of the liberal state, which supports the pluralism necessary for both the popular selection and replacement of governmental leaders and the workings of a market economy, are also important. Rational-choice models provide a useful tool for analyzing the operation of liberal societies. Yet while each of these perspectives makes a contribution, they do not capture all that is important. Democracy works through three central relationships: (1) among individuals and groups

---

[23]When we look closely at the Deutschian social-communication model of the integration process, as well as at the neo-functional model of Haas (1958), we find all the components of the two main theories of the democratic peace. The structural constraints model involves interdependence, organizations, and formal laws or constitutions; the democratic culture argument involves the presence of community, responsiveness, shared values, and norms.

within society, (2) from society and its various components to government, and (3) from government to society. These elements of liberalism also need to be considered.

The first relationship is straightforward. Models of social community account for nationalism (Deutsch 1953) and for how humans form relationships with family, neighbors, and strangers on the street. Three elements of community are shared values, beliefs, identities, and meaning; multiple and multifaceted direct relationships; and recognition of long-term interests, reciprocity, and even altruism (Taylor 1982). Democracies have a particular kind of community based on values such as legal equality, democratic process, and civil and political liberties; but democracies are not free from conflict: "Conflict flourishes at all levels precisely because it is contained within well-accepted limits and channelled through procedures and institutions to which loyalty is assured. The role of those devices is not to turn conflict into consensus; it is to find for limited conflicts solutions that are inspired by the procedural and substantive consensus which keeps the system going, and which solutions strengthen in turn" (Hoffmann 1995, 22).

The second relationship, between society and government, is characterized by legitimacy. If a government is regarded as legitimate, citizens are more willing to respect its laws. They also expect it to take their needs into account when setting policy. Both political culture and the institutional structure contribute to the legitimacy of a political system, and the legitimacy of security communities rests on the same supports. A regime is "legitimate to the extent that it can induce a measure of compliance from most people without resort to the use of physical force" (Jackman 1993, 98). Legitimacy is the "cement of society": a good democracy "requires relatively little punitive or physical coercion. . . . social governance for the majority of citizens is, in essence, noncoercive, voluntary, and compliant" (Nie et al. 1996, 2). Just as the norms and procedures for citizens' interactions with one another in a democratic society are externalized, so are the norms and procedures by which citizens in democracies interact with their governments. The responsiveness and legitimacy of these relationships are assumed for other democracies as well, and they fashion relations among democracies.

The third key relationship in the functioning of liberal democracies concerns how government sees and reacts to society—what obligations the government has to the individual in a liberal state (Onuf and Johnson

1995). Doyle (1995, 84) calls liberalism "a family portrait of principles and institutions" recognizable by "a commitment to individual freedom, government through democratic representation, rights of private property, and equality of opportunity."[24] Ruggie (1982) adds, with his concept of "embedded liberalism," the idea of a shared social purpose. A shared social purpose is essential for a successful political and economic system, as Western countries learned in the Great Depression of the 1930s. Individuals must be allowed to pursue their own interests, to pursue happiness, as Jefferson put it in the Declaration of Independence, but unbridled economic competition is dangerous economically and politically. A successful economy, certainly one that is open internationally, requires a degree of social protection if there is to be social peace (Polanyi 1944). Garrett (1998) contends that the success of the rich industrialized countries was built on interdependence, growth, and social democracy.

From the societal integration that orders behavior among individuals in a democracy and the legitimacy that establishes society's obligations toward government, there emerges the responsibilities of government: how it ought to behave, both toward its own citizens and toward other states internationally. In economic terms, a democratic state must insure domestic stability by promoting economic growth, providing the greatest good for the greatest number, but it must also maintain a minimum standard of social welfare for those least well-off. We expect democratic governments to serve the people in ways that go beyond the mere calculation of utility. As Kant affirmed in his "moral imperative," we are not to treat others as mere means to our own ends. Each individual is to be treated with dignity. This moral imperative applies not only to us as individuals but also to our agents, especially governments because of the extensive powers they are granted.

Democratic governments approach this ideal most closely. Major famines have occurred only in authoritarian states in the twentieth century (Sen 1981), where information could be suppressed and protest repressed. Over twenty-five million Chinese starved as a result of misguided agricultural policies that could not be challenged under the Communist rule of Mao Zedong (Rummel 1991, 249). At all levels of development, democracies have lower infant mortality rates than autocracies, partly be-

[24]See also Moravcsik 1997 and McMillan's discussion (1997) of "sophisticated liberalism."

cause fewer citizens are hungry (Zweifel and Navia 2000). Internationally, the inclination of democratic governments to observe the Kantian imperative underpins the democratic peace and explains why they are more respectful of international laws regarding human rights (Arat 1991; Poe, Tate, and Keith 1999). Democracies may also be better able to resist forces causing environmental degradation (Gleditsch 1997).[25]

A sense of community among individuals, the respect of citizens for legitimate authority, and the responsibility of government toward society are central to our understanding of democracy. Together they form the basis for both cultural and structural theories of the democratic peace and their derivatives. In sum, democracy promotes cooperation and peaceful conflict resolution internationally through (1) its domestic legitimacy and accountability, (2) institutional checks and balances, (3) the transparency that emerges from free communication and political competition, (4) the crediblity of its international agreements, and (5) its sensitivity to the human and material costs of violent conflict (Solingen 1996, 84). No democracy is perfect, but to a significant degree these forces shape the preferences and perceptions of democratic leaders and thus the choices they make globally. Similar elements in a liberal international system, which seems in the process of emerging, may also provide for a more just international society (Brilmayer 1994; MacMillan 1998).

All good things do not necessarily go together. There is no free lunch. Democratic liberties can be debased. The inequalities of capitalism may run wild. A global authority or hegemon could become a Leviathan. Peace does not always mean justice. There are trade-offs and hard choices to be made. Yet in the world as it is, the roots of peace lie not simply in force and the mechanisms of realpolitik but also in the structures and culture of freedom.

[25]Midlarsky (1998b) disputes this; however, his data exclude Communist countries.

Democracy Reduces Conflict

As terrible as it is, war sometimes seems necessary to most people. Certainly, national governments, and the people who support them and die for them, sometimes wage war or use lower levels of military force to protect their sovereignty and security or to promote national interests. Nevertheless, most countries at most times are at peace. A few, like Switzerland, have not engaged in a major military confrontation with another state for a century or more. Many others have experienced a serious military dispute more recently, but the vast majority of even these states have been at peace during most of their existence. In 1997, for example, there were no international wars and few serious crises. The usual condition of interstate relations is, therefore, peace, though "peace" is a broad category that includes the "special relationship" of the United States and Britain, indifference (Burundi and Ecuador, for example), as well as a lull in ongoing hostilities (Israel and Syria over much of the last few decades). And though most people think war is occasionally necessary, the great majority would prefer to have few of them. People typically desire peace not just for the absence of killing but for the chance to live normal lives. Peace is not only common; it is desirable. Accordingly, most people expect their governments to preserve it as long as they can without making unacceptable sacrifices.

Though governments use military force on occasion, there are constraints on their ability to do so. In this chapter, we consider the importance of some obvious constraints, those usually emphasized by the realists. These include geographical distance, alliances, and the balance of power. But we also consider the more voluntary constraint posed by democratic government, the influence found on the lower left of the Kantian triangle at the head of this chapter. To illustrate that it is the focus of this chapter, the arrow from that lower left corner is darker here. We find that democracy has a great impact on reducing conflict: democracies do not fight other democracies and they are more peaceful in general. On average, democracies fight less than autocracies, other things being equal. The evidence also shows that newly democratizing countries are not more prone to international disputes than older democracies are. Before we present these results, however, it is first necessary to think about how some kinds of researchers, as in medicine, or politics, analyze evidence in order to generalize about the causes of disease or, in this case, conflict.

The Epidemiology of War and Peace

To understand some of the influences that promote or inhibit interstate conflict, in much of this book, we will be using the same methods that medical scientists use to understand the causes of disease. More and more, international relations scholars are adopting such scientific methods to investigate the causes of war. There are some differences, but it is enlightening to consider the similarities between our approach and those of medical epidemiologists. As with nations and peace, the usual condition of most individuals is health, though, as with peace, the quality of people's health varies from vigorous physical and mental fitness to the mere absence of disease. One difference between the study of international relations and medicine is that some fortunate and wisely governed nations may avoid war indefinitely, but individual human beings ultimately die. Still, most of us try to delay that day by all reasonable means, and the practitioners of medical science help us do this. They attempt, by a combination of theory and empirical research, to identify the conditions that promote or prevent disease. Their job is to find out how we can avoid illness and postpone death. Our job, in trying to understand international relations, is to find out how to prevent or mitigate violent conflict.

Much of medical research is experimental, or it is clinical and focused on the details of particular cases, but a large proportion is "epidemiological" in character. Epidemiological research analyzes the distribution of particular diseases in large populations in order to understand why some individuals contract a disease while others do not. Very large computerized databases containing information on who has died, where, and when of various diseases and about the life experience and genetic heritage of those individuals are now available. They allow scientists to use statistical methods to uncover the causes of disease and, ultimately, to devise regimes for their prevention or treatment. Frequently, these databases include records on hundreds of thousands of individuals. These are never fully accurate and complete, but if they are reasonably so, a skilled researcher with keen intuition or a sharply honed theory can perform statistical analyses to discover conditions that are correlated with disease. Indeed, statistical tests are valuable because they do not require the data to be perfectly accurate. They are designed to reveal the message in the midst of considerable noise.

If her theory is sound and well developed, a researcher may be able to move beyond simple correlations to suggest the causal mechanisms whereby something in individuals' heredity, or their environment, actually causes a disease. Epidemiological or "macro" research is rarely conclusive in establishing a causal mechanism, which typically must be confirmed in controlled experiments and micro-level studies of individual patients or by laboratory research at the level of the cell. Nonetheless, good macro-level epidemiological work can provide strong indications of causality and, even before the micro-level mechanisms are well understood, can offer practical advice about what kinds of exposures or behaviors individuals should avoid if they wish to stay healthy. Reports of this kind of work appear almost daily in newspapers.

Consider the kind of results one might see from a large-scale epidemiological investigation of the causes of heart disease. Certain characteristics of individuals have been shown to be strongly associated, probably causally, with the incidence of this disease. One obvious relationship is that a person's chances of dying from heart disease increase as he or she ages. A second is that the probability of a person's having a heart attack is greater if one or both parents died of heart disease: heredity is important. The researcher might not be able to tell just why having a parent with heart disease increases the likelihood that an individual will also experience it, but the empirical correlation itself is important. We also know that on average males are more likely to have heart attacks than females are, at least when such other influences as age and heredity are held constant in the analysis. All these "risk factors" are influences over which the individual and his medical advisers have essentially no control. One cannot keep the years from advancing, change one's parents, or—except at high costs of various kinds—change one's gender. With only this information, a physician can do little more than advise those patients at high risk to be sure they keep their life insurance paid up. And for some patients that would be valuable—if unwelcome—advice.

But of course neither patient nor physician will stop there, and other findings of epidemiological research have been found to be helpful in the prevention of disease. We now know that certain lifestyles or habits are associated with the risk of heart disease and that these habits can be modified if an individual is sufficiently motivated. For instance, smokers run a much higher risk of heart attack than do nonsmokers. So, too, do those who consume a diet high in cholesterol and saturated fats or those who engage in little physical exercise. Each of these influences to a substantial degree operates independently of the others. That is, smoking by itself increases the risk of a heart attack whether or not one has a family history of heart disease and regardless of diet. Therefore, a doctor can say to a patient, "Based on your age, sex, family history, and lifestyle, statistically you run a two percent risk of having a heart attack in the next year. You can't totally eliminate the danger, but if you will quit smoking (or go on a diet, or get off the couch), you can cut that risk in half. In fact, if you change your lifestyle dramatically—quit smoking, go on a diet, *and* get off the couch—you can cut your risk by three quarters." In other words, some things are beyond the ability of either the doctor or the patient to change or control, but a lot of other things can be done to improve our health, if we want to do them badly enough.

None of this implies that any one of these influences is a perfect predictor of contracting heart disease. Some people who have never smoked nevertheless have heart attacks. And many smokers live a long time. The predictions are probabilistic; they are about greater and less risks, not about certainties. We should also acknowledge that the research that forms the basis for the doctor's advice is never final: estimates of the relative importance of the different risk factors may change on the basis of subsequent research. New, more reliable data may become available, for example, data gleaned from actually monitoring what people eat or how much they exercise rather than from what people report about their habits to an observer. Further research may also identify new influences that affect the probability of acquiring heart disease, or it may show that relationships thought to be important are actually spurious. It will never be possible to develop a perfect model that will predict all heart attacks. For such a complex biological phenomenon, the theory can never be complete. There are too many unique qualities of our heredity and experience, and chance events play a significant role. Yet at some point, physicians and patients decide that the science is sufficiently conclusive to use as a guide for behavior. Political scientists, too, can provide only partial, tentative conclusions about what countries can do to avoid violent conflict; nevertheless, the science seems sufficiently clear to warrant certain prescriptions.

What Causes or Constrains States' Use of Force?

Most people are reasonably healthy most of the time, but the possibility of serious disease or even death is always present; it is inherent in the human condition. Similarly, though most states are at peace most of the time, the possibility of a serious military confrontation or war is inherent in international relations. International relations for many centuries has been anarchic because countries cannot look to a higher authority to protect them. The constancy of the danger of war is a central theme of writers on international relations, from the time of Thucydides, historian of the Athenian wars with Sparta, to the present. A great twentieth-century scholar, Quincy Wright (1965, 1518), put it very strongly: "Peace is artificial; war is natural." States must find the policies, and the material means, to look out for themselves. By force of arms, the assistance of allies, or appeasement, they must seek to prevent the inherent possibility of international violence from becoming manifest. In considering whether to use force in their relations with another state, national decision makers must consider various constraints on their freedom of action.

Geography

Both distance and topography affect the probability that two states will become involved in a militarized conflict. The effect of distance is straightforward: the farther two states are from one another, the less likely they are to fight. Neighboring states are more likely to fight each other, unless other constraints discourage it. Among individuals as well, most violence occurs between people who regularly interact. There are two reasons why distance reduces the probability of conflict. First, it is hard to exert great military power at a substantial distance. It is one thing to mount an incursion against a bordering state, but it is quite another to conduct military operations against a country thousands of miles away, as the United States discovered in its war in Vietnam. The cost of using military power increases with distance for logistical reasons. Second, interstate conflict is unlikely between widely separated states because in most cases they have few reasons to fight.

The great majority of international wars arise over territorial issues, chiefly the location of a disputed border (perhaps involving territory that has changed hands in previous wars) or the ownership of valuable natural resources (oil, minerals, water, or fishing grounds, for example). Many other conflicts between contiguous states arise over the treatment of ethnic minorities, groups of people who may be a majority in one country but are an ill-treated minority in the other. For a variety of reasons, the border between two countries may have been delineated in a way that divides people from ethnically similar groups across the border. From the late nineteenth to the mid-twentieth century, Prussia (later Germany) repeatedly fought its neighbors in an attempt to unify Germans under a single government. Wherever borders have been recently constructed and create ethnically artificial divisions—as many have been in contemporary Africa because of colonialism—there is the possibility that one country will intervene in another on behalf of an ethnically related minority. The current conflict in the Republic of the Congo is an example. At times, ethnic ties provide an excuse if not the actual cause for war. Again, the fighting in the Congo provides some examples.

Geographical proximity, then, increases both the opportunity and the willingness for states to fight. As a consequence, distance is the most important constraint on the use of military force. Clearly, however, the constraining influence of distance is much greater for small or poor countries (which includes most of those in the world) than it is for those few states we call "great powers." A great power has the ability to exercise military force even over long distances. The cost of doing so is higher than against a neighbor, all other things being equal, but a great power, by definition, has the resources to exercise its influence widely. Napoleon had a big enough army to permit him to move across Europe all the way to Moscow (though extending his lines of supply so far ultimately cost him dearly). In the eighteenth and nineteenth centuries, great navies provided Britain with the capacity to build an empire—protected by the threat to use force—upon which the sun never set. In the twentieth century, air power and eventually intercontinental ballistic missiles armed with nuclear weapons provided the instruments whereby a few states, big enough or rich enough to afford them, could strike anywhere. Although even the great powers are constrained by distance, they have the ability to mitigate that constraint. In addition, by acquiring colonies—or spheres of influence, or allies, or markets, or sources of vital raw materials—great distances away, they are more likely to have reasons, and the willingness, to fight adversaries at a distance.

Power

Another important constraint on states' ability and willingness to use force, emphasized in traditional accounts of international relations, is power. The balance of military capabilities undoubtedly influences decision makers contemplating the use of force against a rival. States seek to constrain their adversaries by increasing their military strength. Deterrence has been an element of statecraft as long as there have been states. The line of thought runs like this: "I will make myself strong enough to deter others from attacking me. I will create military capabilities that will deny them the ability to invade me successfully. Or if that is not possible, I will at least be able to impose such a high cost on an attacker that the potential gains will not be worth the price." In the nuclear era, even the most powerful states have had to settle for the threat to punish rather than the ability to deny an attack. Topography can help a state succeed at deterrence. Contrast the situation of Switzerland, surrounded by the Alps;

the strategic benefits enjoyed by the United States from having two oceans on its borders; or the safety provided by the great depth of the Russian territory with the vulnerability of such small states as Belgium or the Netherlands, located on the northern plain of continental Europe. But topography must be supplemented by real military power.

Saying that military power is an important constraint on interstate relations does not answer a key question, however, and one that has been debated for thousands of years: Is the probability that two states will fight lowest when there is an equal balance of power between them, or is it lowest when one side has much more power than the other? Many realists, including Waltz (1979), believe that international peace is best maintained by a balance of power. When two states have equal military capabilities, each will be uncertain whether it can defeat the other in a war, and thus they will both be reluctant to start one. If one state had a preponderance of power, it would, according to this view, use its advantage to conquer its weaker adversary. Other realists, such as Organski and Kugler (1980), contend that wars are actually tests to determine what the real balance of power is. According to this school of thought, militarized disputes are most likely when two states have different expectations about which would win a fight. When one is clearly predominant over the other, the outcome of a military contest is predictable, so the weaker side will not fight a war it knows it will lose. Better to concede what the more powerful state demands and at least avoid the cost of fighting a losing battle. Power preponderance, in this view, is associated with peace. As the emissary of the powerful Athenian empire said harshly to the weak city-state of Melos in Thucydides's famous "Melian dialogue," "the strong do as they will and the weak do as they must."

Most recent research supports the view that preponderant power is more likely to discourage military conflict than is a balance of national capabilities. A strong state is usually able to deter a weaker one from challenging it by using or threatening to use military force (Fearon 1994b). Clearly, however, peace for the weak often comes at the price of domination and exploitation. We will see, through the use of statistical tests reported in the rest of the book, whether the evidence generally supports the view that preponderant power induces peace. Here, we simply leave it as a hypothesis.

Alliances

Another constraint on the use of force is an alliance. A major motive for many states to form an alliance is protection. Small states may seek to ally themselves with bigger protectors. Or, preferring to avoid too close a relationship with a great power, they may seek to put together an alliance with several smaller states. Even the great powers may see an advantage in becoming allied, either with another major power or with small but strategically located states. They may also form alliances to insure that a country important to their security will not join an opposing coalition. Sometimes, too, a big power brings a smaller state into an alliance as a means of controlling it, perhaps to keep it from provoking a regional adversary in a way that might drag the big state into a war it wishes to avoid. The United States and its European allies brought West Germany into NATO in 1955 partly to bolster Western defenses against the Soviet bloc but partly also to insure that Germany would not take actions that would endanger the peace in Europe. Alliances thus are partly a way of constraining the likelihood of war with nonallies and partly a way of reducing the likelihood of war among their members.

Not all alliances succeed in deterring or constraining military action, however. Indeed, sometimes they make conflict contagious, dragging states into ongoing wars that they would otherwise have avoided. In the world wars of the last century, the fighting spread rapidly beyond the initial protagonists. Most countries in central and Eastern Europe were drawn into war, even though their small size meant they had little to contribute.

Geographical location, distance and topography, and to a large degree the ability to be a great power are not matters over which states have any real influence. They are more like givens, more like an individual's age, family history, and sex in our medical analogy. Building up relative military power and forming alliances, however, are more like diet and exercise; they are influences over which a state can, over time, exercise some degree of control. Yet all these factors—the importance of distance, the historical role of the great powers, the central place of power and alliances—share the common characteristic of being familiar elements of realist theories.

Kantian influences

In this book, we combine the realist and liberal perspectives. Realism and liberalism are sometimes presented as antithetical understandings or theories of international relations, but that is not the position we adopt. Kant and other classical liberals did not deny the importance of the realist outlook in attempting to understand and avoid war. Realism presents a baseline against which the effect of the liberal influences can be compared. Kant, for example, shared Hobbes's understanding that anarchy meant the continued threat of war. Like Hobbes, he believed that in the state of nature, nations "like lawless savages, exist in a condition . . . of war" (Kant [1797] 1970, 165). And he agreed with Hobbes that great power could sometimes be used to prevent war, but even Hobbes and other realists acknowledge that this sort of "peace" is tenuous. Kant and other liberals have stressed this point and insisted that the realist perspective alone is incomplete, that it misses too many important elements of international relations. Kant was convinced that a stable, genuine peace—a "perpetual peace," as he put it—could be developed within a "federation" of liberal republics. For countries that share democratic institutions and are economically interdependent, powerful constraints limit the use of force (Doyle 1997, chap. 8; Huntley 1996). According to liberals, then, theories of realpolitik do not identify all the factors that affect whether states will engage in violent conflict. Perhaps even more important, they do not emphasize the constraints over which states can exercise the most control.

A positive peace, we believe, must rest more on the three Kantian supports—democracy, interdependence, and international law and organizations—than on power politics. The pacific federation Kant envisioned was not a world state, which he expected would be a "soulless despotism." Its members remain sovereign, linked only by confederational arrangements relating to their collective security, economics, and social interactions. The difference between realism and liberalism is that liberalism sees democratic governance, economic interdependence, and international law as means by which the security dilemma rooted in the anarchy of the international system can be mitigated or even superceded—although the threat of violence remains among states not much linked by these ties.

Thus, we begin by assuming that the international system is anarchic and power politics is important over much of the globe. The possibility of violence is inherent. Yet states do not fight all others at all times even where and when realist principles dominate; they are constrained by power, alliances, and distance. Ultimately, realists are concerned only with states that have the opportunity and incentive to become engaged in conflict (Most and Starr 1989, chap. 2). Accordingly, we incorporate these constraints as central features of our theoretical model. But to these realist variables, we add measures of the three Kantian influences, hypothesizing that democracies will be constrained from using force, at least against other democracies; that economically important trade creates incentives for the maintenance of peaceful relations; and that international organizations constrain decision makers by positively promoting peace in a variety of ways. Since the modern international system is far from being a "pacific federation" of democratic states, we expect both realist and Kantian factors to affect interstate relations, and we include both in our analyses. We also consider the effects of characteristics of the international system, both realist and liberal, on the incidence of conflict. For instance, if more states become linked by Kantian ties over time, does their example or influence help change the behavior of other states in the system? Has the deepening of such ties among interdependent democracies over the last half century induced some change of behavior even in states that are not especially interdependent or democratic? Or, as many realists believe, is a powerful international leader or hegemon able to constrain other states from fighting?

The first of the Kantian variables is the character of states' political systems. We hypothesize that democracies will rarely fight or even threaten each other, and perhaps also that democracies will be more peaceful in general. In this chapter, we concentrate on the effect that democracy has on the likelihood that two states will become involved in military conflict. We save for subsequent chapters consideration of the effects of trade and international organizations.

A Database for Epidemiological Studies of Interstate Conflict

Just as medical researchers create and examine data on the life histories of individuals, we need information on the relations of countries: whether they were peaceful or in conflict, the character of their governments, their level of trade, and other characteristics. Most early analyses were confined to the cold war era (1950–85), but we now have information for most independent countries in the world over the period 1885–1992. This allows us to see whether the patterns initially discovered hold in other periods and, if so, to make generalizations regarding countries all over the globe and over a long span of time. We can, therefore, examine the effects of democracy on conflict as this form of government has spread around the world and as democratic institutions have evolved and deepened. We take a special interest in whether the effect of democracy on the likelihood of conflict is the same in different historical periods.

One important thing that has changed over time is the fundamental configuration of power in the international system. Realists contrast multipolar systems with bipolar systems, though they disagree on how best to determine polarity. Polarity is sometimes defined according to the number of major alliance systems confronting each other. If alliances are the defining characteristic, then in the decade or so immediately preceding World War I, the system was bipolar because the alliance of Austria-Hungary, Germany, and Italy was arrayed against the competing coalition of Britain, France, and Russia. But alliances can shift and be broken. Italy actually fought on the other side in the Great War, against Austria and Germany. Therefore, it is preferable to determine polarity not by the number or relative power of alliances but by the number of major powers in the system (Waltz 1979, 98–99). If there are several—as there were before World War I—then the system is multipolar. On the other hand, if there are only two states whose power substantially exceeds all others, then the system is bipolar. By this criterion, the international system was multipolar for centuries preceding 1945 but bipolar during the cold war. We should consider, therefore, whether international relations were different in the two eras.

Since the end of the cold war, the global system has no longer been bipolar. The cold war ended sometime between 1988 and 1992, depending on how one judges the importance of various events. Communist governments in most of Eastern Europe collapsed over the course of 1989. The Soviet Union proved unable or unwilling to preserve even its important client state East Germany, which in 1990 reunited with West Germany to form again a single country. The Warsaw Pact, created by the Soviet Union to counter NATO, was formally disbanded in July 1991, but for almost two years previously, it had had no military significance. Finally, at the end of 1991, the Soviet Union itself was dissolved. It is hard to determine a single date for the end of the cold war, but the tearing down of the Berlin Wall in 1989 is probably as good as any other. It effectively marked the end of the bipolar system. After 1989, the world has been neither bipolar nor multipolar. Perhaps it is best understood as unipolar, at least as indicated by the relative power of the United States if not its will to control or shape the international system. Therefore, we also need to consider whether interstate relations have been different since the cold war ended. This will be hard to do with no more than four or five years of post–cold war data, but it is important to try.

Our information about the international system has two short gaps: all but the first year of both World War I and World War II are missing from our analyses because good data on who traded with whom are unavailable. What information does exist is greatly distorted by the worldwide disruption of normal commerce caused by the war. For similar reasons, we omit the years immediately following those wars, 1919–20 and 1946–49. Even though we postpone analyzing the effect of trade to the next chapter, we limit our analyses in all chapters to the years 1885–1914, 1921–39, and 1950–92. It is best to use a consistent database for all our analyses rather than to drop or add cases as the available information contracts or expands. If omitting these years biases our results in any way, it biases them *against* finding evidence to support the democratic peace. During the world wars, peace between the democracies was especially strong: all the warring pairs of countries were composed either of two autocracies or of a democracy and an autocracy.[1]

Since our basic perspective is that countries can in principle fight any other country (although they are usually constrained from fighting particular countries), all our analyses will be carried out using data regarding *pairs* of countries. For example, we are concerned not with Germany individually but with Germany's relations with Austria, Belgium, France, Italy, Japan, Russia, Sweden, Turkey, and so forth. Thus, a case (or observation) is the experience of two states in a single year, say, Germany and Austria in 1890, or the same two countries in 1891, or Germany and France in 1892. From a statistical analysis of thousands of historical cases, we can compute the likelihood that a pair of countries having certain constraints on conflict (for example, two contiguous states, members of a

[1]The only exception is Finland in World War II, which fought against some of the Western Allies, but democratic Finland's real quarrel was with the Soviet Union, and no deaths arose from conflict between Finland and other democracies.

common alliance, two democracies) will have experienced a militarized dispute in a year, and how this probability compared to the risk of a "typical" pair of countries or to the risk of conflict for a pair of states that experienced other constraints.

Militarized Disputes

Our information base was compiled by many scholars and organizations. We are particularly indebted to those who have worked so hard to make the study of war a science. To determine which states were involved in conflicts in which years, we use data compiled by the Correlates of War (COW) Project regarding militarized interstate disputes (MIDs). We are interested in all international militarized disputes, not just wars. Wars, as we have noted, are (fortunately) rare events; consequently, as with rare diseases, it is hard to find patterns in where and when they erupt. Casting our net more widely, to include all organized uses of violence between countries, including the threat to use military force, gives us a better chance to discern the causes of interstate conflict. Militarized disputes short of war are about thirty times more common than wars. Also, most wars begin with some threat or more limited use of violence. War virtually always starts with a sequence of symbolic words and acts that serve as threats or warnings that more damaging acts may follow (O'Neill 1999, 16).

World War II is a good example. It was preceded by a long series of diplomatic threats, military moves, and crises. They began with Germany's remilitarization of the Rhineland in March 1936. This was followed by Hitler's annexation of Austria in March 1938 and then, in more rapid succession, by the Munich crisis that fall, the occupation of Czechoslovakia in March 1939, and German territorial demands on Poland in the spring of 1939. Finally, in September, the Germans invaded Poland and full-scale war began. As with each of these events, many militarized disputes have the potential to escalate to war. Overall, the influences and constraints that affect the occurrence of wars do not appear to differ much from those that are relevant to militarized disputes in general. Therefore, it makes sense to investigate the more inclusive but still dangerous phenomena of militarized disputes.

The COW data record each year a dyad was involved in a dispute, that is, when one state threatened to use force, made a demonstration of force, or actually used military force against another. For our analysis, a militarized dispute requires an action that is explicit, overt, not accidental, and government approved. (For example, cross-border attacks by independent guerillas, not under the control of the government on whose territory they are based, are not counted; nor are civil wars.) In this electronic database, a 1 is entered for the variable DISPUTE if any kind of militarized dispute was ongoing between two states in a particular year and a 0 is entered if there was no dispute.[2] Many disputes are purely bilateral, that is, between only two countries. Many others, however, are multilateral, bringing in allies or adversaries of one or both of the initiators. We count every conflicting pair that was involved in a dispute, deliberately giving full weight to expanded, contagious, multistate disputes. Our MIDs data are dominated by events short of war, with about 70 percent of these falling into the category of a use of force but not war. (Recall that a "war," according to the COW Project, involved at least 1,000 deaths in battle.) The rest of the disputes are mostly demonstrations of force, such as posting a warship offshore of another country as a warning but not actually firing any shots.

Most explanations of the democratic peace predict that democratic dyads will be less willing to threaten each other militarily or to use force even at low levels than pairs of nondemocracies. In this view, pairs of democracies should experience fewer militarized disputes of any type, and they should be less likely to escalate low-level disputes (say, those involv-

---

[2]These and other data from the COW Project are available at http://pss.la. psu.edu/MID_DATA.htm. Some researchers urge that only the initial year of a dispute be used, since a dispute in one year increases the chances of another or continued dispute in the next year and events in each year are not statistically independent. But rational leaders frequently reevaluate their positions, whether to escalate, deescalate, halt, or maintain the existing strategy. Fully half of all militarized disputes involve a change in the level of force employed over the course of the dispute or a new dispute that arises before the first has concluded. We have performed many analyses using only the first year of disputes and found few material differences from those reported below (see Oneal and Russett 1999a, 1999c). Because, for other reasons noted above, we exclude all but the first years of the two world wars from our data, the impact of continuing disputes on our analysis is much reduced.

ing a verbal threat) to a higher level that actually causes casualties. Other theories, emphasizing the ability of democracies to signal their resolve by threats or low-level uses of force, suggest that precisely because one democracy normally does not expect another to go to war with it, it may be willing to initiate low-level disputes as part of diplomatic bargaining and posturing.

We disagree with this second view. If even low-level disputes carry some potential to escalate into war, we predict democracies will avoid stepping onto this slippery slope with each other. Moreover, if democracies are confident that they will not go over the brink to war, the initiation of a low-level MID by one democracy would be recognized by another as a bluff, what game theorists call "cheap talk." Insofar as normative theories of the democratic peace are correct, it would also be seen as a threat lacking legitimacy in domestic politics, where peace with other democracies is expected and desired. Diplomatic actions by one democracy against another—ceasing to cooperate in an international organization, cutting aid, or applying trade quotas—may be common, but threats to use military force will not be.

Democracies are raucous, contentious places, where the public expression of competing interests is common, but those conflicts are generally resolved nonviolently because of the nature of democratic institutions and culture. It would hardly be surprising if democracies experienced a variety of conflicts with one another over matters such as environmental controls or trade policy. Such conflicts may even be voiced more frequently among democracies than among nondemocratic states. We are concerned with the threat and use of military force that may lead to war. We do not consider in our analyses mere diplomatic disputes. This, then, is our prediction: democratic dyads will be much less likely to cross the threshold between nonviolent and violent acts than other pairs of states. Because there is theoretical disagreement about how democracies behave with regard to low levels of violence, our prediction in one sense poses a harder test of the democratic peace than does just the prediction that wars will be rare.[3]

---

[3]We do not examine patterns of escalation short of war within disputes, in part because we do not believe that portion of the COW scale is truly ordinal; for example, a threat to initiate a nuclear war is coded lower than a forcible seizure of a fishing boat without casualties in the COW data.

Influences and Constraints: Democracy

In our statistical analyses, we consider a variety of influences that affect the likelihood that two states will become involved in a militarized dispute. These are suggested by theory and, in many cases, previous work by ourselves and others.[4] Because some factors can themselves be influenced by the occurrence of a dispute (for instance, conflict can reduce trade just as trade can reduce conflict), we assess all the explanatory variables in the year prior to that in which the existence of a dispute (or peace) was recorded. This precaution cannot settle all the questions we might have about the direction of causality, but it is a reasonable beginning. Later in the book, we will look at some of the most important reciprocal relationships, such as the effect of conflict on trade, to get an idea of the importance of the feedback loops discussed in Chapter 1.

Democracy is our special concern in this chapter. We use the Polity III data to compute a summary measure of the political character of regimes.[5] The codes are based on three characteristics of national governments: (1) the competitiveness of political participation, (2) the openness and competitiveness of executive recruitment, and (3) the level of institutionalized constraints on the chief executive. The evaluation of states according to these criteria allows us to distinguish democracies from autocratic (or authoritarian) governments.

These criteria, as we noted in the last chapter, are standard elements of the concept of democracy as it has evolved in the West and spread across the globe. Not every state that has the word "democratic" in its name qualifies. The "people's republics" and "people's democratic republics" of the Communist bloc during the cold war are excluded. The underlying

[4]In this book, we keep to a minimum the technical discussion of the sources, definitions, and measurement decisions necessary to turn concepts and theory into variables and hypotheses we can employ in a systematic scientific study. Readers who wish to examine these matters further can do so in previously published reports of our research. The information used here is described extensively in Oneal and Russett 1997, and as noted in the preface, all the data are on our Web sites.

[5]This method is recommended by the originators of the Polity III data (Jaggers and Gurr 1995). The data are available from http://isere.colorado.edu/pub/datasets. polity3/may96.data. It is important to note that these data, like those on disputes, were created by scholars who were not pursuing research on the democratic peace and thus were not subject to bias in its favor.

idea behind the Polity III codings is that the institutions, principles, and practices of Western-style democracy provide powerful constraints on arbitrary government. The constraints on the leaders of autocratic states are usually much weaker. While the concept and its measures are creations of Western political thought and scholarship, there is, nevertheless, a great deal of agreement among alternative indicators of democracy. They do differ to a degree on individual cases, but there is little evidence that the Polity data are systematically biased in the way they score different countries. If we were to use the data of other scholars, our conclusions would not be much affected.

No democracy is "perfect," and even the most totalitarian government has some limits on arbitrary rule. Indeed, many states are a mixture of democratic and authoritarian features, and sometimes the balance is so close that one cannot really put a country into either one category or the other. Therefore, democracy must be understood as a matter of degree, and our measure of it should reflect this. Referring back to our medical analogy, one can smoke (or exercise) a lot, very little, or some amount in between. In the Polity data, each country is coded on a scale of 0 to 10 according to various characteristics of democracy and on an autocracy scale that also runs from 0 to 10. Subtracting each country's score on the autocracy scale from its score on the democracy scale gives us a country's summary evaluation on a twenty-one-point democracy-autocracy continuum. We refer to this measure as DEMOC. It ranges from −10 for an extremely autocratic or authoritarian state to +10 for those that are the most democratic. During the cold war, most European democracies were +10, and most communist states were −10. Our hypothesis is that the higher the degree of democracy, as indicated by the DEMOC variable, the greater the constraint on a country's leadership's use of military force and, hence, the less likely it is to become engaged in militarized disputes with other countries.

We should note that the Polity III scores are not perfectly comparable over the many years, 1885–1992, that we study, and this has implications for our effort to make generalizations about this long period. Even in the few republics of Kant's time, the voting franchise was tightly restricted, with little philosophical or political challenge. As late as 1918, about 40 percent of British males (mostly working class) were disfranchised by residence requirements; female suffrage was granted partially in 1918 and fully only in 1928. In the United States, women achieved the vote only in

1920, and blacks were systematically excluded in many parts of the country until the 1960s. In most Western democracies, women did not obtain the vote until after World War I. Swiss women obtained the franchise only in 1971. In the Polity data, the United Kingdom goes from 6 to 7 on our democracy scale in 1880, to 8 in 1902, and jumps to 10 only in 1922. But Switzerland is coded at 10 from 1848, and the United States from 1871, despite the limitations on the right to vote. The consequences for foreign-policy making of these restrictions on the participation of women and minorities may not be trivial. In the contemporary United States, women are significantly more averse to the use of military force than men are, and they vote in part on this basis (Chaney, Alvarez, and Nagler 1998). Thus, the exclusion of women from the franchise in earlier periods could have profoundly reduced the constraint on even the most "democratic" states to avoid the use of force. Unfortunately, this state of affairs is only partially reflected in the data.[6]

In order to specify precisely how we will test the democratic peace, we need to think about how a dispute might occur. The key point is that it can result from the actions of a single state. Either state in a dyad can issue a threat, make a show of force, or launch an attack. It may take two to tango, but it only takes one to start a military conflict. If we are trying to assess the probability that a conflict will occur, we must be particularly concerned with the state that is less constrained from using force. This state is the principal threat to the peace. We hypothesize, therefore, that the likelihood of conflict depends primarily on how strong the constraints are on the less constrained state in each pair. In effect, that state is the weak link in the chain of peaceful dyadic relations. We expect, therefore, that the probability of a dispute depends mainly on the lower democracy score ($DEMOC_L$) in each dyad. The more democratic the less democratic state is, the more constrained it will be from engaging in a dispute and the lower we expect the chance of a militarized dispute to be.

In some of our previous studies, we found that the *difference* between

[6]New data on government type compiled by a European (Vanhanen 2000) correlate fairly well with the Polity III data (usually above .80) from the 1920s onward, but much less so (under .60) from the 1880s to World War I. (A perfect correlation would be 1.00, a perfect negative correlation −1.00, and no correlation 0.) Vanhanen's measure identifies substantially fewer states as democratic in the earlier period. Doorenspleet (2000) concurs.

states' political regimes also affects the likelihood of conflict: democracies and autocracies seem to fight like cats and dogs. To explore this, we also include in some analyses the democracy score of the more democratic state in each pair: $DEMOC_H$, the higher democracy score of the two. Using both the lower and the higher democracy score in a single equation allows us to see whether the "political distance" separating two states along the democracy-autocracy continuum affects the likelihood that they will fight. We expect that two democratic states will fight least, but we also want to determine the chance of conflict for two autocracies and for a mixed pair of one autocracy and one democracy. This allows us to see not only whether two autocracies get along better with one another than they would with a democratic state but also whether there is an "autocratic peace," in which pairs of autocracies are as peaceful as pairs of democracies are. Finally, analyses that include both $DEMOC_L$ and $DEMOC_H$ enable us to determine whether democracies are more peaceful in general or whether the democratic peace operates only between democracies.

Realist Constraints

We do not, of course, look only at the effects of states' political systems on interstate conflict. International politics takes place in an environment heavily influenced by realist considerations. These are influences that apply to some degree to all countries, democracies and otherwise. In assessing the democratic peace, we must address the concerns of the realists.

Contiguity and distance

The potential for international violence exists when at least one member of a dyad can reach the other with military force. For most states, the ability to do so is determined foremost by geographical proximity. Many countries are virtually irrelevant to each other's security concerns because of the effects of geography. The importance of distance is apparent. You do not need a Ph.D. in political science to know that, but many tests have confirmed that geographical proximity has the greatest, most consistent influence on the likelihood that conflict will occur. To take it fully into account we use two different variables. One is the great-circle distance separating two countries. This is the shortest distance around the surface of the globe between their capitals; it is the route a plane would fly if it were to fly directly from one capital to the other.[7] This variable measure of distance is a good indicator of the constraints imposed by geography, but we also need to recognize the effects of colonial holdings on the likelihood of conflict, especially as we move back in time.

In the late nineteenth and early twentieth centuries, several of the great powers controlled territory far from the metropolitan country. Countries may have both reasons and the ability to fight each other across colonial boundaries as well as from one home country to another. Many international disputes, and some wars, began that way. So we created an additional measure to capture this influence. It is a simple indicator of contiguity that equals 1 if two states are *not* contiguous. If they share a boundary on land or are separated by less than 150 miles of water, our indicator takes a value of 0. In making this determination, we consider both the geographical locations of the home countries and their colonies or other dependencies. We call this measure "*non*contiguity" because we want to think consistently in terms of constraints on the use of force. Being contiguous facilitates conflict. Since it takes colonies into account, our measure of noncontiguity is only moderately correlated with the distance between states' capitals. These two variables are not redundant, therefore, but complementary.

Distance constrains great powers, which have the ability to deliver substantial military forces to targets far away, much less than it does small states. The major powers have been identified by the COW Project based on the consensus of historians. For the entire period of our analysis, 1885–1992, Great Britain, France, and Russia/Soviet Union qualify as

---

[7]Actually, we modified this procedure in two ways. For the largest countries, we considered the location of their major ports and used the distance from one of these ports to the capital of another country when the port was closer to the other member of the dyad than its capital was. Thus, we sometimes use Vancouver instead of Ottawa for Canada, Vladivostok for Russia/Soviet Union, and New Orleans or San Francisco for the United States in computing the distance to another country. Also, for all dyads, we use the natural logarithm of distance to capture the effect of geographical separation. While the cost of moving troops and equipment increases with distance, the rate of increase drops because fixed costs are important.

great powers. Austria-Hungary is included until its defeat and dismemberment in 1918. Italy and Germany are included until 1945. (Italy had been somewhat marginal as a great power anyway, and West Germany ceased to play a significant military role beyond its own borders.) Japan is considered a great power after defeating China in 1895, but it lost this status after its defeat in 1945. The United States remains a great power from its victory over Spain in 1898 to the present. China is counted after the Communist takeover in 1949. It is worth emphasizing the importance of major or minor power status. Because of their wide-ranging interests, the great powers become engaged in many more disputes than small states do. A major power is more than five times as likely as a minor power to become involved in a militarized dispute. Thus, despite its democratic institutions and culture, the United States gets into more militarized disputes than many smaller states do. Because major and minor powers behave so differently, we include a variable that distinguishes two kinds of dyads. It is coded 1 when a dyad includes only minor powers (because they are the states more constrained from fighting); it equals 0 otherwise. Some contiguous dyads also include one or two major powers; these are the dyads most at risk.

Two types of dyads have a particularly high potential for conflict: dyads containing contiguous states and dyads containing at least one major power. Together, they constitute a set of cases that we characterize as "politically relevant dyads" because these include most of the pairs for which security relations are especially important. They are easily the most dispute-prone dyads in the international system. While they constitute just 22 percent of all the dyads for which we could compile data, they account for 87 percent of all the disputes. In other words, the politically relevant dyads are twenty-four times as likely to experience a militarized dispute as those deemed to be "irrelevant." Overwhelmingly, then, these are the dyads at risk. Furthermore, some disputes among the nonrelevant dyads are the result of the "contagion" of large conflicts: distant small states getting drawn into disputes. Often these small states do not take much military action or incur casualties. The disputes involving contiguous states or a major power are the most serious and the ones on which we should focus our attention.

The statistical analyses in this book, therefore, are limited to the set of almost 40,000 observations we have for the politically relevant dyads over the period 1885–1992. These are the cases for which our theories of conflict are most applicable. Elsewhere (Oneal and Russett 1999a, 1999c), we have analyzed all possible pairs of states, not just the politically relevant dyads. Those results are very similar to what we report here.

Power ratio

Realists are always concerned with the balance of power. To measure the military capabilities of dyadic members, we use the COW composite capabilities index (Singer, Bremer, and Stuckey 1972). It is composed, in equal weights, of a country's share of the international system's total population, urban population, energy consumption, iron and steel production, military manpower, and military expenditures. Together, these six dimensions of power tap a variety of elements that contribute to national power. Some can be utilized immediately for military purposes (manpower and expenditures); others indicate the longer-term military potential of states. In a protracted conflict, a state can mobilize substantial parts of its total population, particularly if many people live in cities, and divert its industrial base (indicated by energy consumption and iron and steel production) to the war effort. No measure of power is perfect, especially over a century-long period that witnessed major innovations in technology and strategy, but this measure is reasonable and is the standard way of tapping this important element of international relations. Our variable POWER RATIO is the logarithm of the ratio of the stronger state's capability index to that of the weaker state. We use the logarithm of the power ratio because we think having more and more power brings only declining marginal gains.

Alliances

Allies do not usually fight or threaten one another with military action. The fact that they are allied indicates that they share common strategic and security interests. Were they to have military disputes among themselves, they would weaken the common front they have formed against their enemies. During the cold war, the NATO allies rarely became involved in disputes among themselves, and except for those between Greece and Turkey, these never reached the point at which casualties were inflicted. Some potential conflicts may have been averted not just by the efforts of the two countries directly involved but also by the efforts of other, especially larger, allies. Usually this involved an offer to mediate or arbitrate a disagreement, but other forms of diplomatic pressure were also used. Militarized conflicts among the Warsaw Pact countries were also rare, but not unknown. There were few open disputes between the smaller members of the pact, but several times the Soviet Union intervened with military force (Hungary in 1956, Czechoslovakia in 1968) or with military threats to keep its smaller allies from changing their governments and weakening or leaving the alliance.

Sometimes countries switch their allegiance despite the existence of a formal commitment to provide military support. For example, at the start of World War I, Italy had a treaty with Germany and Austria-Hungary, but it did not enter the war on their side. Despite the alliance, Italy regarded Austria-Hungary as an adversary because the Austrians still claimed and occupied big sections of territory populated by Italian-speaking people. The Italian government wanted to incorporate this territory and its people into Italy. So in 1915, it joined the British-French-Russian side against its "allies."

An alliance may reduce the likelihood that two states will become involved in conflict with one another, but it is clearly no guarantee. Ultimately a treaty is just a "scrap of paper." As a result, we need to find out just how important a mutual alliance really is in reducing the risk of a militarized dispute. We do that here by using an updated set of data on alliances, information initially compiled by the COW Project. These data tell us which states were allied and how long the alliance lasted. Our variable ALLIES is coded 1 if the members of a dyad were linked by a mutual defense treaty, a neutrality pact, or an entente in a particular year; otherwise, it equals 0.[8]

Analyzing the Global Experience of a Century

To uncover the relative importance of the Kantian and realist influences on the likelihood of international conflict—the risk that a dyad will en-

---

[8]The original data are from Singer 1995, which we updated based on Rengger 1995.

gage in a militarized dispute—we use a method like that employed by epidemiologists to study the influences of environment, heredity, and lifestyle on illness. Logistic regression is one type of what statisticians call multiple regression analysis.[9] It allows us to estimate the independent effect of each one of our variables on the likelihood of a militarized dispute, while holding all the other variables constant. By "independent effect," we mean the change caused by one variable while simultaneously taking into account the effects of the other variables in the equation. With our example of heart disease, such an analysis tells how much the average patient's risk of a heart attack would be reduced if his blood cholesterol level were twenty points lower while nothing else changed (e.g., the amount of exercise, smoking habits, etc.). With militarized disputes, we can ask how much lower the risk of a dispute would be if both states were very democratic, or if they were allied, while holding constant all other influences, such as the capability ratio and the distance between them.

Our unit of analysis is the dyad-year; that is, an observation about the behavior of a pair of states in a single year. For example, we know whether or not Germany and France were involved in a militarized dispute in 1910. Combining information about different pairs of states with information regarding these pairs through time gives us a "pooled" data set. This kind of analysis is mathematically complex and requires statistical adjustments because many of the observations are not truly independent of each other, as we assume they are when we use regression analysis. For instance, a German attack on Belgium was certain to bring France into a war, and once Germany and France were at war, it was more likely that they would be at war in the next year as well. The analysis here employs standard statistical adjustments that are discussed in the appendix. This area of statistics continues to develop, and there are difficult issues involved; but we have conducted our tests in a variety of ways, and as we have reported in various other publications, we are confident

[9]Logistic regression is appropriate when the dependent variable, i.e., the variable to be explained, is nominal (dispute or no dispute) rather than continuous (fine gradations in the scale of violence from no conflict to big wars). We use the routines for logistic regression found in the statistical package Stata (*Stata Reference Manual* 1999).

that the results we will discuss here are robust. In general, different corrections for various statistical problems do not affect our results very much.[10]

In adopting the scientific method, we do not mean to suggest that all of international relations is amenable to the kind of statistical analysis presented here. Historical and philosophical studies are also important. Here, we try to formulate an explanation (or model) of militarized interstate disputes that incorporates the most important influences identified by both realist and liberal scholars. Each of these factors is thought to make an independent contribution to the pattern of conflict around the globe at any one time and for pairs of states through time. We consider only theoretical influences that are amenable to measurement, albeit imprecisely. This permits us to conduct statistical tests. We think this is important because it aids in the accumulation of knowledge, but we acknowledge that many things are missing from our model. First, some important influences, for example, decision makers' perception of events, are difficult to measure and so are excluded. Second, we do not look in any detail for different patterns of behavior for particular subgroups of states within the global system (say, by geographical region), and our analyses of the effect of change over time, even in the variables we believe are important, are limited. There is as yet little agreement on satisfactory methods for addressing some of these important issues. Finally, we acknowledge that there is an important element of unpredictability in all of human affairs. Small changes sometimes have big effects. "For want of a nail the shoe is lost, for want of a shoe the horse is lost, for want of a horse . . ." These limits to the scientific study of international relations will undoubtedly be pushed back as our methods and understanding develop. This

[10]These include corrections to produce robust standard errors and for clustering by dyads, and controls for time dependence using the general estimating equation (GEE). We reestimated our basic 1885–1992 equations for democracy and for trade (in Chapter 4) with the fixed-effects model (Oneal and Russett 2000a, 2001) and also found the results robust in this regard, as have Bennett and Stam (2000). Also see Beck and Katz 2001 and King 2001. These results are also not significantly affected by using the peace-years method of adjusting for temporal dependence (Beck, Katz, and Tucker 1998). These and other methodological decisions are discussed in the appendix to this book.

book is no more than a building block in an ongoing process of discovery.[11]

With these cautions, we now look at our first set of results. Table 3.1 presents the effects of the various risk factors on the likelihood of conflict. They are expressed in terms of the increase or decrease in the probability of a militarized dispute induced by a change in the factor of interest. This is the clearest way to consider the consequences of democracy and the realist variables and is how epidemiological results are given. Table 3.1 shows the effect of each of the variables that is, at least in principle, subject to policy makers' intervention if they wish to lower the probability that a military dispute will occur. (Distance, contiguity, and major power status were included in the analysis, and as expected, all strongly affected the probability of a dispute. But since these variables are not amenable to change by a state, we do not include them in this table.)

To show the effect of one influence on the probability of conflict, we must first compute a baseline probability against which to make comparisons. We want to know what the chance of a dispute is for some "typical" dyad; then we can see how each of the variables of interest affects this. We assume that our typical dyad is contiguous. Since these are the states most prone to conflict, they warrant particular attention. We also assume that the typical dyad is not composed of allies and does not include a major power. (Minor power dyads are more common in the international system than are those containing a major power.) Next, we set the democracy score at its midpoint (0) and set every other continuous variable at its

---

[11]We owe this threefold analytical distinction to Allan C. Stam. Jervis (1976) is identified with the view that decision makers' actions depend heavily on their perceptions. This adds to the complexity of international relations (see also Jervis 1997 and Cioffi-Revilla 1998). Wendt (1999) develops the constructivist argument that certain pairs of states may develop a sense of mutual identity that causes their baseline behavior to evolve in a cooperative direction. He is not sanguine that these effects can be established by social science, but the recent work of Green, Kim, and Yoon (2001), looking for what statistical analysts call fixed effects, is an effort to measure them. Nonetheless, fixed-effects models may not capture the phenomenon, noted by Wendt, that shared identities can be reversed as well as developed over time. Gartzke (1999) argues that uncertainty is inherently unmeasurable and so cannot be included in systematic analyses. Debates about the proper methods for studying international relations will surely continue.

average value for the contiguous dyads. With these values and the coefficients from Table A3.1, in the appendix, we can estimate the annual probability that this typical dyad would experience a military dispute. The baseline probability is about .06—six chances in a hundred of a dispute's arising during any given year. Next, we change the variables one at a time, making the dyad allied or adding a comparable amount of change (one standard deviation) to each of the continuous measures.[12] This allows us to compute the change in the risk of conflict induced by each alteration in the dyad's characteristics.

Table 3.1: Percentage Change in Risk for Annual Involvement in a Militarized Dispute, 1886–1992: Contiguous Dyads, Realist Variables and Democracy

All variables at baseline values except:

ALLIES equals 1	−46%
POWER RATIO increased by one standard deviation	−29
$DEMOC_L$ increased by one standard deviation	−42
$DEMOC_L$ decreased by one standard deviation	+69
$DEMOC_L$ increased to +10	−54
$DEMOC_L$ decreased to −10	+109

Our results correspond well with both Kantian and realist perspectives. As noted above, contiguity strongly increases the chance of conflict, distance strongly decreases it, and major powers fight more than smaller states do. Of the realist variables subject to policy action, an alliance between two states is associated with a drop of nearly half from the baseline

[12]Standard deviation is a statistical measure that allows us to compare the effect of changes in indicators that have different units of measurement: units along the democracy-autocracy continuum, fractional changes in the ratio of national capabilities, etc. The "normal" or bell-shaped curve is a statistical distribution that has a bulge at the mean (or average) of the distribution and then trails off to the sides in either direction. Under the normal curve, 68 percent of all observations fall within one standard deviation of the mean, and 95 percent lie within two standard deviations. By using a standard deviation as our unit of comparison, we consider the effect of changes that are plausible and substantively meaningful, neither trivial nor extreme.

rate—46 percent—in the likelihood that they will have a dispute. (Remember that this reduction in risk results from changing the dyad from unallied to allied, while not changing any other variables from their baseline values.) It is not entirely clear to what extent allies are less likely to become involved in disputes *because* they are allied and to what extent states ally with one another because they share common interests and common adversaries and already maintain friendly relations. Too quickly attributing causation for this relationship would be like saying that people who don't exercise much are more likely to get heart attacks. That is true, but it is also true that people who are already sick, with bad hearts, may not be able to exercise. For them, lack of exercise would be more the consequence than the cause of illness. The alliance-dispute relationship probably also works both ways.

The next relationship, that between relative power and the likelihood of a dispute, also lies at the heart of realist theory. Our findings are clearly consistent with the hypothesis that a preponderance of power inhibits the overt expression of a militarized dispute, while a balance of power is dangerous. If both sides can confidently predict which would win a military showdown, there is little need to pay the high price that armed conflict entails. The weak state will usually concede what is demanded by its strong adversary, without a fight. That way, at least it avoids the financial cost and human casualties of war. The result—29 percent lower probability of conflict—however, is somewhat misleading because it comes from a very big difference in power. It reflects to a large degree the success of the five major powers in deterring conflict with the many small states of the world. Adding one standard deviation to the capability ratio increases the advantage of the larger state from about 6:1 to over 26:1. Apparently, securing peace by deterrence requires a substantial military advantage. Because our measure of national capabilities includes measures of population and industry, which are very slow growing, it would certainly not be practical to advise policy makes who wish to prevent disputes to increase their military superiority fourfold.

Now look, in Table 3.1, at the effect of democracy on the likelihood that two states will be involved in a military dispute. First, we report the effect of making the less democratic state in the pair more democratic by one standard deviation. As reported, the probability of a dispute drops by 42 percent. This means that if we change the less democratic state from a neutral reading of 0—the midpoint on the democracy-autocracy scale—

to +7, there is a greater change in the likelihood of peace than if the balance of power is increased from 6:1 to 26:1. The difference between 0 and 7 on our scale is, for example, the difference between Pakistan under the "tutelary democracy" of the 1960s, when it had a centralized presidency and a rubber-stamp legislature, and its more democratic regime of the 1990s, before the 1999 military coup. Seven and higher readings on the democracy-autocracy scale are what Jaggers and Gurr (1995) call "coherent" democracies. If the less democratic state in a dyad is a true democracy, of course, the more democratic state will be one as well. Thus, this is strong evidence that two democratic states are unlikely to become involved with one another in a dispute. The effect on the likelihood of conflict is even larger if we make the less democratic state in our pair an autocracy, reducing its democracy score from 0 to −7, again holding the other variables constant. In this case, the two states would be about 69 percent more likely to get into a militarized dispute. The chance of a dispute in a year rises from six chances in a hundred to ten chances in a hundred.

These effects are even stronger if we make the less democratic state a full democracy at the +10 end of the scale (like Japan or most of Western Europe), or extremely autocratic at the −10 end (like the old Soviet Union and most Communist states of Eastern Europe). With full democracy, the likelihood of conflict drops 54 percent below the baseline probability, but when the less democratic state is fully autocratic, the chance of a dispute rises 109 percent above the baseline. The most autocratic states are therefore much more dispute-prone than are less extreme autocracies.

Another common way to estimate whether the influence of one variable on another is important is by computing the variable's statistical significance; that is, how often one would by chance find a positive (or a negative) relationship in a sample even if there were in fact no such relationship in the full "universe" of cases. This is a useful procedure for survey research, for instance, where a sample of perhaps 1,000 voters is interviewed, out of the millions of voters in a country. The meaning of statistical significance is less clear when, as in our tests, nearly the complete universe of cases is being analyzed. Nonetheless, computing the level of statistical significance helps us gauge the likelihood that our results are really just due to chance. As it happens, all the variables in Table 3.1 are statistically significant at the .001 level. This means, for example, that when we say allies are less likely to get into military disputes with each other, the odds are less than one chance in a thousand that there is actually no relationship between these two variables.[13]

Was the Effect of Democracy Different in Different Periods?

Do these relationships hold true throughout the long period we are considering, or are there different patterns within different subperiods? Do we have the basis for strong generalizations or only for ones limited to particular historical eras? The long period, from 1885 to 1992, covers several different eras of international relations. We noted earlier that the cold war ran from after World War II to around 1988 or 1989 and that conditions in the international system have been markedly different after the cold war. They were also different before it.

As noted in the previous chapter, some observers of international politics have argued that peace among democracies is primarily a product of the cold war, when democracies shared similar security interests and sought to protect their interests and sovereignty against an opposing alliance that was composed of authoritarian states. In this view, the democracies did not fight much among themselves because they were too worried about the security threat from their common enemy. But this begs an important question: Why did the Western democracies share common interests? Was it only because of the existence of the Warsaw Pact, which was coincidentally composed of autocracies? Or did democracies oppose the Warsaw Pact because they shared an interest in maintaining their democratic practices and institutions as well as the network of international economic relations within the "free world"? Surely both influences had an effect: they had common interests because they were allied against a common foe, but they were also allied because they had common interests that went beyond issues of national security. To address this criticism of the democratic peace, we must ask whether democracies have been more peaceful toward each other outside of the cold war era.

We will summarize several additional analyses designed to answer that

---

[13]Because most of our hypotheses predict either a positive or a negative relationship between a variable and the risk of a dispute, we use one-tailed tests of statistical significance rather than two-tailed tests, which are appropriate when no particular direction is anticipated.

question. In short, the democratic peace is not just a phenomenon of the shared interests particular to the bipolar cold war years. We do not have dispute data for 1993 and more recent years, but we can ask whether the pacific benefits of democracy were evident during the four years from 1989 to 1992. This means treating 1989 as the first year in which a different pattern of disputes, characteristic of the post–cold war era, might have emerged. This is consistent with most Europeans' views and with an analysis that found a clear shift in the pattern of Soviet-American interactions at this time (Dixon and Gaarder 1992). Analysis of the 1989–92 period, admittedly a short span of time, reveals that democracies became somewhat *more* peaceful among themselves with the end of the period of bipolarity.[14]

A democratic peace is also evident when one examines the years before the cold war, 1886–1939, in their entirety. This is an appropriate period over which to conduct a separate analysis. There is an abundance of cases for these years, nearly 12,000, and they differ from the cold war era in at least two important ways. First, relations among the great powers then were multipolar, not bipolar. There were always at least six great powers in the system and sometimes as many as eight. No two states were ever nearly as dominant as the United States and the Soviet Union were after 1945. At times (just before the two world wars), the great powers did form into two opposing alliances, but these were not rigid and fully predictable, as we have noted. If the polarity of an international system is judged by the relations among the great powers and not by the number, power, or configurations of the alliance systems (Waltz 1979), then all of the 1886–1939 period constitutes a period of multipolarity. The second big difference between these early years and the post–World War II era is the existence of nuclear weapons. The destructiveness of nuclear weapons markedly changed the calculus of peace and war from that which had operated previously.

---

[14]The difference in the peacefulness of democracies in the cold war and post–cold war eras is not statistically significant; the important point is that there is no indication that democracies have become less peaceful. Technically, the analysis is done by adding an interactive term, the lower democracy score times a dummy variable that identifies cases in the post–cold war period, plus this dummy variable, to the basic equation. We use the same technique to analyze the democratic peace in the other time periods discussed below.

Analysis of our data clearly shows that the peace among democracies also held during the pre-1945 period as a whole, and this relationship was statistically significant, though not as strong as it became after 1945. The most important difference between the years before and after World War II concerns not democracy but alliances. After World War II, allied states had fewer disputes with each other than did nonallies, but alliances made no statistically significant difference in the incidence of disputes over the full pre–World War II era. In those years, allies were as likely to fight or threaten each other as they would have been had they not been allied.

Breaking the pre–cold war era down further is problematic. If one cuts up any set of data into very small subgroups, the relationships one finds become unstable—sometimes positive, sometimes negative—and ultimately it becomes impossible to find *any* statistically significant relationships. This is especially true in the analysis of uncommon events. To avoid this, the choice of subgroups must be informed by theory, either about the key explanatory variables themselves (is there some reason, for example, why our measure of democracy might not be accurate in certain years?) or about other influences that might affect their operation (does the structure of the international system change the effect of democracy?).

There is no reason to divide the pre–World War II era on grounds that the character of the international system changed significantly. Throughout, it was multipolar and nonnuclear in nature. There may be reason to believe, however, that the characteristics of democracy changed in important ways. In discussing the measurement of democracy earlier in this chapter, we noted that in Britain roughly 40 percent of males did not have the vote before World War I, and that there, as well as in many other countries that are coded in the Polity III data as democratic, women did not get the vote until after 1919. Widening the franchise to this degree, making it nearly universal, is a major change in the character of democracy, one that might affect countries' international behavior. Therefore, it does make sense to break the pre–World War II era into two groups: the years 1886–1914 and the interwar era 1921–39.

The interwar period contains nearly 8,000 observations, and as we would expect from the expansion of the right to vote, the influence of democracy remains strong. While the relationship is somewhat weaker during the interwar era than it is during the cold war era, the difference between the two periods is not statistically significant. It is clear that democracies enjoyed relatively peaceful relations with each other between the two world wars. In the pre–World War I years, however, the democratic peace is much less evident. But on closer scrutiny, it appears that although democracies fought at a somewhat greater frequency than the typical nondemocratic pair during the first decade or so for which we have data (1885–95), they then began to experience the peacefulness that characterizes their relations to the present. For the politically relevant dyads, the turning point came around 1896: after that time, democracies avoided militarized disputes with one another.[15] This is close to our earlier results (Oneal and Russett 1999c) in analyses with all pairs of states, when we placed the turning point at around 1900. Gowa (1999, 98–100) also reports that democracies became less likely to engage in militarized disputes with each other in the decade leading up to World War I and that this democratic peace continued during the interwar years. This important shift is obscured by treating the years 1886–1914 as a whole.

In light of this evidence, if the democratic peace was absent through much of the nineteenth century, it is that absence—not its presence in the cold war era—that is the unusual result or anomaly to be explained. The explanation may lie in the restricted suffrage that existed during that century, rather than in characteristics of the international system. Even in the nineteenth century, a careful look at the evidence (see Gowa 1999, Table 6.7) discloses that disputes between democracies were *far less likely* to escalate to high levels of violence than were those involving autocracies.

Peaceful Autocracies?

As noted earlier, we expect the political character of the less democratic state in each dyad to be primarily responsible for determining the likelihood of conflict. This is the state that is less constrained from using force. But we also noted that the political regime of the other state, the one with the higher DEMOC score, might also affect the prospects that force will be used. In a previous study, we found that the most dispute-prone pairs of states were those that contained one democracy and one autoc-

---

[15]Looking for a break at other years, such as 1891, 1901, and 1906, shows that the shift to greater peacefulness occurred no later than 1896.

racy. We called this the "cats-and-dogs effect" (Oneal and Russett 1997). Other analysts (Bueno de Mesquita and Lalman 1992; Leeds and Davis 1999) have reported similar results. It is certainly plausible that two states with very different political systems would have a lot to fight about. The cold war, as we have argued, was not just about security and foreign policy but also about how national political and economic systems should be organized, the rights of citizens, and other domestic issues. Because there are a variety of such issues in contention, it also seems reasonable that democracies and autocracies would mistrust one another. Finally, if democratic states are reluctant to go to war or are inhibited from doing so by the institutional restraints of their systems, their slowness to engage in military action might be exploited by less constrained, authoritarian states.

To discover whether democracies and autocracies are particularly prone to fight, we added the variable $DEMOC_H$ to our basic equation. If the hypothesis is correct, then the higher the level of democracy in the more democratic country ($DEMOC_H$), controlling for how democratic the less democratic country ($DEMOC_L$) is, the more dispute-prone the dyad will be. This is because if $DEMOC_L$ is held constant, the "political distance" between the two states will increase as $DEMOC_H$ increases.

The cats-and-dogs effect was not confirmed, either for the post–World War II era in particular or for the whole period 1885–1992. Pairs of democracies are much more peaceful than either pairs of autocracies or mixed democratic-autocratic pairs. In the analysis for all years, when both states are +7 democracies, the rate of disputes is 41 percent below the rate for the typical dyad. The rate for mixed pairs is 73 percent above this baseline, and the rate for a pair of autocracies is 67 percent above it. The slight difference between mixed and autocratic dyads is not statistically significant.[16] *Thus, there is no evidence of an "autocratic peace" to match the peace among democracies* (Gowa 1999, 106–8). Nothing comparable to the effect of democratic norms and institutions produces a generalized pattern of dispute-avoidance among authoritarian states. This is not surprising. Many different types of political regimes are characterized as autocracies.

[16]Earlier indications (e.g., Oneal and Russett 1997) that mixed autocratic-democratic pairs were significantly more dispute-prone than autocratic pairs were primarily due to the absence of statistical adjustments for heteroskedasticity and temporal dependence that are now standard and are applied here.

These include fascist states and Communist ones, which had many conflicts between them; Islamic theocracies; monarchies; Latin American juntas; and governments dominated by a single, charismatic ruler.

The results of our analyses of the influence of the level of democracy for both states in a pair also mean *that on average, democracies, as individual states, are more peaceful than autocracies.* This is true in the sense that the likelihood of conflict goes down or remains unchanged if we replace an autocracy with a democracy in a dyad. Consider first the consequences of starting with an autocratic-democratic dyad. If we replace the autocracy with a democracy, this creates a democratic-democratic pair. The likelihood of conflict would drop from 73 percent above the baseline rate (or a probability of .103) to 41 percent below it (a probability of .035). If, however, we start with two autocracies and make one of them democratic, the risk of a dispute stays essentially unchanged. Apparently, democracies act according to realist principles in their dealings with autocracies but are no more prone to fight them than are other autocracies.

Perhaps most important, the fact that democracies are indeed more peaceful generally means that *the incidence of conflict should go down over time if more countries become democratic.* Newly established democracies can be peaceful with their democratic neighbors, and being democratic will not make them more prone to fight autocratic neighbors than if they themselves had remained autocratic. If instead autocracies and democracies were especially likely to become involved in disputes, as previous results indicated, then the incidence of conflict would rise in a region originally populated solely by autocracies as each state became democratic. This rising incidence of regional conflict would continue until the democratic states had mostly democratic neighbors and were at peace with them. Our latest results are very encouraging, then, because it seems likely that more and more states will become democratic.

Are Political Transitions Dangerous?

This observation about the effects of having more states become democratic returns us to an important question raised in Chapter 2: Do states that have recently become democratic behave less peacefully than do countries that have long been democratic? In the results we just discussed, we did not consider whether a democracy was newly established or of long standing. We need to investigate the idea, associated with Mansfield and Snyder (1995, 1996), that countries in transition from dictatorship to democracy are war-prone. We also want to consider whether political change in the opposite direction, from democracy to autocracy, affects the likelihood of conflict. Perhaps dramatic political change in the regime of a state in either direction, indicative of political instability, makes for a dangerous situation.

The "diversionary" theory of war has long been of interest to international relations scholars, but Mansfield and Snyder offer a new reason to consider the effects of domestic politics on the foreign behavior of states. They carefully discuss the role that nationalist ideology and coalition politics in newly democratizing states might play in producing a heightened danger of conflict with their neighbors. It is easy to imagine reasons why democratization, or political change generally, might affect a state's foreign policy. A newly installed political system, whether democratic or autocratic, is more likely to be unstable. This could tempt neighbors to threaten or attack it while it is weak and not fully in control of the resources of the government and the nation. This temptation seems to have seduced Iraqi president Saddam Hussein when he attacked the new revolutionary government of Iran in September 1980. In addition, dramatic changes in government often occur at times of social and economic turmoil, when the populace's standard of living is sharply reduced or endangered. A domestic crisis may encourage a new regime to pick a quarrel with another state in order to solidify its support at home. This may be especially true of new democracies, dependent on popular support for their continued survival.

Examples concerning the dangers of democratizing and autocratizing states abound. The French Revolution of 1789 began a chain of events that can be cited in support of the heightened belligerence of both types of new regimes. It started with the installation of a democratic government that first sharply restricted the power of the monarchy and then violently abolished it. By April 1792, France was at war with Austria, a war that both sides apparently wanted; the war quickly widened, and by February 1793, Britain, the Netherlands, Sardinia, and Spain were added to France's adversaries. The revolutionary ideology promoted by France threatened all the monarchies of Europe. They, in turn, sought to eliminate the threat at its source. Meanwhile, the French republicans became increasingly radical and violent toward their domestic opponents and rivals, and France deteriorated into a reign of terror and dictatorship. In 1798, Napoleon staged a coup d'état and eventually crowned himself emperor. The Napoleonic Wars soon swept over Europe, reaching from Spain to Moscow. Peace was only restored in 1815, with Napoleon's final defeat at Waterloo. From 1789 to 1815, France, in both its democratic and imperial periods, waged war on many states.

Germany and Japan in the 1930s, too, illustrate well the turn to external violence that can follow the installation of autocratic regimes. When Adolf Hitler came to power in 1933, for example, he quickly moved to end the Weimar Republic and consolidate a dictatorship. Within three years, he had precipitated the first of a string of major foreign policy crises with Britain and France by reoccupying the Rhineland, which had been demilitarized by the Versailles Treaty ending World War I.

The political changes associated with the end of the cold war and the wave of democratization in Eastern Europe and the former Soviet Union led to fears in many quarters of a consequent surge of international disputes and wars fueled by ethnic conflicts. There are a lot of new democracies in the region, and there have been a number of disputes. The question is: Are these phenomena causally related? In fact, democratization cannot be implicated in any of the wars that have arisen. Certainly, there have not been any wars by newly democratic states against democratic neighbors. Conflicts did loom between a newly democratic Hungary and several of its neighbors over the status of large Hungarian-speaking minorities in semidemocratic Romania and Slovakia and in authoritarian Serbia. Yet none of these were allowed to escalate to war, and conflicts with the first two have largely been resolved by diplomacy.

So many examples and counterexamples exist that the effect of democratization must be determined through a systematic analysis. Also, it is not obvious theoretically that new democracies, even if they are unstable, will be prone to conflict. The opposite possibility also exists: being weak, new democracies may be cautious and avoid becoming engaged in conflict with their neighbors precisely because they cannot count on a lot of popular support. To address the question scientifically, we must consider all militarized disputes and not just those that come easily to mind. It is also important to control for those influences that we expect to affect the likelihood of conflict. One is whether a new *shift* or transition toward democracy has any effect over and above the effect of the *level* of democracy in the current governments of the two states in the pair. Unlike virtually all previous analyses (Oneal and Russett 1997 is an exception), we control for such influences here.

To get some sense of the matter, we modify our basic analysis by adding two new variables; these identify states that have undergone a dramatic political change over a five-year span. We ask whether either member of a dyad markedly changed its position on the twenty-one-point democracy-autocracy scale over the previous five years. The first new variable, AUT-to-DEM, identifies those dyads that experienced a change in at least one state from autocracy (-7 or less on the democracy-autocracy scale) to democracy ($+7$ or more). This variable takes a value equal to the magnitude of the shift, if there was one. That is, if a state shifted from -7 to $+7$ at any time in the previous five years, AUT-to-DEM equals 14. This allows the size of the shift to affect the likelihood of conflict, because the theory suggests that a bigger shift should have a greater effect on foreign policy. If there was no dramatic change from the autocratic to the democratic side of the political spectrum, AUT-to-DEM equals 0. Because we also wish to consider whether the process of autocratization influences the likelihood of conflict, we created a second new variable, DEM-to-AUT, which records in a similar fashion dramatic shifts in the autocratic direction.[17]

This procedure is not designed to pick up small shifts in political regimes. Most versions of the theory talk about substantial movements from autocracy to democracy, not merely a strongly autocratic regime undertaking mild liberal reforms. Minor changes in the character of political regimes are not expected to affect the incidence of militarized disputes. Also notice that our test does not set an unrealistically high level for a new democracy and does address the possibility of short-term instability. Remember that a score of $+7$ is equivalent to Pakistan in the 1990s, not to Sweden or the United States; also, the effect of a transition runs for only five years.

To discover whether the process of democratization increases the prospects of conflict, we added to the basic analysis of Table 3.1 the two variables that identify political change. Adding indicators of autocratization as well as of democratic change allows us to find out if democratiza-

---

[17]If fewer than five years' information on government type is available and no shift in the character of either regime occurred in the shorter period, we drop the dyad from the analysis.

tion leads to international conflict and also whether "backsliding" from democracy to autocracy is dangerous. Perhaps it is not democratization but political instability in *either* direction that is the cause of disputes. The results, which do not require a new table, lend little support, however, to either theory. Over the entire 1886–1992 period, the effect of democratization was effectively nil. If the less democratic state in a dyad scored at least a +7 on the democracy-autocracy continuum, the probability of a dispute was almost 46 percent below the baseline rate for the typical dyad. Yet if one of the states had only become democratic within the last five years, the effect of that alone was to raise the chance of a dispute by just a single percentage point—a trivial and statistically insignificant change. Much the same was true if one state shifted from democracy to autocracy. If the less democratic state was a −7 on the political spectrum, the dyad's dispute rate was 80 percent above the baseline. If either member had recently become autocratic, there was no additional effect.[18]

These results do not change appreciably if one uses shorter or longer periods over which to measure political change. If anything, the influence of democratization is usually to lower the risk of disputes, but the effect becomes statistically significant only if the time period is lengthened to ten years or more, as the newly democratic regimes have had more time to stabilize. Nor does it matter much if smaller shifts in domestic politics are studied, as, for example, a shift from very autocratic (−8 to −10) to the middle of the scale (−3 to +3). And no difference emerges if the shifts are bigger, say to +8 or +10. Consistently, it is the *level* of democratic government achieved by both members of a dyad, not whether this was achieved recently, that affects the likelihood they will experience a dispute.

Other measures of democratization and autocratization might give somewhat different answers. Some studies have found that differences in the time period, the way political change is measured, or the precise form

[18]These percentage changes in risk are a little greater than those reported in Table 3.1, perhaps due to a reduction in the sample size as a result of measuring political change over several years. The percentages are always only approximate estimates, varying somewhat for different samples, measures, and analytical techniques. What matters is that they stay consistently at about the same level and have the same theoretical implications. All the statistical significance levels for regime change use two-tailed tests, since competing hypotheses expect opposite effects.

of the equation can affect the results. But few find anything consistent, and none offers a convincing theoretical argument as to why any particular method should be preferred. How then can we square our statistical results with the impression, backed by fairly numerous examples, of conflicts involving new democracies?

First, the existence of some instances of newly democratized states engaging in militarized disputes is consistent with our statistical results. As we have seen, relations between a democracy and an autocracy are dominated by the same realist logic as are relations between autocratic states. It matters whether one's geographical neighborhood is populated largely by other democracies or by autocracies. Consider the situation in Eastern Europe, where most of the post-Communist countries have experienced little militarized international conflict. The highly democratic states in the area (the Czech Republic, Hungary, Poland, and Slovenia) have had no militarized disputes with one another and few even with their less democratic neighbors (Slovakia, Romania, and Croatia). The vast majority of their disputes have been with nondemocratic Serbia. Likewise, the three democratic Baltic states that split off from the old Soviet Union (Estonia, Latvia, Lithuania) have avoided militarized disputes among themselves and largely even with Russia, their less democratic but powerful neighbor. Our analysis accounts for this by embedding changes in a single government within a larger political context that controls for whether *both* states have reached a high *level* of democracy, even recently.

Furthermore, when we say that there is no general relationship between democratization and conflict, we mean just that. While there are examples of conflict involving new democracies, there are also counterexamples where democratizing states have been peaceful. Overall, these two tendencies cancel each other out, leaving us with no evidence that democratization in general is dangerous. Because democratizing states sometimes do get involved in disputes, it would be useful to have an additional theory to understand the particular circumstances under which this process might be dangerous. Snyder (2000) makes an important start in this effort. He considers how democratization can combine with exclusionary nationalism to incite either domestic or international violence. We have only examined international conflict here.

Finally, most of the examples of democratization and violence involve states that are still incompletely democratic, where democracy has not been consolidated at a high level. This means these examples tell us less about the danger posed by new democracies than about the risk of conflict for states that have not yet reached a high level of democracy. Our analyses and those of others (Beck, King, and Zeng 2000) indicate that once a state becomes a well-institutionalized democracy, the likelihood of conflict falls sharply. States that are only partly democratic will be more conflictual than coherent, institutionalized democracies but more peaceful than autocracies. Democratization is, therefore, good, but it is best when complete. In short, the higher the level of democracy a state achieves, the more peaceful that state is likely to be, regardless of whether or not its transition to democracy occurred recently.

The results we report, then, are consistent with most other analyses: neither a transition to democracy nor a turn toward greater autocracy makes much difference in whether states get themselves into militarized disputes. Thus, there is no compelling evidence to support a "go slow" policy toward democratization in Eastern Europe or elsewhere. Transitions in themselves do not appear dangerous. It is important, however, that a transition become consolidated at a high level of stable, institutionalized democracy. Democracy, old or new, strongly encourages peace. Peace will prevail throughout a region when all the states there are democratic.

More Democracy and More Peace

We discussed several theories of the democratic peace in the previous chapter. To some degree they are competing explanations, but for the most part, they can be considered complementary. We also considered some of the evidence that has been offered for them. In this chapter, we focused on new empirical analyses. These provide further evidence for the pacific benefits of democracy. Pairs of democracies are much more peaceful than other kinds of dyads. This generalization applies to the whole twentieth century. In addition, democracies are in general more peaceful than other kinds of states. If an autocratic state becomes democratic, its chance of conflict with another democracy drops dramatically, while its risk of a dispute with an autocracy remains unchanged. And we find no evidence that transitions in political regimes—either democratization, backsliding to autocracy, or political instability generally—endanger the

Figure 3.1: Global Democracy and Autocracy, 1946–1998

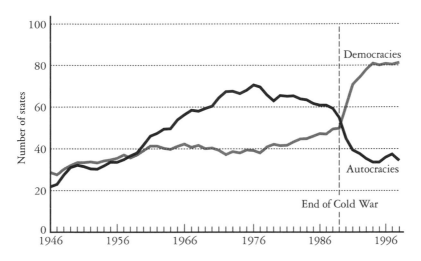

Source: Adapted from the figure titled "Global Democracy and Autocracy, 1946–1998" by Monty G. Marshall and based on Polity98 data of the Polity IV Project, Center for International Development and Conflict Management, University of Maryland.

peace. The analyses reported in this chapter serve as the basis for additional empirical tests in the following chapters, where we explore the effects of the other Kantian influences.

The emergence of new democracies in the last decade of the twentieth century presents the possibility for widespread peace in the international system. For the first time in world history, a solid majority of states are democratic. As shown in Figure 3.1, the proportion of Western-style democracies among the world's governments has grown dramatically. By 1998, slightly over half of the world's population lived in democracies (Freedom House 1998). In 1999, some big countries, notably Indonesia and Nigeria, made precarious but promising transitions away from authoritarianism. Of course, the process of democratization is far from complete in many parts of the developing world, and some of the new democracies rest on tenuous foundations. Consequently, this global democratic wave may crest and then fall part of the way back, as earlier ones have done. Even so, this is a remarkable achievement, and the prospects for sustaining democracy globally are more favorable than in earlier eras.

Imperialism, balance-of-power politics, the fear of communism, and the absence of accepted norms of human rights—all hampered democratization in previous periods. All of these impediments are now substantially gone (Green 1999). This provides hope that the zone of democracy can be sustained and even further enlarged. If that effort succeeds, world politics will be very different.

Both Democracy and Economic

Interdependence Reduce Conflict

The results we reported in Chapter 3 indicate that democracy is a strong force for international peace. Yet we should resist the temptation to accept that evidence as conclusive until we consider at least one other influence: commercial relations that create a high degree of economic interdependence. Perhaps what looks like the effect of democratic institutions and culture is really the result of the interdependence that arises most naturally between states with open economies. Almost all democracies, though varying to a degree in the role played by the state, have capitalist economic systems that involve extensive competition in free markets among economic agents, including those in other countries. Consequently, democracies tend to trade extensively with one another. Because of the correlation between democracy and open markets, we need to reconsider the consequences of democracy through tests in which we control for the influence of interdependence.

There are three possibilities. The first is that the apparent benefits of democracy for interstate relations are mostly, or even entirely, the effect of economic interdependence. The second is that economic interdependence and peace are both consequences of democracy, so that consideration of interstate commerce adds nothing to our understanding of the causes of war; it is only democracy that is important. The third possibility, the one most consistent with the Kantian perspective, is that democracy and economic interdependence make independent contributions: both constrain the use of force by creating powerful incentives for peace. In this case, those pairs of states that are both democratic and economically interdependent would tend to be more peaceful than pairs that are either only democratic or only interdependent. This chapter seeks to determine which of these three possibilities is correct. Here we expand our examination of the democratic peace to consider the effects of economic interdependence on the likelihood of conflict.

In the liberal view, trade and foreign investment, as well as the institutions and practices of democratic governance, should reduce the incidence of militarized disputes between countries. This thesis, like the liberal account of the peacefulness of democracies, has its origins in a classical literature that most clearly addressed the individual characteristics of states, arguing that democratic states and those economically open will be more peaceful in their diplomatic and military relations with others. But consideration of the pacific benefits of trade, as with the study of the democratic peace, has progressed through careful attention to the conflict-reducing potential of interdependence in dyadic analyses. Indeed, the effects of either democracy or interdependence on states' behavior can be obscured unless careful attention is paid to their bilateral consequences.[1] Consequently, we begin the empirical analyses reported below by examining the effects of economically important bilateral trade. We consider as well, however, whether a country's openness to trade with all countries, not just its relations with the other member of a dyad, also reduces the likelihood of conflict. Together, these analyses mirror our earlier interest in the peaceful relations that occur when both members of a dyad are democratic and the finding that democracies are generally more peaceful than autocracies.

---

[1]The importance of analyzing the behavior of pairs of states is all the more evident when the liberal peace is evaluated within the wider context of international relations theory. Realism stresses the importance of alliances, relative power, and geostrategic location—influences best represented dyadically.

Our analyses here develop and build on those of the previous chapter. To reflect our attention to the second of the Kantian variables, the graphic at the head of this chapter includes a second dark arrow, from the lower right corner of the Kantian triangle to the center. The principal question of this chapter is whether trade makes an independent contribution to the probability that a pair of states will experience a militarized dispute. We also want to know if democracy, alliances, and the balance of power continue to be important influences when our measures of the economic importance of trade are added to our explanatory model. The tests we report below allow us to compare the relative benefits of the liberals' political and economic prescriptions for peace. Other questions, notably whether economic growth also contributes to peace—or provides the means for the exercise of power—are also explored.

If trade does appear to contribute to peace, we need to consider the reciprocal relation. Perhaps economic interdependence is largely a consequence, rather than a cause, of the absence of international disputes. After all, commercial agents can be expected to avoid the risks and costs of international violence where possible, and trading with the enemy is usually prohibited or extensively regulated by national governments. There may well be an association between trade patterns and conflict, but it may be primarily conflict that affects commerce, rather than the other way round. This chapter will not fully resolve that question, but it provides a good start, and we shall return to this issue later in the book.

The Liberal Peace: Classical Perspectives and Recent Research

The classical liberals advocated policies to increase liberty and prosperity. They sought to empower the commercial class politically and to abolish royal charters, monopolies, and the protectionist policies of mercantilism so as to encourage entrepreneurship and increase productive efficiency. They also expected democracy and free-market economics to diminish the frequency of war. Political scientists have addressed the connection between democracy and international conflict in recent years, but they have shown less interest in the consequences of free trade and economic interdependence. Yet, expanded trade was advocated as a remedy for war even before democracy was a realistic possibility in most countries.

In the early seventeenth century, Emeric Crucé concluded that wars arose from international misunderstandings and the domination of society by the warrior class and that both could be reduced by expanding commerce: trade would create common interests and increase the prosperity and political power of the peaceful, productive members of society. Similarly for Kant,

> The *spirit of commerce* sooner or later takes hold of every people, and it cannot exist side by side with war. And of all the powers (or means) at the disposal of the state, *financial power* can probably be relied on most. Thus states find themselves compelled to promote the noble cause of peace, though not exactly from motives of morality. And wherever in the world there is a threat of war breaking out, they will try to prevent it by mediation. (Kant [1795] 1970, 114; italics in original)

Kant's view is especially interesting because of when and where he wrote. He lived in Königsberg, a city in Prussia in the late eighteenth century. (Königsberg is now a part of Russia and is called Kaliningrad.) Königsberg was no democracy, but was part of a hereditary monarchy. International law was not extensively developed at the time, and there were essentially no international organizations. But Kant knew firsthand about the political effects of foreign commerce, for Königsberg had long been an independent trading state and was involved in economic exchange with much of Europe. In thinking about the causes of peace, he embedded trade within the right to "hospitality," or temporary sojourn, whereby foreigners could carry on the peaceful pursuit of their livelihoods while temporarily on the territory of other states. Königsberg had been a member of the Hanseatic League during its heyday from the thirteenth to the seventeenth centuries. The Hanseatic League was a loose confederation of independent, self-governing trading towns, devoted to promoting and protecting its trading monopolies in northern Europe. It was able to coordinate economic sanctions or even war against nonmembers, and it had sufficient dispute-settling mechanisms to avoid wars among its members (Lister 1999, chap. 3).

François Quesnay, Anne Robert Turgot, and the French Physiocrats; Adam Smith, David Ricardo, and John Stuart Mill, in England; and Thomas Paine, in the United States, were other theoreticians or political figures who emphasized the role of economic relations in promoting peace (Howard 1978). In the mid-nineteenth century, Richard Cobden and the Manchester school of "commercial liberalism" argued that the cost of war made it anachronistic, as did Norman Angell and Joseph Schumpeter somewhat later. In Cobden's terms, "Besides dictating the disuse of warlike establishments, free trade (for of that beneficent doctrine we are speaking) arms its votaries by its own pacific nature, in that eternal truth—*the more any nation traffics abroad upon free and honest principles, the less it will be in danger of wars*" (1886, 222; italics in original). Over time, trade also encouraged the development of international law and organizations, because these were needed to regulate and manage commercial relations, just as similar institutions were necessary in domestic economies.

The free traders—especially of nineteenth-century Britain—had an economic interest in the ideology they promoted. They sought a commercial republic of the world, of economic attraction rather than political rule (Semmel 1970), because economic interdependence was thought to create transnational ties that encouraged accommodation rather than conflict. In this way, economic interdependence reinforces the pacific benefits of democratic institutions and norms. Thus, material incentives add their force to law and morality. The benefits of interdependence are also central to functionalist accounts of political integration in Europe (Mitrany 1966) and are reminiscent of some socialists' emphasis on the virtues of internationalism (Domke 1988, 43–51).

Despite this impressive intellectual pedigree, the role of economic interdependence in preventing conflict has until recently been neglected (Levy 1989a). The benefits of trade may not be symmetrical and may favor the side with the stronger economic power in the market, but trade is always to some degree a mutually beneficial interaction; otherwise, it would not be undertaken. This gives each party a stake in the economic well-being of the other—and in avoiding militarized disputes. The nineteenth-century liberal argument derived primarily from a view that individuals act rationally in accordance with their economic interests. It is hardly in a state's interest to fight another if its citizens sell their goods, obtain imports (raw materials, capital goods, intermediate products, or consumer goods), or have financial investments or investors there. If my factory is located in your country, bombing your industry means, in effect, bombing my own property. Of course, trade can be redirected, at least over time, by political leaders who see the clouds of war on the horizon. But goods and services from alternative suppliers would cost more and/or be inferior in quality, and shifting exports means competing with

existing suppliers elsewhere, lower prices, and less profit. Indeed, the need
to switch to the second-best trading partner may involve such high costs
that a state is seriously vulnerable to a disruption of trade (Keohane and
Nye 1977, 8–13).

Many interest groups, economic and otherwise, compete for the attention of government leaders and seek to influence their choices. Some of
these interest groups will not care much about foreign policy, and some
may even have economic interests linked to international conflict (for instance, arms manufacturers or those whose products could, in times of
conflict, be sold in place of goods currently imported). The political influence of domestic economic interests will always be most important;
this is especially true in large countries, which tend to be less dependent
upon international trade. Yet if commerce between two countries constitutes a substantial share of the national income of one or both, important
commercial interests will have a political stake in maintaining good relations. Commerce increases the power of special interest groups that benefit from foreign trade and investment. This includes not just bankers and
the captains of industry but also their workers, consumers, suppliers, and
the whole network of secondary economic beneficiaries: the automobile
dealer who sells cars to those who work in factories that export abroad,
those workers' grocers and restaurant owners, and many others. Rational
political leaders want to stay in office, and to do so they must respond to
the demands of constituents who are economically and, hence, politically
powerful. If maintaining trade is important to continuing national prosperity and growth, leaders will be responsive to its beneficiaries. They
may also see this as an important element of national security.

A somewhat different argument linking economic interdependence
and peace focuses on the role of trade and foreign investment as media for
communicating on a broad range of matters beyond the specific commercial exchanges that take place. Trade exposes a state's citizens to the ideas
and perspectives of citizens of other countries on a wide range of issues
(Lerner 1956; Russett 1963; Rosecrance 1986). These communications,
too, form an important channel for averting interstate conflict. Economic
interdependence contributes to the construction of a "security community" (Deutsch et al. 1957), in which shared values make the resort to
force unimaginable. Common values create a shared sense of identity,
which Deutsch calls "we-feeling." Very likely, both rationalist and constructivist arguments are correct. One influence may be stronger than the

other in one situation or another, but ultimately they are complementary.

Democracy, with its commitment to individual liberty, may reduce conflict not just directly but indirectly by encouraging interdependence. In democracies, economically powerful groups are likely to be politically powerful as well (Papayanou 1996). Political and economic freedoms allow individuals to form transnational associations that may be able to influence policy (Verdier 1994; Risse-Kappen 1995a). Trade agreements among democracies may be particularly long lasting. Because executives in democratic countries must persuade and accommodate other powerful groups—the legislature, their political party, interest groups, the public—they may be more likely to abide by their international commitments than nondemocratic leaders, whose power is less subject to checks and balances. Consequently, democracies should be better at promoting and sustaining interdependence because economic ties require credible commitments regarding the terms of trade, regulation of capital flows, and the adjudication of contractual disputes (Martin 2000). As we shall see later, democracies are indeed inclined to trade with one another.

A challenge to the liberal view comes from those who emphasize that economic ties not only offer the prospect of mutual gain but may also transmit economic ills and create rivalry over the division of benefits. In the seventeenth century, England and Holland—both major trading states—fought heavily over colonial territory and access to foreign markets. Some analysts of the age of Western imperialism, such as the liberal J. A. Hobson (1902) and the Marxist revolutionary V. I. Lenin ([1916] 1929), vigorously developed such arguments. Lenin, in fact, regarded imperialism as the "highest stage of capitalism." He considered imperialism an inevitable consequence of the growth of monopolies in capitalist economies and believed that it would lead to such terrible wars among the great powers, all of whom were scrambling for economic gain abroad, as to destroy the capitalist system and open the door for socialism worldwide.

More recently, critics of capitalism have shifted their attention away from the potential for conflict between imperial powers and focused instead on the likelihood of conflict between a powerful state and a much smaller economic partner. When the political, military, and economic power of states is vastly different, dependency theorists suggest, trade and investment create not interdependence but dependency. This disproportionately benefits the larger country because it is able to use its power to manipulate the terms of exchange. In this view, too, trade can be a source of conflict (Hirschman 1945; Keohane and Nye 1977; Kroll 1993): asymmetrical economic relations lead to dependency, exploitation, and militarized disputes (dos Santos 1970; Rubinson 1976; Mearsheimer 1992). If a small economy is dominated by a big one, popular resentment may bubble over and lead to violence. Or a revolutionary government may seize great agricultural estates, mineral assets, or factories owned by nationals of the great power, provoking military threats or retaliation. Consequently, conflict can arise because the weaker party resists what it sees as unfair treatment and exploitation or because the stronger state seeks to enforce its advantage. Some analysts doubt, therefore, that trade makes an important contribution to world peace, at least between states of greatly unequal size.

It is certainly possible to find historical examples that support dependency theorists' view. Something like this happened in Cuba after Fidel Castro's revolution in 1960. Castro was committed to a program of socialism, which entailed large-scale expropriation of private property and of Americans' property in particular, because they owned much of the agricultural land that was used to produce sugar, Cuba's principal export. Castro not only nationalized foreign holdings but he also switched Cuba's pattern of trade. He bartered Cuban sugar—no longer given a privileged position in the U.S. market—to the Soviet Union in exchange for oil, which had previously been imported from the United States. The result was a rapid deterioration in relations between the United States and Cuba, leading to a series of economic sanctions. In 1961, the United States sponsored the disastrous Bay of Pigs invasion by Cuban exiles. Castro then openly allied himself with the Soviet Union, accepting the Soviet weapons that prompted the Cuban missile crisis of 1962. The possibility of disputes arising out of asymmetrical economic relations must be considered in any systematic examination of the consequences of trade for interstate conflict.

However, despite some examples to the contrary, recent social scientific research has generally concluded that trade does reduce conflict.[2] Nor is the evidence for this beneficial effect limited to the post–World War II era. Way (1997) found strong support, in both the nineteenth and twen-

[2]Polachek 1980; Gasiorowski and Polachek 1982; Gasiorowski 1986; Polachek 1992; Polachek and McDonald 1992.

tieth centuries, for the pacific benefits of bilateral trade as well as democracy. Similarly, Domke (1988) reported that countries with high levels of total exports relative to the size of their economies were less likely to initiate wars than countries that were relatively self-sufficient. Indeed, he found that countries that were open to the global economy were more peaceful than democratic states that were not open. Looking at the international system as a whole over nearly two centuries, Mansfield (1994) found that a high level of world trade reduced the number of wars initiated in the subsequent five years. One recent review, while cautioning that "outstanding empirical and theoretical questions" make "elevating this hypothesis to the status of a social scientific 'law' . . . premature," concludes that "the position advocated by liberalism is strongly supported by the existing literature."[3]

Analytical Problems

In accord with the findings of most—though not all—social scientific studies regarding this link, we, too, have found that economically important trade reduces interstate conflict. In previous articles, we reported the results of analyses using different sets of cases, over different periods, and with a variety of measures of interdependence. Below we report new empirical analyses that provide additional support for this conclusion. First, however, we must address some important analytical issues.

One involves how the effect of trade is to be assessed. If trade is to affect national decision makers, its beneficiaries must be politically important. They will be more influential, as we suggested above, when trade is more important to the national economy. For instance, the value of France's exports to Belgium is, allowing for shipping costs, reporting errors, and some technicalities, identical to the value of Belgium's imports from France. Likewise, France's imports from Belgium are the same as Belgium's exports to France. But since France's total economy is six times larger than Belgium's, this trade is more important economically to Belgium than it is to France. Consequently, Belgium's leaders are more subject to the political influence exercised by the economic actors who

---

[3]McMillan 1997, 34; for more recent reviews, see Oneal and Russett 1999a; Barbieri and Schneider 1999.

benefit from this exchange. Therefore, unlike Barbieri (1996), in assessing the impact of trade on the decisions of national leaders, we must calculate the value of trade relative to the size of a nation's economy, usually as measured by its gross domestic product (GDP). Presumably, the smaller country will have more incentive to avoid the costs of conflict with the bigger country than vice versa.

In assessing the effects of trade on dyadic relations, it is also important to control for the distance separating two countries. As common sense and the evidence of the previous chapter tell us, countries' ability to fight one another depends heavily on how near they are. Distance limits their ability to exert effective military power against one another. Trade, too, is clearly affected by distance. Distance increases the costs of trade, even to-day when technological innovation has dramatically reduced the expense of shipping by air or sea; distance influenced economic relations much more fifty or a hundred years ago. As a result, countries that are far apart trade less with each other than do close ones, all other things being equal (Tinbergen 1962; Deardorff 1995). Because proximate states tend both to fight more and to have higher levels of trade, if we are not careful, we might conclude that trade increases the likelihood of conflict. This would be a mistake, and it is a common one when analysts (e.g., Gaddis 1987, 224–25) note that states that have high levels of mutual trade (and, not coincidentally, are contiguous) often fight each other. To estimate the benefits of trade properly, we must control for the effect of distance on the frequency of militarized disputes. The right question is: With distance held constant, is trade positively or negatively related to the probability that two states will fight? In other words, of two states that are equally distant, which is more likely to become a country's military adversary, the one with which there is a high level of trade or the one with which commercial relations are minimal?

It is especially important to control for distance when investigating the effect of trade. There is little need to worry that distance is an important influence on whether two states are both democratic and on whether they are likely to fight. Two countries can be democratic even if they are on opposite sides of the globe, though to a degree, democracy does seem to be "contagious" among neighbors. But in investigating the effect of trade on conflict, not only do we run the risk of finding a correlation between high levels of trade and conflict if we fail to control for distance, we could also observe many "false negatives," where we mistakenly attribute the lack of conflict between, say, Iceland and China to their negligible economic ties. Much of the confusion about the benefits of trade arises from not recognizing the importance of distance.

In testing the liberal thesis regarding the pacific benefits of interdependence, it is also important to think carefully about the direction of causation. Economically important trade is expected to reduce military conflict because conflict would disrupt this trade and impose significant economic costs on those involved. Thus, the theory argues not only that trade will limit the use of force but also that conflict will reduce the level of trade. Indeed, it is because militarized disputes are likely to reduce trade and adversely affect economic interests that interdependence is expected to lower the chance that disputes will occur.

There are two reasons why this feedback of reciprocal relation between the two variables should occur. The first is simple enough: traders are assumed to be rational economic actors. They will stop trading if their goods (or their lives) are endangered by military hostilities. At a minimum, they will seek a greater profit margin to compensate for the greater risk, but these higher costs will lower demand and reduce commerce. Indeed, traders may see war clouds on the horizon and, out of self-interest, limit their commercial activity so as to cut their risks. Thus, trade may fall in response to conflict, and it may fall in anticipation of it. Accordingly, declining trade may signal deteriorating political relations. It may even exacerbate interstate tensions by reducing the flow of valuable communications or heightening the alarm of national leaders, who may be encouraged to turn to military action to limit or reverse the economic consequences of the lost trade (Copeland 1996).

Conflict will also influence the level of trade because states usually take steps to prevent their citizens from "trading with the enemy." Commerce between states at war was not uncommon in earlier centuries (Barbieri and Levy 1999), but modern states are more effective in limiting such activity. States can impose a variety of economic sanctions to weaken or punish their adversaries, including a complete embargo on trade and investment. States can also act against countries with which they are not actually at war; for example, by limiting the sale of goods that are considered strategic: key raw materials or technological products with possible military applications. Many restrictions of this type were imposed on East-West trade during the cold war, and there are still significant limitations on U.S. trade with China, Russia, and other countries. The United

States also maintains a virtual embargo on trade with Cuba, Iran, Iraq, Libya, North Korea, and Serbia. Indeed, many types of military equipment can only be sold to members of the NATO alliance, Israel, and a few other countries that have a "special relationship" with the United States.

These are all examples of how conflict or governments' fear of conflict can lead to policies that reduce the level of trade with another state, but states can also act to increase their economic interdependence with those with which they have good relations. Various political scientists, such as Pollins (1989a, 1989b), Gowa and Mansfield (1993), and Gowa (1994), have shown that trade is influenced by states' security interests. A state is apt to trade more with an ally because it need not fear that the economic gains that arise from their commercial relations will be used to threaten its security. After World War II, the United States deliberately opened its markets to Japan to facilitate that country's revival as a prosperous and democratic ally. Consequently, we need to look at whether interdependence has important pacific benefits when the influence of alliances is held constant, just as we controlled for the influence of alliances in assessing the effects of democracy.

There is substantial evidence that the peace-inducing effects of trade remain significant even when the reverse impact, of both conflict and the state of political relations on trade, is estimated simultaneously (Polachek 1992; Mansfield 1994; Reuveny and Kang 1996; Kim 1998). In order to get the temporal sequence right in the analyses we report, we explain conflict in one year by referring to conditions, namely, the level of trade, in the previous year. This precaution is particularly important in evaluating the effects of trade on interstate conflict and helps us avoid clearly erroneous causal inferences. In Chapter 6, we explore further the reciprocal effect of conflict on trade with an analysis that predicts the level of bilateral trade from looking at conflict in the previous year and other influences.

We adopt one other method in this chapter in an effort to get the causal inference correct. We look at the effect of a country's total trade, that is, its exports to and imports from all other countries, on the likelihood of military conflict. In the discussion so far, we have emphasized the role that the trade between two states is expected to play in their relations with one another. That is where the effects of trade on conflict should be most evident. But the classical liberals thought that states that were integrated into the world economy would be peaceful. Economic openness, as indicated by the ratio of a state's total trade to its GDP, should also constrain the use of force, even against another state with which bilateral trade is limited. This is because an ongoing dispute is apt to discourage some traders and investors from third countries from engaging in economic activity with the disputing states. States with open economies must be concerned about these indirect costs of resorting to military measures. Consequently, the total trade-to-GDP ratio, as well as states' dependence on bilateral exchange, indicates the costs associated with the use of force. This provides a valuable test of the causal influence of economic interdependence on the likelihood of conflict because it is difficult for a state to manipulate the economic importance of its trade with all countries simultaneously. It is relatively easy for a state to restrict its bilateral trade with a potential adversary while increasing its commercial relations with others, but it would be much more costly to reduce trade with all states in anticipation that conflict were imminent. National economies are not so easily restructured.

For example, by the end of the nineteenth century, Great Britain worried about the effects that conflict might have on its trade and on its economy. Having adopted the policy of free trade, with few artificial supports for domestic agriculture, Britain had become largely dependent on imports of food to feed its people and on the export of manufacturers to pay for those imports. This dependence on trade—and its vulnerability to disruption—meant that a protracted war in Europe would seriously hurt the standard of living of the British people. Britain's leaders must have been mindful of this danger. Russia, by contrast, was much more self-sufficient in this period because of its great continental territory and had less to fear from a disruption of foreign trade.

The vulnerability of a state that is dependent on trade was illustrated more recently, when in 1996, Taiwan too openly asserted its independence from the Chinese government on the mainland. In retaliation, Beijing fired missiles into the ocean near Taiwan. This did not so much disrupt commerce between the two countries, which was not very great, as frighten Taiwan's important trading partners. The possibility of conflict in the Taiwan Strait made that commerce much more risky and costly, for both Taiwan and its commercial partners, as shipping and insurance costs rose sharply. Because Taiwan is heavily dependent on trade with many countries, this proved to be a significant threat.

Much of the theorizing in the nineteenth century about the influence of trade on interstate relations centered on the effects of openness to the global economy generally rather than on the effects on bilateral relations. The liberals advocated free trade because it would lead to specialization according to comparative advantage and higher levels of international trade and investment. This would encourage economic growth and create in each state a large political constituency for maintaining the interdependent global system. All this necessitated peace. Thus, high levels of economically important trade were expected to create broad commercial interests that would encourage peace with everyone, not just with a state's closest trading partners. As David Ricardo put it, "The effects of war may so raise the freight and insurance on its conveyance, that it can no longer enter into competition with the home manufacture of the country to which it was before exported. In all such cases, considerable distress, and no doubt some loss, will be experienced by those who are engaged in the manufacture of such commodities" (Sraffa 1951, 255). Thus, in the analyses we report below, we consider the effect of economic openness, as indicated by the ratio of state's total trade (exports and imports) to its GDP, as well as of bilateral interdependence, on the likelihood of interstate conflict.

Testing the Effects of Trade

To sort out the evidence for these varied claims about the effect of trade requires analyses like those in the previous chapter. We will look at the same set of politically relevant dyads over the years 1885–1992, using the same method of logistic regression analysis. This means that we explain the probability of a dyadic dispute with the same control variables—a measure of the distance separating the members of a dyad, an indicator of whether they are contiguous states or not, and one showing whether the dyad contains only minor powers—and the same policy-relevant influences—level of democracy ($DEMOC_L$), whether the pair was allied, and a measure of the bilateral balance of power.[4] To these we add trade

---

[4]We omit the higher democracy score ($DEMOC_H$) from the analyses in this chapter because it did not prove to be statistically significant. Adding it makes little difference to the effects of the other variables considered below.

and economic growth. As before, we lag all explanatory variables by one year to give us some protection against confusing the direction of any causal relationship, so the first year of disputes we explain is 1886.

Our hypothesis, derived from Kant and other classical liberals, is that the probability two states will become embroiled in conflict is inversely related to the degree to which they are economically interdependent. Interdependence both raises the economic interest countries have in continuing peaceful exchange and provides a medium of communication that can be useful in preventing or resolving disagreements short of violence. For the post–World War II era, we use International Monetary Fund data regarding the direction and value of trade as the basis for our measure of bilateral economic interdependence (IMF 1997). The IMF reports reasonably complete information on its member countries' exports to and imports from their trading partners.[5]

Information about international trade becomes more problematic

[5]The IMF does not report the value of trade for all possible pairs of states; data are sometimes missing. IMF members sometimes report that the value of their trade with a particular country is zero, but often they do not report the absence of trade. This is true both for small, distant countries and for dyads involved in long-term rivalries, such as many of the Arab-Israeli dyads. Syria, for example, does not report that it had no trade with Israel. It makes no mention of Israel at all in its report to the IMF, unwilling even to acknowledge the existence of the Jewish state. For both types of dyads, no entry in the IMF statistics really indicates that no significant trade took place. To minimize the loss of cases due to missing trade data, we first supplemented the IMF statistics with data collected by Katherine Barbieri, which are available at http://pss.la.psu.edu/TRD_DATA.htm. Then we assumed that trade data for IMF members that were still missing indicated zero (or near zero) trade. According to an official in the IMF's Statistics Department, this is a reasonable assumption because IMF members are required to report trade and a variety of other statistics to the IMF by the terms of their agreement with the fund. If neither member of a dyad belonged to the IMF, we made no assumption about their level of trade. Most notably, this meant the loss of about 2,500 observations (dyad-years) involving two Communist countries during the cold war. Many dyads involved in the Korean and Vietnam Wars are omitted because of missing data on the gross domestic products of the Communist states. As shown in Oneal and Russett 1999a, evidence for the pacific benefits of trade does not depend upon assuming that missing data means that there was no trade. In our earliest analysis (Oneal et al. 1996), we used other assumptions to reduce the problem of missing data and there, too, found strong support for the pacific benefit of trade.

when we move to the years before World War II. The League of Nations contemporaneously compiled data on bilateral trade in current values, along with exchange rates, during the years 1920–38 (League of Nations, various issues). While the accuracy and comparability of these data are undoubtedly not as good as the later IMF reports, they are the best available. There are no institutional compilations of trade data for the years of the two world wars or for the period before 1914. Before World War I, the annual editions of *The Stateman's Yearbook* (Epstein 1913 and other editors and years) are the closest approximations, but the data there are less standardized, the appropriate exchange rates for converting them to a common currency are less certain, and there are more missing data. So we took several steps to minimize the effect of missing data and to insure that what we had was as accurate as possible.[6]

We expect trade to influence dyadic relations to the degree that it is economically important. Only then will the economic agents involved— the exporters and importers, shippers, and consumers—be politically powerful and motivated to influence national leaders. To calculate the economic importance of trade, we divided a country's trade (exports plus imports) with its dyadic partner by its gross domestic product. This gives

---

[6]We took several steps to minimize the effect of missing trade data in the 1885–1949 period. We used information about one state's exports to another to infer its partner's imports. We collected estimates from other sources, compared them to the data from *The Stateman's Yearbook* and the League of Nations, and adjusted the data from our principal sources as appropriate. These sources include Mitchell 1981 for Europe and other volumes by Mitchell for all other regions of the world and for the United Kingdom; U.S. Department of Commerce, *Historical Statistics of the United States: Colonial Times to 1970*; and Katherine Barbieri's data. Exchange rates come from U.S. Federal Reserve Bank sources, *The Stateman's Yearbook*, and Global Financial Data Company (www.globalfindata.com). We also interpolated between known values of trade and used the average value of a dyad's trade to extrapolate. Finally, if neither state in a dyad reported exports to or imports from the other, we assumed that there was no trade between them. We conducted several tests to see if these methods might have biased our results. First, we dropped all zero values of trade, and then we dropped all interpolations and extrapolations. Analyses with the remaining "real" data for the pre–World War II period were consistent with those discussed in the text.

us a measure of the degree to which it is economically dependent upon this bilateral commerce (DEPEND).[7]

We must acknowledge that dyadic trade, even when adjusted for the size of the overall economy, is an imperfect indicator of economic interdependence. For one thing, the composition of trade is not considered. A country like Japan that imports large quantities of oil and food, for example, may experience greater vulnerability than our measure of dependency indicates. Yet to the extent that international prices reflect the true value of commodities, including the possibility of disruptions to existing channels of supply, the dyadic trade-to-GDP ratio will accurately measure a country's dependence on its trading partner.

It would also be good if we were able to analyze the effect of foreign investment on the likelihood of conflict. This type of interdependence has become increasingly important in recent decades. Between 1970 and 1997, worldwide GDP more than doubled in constant dollars, and trade quadrupled, but foreign direct investment expanded to more than 700 percent of what it had been (Rosecrance 1999, 37). Foreign investment and the globalization of production, like trade, should increase the incentive for peace. Investment creates similar networks of shared interest and communication. Military conflict raises the risk that foreign investments will be expropriated or destroyed. Unfortunately, dyadic investment data comparable in coverage to the trade data simply do not exist; they are particularly sparse and unreliable prior to the 1950s. Yet trade and foreign investment are highly correlated, so consideration of this important influence is not completely absent from the analyses we conduct. It is true that trade and foreign investment are to some degree substitutes: a manufacturer may export goods to another country rather than make them there. But even traditional forms of trade often involve the establishment of for-

---

[7]We used GDPs in current dollars to be consistent with the trade data. We began with the estimates of constant dollar GDP in Summers et al. 1995 for the years after 1949 and with Maddison's estimates (1995) for fifty-six countries in all regions of the world for 1870–1992. We regressed those estimates on year and COW's estimates of annual energy consumption to predict data for additional years and additional countries. Energy consumption is a good correlate of incomes, as Morgenstern, Knorr, and Heiss 1973 note (see also Oneal 1989), but the efficiency with which energy is converted to useful output (GDP) varies through time. We converted these constant dollar GDPs to current dollars using Maddison 1991b.

eign commercial operations. Increasingly, however, trade takes place within multinational corporations. Some 40 percent of all merchandise trade involves transactions between subsidiaries of the same company (Alworth 1988, 208; Spero 1990). We can be reasonably confident, therefore, that our trade measure reflects this important dimension of international economic relations, too.

We assume that the state with the lower bilateral trade-to-GDP measure is the one less constrained from using force and, therefore, that it has the greater influence on the likelihood of dyadic conflict. This state has greater freedom to initiate violent conflict because its economic costs and the beneficial effect of communication would be less. An example is provided by events in Guatemala in 1952. The leftist government of Jacobo Arbenz seized vast areas of agricultural land, including a quarter of a million acres belonging to United Fruit, an American multinational corporation. Only small sums were paid for the land, which was then turned over to landless Guatemalan farmers. The economic stakes for the United States were small relative to its huge economy, so there was no significant constraint preventing the Eisenhower administration from adopting a tough line. Severe economic sanctions were imposed on Guatemala. The Guatemalan government fell increasingly under Communist influence, and in August 1953, the U.S. National Security Council defined the situation, which took place at the height of the cold war, as a threat to national security.

Arbenz tried to avoid worsening his relations with the United States, but diplomatic conditions deteriorated, and the U.S. government increased its military assistance to a group of rebels, led by Castillo Armas, which operated from bases set up with CIA support in Nicaragua. In January of 1954, Arbenz made arrangements to buy arms from Communist Czechoslovakia. In turn, the United States set up a naval blockade of Guatemala to stop arms shipments from Eastern Europe, concluded a military assistance agreement with Guatemala's neighbor Honduras, and began shipping tanks and planes to Honduras to support an invasion. In June, with heavy covert support from the CIA and the Pentagon, Armas invaded Guatemala and the Arbenz regime collapsed (Cullather 1999). Although the Arbenz government certainly provoked U.S. displeasure, it was the United States that militarized the dispute: supporting Armas and his rebels, initiating the blockade, and ultimately encouraging the invasion. While Washington was not prepared to commit the U.S. Army to the effort, the invasion could not have occurred without U.S. support. The United States was far less constrained from using force than Guatemala was.

This example illustrates why we expect the less constrained state in each dyad to be primarily responsible for the presence or absence of conflict between them. It is the weak link in the chain of peace. Accordingly, we include in our statistical analyses the bilateral trade-to-GDP ratio for the state with the lower dependence score ($DEPEND_L$). To determine if asymmetric economic relations increase the probability of conflict, as dependency theorists suggest, we can add a second trade variable ($DEPEND_H$) to our model of conflict. If one country is much more dependent on existing commercial relations than the other, exploitation (or a perception of exploitation) may make political relations subject to conflict, or it may at least reduce the benefits of economic exchange from what they would be if their trade were equally important to both and the two states were truly interdependent. Since the numerator (dyadic trade) is the same for both countries, the state with the smaller economy will have the higher trade-to-GDP ratio. The difference between $DEPEND_L$ and $DEPEND_H$, as in the case of the United States and Guatemala in 1953, can be very great.

The recent trend in economic relations, as well as their most recent level, may also affect the likelihood of military conflict. To measure the trend in relations, we calculated the change in the bilateral dependence of states over a three-year period, from four years prior to the current year, when the state of dyadic relations (peace or a dispute) is being assessed, to the year just before a possible conflict. A decline in the economic importance of bilateral trade should be associated with an increase in the likelihood of dyadic disputes. On the other hand, a rising level of trade may signal improving interstate relations. The relatively long four-year span helps to maximize the chance that a decline in trade may be more a cause of worsening political relations than simply a near-term reflection of an anticipated violent conflict.[8] We assess the consequence of change in the economic importance of trade by including in our analyses the magnitude of the change in the trade-to-GDP ratio (negative or positive) for whichever state in each dyad experienced the greater change.

---

[8]To minimize the loss of cases, we substituted the change in trade over a three- or two-year span when values were missing at the beginning of a dyadic time series.

We also consider the effect of total trade on the likelihood of a dispute in order to take into account the economic effects of conflict on third parties. Economic openness, a state's trade with all countries as a fraction of its GDP, is a measure of a state's interdependence in the global economy generally. As with Britain in the late nineteenth century or Taiwan in the twentieth, open economies are subject to disruption by wars and rumors of war (Rosecrance 1999). We measure openness (OPEN) as a country's total exports plus its total imports divided by its GDP.[9] We expect the less open state ($OPEN_L$) to be less constrained from resorting to violence because its economy is less subject to the disruption that hostilities might cause.

The degree to which a country depends upon international trade is influenced by the size of its domestic market. Small countries tend to be more open than larger ones. A small country will find it difficult to be highly self-sufficient. It will need many goods and services that it cannot produce efficiently on a small scale, so it will import them. To be able to afford these imports, it will have to specialize in making goods that it can produce relatively efficiently and sell abroad what it does not need for its own consumption. Consequently, small countries have little choice but to concentrate on the export of natural resources (oil, mineral, specialized agricultural products) if they have them (as does Kuwait) or on a set of high-tech manufacturers or services for which they possess a comparative advantage (as does Singapore). Big economies, with internally varied climates and resource endowments and a large number of consumers, can produce a wide range of products at close to the prices that prevail in the world market, so they are usually more self-sufficient.

Some states make a greater political commitment to the liberal principles of free trade and comparative advantage than do others, so the correlation between economic size and openness is far from perfect. At the end of the nineteenth century, Great Britain had a substantially more open economy than its competitor Germany, although they were comparable in size. In 1968, the United States, with a GDP more than twice that of the Soviet Union, imported and exported goods equal in value to 8 percent of its GDP, whereas the openness of the Soviets was under 3 percent.

[9]Our data for total trade for 1950–92 are from Summers et al. 1995. For the years before 1950, we relied primarily on the volumes by Mitchell identified above.

For West Germany and Japan in the same year, then with very similar GDPs, the trade percentages were 33 percent and 18 percent, respectively. Thus, the relative impact of the international economy on a state's politics depends not just on the size of its GDP but also on other economic and political factors, including the policies adopted by the national government. This is fortunate because we want to be sure we are measuring economic interdependence, a liberal variable, and not size, which is associated with national power and the argument of the realists.

Trade Does Reduce Conflict

We are now ready to evaluate the liberal thesis that trade reduces the likelihood of military conflict. First, we consider the consequences of economically important bilateral trade by adding the bilateral trade-to-GDP ratio for the larger and thus less dependent state to the basic regression equation we used in the last chapter. Thus, the variable $DEPEND_L$ is combined with our measure of democracy and the various realist variables. We use the entire 1885–1992 set of politically relevant dyads. Then, in turn, we ascertain the effects of asymmetric trade (as indicated by $DEPEND_H$), of openness, and of growth in dyadic trade. As in the previous chapter, we evaluate the effects of each of the theoretically interesting variables by first setting them all to their baseline values and then estimating the likelihood of a dispute for this "typical" dyad. Thus, we make the measure of democracy equal to 0, assume the dyad is unallied, and set each of the continuous variables at their means for the contiguous subset of dyads.[10] Then, one by one, we add one standard deviation to each of the risk factors while holding the others constant. This tells us the independent risk-reducing effect of that variable. This information is reported in column 1 of Table 4.1.

These results provide strong support for the liberal peace. Both democracy and economically important trade are strong and statistically significant constraints on the use of force. The likelihood of a dispute is much lower when states are dependent on bilateral trade or are democratic.

---

[10] We use the median of $DEPEND_L$ as its baseline value. It is more representative than the mean because of the skewed distribution of this variable.

Table 4.1: Percentage Change in Risk for Annual Involvement in a Militarized Dispute, 1886–1992: Contiguous Dyads, Realist Variables, Democracy, and Economic Interdependence

All variables at baseline values except:	*(1)* *With Dyadic Variables*	*(2)* *Adding Openness*
ALLIES equals 1	−47%	−35%
POWER RATIO increased by one standard deviation	−34	−33
$DEMOC_L$ increased by one standard deviation	−36	−31
$DEMOC_L$ decreased by one standard deviation	+54	+44
$DEPEND_L$ increased by one standard deviation	−44	−35
$OPEN_L$ increased by one standard deviation		−27
$DEPEND_L$ and $OPEN_L$ both increased by one standard deviation		−52

Both influences are substantial despite the fact that democracies tend also to have higher levels of trade than other states. Controlling for the benefits of interdependence, democracy still reduces the probability of a dispute by 36 percent. The impact of the bilateral trade-to-GDP ratio is even bigger: an increase of one standard deviation makes a dispute 44 percent less likely. There is less than one chance in a thousand that the close association between either interdependence and peace or democracy and peace would have occurred by chance. Kant and the other classical liberals were right: both democracy and trade increase the prospects for peace. The other variables perform as expected: alliances are strongly associated with less dyadic conflict, and an overwhelming imbalance of power (POWER RATIO) still has an important deterrent effect. The reductions in risk associated with these influences are 47 percent and 34 percent, respectively. All the variables (including distance, contiguity, and minor power dyads, which are not shown in the table) are statistically significant at a very high level (.001).

The pacific benefits of economically important bilateral trade seem well illustrated by the experience of the United States with China over the past twenty years. After the Communist government began to open its economy in the late 1970s, its political relations with the United States became far more peaceful than they had been during the cold war. This thaw in relations began with a deliberate political decision to improve them, but as trade increased, both sides gained a greater stake in keeping them peaceful. This happened despite the fact that China did not become significantly more democratic.

Next we assess the view of dependency theorists that asymmetric dependence on trade reduces the pacific benefits of commerce. Asymmetry is said to give a powerful state the opportunity to exploit its trading partner. This may provoke disputes as either the disadvantaged state rebels or the powerful state uses military force to enforce its advantage. The example of U.S.-Guatemalan relations in the early 1950s might be an example of a general tendency. To test whether trade between a large and a small state has different implications for interstate relations than trade between states of equal size, we add to our equation the higher bilateral trade-to-GDP ratio ($DEPEND_H$) in each pair of states. The coefficient of this variable will be positive if, holding the trade-to-GDP ratio of the bigger state constant, greater dependence on the part of the smaller state increases the likelihood of interstate conflict. This analysis is similar to the one in the preceding chapter where we asked whether autocracies and democracies are particularly prone to fight.

Contrary to the expectation of dependency theorists, the benefits of trade do not depend upon the states' being of similar size. The estimated coefficient of $DEPEND_H$ was not significantly different from zero. This means that the benefits of trade are not importantly affected by the higher trade-to-GDP ratio, only the lower one. Indeed, the coefficient was negative, not positive. What little effect an unequal balance of trade has is to reduce the likelihood of conflict further. Economically important trade between large states and small states increases the prospects for peace just as it does for states of equal size.

We can only speculate why this is true. One possibility is that the economic domination of small states by big trading partners is so complete that acts of resistance are not undertaken. If the political system of a small trade-dependent state is heavily dominated by an elite (such as plantation owners or mining companies in Central American countries) trading with

the big country, that state's restraint in avoiding overt conflict may deter
it from any actions that would cut off profitable trade. If the small country does not resist the powerful one, there may be no need for the latter to
exercise its military might.

The alternative explanation, and the one that would be emphasized by
liberals, is that trade really does significantly benefit both partners. Trade
is not forced. It is voluntary. If a buyer and a seller agree to a transaction
in a free market, it is because both expect to be better off than they would
have been without the exchange. If both are better off, neither one would
prefer to see the relationship disrupted by hostilities. We cannot settle this
debate here, but this second explanation coincides with doubts that the
international economy works to the disadvantage of developing countries
(de Soysa and Oneal 1999).

Are Open Economies More Pacific?

Next we ask whether pacific benefits also accrue from a high level of economic openness generally, or whether it is only bilateral trade that affects
the likelihood that two states will become involved in a militarized dispute. We report in column 2 of Table 4.1 the results of estimating the independent effect of high levels of total trade, controlling for bilateral
interdependence, democracy, and the realist variables. Adding openness
($OPEN_L$) to our model of interstate conflict provides strong support
for the general thesis that economic interdependence reduces the likelihood of military conflict. All of the variables that had a statistically significant impact in the analysis reported in column 1 still do. As before, all
the variables are significant at the .001 level, meaning that there is less
than one chance in a thousand that such strong correlations would be
found if the information used was just a randomly generated series of
numbers.

Even when both dyadic trade and general openness are included in the
same analysis, each makes a substantively important independent contribution to reducing the probability of a militarized dispute. Again, dyadic
trade has the greatest impact, reducing the risk of a dispute by 35 percent,
as much as if the two states were formally allied. A higher level of democracy reduces the likelihood of conflict by 31 percent, but openness to the
world economy also has a notable impact: an increase of one standard de-

viation reduces the risk of a dispute by 27 percent.[11] The impact on the likelihood of conflict of democracy, bilateral trade, and the existence of an alliance all fall slightly because these variables are correlated with one another. That is, states that are democratic trade more with one another, tend to be allied, and have more open economies generally.[12] The most important thing to note is that, despite these interrelationships, the independent effect of each variable is still quite dramatic.

It is not surprising that bilateral economic relations are a better predictor of the tenor of dyadic relations than openness is, but it is encouraging that total trade also has an independent, statistically significant, and substantively important impact. Countries that are open to external economic relations are constrained from using force even against rivals with whom commercial ties are limited. It is worth estimating the combined effect of high levels of dyadic trade and openness. Because we are estimating the probability of a dispute, which must lie between 0 and 1, their combined effect is not as big as adding 35 percent and 27 percent together. Nevertheless, if both dyadic trade and openness are increased above their baseline levels, the likelihood that two countries will experience a dispute falls by more than half (52 percent). It is the isolated countries of the world that represent the greatest danger to peaceful international relations.

We also looked at whether the trend in bilateral trade dependence affects the probability of conflict. To do this, we performed new analyses that included measures of the level of economic interdependence and of the change in the level over the previous four years. There is no need to present these results in a table; they are easily summarized. Contrary to

[11]As noted earlier, smaller states tend to have more open economies than large states. To make sure that our measure of openness was not acting as an additional measure of national power, rather than interdependence, we conducted an analysis adding the ratio of the larger state's GDP to the smaller state's GDP to the model. If openness were really indicating just economic size, this measure would have been negatively related to the onset of conflict, as is the POWER RATIO derived from the COW data. In fact, the GDP ratio had the wrong sign and was far from statistical significance; $OPEN_L$ remained significant at the .002 level.

[12]A country's total trade is, of course, the sum of all its bilateral commercial exchanges, but $OPEN_L$ and $DEPEND_L$ are only moderately correlated ($r = 0.33$) since trade can be shifted from one country to another while maintaining the same level of total exports and imports.

our expectations, we found no significant evidence that the trend in trade makes a difference in the likelihood of dyadic conflict. We measured change in economic relations in several ways. None of them indicated that falling levels of trade are an additional portent of danger or that rising levels per se reduce the probability of a dispute. In these analyses, it was the level of trade, not recent changes in it, that proved useful in accounting for interstate violence.

This does not mean that falling levels of trade are unimportant. If economic interdependence declines, the prospects of conflict do increase, because the level of trade is closely associated, as we have seen, with the incidence of conflicts. It is just that low and declining trade does not herald greater danger than does trade that has been low over all of the four most recent years. The Great Depression, as we briefly noted earlier, is a dramatic reminder of the dangers that attend economic crises. In the 1930s, there was a sharp decline in living standards and then an even sharper drop in the volume of international trade, as states imposed new tariffs and other trade restrictions to protect their domestic markets from foreign competition. These "beggar-my-neighbor" policies invited retaliation in kind. As the retaliatory policies took effect, states became less dependent on maintaining good political relations with each other. This led to a downward spiral or vicious circle of hard economic times, failed democracies in much of Europe and in Japan, and darkening clouds of war. International organizations, notably the League of Nations, were too weak to act effectively. Interdependence reduces the prospects of violent international conflict. If the links of interdependence are broken, however, so too are important constraints on conflict.

As with the democratic peace, one of the key questions about the consequences of trade is whether the benefits of interdependence are confined to the post–World War II period. It is often noted, for example, that World War I occurred at a time when the countries of Europe were more interdependent than they had ever been before and more interdependent than they would be until many years after the end of World War II. We will look at this matter in detail when we consider the effects of the full set of Kantian influences, including international organizations, in the next chapter. For now, we will say only that the benefits of trade have been greatest in the years after 1950, but they were substantial for the years 1886–1939 as well. We do not find any reason to think that the liberal peace is limited to the cold war. As we noted in the last chapter, the biggest difference between the cold war and earlier periods was that alliances became associated with reduced conflict only after World War II.

Economic Growth and Conflict

Our consideration of the influence of economic conditions on the likelihood of international conflict should not stop with trade. The role of economic growth also warrants attention. States with strong economies, those that enjoy prosperity and are experiencing economic growth, may be disinclined to fight. Their populations are likely to be satisfied with the economic and political status quo, and as liberals have emphasized, violent conflict is inconsistent with many financial and commercial relations. One reason why the rich industrialized countries gave up wars of imperialism in the latter part of the twentieth century was that their prosperity and continuing growth made such wars look unattractive from any reasonable cost-benefit perspective (Mueller 1989). The higher the rate of economic growth, presumably the greater the popular satisfaction and the less inclined the people should be to engage in militarized conflicts.

Moreover, leaders do not have an incentive to start a conflict if the economy is prospering. In Chapter 2, we discussed the substantial literature on the hypothesis that some wars stem from an effort by leaders to divert attention from domestic difficulties, such as a failing economy, toward foreign adversaries (or scapegoats). Presumably, the greater is the rate of economic decline, as indicated by falling personal incomes, the greater will be the incentives for leaders to divert attention from economic conditions. The evidence for that effect from previous research is mixed, as we noted, but the hypothesis is interesting and plausible, so we want to explore the possibility here. Both these considerations—about the conflict-mitigating effect of economic growth and about the conflict-inducing effect of economic decline—suggest that the state with the lower rate of economic growth will be the greater danger to peace.

Although the diversionary theory of war seems a plausible account of some individual cases, such as the Argentine invasion of the Falkland Islands in 1982, the effect that we should expect the economy to have on the likelihood of conflict is not entirely obvious. Some have suggested that economic growth *increases* the prospects of war and that economic decline reduces it. If a country's economy is deteriorating, its industry may be incapable of producing the war material necessary to support an extended conflict with another country. Or domestic dissatisfaction with the government could be so serious that the public will not support it in a foreign dispute. It is commonly believed that the war with Germany in 1914–17 only added to the dissatisfaction of the Russian people with the tsar; it did not divert attention away from the economic suffering and instead provided an additional reason for a revolutionary explosion.

Rapid economic expansion, on the other hand, may provide the "fuel," in the form of greater material capabilities, for military adventures and may encourage a general sense of optimism about the strength of the country that would embolden them. To this could be added the hypothesis that rapid economic growth intensifies the need for imports of vital commodities. Both Hobson's and Lenin's theories of imperialism, formulated at the height of the era of imperialism at the turn of the last century, stressed the danger of international conflict inherent in efforts to acquire colonies in a diplomatic and military competition with other imperial powers. This idea was taken up by later social scientists (Choucri and North 1975; Goldstein 1988; Pollins and Schweller 1999), who argue that economic growth creates "lateral pressure" that forces states to look abroad for resources, raising the danger of war as they encounter others on the same quest. These various considerations agree in predicting a greater danger of conflict with greater economic growth and less conflict when states are in decline.

When faced with such conflicting predictions about the effect of economic growth on conflict, empirical analysis is particularly important. To evaluate the rival hypotheses, we used information regarding personal incomes—real GDP per capita—to calculate economic growth rates over three years. The term "real" indicates that the effects of inflation have been factored out and that the variability of prices in different countries is also taken into account; thus, we are assessing change in the average person's actual standard of living. The initial hypothesis was that a strong economy discourages conflict and economic decline encourages it. We conducted a couple of tests of this view. In the first, we assumed that the likelihood of conflict depended mainly on actions by the less constrained state in each dyad. According to liberals and those who think wars occasionally serve a diversionary purpose, this would be the state with the lower rate of growth. Thus, in our first test, we used the variable

GROWTH$_L$. As in our other tests, we sought to insure that the disputes we were trying to explain had not influenced the variables we were using for that very purpose, so we used the lower rate of growth in each dyad over the three years *preceding* the year in which conflict might have occurred.

We wanted to consider carefully the experience of both members in each dyad, so we also conducted a second test. In this analysis, we created one variable that recorded the faster rate of growth in each dyad and a second that measured the severity of the worse decline.[13] In this way, we hoped to capture the effect of growth on interstate conflict in more complex situations, for example, if one member of a dyad is growing rapidly while the other is experiencing a declining standard of living. These variables also allowed us to investigate the alternative hypothesis that economic growth creates wealth that enables states to act more aggressively and that a declining economy limits the use of force.

However we measured the effect of growth, we found no significant influence on the occurrence of militarized disputes. There seems to be no systematic relationship between conflict and either a successful, growing economy or economic decline. Our measures of growth in both tests never approached statistical significance. Consequently, we do not report any effect of this factor on the risk of disputes. This evidence suggests that *economic growth is neither the enemy of peace nor essential to it.* More important are the ties of interest and communication that derive from substantial commercial transactions with other states, the character of states' political regimes, whether they are allied, the balance of power, and the other influences we have been discussing.[14]

---

[13]Heldt (1999) suggests that the effect of growth be assessed in this way. One variable indicates the higher rate of growth in the dyad if one or both states experienced growth at a positive rate. If both states experienced a decline in their per capita GDPs, this variable equals 0. Similarly, the other variable equals the change in GDP per capita of the state that experienced the greatest economic decline. If both states experienced actual growth in incomes, this variable is set equal to 0. Heldt also asks whether democracies are more prone to use force under various economic conditions than autocracies are, but he finds no systematic effect.

[14]Mousseau (2000) and Hegre (2000), however, suggest that democracy and economic interdependence may have little dispute-reducing effect for very poor countries, such as Bangladesh.

Economic Interdependence and Peace

We can now summarize the results we have reported in this chapter. They
are important and encouraging. There is strong, consistent evidence that
economic interdependence, like democratic institutions and norms, significantly reduces the risk that two states will become involved in a militarized dispute. Over the years, liberals have claimed that democracy and
free trade not only increase individual liberty and prosperity but also
ameliorate international conflict. Our analyses indicate they have been
right: the pacific benefits of both democracy and economic interdependence are evident and substantial. In addition, neither variable eliminates
the importance of the other. Higher levels of economically important
trade, as indicated by the bilateral trade-to-GDP ratio, are associated with
fewer incidences of militarized international disputes. A one standard deviation increase in the bilateral trade-to-GDP ratio reduces the annual
probability of a dispute more than one-third below the baseline rate.
Such a powerful benefit appears even when we control for a variety of
potentially confounding, theoretically interesting influences, such as
geographic contiguity, the balance of power, alliance bonds, democracy,
and economic growth rates. Nor are the pacific benefits of trade reduced
by asymmetric economic relations, as dependency theorists have feared.

Economic openness (the total trade-to-GDP ratio) is also associated
with a reduced risk of conflict. Even when we hold constant the effects of
bilateral interdependence, a one standard deviation increase in openness
makes a dispute 27 percent less likely. If both bilateral trade and openness
are increased, the likelihood of dyadic conflict drops by 52 percent. This
evidence for the pacific benefits of openness is important for two reasons.
First, it indicates that states recognize the consequences of militarized disputes for their economic relations with third parties. As a result, even
when bilateral trade and investment is limited, states can be constrained
by wider economic forces from taking military action. Second, the significance and substantive importance of openness as a predictor of peaceful
relations increases our confidence that economically important trade affects the probability of conflict and is not just a consequence of peaceful
relations. Deteriorating political relations might cause a state to reduce its
economic dependence on a potential adversary, but it is much harder for
a state to manipulate its total trade-to-GDP ratio by restricting economic
ties with all states simultaneously. Our analyses with openness do not dis-

pel all doubts about the causal influence of trade on conflict. We want to get a better indication of the strength of the influence of conflict on trade, and so we return to this issue in Chapter 6 when we investigate the influences that shape bilateral trade.

We found no support for some other hypotheses. The short-term trend in bilateral interdependence has little impact on the likelihood of conflict. We found no evidence that change in the level of the bilateral trade-to-GDP ratio indicates states' expectations regarding the future of their relations or that declining trade exacerbates interstate relations. It is the economic importance of current levels of trade that affect the prospects for peace, not change in the level. Nor did we find a systematic relation between economic growth (or decline) and states' involvement in militarized disputes with each other. Neither liberals, who think growth might have significant benefits, nor those concerned that growth might trigger conflict as states compete for resources can find support here. Nor is there evidence that the leaders of states are inclined to divert attention from economic difficulties by engaging in foreign military adventures. Perhaps the benefits are too uncertain.

Overall, evidence we have presented in this chapter provides a strong indication that both elements of the liberals' agenda—interdependence and democracy—make independent contributions to the prospects for peace. Indeed, the pacific benefits of trade are not limited to the countries normally considered liberal—the Western democracies—or relations among them. *Countries that are interdependent bilaterally or economically open to the global economy, whether democratic or not, have an important basis for pacific relations and conflict resolution.* Still, as the liberal theorists anticipated, those that are democratic, interdependent, and economically open—as are the economically advanced democracies of the West—are most likely to be at peace.

International Organizations

Also Reduce Conflict

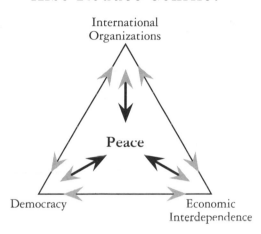

The final element in Kant's vision of "perpetual peace" is international law, which, building on an understanding of the legitimate rights of all republics and their citizens, provides a legal framework for the peaceful resolution of interstate conflicts. In Kant's view, the three legs of the tripod are not truly independent elements that are individually useful in preventing wars. Rather, they are integrally related. Democracy, by its recognition of individual liberty and responsibility, encourages entrepreneurship and the expansion of commerce, ultimately beyond the boundaries of a single state. As the economic activities of citizens make countries more and more interdependent, there is an increasing need for institutions that can regulate and facilitate trade and investment. Thus, international law and institutions are established in response to the actions of the citizens of democratic states pursuing their interests over a constantly expanding geographical area. The three elements of the Kantian peace are, therefore, part of a whole that contributes to a stable peace (Kant [1795] 1970; Doyle 1992). In the contemporary world, international law is often expressed in international organizations. So we now expand our analysis of the Kantian peace to include the contribution of international organizations, as illustrated by the third dark arrowhead in the triangle above, pointing from the apex of the triangle to the center.

Kant believed that international law would operate most powerfully among democracies (republics), which would form a loose "federation" of sovereign states (an international organization) to facilitate their peaceful relations and provide a framework for collective security against threats from states that were not republics. These same elements inspired the practical vision and actions of the leaders of Europe following World War II. Establishment of the European Common Market—and its evolution into the European Union—required that they restore stable democratic governments; ease the flow of goods, services, capital, and labor throughout Western Europe; and establish a network of multinational institutions that could solidify democracy and facilitate markets. The experience of Europe over the last fifty years records their success. The creation of a security community has made armed conflict between France and Germany, for example, unthinkable. The absence of war—or even the serious possibility of it—among members of the EU is a remarkable achievement, particularly in light of the continent's earlier history. It has freed tremendous resources from preparations for armed conflict to more productive activities. Europeans in the postwar period have demonstrated the efficacy and practicality of a liberal response to the problem of war, one that others beyond the borders of Europe can emulate.

In examining the conditions that promote peace, we have concentrated to this point on the effects of democracy and economic interdependence. We have seen that each makes an important, independent contribution to reducing the frequency of interstate conflict. In this chapter, we turn our attention to the third Kantian element, asking whether dense networks of intergovernmental organizations (IGOs) also reduce the incidence of militarized disputes. To answer this question, we gathered information on states' participation in IGOs and then counted for each pair of states the number of organizations to which they both belonged. This gives us a measure of the availability of institutions that can resolve potential disputes. In the analyses reported below, we show that shared IGO memberships do reduce the risk of interstate violence, completing the Kantian tripod for peace.

After incorporating all the Kantian elements, we undertake several additional tests designed to differentiate their dyadic effects, which we have been considering until now, from those connected with the international system generally. We want to know whether peace is more likely when the system has a higher proportion of democratic states, the average level of interdependence is greater, and there are more IGOs. Can the norms and institutions of the system under these conditions exercise a beneficial influence on pairs of states that are not themselves democratic, or interdependent, or closely linked by international organizations? Once we have distinguished the systemic consequences of the Kantian variables from their purely dyadic effects, we next consider several important realist theories regarding the influence of the international system on the likelihood of conflict. Is peace more likely when there is a very powerful state, a "hegemon," that can reduce interstate conflict by its management of the system? Does the political character of the hegemon account for the democratic peace? In answering these questions, we have new opportunities to assess the relative importance of realist and liberal theories of international politics.

In this chapter, we focus on intergovernmental organizations (IGOs), not on the far more numerous international nongovernmental organizations (INGOs). While many of the latter also can be expected to make a direct or indirect contribution to international peace, their membership consists chiefly of individuals or private organizations rather than states, and their functions are even more diverse than those of IGOs. It is better to begin, in an analysis of states' actions in the realm of war and peace, by considering the effects of organizations that are composed of states and that directly address the responsibilities of states.

Networks of Intergovernmental Organizations

Arguably, the first IGO was the "congress system" in Europe. It was inaugurated with the Congress of Vienna in September 1814 and was designed to bolster the peace that followed the end of the Napoleonic Wars. It continued with regular institutionalized consultations among the great powers. The congress system ended with the assembly in Verona in 1822; its successor, the Concert of Europe, lacked significant institutional structure. Proposals to establish international organizations in order to maintain the peace are much older, however, going back as far as Pierre Dubois in the thirteenth century (Jacobson 1984). The oldest extant IGO, the Central Commission for the Navigation of the Rhine, was formed in 1815 in response to the economic interdependence of states along one of Europe's most important rivers. Although other important IGOs were created in the nineteenth century, the phenomenon is primarily a twentieth-century one. Growth in the number of international organizations has been especially great since the end of World War II.

The growth in the number of international organizations has even exceeded that of democracy and economic interdependence. The number of democratic states has expanded rather steadily since 1885, but more slowly than has the number of IGOs. Interdependence, on the other hand, was greater in the years before World War I; but by the 1970s, it had surpassed its earlier peak, especially among the European states. By one common count, there were 37 IGOs in 1909, 132 in 1956, and 293 in 1990. The last figure is somewhat below the total achieved in the early 1980s; some specialized organizations later curtailed their activities or were absorbed into more comprehensive institutions (Union of International Associations 1992–93, 1610–11). The decline in the number of IGOs in the 1980s shows that it is not inevitable that their number will increase. They can cease to exist or become dormant as states' interests change. Nevertheless, most IGOs have proven to be fairly stable and long-lived. According to one study, of the 34 IGOs that existed in 1914, 18 were still operating in 1989. The average age of those that disappeared was about twenty years (Cupitt, Whitlock, and Whitlock 1996).[1] This is consistent with the requirement that a political actor must have "a claim of institutional coherence and authority" and with a definition of institutions as "persistent and connected sets of rules, formal and informal" (March and Olsen 1984; Keohane 1990).

An intergovernmental organization can be defined as a formal, continuous institution established by treaty or other agreement between governments with a long-range purpose. IGOs are multilateral; the Union of International Associations specifies that there must be three or more members. They have secretariats to record their activities and monitor their affairs, and they meet more or less regularly. Legally, they are con-

---

[1]Using a broader definition of IGOs that includes "emanations," Shanks, Jacobson, and Kaplan (1996, 599) find that, of all the IGOs extant in 1981, only 68 percent were still alive in 1992.

sidered to be international "persons," which means they have standing in law (Feld, Jordan, and Hurwitz 1994, 10–11). The system of international organizations can be characterized as decentralized and nonhierarchical; it is composed of quasi-universal as well as regional organizations. An organization's purposes or functions may be general or limited to specific economic, social, cultural, political, or security matters. The League of Nations was the first multipurpose, quasi-universal intergovernmental organization. In the post–World War II era, the most prominent universal organization has been the United Nations. In addition to the UN proper, there are its various specialized agencies, whose memberships vary to some degree. Switzerland, for example, does not belong to the United Nations itself but has joined many of its affiliated institutions.

The creation of the UN and a substantial number of other, nearly universal organizations means that by the 1950s the great majority of states shared some common memberships with almost all other states. That base of institutional association has expanded in various degrees by memberships in regional groupings defined primarily in geographical terms (such as the Americas, Europe, the North Atlantic, or Southeast Asia). For the period of our analysis, 1885–1992, the number of shared IGO memberships ranges from zero to 130. The densest network of international organizations is found in Europe (particularly in Western Europe), followed at some distance by Latin America. Interestingly, these are the areas of the world exhibiting the least interstate conflict since World War II. At the other end of the spectrum, some pairs of states are not members of any of the same IGOs. Despite the existence of several "universal" organizations, a few states choose not to join or are not allowed to do so. Most notably, the People's Republic of China was excluded from almost all before 1971. Consequently, the United States (and many of its closest allies) shared no memberships in IGOs with the PRC during this period. There were far fewer IGOs in the nineteenth and early twentieth century, so the number of dyads that shared no common memberships was greater then, too.

Why and How IGOs Might Matter

The literature on the contribution of particular IGOs to world peace is vast, but there are few social scientific studies of how IGOs in general af-

fect interstate relations. Previous research shows that IGOs are often established during the peaceful periods following major wars; hence, one
would expect to see a correlation between IGOs and peace, but this does
not necessarily show a causal link from IGOs to peace (Vasquez 1993,
269 ff.; also Jacobson, Reisinger, and Mathers 1986, 156). Domke (1988,
chap. 6) found in his study of the nineteenth and twentieth centuries,
however, that rapid growth in the number of IGOs in the international
system was followed by fewer outbreaks of war. Other studies show that
shared IGO memberships increase the level of cooperation among allied
nations (Oneal 1990a, 1990b; Oneal and Diehl 1994).[2]

Before undertaking new statistical analyses, it is essential to consider
how international organizations might promote peaceful relations. Like
other institutions, IGOs serve various purposes. These range from acting
in a quasi-supranational capacity to enforce established agreements by
military action, through facilitating members' pursuit of their individual
self-interests in ways that are consistent with their common cause (a standard liberal understanding of the role of institutions), to "teaching" a set
of norms that may sharply revise states' conception of their interests and
preferences (Finnemore 1993; Finnemore and Sikkink 1998).

Many commentators on world politics (for example, Mearsheimer
1994–95) believe that international organizations are unimportant because they typically lack independent means of enforcing their own decisions in particular or international law in general. Whatever authority
they have, it is argued, is simply derivative of the power of their members.
They are not, therefore, independently important. But most international
organizations, while rarely able to exercise centralized means of coercion,
fulfill many other functions of "government" (Milner 1991). Relatively
decentralized institutions may encourage cooperation by enhancing facilities for consultation, coordination, and the creation of norms. They may
make it possible for member states to make and enforce cooperative
arrangements among themselves. Somewhat more centralized organizations may produce instruments of efficiency, legitimacy, and weak en-

---

[2]General dyadic studies are few. One early investigation reported a positive relationship between dense IGO memberships and the frequency of conflict (Russett
1967, 200), but that relationship is apt to be spurious because IGO memberships—
like alliances and trade—are found predominantly among countries that are geographically close to one another.

forcement (Abbott and Snidal 1998; Snidal 1997). Indeed, international organizations can serve any of six functions. We consider these in turn.

Coercing norm-breakers

The use of coercion to maintain or restore peace is straightforward. It is an aspect of international relations more easily derived from realist theories than from the liberal view of global politics. Realists and liberals, of course, disagree on how important IGOs are likely to be in this respect. In theory, the UN, with the Security Council acting as the agent of its collective security system, acts on the principle of unified action of all against *any* state, even a member, that breaches the peace. The organization may also act to deter a threat to the peace. The founders of the United Nations were realistic enough to recognize the difficulties the institution would face if the great powers, which constitute the core of the Security Council, were in serious conflict. In this they anticipated events as they actually transpired, with the outbreak of the cold war. Nonetheless, those who wrote the UN Charter gave the organization the power to act forcefully when circumstances were right. Alliances such as NATO and the former Warsaw Pact also may act coercively. They are directed against states outside the alliance, of course; but in the interest of solidarity, they may operate to suppress violent conflict among their members, too.[3] They use various mechanisms for this purpose, including overt military coercion. Institutions with coercive powers often exercise many of the following functions as well.

Mediating among conflicting parties

International organizations may play a legal role, adjudicating and arbitrating disputes. These activities are important because they reduce the cost of enforcing contracts, encourage their creation, and promote exchange (Stone Sweet and Brunell 1998a). This in turn facilitates interde-

---

[3]The line between collective security organizations and alliances, like the difference between internal and external targets of action, is often blurred (see Kupchan and Kupchan 1991 and Claude 1984). The congress system was not very institutionalized, and the Concert of Europe was even less so. On their role as collective security institutions, see Schroeder 1994.

pendence and adds to global prosperity. Institutions such as the European Court of Justice or the Permanent Court of Arbitration may incorporate a degree of voluntarism in states' participation, and rarely is enforcement carried out by the threat or use of military force. IGOs can also mediate disputes or provide diplomatic "good offices," where the capability of enforcing settlements is explicitly absent.[4] For example, Manlio Brosio, as secretary general of NATO, helped mediate the dispute between Greece and Turkey over Cyprus in 1967 and was able to avert the widening of the war. Even while caring for refugees fleeing across interstate borders from civil wars, as in Rwanda, IGOs may provide useful services of mediation.

Reducing uncertainty by conveying information

The International Telecommunication Union, established in 1865, and the International Telecommunication Satellite Organization (INTELSAT), since 1964, are examples of IGOs primarily concerned with facilitating international communication, but every institution constitutes "a set of channels for processing information, solving problems, and transmitting capabilities" (Russett 1967, 98). All institutions reduce transaction costs (Coase 1937). "Information-rich institutions . . . may help governments pursue their own interests through cooperation" by reducing uncertainty (Keohane 1984, 146–47). In this way, IGOs make it easier to identify states that are not abiding by their international agreements and increase the opportunity for other states to impose sanctions. During the cold war, NATO's annual report was designed to show every member's contribution to the alliance in order to encourage cooperation and discourage free riders. As with trade, in their information-carrying roles, IGOs may be important in promoting accurate perceptions of states' political characteristics and thus more correct expectations of how they will behave in crises. Democracies are more likely to use IGOs in resolving their conflicts than are other kinds of states, and regional IGOs (though not universal ones) are reported to be more successful in preventing violence in crises that involve democracies.[5]

---

[4]Bercovitch and Langley 1993; Haas 1993; Miall 1992; Young 1967.
[5]Coplin and Rochester 1972; Bercovitch 1991; Dixon 1994; Raymond 1994; Hewitt and Wilkenfeld 1996.

Problem-solving, including expanding states' conception of their self-interest to be more inclusive and longer term

"International organizations may provide arenas within which actors learn to alter perceptions of interest and beliefs" (Caporaso 1992, 602). From the perspective of rational choice theory, institutions may establish expectations for gain and a congruence of interests that did not previously exist. For example, to the degree that the World Trade Organization succeeds in promoting economic interdependence, all its members come to share a common interest in the long-term prosperity of other economies. They become, among other things, reliable sources of imports and markets for exports. These common interests encourage a growth in IGOs because the requirements of coordination "spill over" from one issue into related areas, as anticipated by functionalist and neo-functionalist writers (Mitrany 1966; Haas 1964, 1990). Institutions with responsibilities in several areas create the possibility of linking negotiations on one issue to others, permitting trade-offs and side payments that facilitate agreement (Keohane 1986; Kupchan and Kupchan 1991; Martin and Simmons 1998).

Socialization and shaping norms

Institutionalists "emphasize the discursive, deliberative, and persuasive aspects of communication and argument. The interstate system is a forum as well as a chessboard, and its actors debate, argue, and justify as well as signal moves" (Caporaso 1992, 627). Institutions provide legitimacy for collective decisions and so promote adherence to what has been agreed. Norms and rules developed within IGOs may facilitate arms control and delegitimize the use of force. The Agency for the Prohibition of Nuclear Weapons in Latin America and the Caribbean, for example, helped to free the region of nuclear weapons. Shared norms create common interests and facilitate cooperation. IGOs may develop interests and preferences that are more stable than and to a degree independent of those of their member states (Barnett and Finnemore 1999). These can serve as a basis to influence members in accordance with the original purpose for which the IGOs were created, and they may even create new purposes.

Generating narratives of mutual identification

We have already considered Deutsch et al.'s work (1957) on the importance of building a shared sense of values and identity among peoples.
Mutual identification means that, as others are incorporated into one's
essential reference group, their interests become not just instrumentally
relevant but integral to one's own purpose. Deutsch and his colleagues
were skeptical of the role that "amalgamated" supranational institutions
with coercive powers could play in this process, but they acknowledged
that institutions and people's sense of community can reinforce and
strengthen each other. Recent theoretical works have picked up this
theme, giving greater credence to the ability of international organizations to "construct" mutual identity (Wendt and Duvall 1989; Wendt
1994). This process is evident in the European Union. When people in
the member states were asked whether they saw themselves primarily as
citizens of the EU, their country, or a region, 16 percent identified themselves most strongly with the EU. In addition, 50 percent of those interviewed said that having European citizenship, in addition to their
national citizenship, was necessary for the future of Europe (European
Commission 1996, 86–87). One analyst contends that the porous and
transparent character of democracies makes them, in relations with other
democracies, "likely to develop a collective identity facilitating the emergence of cooperative institutions for specific purposes. . . . Democratic
features of liberal democracies enable the community in the first place.
But the institutionalization of the community exerts independent effects
on the interactions. In the final analysis, then, democratic domestic structures and international institutions do the explanatory work together"
(Risse-Kappen 1995a, 215).

In summary, IGOs are apt to reduce the propensity for states to resort to
force in a variety of ways. Some of these mechanisms will be more developed in some types of organizations than in others. The ways that alliances affect interstate relations, for example, will not be the same as the
ways that institutions with economic functions operate. This makes it difficult to design empirical tests to determine the relative importance of
these institutions. The challenge seems greater even than in previous efforts to distinguish between the normative and structural aspects of the

democratic peace. It will ultimately require more fully developed theory. This might follow from detailed analyses of individual historical cases in which the process of IGOs' influence on events is carefully traced. A refined theory would enable us to improve our measurement of IGOs' involvement in interstate affairs beyond the simple variable we use below and would increase the chance of detecting their influence.

Indirect Effects and Reverse Causality

Risse-Kappen's suggestion, quoted above, that IGOs composed of democratic states can strengthen those domestic democratic institutions is a reminder that IGOs may have important indirect effects on the prospects for peace as well as having the direct effect we will investigate in this chapter. Because democracy and economic interdependence reduce the incidence of disputes, IGOs can have important indirect effects by supporting democracy and interdependence. The evidence that IGOs promote democracy and interdependence is largely unsystematic, but the connection is nevertheless widely asserted. Indeed, it is central to the thesis of three major reports issued by the previous UN secretary general (Boutros-Ghali 1992, 1995a, 1996) and several proposals for reforming the United Nations (Russett 1996b). The current secretary general, Kofi Annan (2000), also shares this view.

We need to be attentive, therefore, to the possibility that our key variables are complementary: IGOs may promote and strengthen democracy and economic interdependence just as all three help to promote peace. There are numerous historical examples of how IGOs have encouraged the spread of democratic institutions. The Conference on Security and Cooperation in Europe and the human rights "baskets" of the Helsinki Accords legitimated and sustained political dissent in the Soviet Union and Eastern Europe in the 1980s, contributing importantly to the dissolution of the Communist autocracies in the region. The European Union's insistence on democratic government as a condition of membership has certainly discouraged some reversions to authoritarianism. Various agencies of the United Nations have assisted recently autocratic states or colonial territories in making the transition to democracy. A little-appreciated part of the UN system, the Electoral Assistance Division in the Secretariat, for example, has aided and monitored democratic elections in more than seventy states. Its services include far more, however, than the supervision of elections; it also offers advice on establishing political parties, constitutions, electoral laws, and freedom of the press (Boutros-Ghali 1995b; Joyner 1999). Many parts of the UN, and several regional IGOs, have engaged in efforts to rebuild peaceful relations in war-torn regions, creating the preconditions for free elections and democratic governance. Their record, discussed in Chapter 6, includes notable successes as well as conspicuous failures (Bertram 1995; Ratner 1995; Zartman 1995).

There are a large number of IGOs devoted to economic development, financial stability, and the freer flow of international goods, services, and capital. These contribute importantly to global interdependence. They include the Bretton Woods institutions (the World Bank and the IMF), the World Trade Organization (formerly GATT), and numerous regional institutions that provide advice to governments on ways to improve the performance of their economies. They help establish norms and principles for international exchange. Increasingly, they emphasize the necessity of "good government" and "transparency"—virtually synonyms for "democracy"—as well as offer more conventional economic prescriptions. These international organizations have also played a major role in reconstructing war-shattered societies. They have provided badly needed capital but have also built institutions and taught appropriate norms. Arguably the recent creation of such powerful IGOs in the realm of finance and economics provides an institutional basis for an international regime that makes interdependence a more effective force for peace than in earlier decades (Brawley 1993a; Murphy 1994; Wendt 1999). Their accomplishments deserve recognition, though we should not ignore critiques that they have been too attuned to the interests of international capital and the economically advanced countries and insufficiently concerned with those least well-off.

In discussing the multiple paths of causality within a well-articulated Kantian framework, we also need to consider the reciprocal relationship between international institutions and peace. States sometimes form institutional links with other states (e.g., in the United Nations) precisely because their political relationships are *not* peaceful and stable. When this process succeeds, it is possible to say that the institutions contributed to the improvement in relations. But other institutions (for example, the EU and its institutional predecessors) reflect both an aspiration for peace and a readiness to deepen institutional ties because their members already share substantial common interests and confidence that their relations will be peaceful (Keohane and Martin 1995). The Kantian hypothesis linking international organizations to peace is plausible. The six functions performed by IGOs discussed above are means by which this causal influence might take place, but the issue of reciprocal causation is important. Establishing a correlation between joint participation by states in IGOs and the existence of peaceful relations is just the beginning. It is impossible to establish in detail the effects in each direction, but an analysis in the next chapter suggests that the mechanism of causation does work both ways.

The Analysis of Dense Networks

To investigate the effect of intergovernmental organizations on the likelihood of conflict, we use the same basic method of analysis employed in the two previous chapters, where we established the role of democracy in reducing the likelihood of militarized disputes (the democratic peace) and then demonstrated the additional, independent benefits of economic interdependence (the liberal peace). Here we consider how dense networks of IGOs complete the Kantian tripod.

We gauge the importance of international organizations for dyadic relations by counting the number of IGOs in which two states shared membership in a year. We call this variable simply IGO. We include all "conventional international bodies" listed as intergovernmental organizations in Sections A–D of the *Yearbook of International Organizations;* "dormant" organizations are not counted.[6] This is a crude measure, in

---

[6]For 1965 and earlier, we used data compiled by Wallace and Singer (1970) and made publicly available through the Interuniversity Consortium for Political and Social Research. We compiled the subsequent information, as they had done, at approximately five-year intervals. Intervening years were filled in by linear interpolation; other missing data were estimated by extrapolation. IGOs are identified in the *Yearbook* at the bottom of the listing before 1980 or by the designation "*g*" at the end of the code number after that. We did not include purely bilateral organizations, as Wallace and Singer did. The difference is minimal because they found only a few bilateral cases, chiefly organizations that were originally multilateral but temporarily comprised only two members.

which all organizations are weighted equally. This is a necessary assumption at this stage, but it is one that we know to be inaccurate. All IGOs are not equal. Many are weak and only tenuously related to security. One might expect alliances or collective-security organizations to have the greatest impact, but they, too, differ greatly in their effectiveness. Over much of the late twentieth century, some Arab countries saw each other as enemies almost as much as they did Israel. The Arab League, therefore, has not remotely had as great an effect on promoting peace among its members as NATO has. In fact, other types of organizations, such as those promoting human rights or economic interdependence, may have greater pacific benefits than weak security alliances. They may make important contributions to the management and resolution of conflicts in nonsecurity fields, which reduce tensions that might lead to a military conflict. As noted earlier, we lack a theory to guide us in assigning greater importance to different types of IGOs or in differentiating effective from ineffective institutions within particular categories. Any prior weighting, therefore, would be arbitrary.[7] For now, our hypothesis is a simple one: the greater the number of IGOs in which both states of a dyad are members, the more forums there are for peaceful conflict resolution and the greater the prospects for peace.

Save for the addition of the IGO variable, our first empirical test is the same as the basic analysis conducted in Chapter 4. We consider the historical experience of the politically relevant dyads during the period 1885–1992. In addition to hypothesizing that greater involvement in the same international organizations aids states in avoiding militarized disputes, we expect that the other two legs of the Kantian system will also contribute to peace. As before, we assume that the risk of conflict is primarily determined by the state that is less constrained from using force on each dimension: the more autocratic state in the dyad, as indicated by the lower democracy score ($DEMOC_L$), and the state less economically dependent on bilateral trade ($DEPEND_L$). We also test the effects of the balance of power and of alliances on the likelihood of dyadic conflict. All these influences are assessed while controlling for contiguity, whether di-

---

[7]"Designing a simple, unambiguous, workable and satisfactory classification of IGOs as to 'political weight' or strength of political links proves virtually impossible" (Nierop 1994, 100; also Russett 1967, chap. 6). We are not so pessimistic as Nierop, but further research and considerable ingenuity will be required.

rect or through colonies; the distance separating the two states; and whether the dyad contains a major power. Again, we lag the explanatory variables one year behind the year in which conflict is to be explained, so as to reduce the chance of getting the causal direction wrong.

From the coefficients reported in the appendix, in Table A5.1, and the values used to represent our typical contiguous, nonallied pair of states, we estimate the chances of the typical pair's being involved in a militarized dispute in any year to be about three chances in a hundred. By changing, one at a time, each of the theoretically interesting variables from its baseline value, we can estimate the independent effect of each variable on the likelihood of a dispute. Table 5.1 shows the percentage change in the risk of conflict for a change of comparable magnitude (one standard deviation) in these variables.

Table 5.1: Percentage Change in Risk for Annual Involvement in a Militarized Dispute, 1886–1992: Contiguous Dyads, Realist and Kantian Variables

All variables at baseline values except:

ALLIES equals 1	−40%
POWER RATIO increased by one standard deviation	−36
$DEMOC_L$ increased by one standard deviation	−33
$DEMOC_L$ decreased by one standard deviation	+48
$DEPEND_L$ increased by one standard deviation	−43
IGO increased by one standard deviation	−24
$DEMOC_L$, $DEPEND_L$, and IGO all increased by one standard deviation	−71

International Organizations Also Reduce Disputes

Once again, all the variables are highly significant statistically: at the .001 level for all. This tells us that the association observed between each of these factors and the incidence of conflict is unlikely to have occurred by chance. The influences that we are observing are consistent and reliable.

That is important, but we are most interested in the substantive effects of the variables. Do they make considerable difference in the likelihood of conflict? They do.

Alliances and a preponderance of power (not a balance) continue to be important. If two contiguous states are allied, they are 40 percent less likely to be involved in a dispute than if they are not. An imbalance of power reduces the prospect of conflict by 36 percent. But the Kantian variables, too, are important. An increase in democracy has about the same effect (a 33 percent reduction) as a large imbalance of power; a decrease in the lower democracy score makes conflict 48 percent more likely. Greater economic interdependence, too, has a very strong effect, cutting the probability of a conflict by 43 percent from the baseline rate. Our third Kantian variable, IGOs, also has a substantial impact on reducing the likelihood of a dispute.[8] A one standard deviation increase in the number of joint memberships shared by two states reduces the likelihood of a dispute by 24 percent. Again, each of these influences is independent of the others. IGOs make an additional contribution to reducing the frequency of disputes above and beyond those of democracy and trade. If we increase all three of the Kantian influences simultaneously, the effect is quite dramatic: the risk of a dispute drops by more than 70 percent. The prospects for peace are especially good when states are democratic, eco-

---

[8]Unlike our other basic Kantian results, our findings on the dispute-reducing impact of IGOs indicate that this impact is limited to the politically relevant pairs of states (the basis for this book) and does not affect distant dyads. Thus, Oneal and Russett (1999c) did not find it with all dyads, nor do Bennett and Stam (2000). Nor is that impact evident in a fixed-effects analysis, even one limited to the politically relevant pairs. We cannot yet tell whether these differences should be ascribed to theory, methods, or measurement. Also, IGOs are much more closely related to alliances, trade, and democracy than the last three are with one another. A regression of ALLIES, $DEMOC_L$, and $DEPEND_L$ explains nearly one-third of the variance in IGOs ($R^2 = .31$), whereas regressions to explain each of the other variables with IGOs and the remaining two variables have much less power: the equations produce R^2s, respectively, of .19 for ALLIES, .16 for $DEMOC_L$, and .12 for $DEPEND_L$. This collinearity of IGOs with the other variables means that we cannot confidently assign to one or another the effects of the variation that they share in common. It particularly decreases our ability to establish the full explanatory power of IGOs, which is probably underestimated when alliances and the other Kantian variables all are used to explain militarized disputes.

nomically interdependent, and participate together in international organizations.

Kant was also correct on another point. The three Kantian variables are substantially correlated with one another: .35 for IGO and $DEMOC_L$, .30 for IGO and $DEPEND_L$, and .28 for $DEMOC_L$ and $DEPEND_L$. Clearly, these good things do go together. Democracies tend to be economically interdependent, and many IGOs are formed to promote economic relations among their member states. Indeed, half the IGOs in the post–World War II period were functional organizations concerned with the global economy (Jacobson 1984). In addition, democracies are more apt to cooperate with one another generally and within international organizations in particular (Dixon 1994; Raymond 1994).[9] The fact that the three Kantian influences are correlated—that democracies tend to be economically interdependent and to work together in IGOs—makes it all the more remarkable that we can discern a separate, statistically significant, substantively important effect for each influence. Where they converge (as especially for IGOs with trade and democracy), they diminish the apparent effect of one another. But there are enough cases where the Kantian influences do not go together to enable us to see something of their separate benefits.

Allies, too, should share common interests and be members of the same international organizations, and they do. The correlation between the two variables ALLIES and IGO is .43. Some IGOs are, of course, military alliances (NATO, the Arab League, the Warsaw Pact, etc.), so there is some degree of overlap in the two measures. In the previous chapter, when the variable ALLIES was in the analysis but the variable IGO was not, being allied reduced the likelihood of conflict by 46 percent—a somewhat stronger effect than appears here (40 percent). Some of what alliances seem to account for is better attributed to international organizations more generally.

These results are reasonably consistent even if we look at particular periods in the years from 1885 to 1992. IGOs had a strong and significant conflict-reducing effect during the post–World War II era and in the decades before World War I. Before 1914, international organizations were rare, so many states were not constrained by them from using force.

---

[9]Democratic states are somewhat more likely than autocracies to join IGOs. See Jacobson, Reisinger, and Matthews 1986; Shanks, Jacobson, and Kaplan 1996.

For states that did share memberships in IGOs, however, the benefit was substantial. Only during the interwar period—perhaps reflecting the failure and collapse of the League of Nations—were common IGO memberships not associated with lower rates of conflict. Democracy and interdependence, like IGOs, are strongly and significantly associated with reduced conflict in the post–World War II years. With all three Kantian variables in the equation, democracy was strongly related to dispute reduction during the interwar years; it had little impact one way or the other when its effect was estimated for the entire 1885–1914 period. But, as reported in Chapter 3, joint democracy began to be associated with fewer disputes before the beginning of the twentieth century. Finally, interdependence exerted a significant conflict-reducing effect before World War I and in the interwar period, though these benefits were not as strong as after 1950. Before World War II, alliances, in contrast, had no statistically significant effect on the incidence of disputes.

The contributions of the Kantian influences have remained largely intact even after the end of the cold war and the collapse of the bipolar international system. We should not make too much of the precise estimates for the post–cold war period, as we have noted before, because of the limited number of years available for analysis. The basic effects are clear, nonetheless. The influence of democracy actually increased after the cold war years, and the effect of IGOs, though weaker, was still evident. The benefits of economic interdependence were reduced. The principal conclusion to be drawn from these limited results is that the conflict-reducing benefits of the Kantian influences did not disappear with the end of the cold war.

World War I as an Example

It might help to consider our general statistical results in the context of a familiar historical case. An examination of the origins of World War I is particularly helpful, because a frequent criticism of the liberal hypothesis about the benefits of international commerce is centered on this dramatic event. Many observers allege that war began in 1914 despite high levels of economic interdependence among the key major powers. It is often said that interdependence was higher in Europe just before World War I than even in recent years after substantial integration within the European

Union (see, e.g., *Economist* 1997). Luttwak (1999), for instance, contends that "no two economies were more interdependent than the French and German" at the onset of the war. Of course, one counterexample does not disprove the liberal thesis, just as one smoker who does not get cancer does not show that smoking poses no hazards. Both theories are probabilistic in nature, ours being that the risk of conflict is less if states exchange economically important trade. Nonetheless, World War I is held up as a prominent counterexample, and some discussion of the circumstances of its eruption can illustrate our perspective.

Our rejoinder to those skeptical about the benefits of interdependence has two parts. First, the premise that trade was more important before World War I than now is flawed. As a share of their gross domestic products, total exports in 1913 were *not* at an all-time peak for the great powers and other important commercial states. The average value of exports as a proportion of GDP in 1913 for the most important of the European countries involved in World War I was 7.5 percent in 1985 prices, as compared with 10.7 percent for the same countries in 1973 and 15.0 percent in 1987.[10] An examination of dyadic relations must be carefully nuanced. For all countries, the average level of dyadic trade as a proportion of GDP was higher than it would be again until after World War II, but it had been dropping since a peak in 1906. Nor was trade so very great between most of the big 1914 adversaries. Luttwak's characterization of the Franco-German situation is mistaken. Germany's trade with France was much below that with Austria-Hungary and barely above that with the Netherlands, which had a much smaller economy than France's. French trade with Germany was only 75 percent of that with the United Kingdom and not much greater than with Belgium—a state far smaller than Germany. Austria-Hungary's biggest trading partner was its ally, Germany, which accounted for more than five times as much of its commerce as did France, Russia, or the United Kingdom. Of the six warring dyads, only two show high levels of interdependence. Russia and Britain were essentially tied as Germany's closest trading partners, while Germany was the largest trading partner of both Russia and, among the Eu-

[10]The data are from Maddison 1991a, except those for Russia, which are from Maddison 1989. These estimates are in 1985 prices. Estimates in current dollars follow a similar pattern: 13.1 percent in 1913, 15.2 percent in 1973, and 17.8 percent in 1987.

ropean states, Britain. But Britain's trade with the United States was about 40 percent greater than its trade with Germany (Mitchell 1981).

The second part of our rejoinder to skeptics concerns the influence of other factors on the likelihood of war in 1914. An understanding of any war, not least the Great War that began in 1914, requires a multivariate explanation, not consideration of a single factor. The rest of the story of World War I concerns the role of the other influences in our theoretical model, all of which point toward a high probability of armed conflict in 1914. The absence of constraints on conflict between democratic and authoritarian great powers played an important role. Consider the opposing alignments: the democracies—France, the United Kingdom, to a lesser degree Italy, ultimately the United States—against autocratic Austria and Germany. Autocracies fought each other (Russia fought Austria and Germany) and fought democracies, but no democracies, great or small, fought each other. Of the contiguous European great power pairs (Germany-Austria, Italy-France, Germany-France, Austria-Russia, Germany-Russia, Austria-Italy), the members of the last four became involved in the war on opposing sides.

Tightening alliances shaped the wartime alignments (Fay 1928), save for that of Italy, which switched allegiances by entering the conflict against Germany and Austria. The relative power of the opposing alliances was nearly equal, leading to high uncertainty about which side would win a war and thus poor prospects for deterrence. Finally, international organizations, the third element of our Kantian model, were less than 10 percent as numerous as in the 1980s. There were no multipurpose institutions, only narrow functional or regional organizations such as the Rhine Commission and the Universal Postal Union, so this restraining force for peace was quite underdeveloped. Of the Kantian influences, then, only economic interdependence operated as a significant constraint. In light of the few, weak IGOs and the incomplete spread of democracy in the region (and the limits on suffrage and civil rights even where it was greatest), this was not enough.

In sum, the Great War fits our theoretical model well: openness to trade was moderately high but not at levels characteristic of much of the post–World War II period, while a constellation of other circumstances— limited democracy, territorial conflicts, distinct military alliances, and insufficient power for effective deterrence—raised the probability of war. All these elements contributed to the outcome, and their separate influences cannot be neatly disentangled. Together, they indicate that the assassination in Sarajevo in June 1914 provided the incident to trigger a war that was already waiting to happen.[11]

Systemic Changes over Time

Considering the Kantian peace over more than a century provides opportunities to look at the effect of changes in the international system over time. How has the character of national governments, the economic importance of trade, and the number of international organizations changed? In Figure 5.1, we graph over the 1885–1992 period movements in the average democracy score for all states in the system, the average bilateral trade-to-GDP ratio, and the average number of joint memberships that dyads shared in IGOs.

Most apparent is the growth in states' participation in IGOs, with a drop in the late 1980s that was reversed after 1990. The emergence of a large number of international organizations associated with the globalization of the economy after World War II is evident. There is little evidence of a long-term trend toward greater democracy during most of the 1885–1992 period. The number of democracies in the international system did rise in the early decades of the twentieth century, but subsequently the pattern has been sporadic and wavelike (Huntington 1991). Evidence of democratization over the full period may be masked, as noted earlier, by codings that overstate the democratic character of states in much of the nineteenth century, before suffrage was extended to women, ethnic minorities, and those without property.

Nor is there indication in our graph of a long-term trend toward greater interdependence. Such a trend is obscured by two factors. First, the composition of our sample of countries changes over time. Dyads including less developed states of the periphery are underrepresented before World War I. Only with the establishment of the IMF and UN agencies does information on states' wealth and dyadic trade become reasonably complete. Thus, the average level of bilateral interdependence is somewhat overstated in the early years. Second, waves of decolonization cre-

---

[11]See Geller and Singer 1998, chap. 8, for another application of social scientific findings to account for the onset of the Great War.

Figure 5.1: Trends in Average Levels of Systemic Kantian Variables, 1885–1992

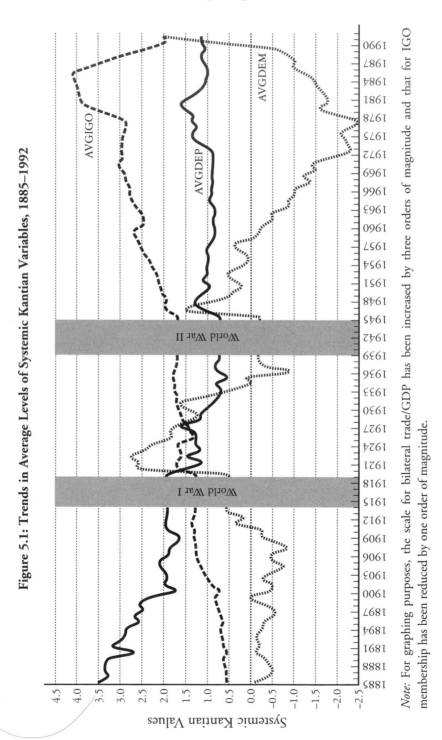

Note: For graphing purposes, the scale for bilateral trade/GDP has been increased by three orders of magnitude and that for IGO membership has been reduced by one order of magnitude.

ated dozens of newly independent states in the late 1950s and 1960s that were less democratic and less integrated into the global economy than the states already in the system, lowering the average score for both democracy and interdependence. Decolonization also helps to account for the leveling off of the number of joint memberships in IGOs shared by the average dyad in those years; the number of years a state has been a member of the global system is the strongest predictor of the number of its memberships in IGOs (Jacobson, Reisinger, and Mathers 1986).

Both democracy and interdependence do show a marked jump in the years just after World War II. The number of democracies has also grown steadily since the late 1970s, with a huge jump after the cold war ended. Similarly, the average level of economic interdependence as measured by the ratio of bilateral trade to GDP fell substantially before World War I and still further after that war, but rose again in subsequent years. Trade grew rapidly in the 1970s before the economic downturn in the 1980s that so adversely affected the many developing countries. Since 1987, growth in the number of democracies and the level of trade has corresponded with a precipitous drop in the number of interstate wars, despite the entry of many new states into the system (Marshall 1999).

Our analysis shows that higher levels of democracy, interdependence, and IGO membership reduce conflict: those states that share these Kantian qualities are less likely to become involved in conflict with one another. But it is also reasonable to expect that when the number of democracies increases, trade grows, and IGOs proliferate in the international system, the beneficial consequences will spill over to other pairs of states. In other words, we hypothesize that the spread of the Kantian influences reduces conflict even among states that are not themselves democratic, interdependent, or members of a large number of international organizations. Having measured the average level of the Kantian variables through time, we can begin to disentangle the effects of change in the international system on the likelihood of conflict from the strictly dyadic influences of the Kantian variables.

Changes over time in the average level of democracy, interdependence, and states' involvement in IGOs are apt to influence the norms and institutions of the international system. Wendt (1999), for instance, contends that world politics has slowly evolved from Hobbesian anarchy to a Lockean system wherein the security dilemma is ameliorated by norms recog-

nizing the right of sovereign states to exist. This effectively limits the use
of military force in interstate relations.[12] States are no longer subject to
elimination. Whereas twenty-two internationally recognized states were
forcibly occupied or absorbed during the first half of the twentieth
century, no state has lost its sovereignty through conquest since World
War II.[13] The emergence of a Kantian subsystem of states, within which
the unprovoked use of force is illegitimate, may have contributed directly
to this evolutionary development. The Kantian states, we believe, have influenced the evolution of both international norms and institutions and,
thereby, affected the probability that force will be used even by states that
are not Kantian.

If democracies are more likely to win their wars than autocracies are,
autocracies will have to be concerned about the security implications of
weakening themselves in war, whether with democracies or other autocracies, especially as the number of democracies in the international system
grows.[14] If most great powers are democratic, their peaceful relations
should reduce the incentive for war for all states within and across their
spheres of influence. If globalization increases and stimulates economic
growth among interdependent states, nonliberal states will have to be
concerned lest they be punished by trading states in global markets for in-

---

[12]See Huntley 1996; Gleditsch and Hegre 1997; Mitchell, Gates, and Hegre
1999; and Cederman 2000 for other discussions of the systemic effects of having a
high proportion of democracies in the system.

[13]Russett, Singer, and Small (1968) provide dates of independence. Germany and
Japan temporarily lost sovereignty after World War II but soon regained it (Germany
as two states). Kuwait was briefly occupied in 1990–91, but a large, diverse coalition
of states forced Iraq to withdraw under the aegis of the United Nations. This action
was intended to protect the sovereignty of established states. South Vietnam is an exception to this generalization if one regards its unification with North Vietnam in
1976 as the result of external conquest rather than an internationalized civil war.
Whereas state extinction as a consequence of international war has become rare, the
ideology of ethnic self-determination has led to the breakup of several states and empires.

[14]A counterhypothesis would be that, as democracies become more numerous and
more confident in their individual and collective strength, they will become embold-
ened and adopt more coercive relationships with the autocracies that remain. Chapter 2 discussed the evidence that democracies win most of their wars.

stigating international violence that disrupts trade and investment. Even antagonistic dyads with little mutual trade, such as Israel and its Arab neighbors, may find it prudent to avoid conflict (Friedman 1999; Brooks 2001). And if international norms and institutions for resolving disputes grow, even nonliberal states may be impelled to use regional or international organizations to help settle their disputes rather than accept the political, military, and economic costs that would be imposed by the liberal community following a use of force. In these ways, increases in the Kantian influences at the system level may constrain the behavior of dyads that are not particularly democratic, interdependent, or involved in international organizations.

To assess whether the evolution of the system affects the behavior of all dyads, we need to determine, for example, whether change in the average level of democracy in the system has an independent effect on the likelihood of dyadic conflict, controlling for the level of democracy in each pair of states relative to the annual average. We will conduct the same sort of tests for interdependence and IGOs. The annual averages of democracy, bilateral trade as a proportion of GDP, and joint memberships in IGOs graphed in Figure 5.1 give us the means to do this. They record the pervasiveness of Kantian changes in the international system and document the success of liberal principles in the competition among nations. In the analyses we report next, these systemic Kantian variables are identified as AVGDEMOC, AVGDEPEND, and AVGIGO. We hypothesize that the greater these systemic averages, the more the global system will reflect the normative and institutional constraints associated with democracy, interdependence, and the rule of law. For example, we would expect the world to be more peaceful in the 1920s, when the norms and behavior of the relatively large number of democracies helped constrain even the autocratic states. Democracies would be less influential in the 1930s and 1940s, when their number had declined as a result of the rise of fascism and communism.

To distinguish the systemic and dyadic influences of the Kantian variables, we need to create three variables that record the standing of each dyad in each year relative to the three annual Kantian averages. These are RELATIVEDEMOC$_L$, RELATIVEDEPEND$_L$, and RELATIVEIGO. They identify the dyads that are most democratic, interdependent, and involved in intergovernmental organizations relative to the systemic average at each point in time.[15] The average number of joint IGO memberships (AVGIGO), for example, captures the changing prominence of international organizations through time, while the involvement of individual dyads relative to this average (RELATIVEIGO) identifies those pairs that are more (or less) linked through a network of IGOs in any year.

To summarize, we want to distinguish between the systemic and purely dyadic influences of the Kantian variables by substituting two new variables for each of the three previous Kantian measures (AVGDEMOC and RELATIVEDEMOC$_L$ for DEMOC$_L$, etc.) in our analysis. Combining systemic and relative measures in a single model of conflict indicates the relative importance of changing values of the Kantian variables through time vis-à-vis the standing of dyads relative to the annual means at any point in time. We expect that both the relative variables and the systemic averages will contribute to explaining which dyads experience militarized disputes.

Table 5.2 reports these results. As usual, the impact of the realist influences—alliances and relative power—is strong. Respectively, they reduce the probability that two states will become involved in a dispute by about 43 percent and 42 percent. In addition, five of the six relative and systemic Kantian variables are very significant statistically (.001 level); the annual average of states' involvement in IGOs is weakly so (.06 level). Each of the first five makes a big contribution to reducing the frequency of militarized disputes. The effect of each Kantian influence is now split between the relative and systemic variables. Among the three relative variables, economically important trade and the density of international organization ties reduce conflict the most (29 percent and 35 percent reductions), but the benefits of democracy are still substantial, too. A dyad is 26 percent less likely to have a dispute if it is more democratic than the systemic average. Two of the three systemic Kantian variables also have important pacific benefits. The likelihood of conflict is much lower when the average level of economic interdependence in the system is high and

---

[15]RELATIVEDEMOC$_L$ = (DEMOC$_L$ – AVGDEMOC) / the standard deviation of DEMOC$_L$; RELATIVEDEPEND$_L$ = (DEPEND$_L$ – AVGDEPEND) / the standard deviation of DEPEND$_L$; and RELATIVEIGO = (IGO – AVGIGO) / the standard deviation of IGO. Dividing by the standard deviations permits us to compare directly the estimated coefficients of these variables.

Table 5.2: Percentage Change in Risk for Annual Involvement in a Militarized Dispute, 1886–1992: Contiguous Dyads, Relative Relationships and Systemic Averages

All variables at baseline values except:

ALLIES equals 1	−43%
POWER RATIO increased by one standard deviation	−42
Dyadic relative scores:	
RELATIVEDEMOC$_L$ increased by one standard deviation	−26
RELATIVEDEPEND$_L$ increased by one standard deviation	−29
RELATIVEIGO increased by one standard deviation	−35
Systemic averages:	
AVGDEMOC increased by one standard deviation	−24
AVGDEPEND increased by one standard deviation	−35
AVGIGO increased by one standard deviation	−10

when there are more democracies.[16] These systemic effects (35 percent and 24 percent, respectively) are about as great as the dyadic ones. Even raising the average level of shared IGOs makes a difference: a 10 percent drop in the risk of a dispute.

These results are important for two reasons. First, they confirm that pairs of states that are relatively more democratic, interdependent, and involved in international organizations at any point in time tend to be peaceful. The benefits we found in our first analysis (Table 5.1) are not just a result of change in the levels of the Kantian variables over time. Sec-

[16]There is a mild downward trend in the likelihood of a dispute over the period 1885–1992. To insure that the systemic Kantian variables were not simply collinear with this secular trend toward decreasing rates of disputes, we reestimated the equations reported in this section with an indicator of the passage of time. The coefficients of the Kantian variables changed very little, and the average democracy score and trade-to-GDP ratio remained highly significant. The indicator of the passage of time, however, was never significant at the .05 level. Estimating this equation for just 1885–1939 did change the impact of the average level of interdependence, primarily because World War I occurred when the level of trade was higher than it was during the interwar years; the average level of democracy remained significant at the .001 level.

ond, our results show that the peace-promoting effects of democracy and trade, and to a lesser extent of IGOs, are important both within the Kantian subsystem and, through their systemic influences, beyond it. Increasing levels of democracy and trade have beneficial consequences for all pairs of states, not just for the liberal ones. States throughout the international system are more peaceful when democracies are more common and there is greater economic interdependence. Only the effect of IGOs is essentially limited to the states that are directly involved. The number of IGOs worldwide does not have a dramatic effect on states that are not extensively involved. Apparently, international organizations promote peace far more by what they do for their members than by their example or by their influence on others.

The results reported in Table 5.2 show that the benefits of the Kantian influences are robust and pervasive. We now have greater reason to believe that states can create more peaceful conditions by policies that increase democracy, interdependence, and participation in international organizations.

Or Is It Hegemony That Reduces Violence?

Throughout this book, we have considered the effects of realist as well as Kantian influences on the likelihood of violent conflict. This enables us to explore how the two theoretical traditions complement each other as well as how they compete. We can also do this when considering the effect of the international system on the likelihood of dyadic disputes. As we have noted, realists have long been interested in how the number of great powers in the system, the system's polarity, affects the incidence of conflict. They have also paid close attention to the influence of the most powerful single state: the hegemon. One prominent realist account of the role of the hegemon is known as hegemonic stability theory. It holds that the hegemon will often constrain weaker states from resorting to violence because it is in its interest to do so (Gilpin 1981). Realists argue that the hegemon is influential in the creation of the international system after major wars, such as those fought against Napoleon or World Wars I and II, and in its subsequent operation. Presumably, the hegemon creates a system that operates to its advantage. Its consequent satisfaction with the status quo leads the hegemon, as a rule, to adopt conservative policies designed to maintain the system as it is.

Because wars disrupt the international system—by breaking economic ties beneficial to the hegemon, for example—the hegemon has an incentive to maintain the peace. The hegemon's efforts to do this manifest themselves in two ways. First, it uses its power to suppress wars within its own sphere of influence and, through its network of alliances, in the spheres of interest of allied states. Second, the hegemon actively deters potential adversaries from using military force in a way that would be detrimental to its interests. Whether through domination or deterrence, the ability of a powerful state to preserve peace in the system will depend upon its power relative to others. Thus, a simple but reasonable measure of the power of the hegemon is its share of the capabilities of all the major powers. As noted earlier, data regarding states' armed forces and their population and industry—indicators of immediately available military capabilities and the potential to develop greater might over time—are available from the Correlates of War Project. With these data, we have calculated the power of the hegemon relative to its principal rivals for each year in the period 1885–1992.

It is not always easy to identify a hegemon. Most scholars agree that in the thirty years before World War I the United Kingdom was closer to being hegemonic than was any other country, although its power relative to both Germany and the United States declined as time passed. During the interwar era, 1919–39, the United States clearly had greater economic strength and military potential than the United Kingdom, but their actual military capabilities were about equal. Moreover, the geographical position of the United States and its isolationist policy limited its involvement in the central European system. Consequently, we accept the judgment (Organski and Kugler 1980) that Britain was more nearly hegemonic than any other power during the interwar period as well. If any country can be said to have been truly hegemonic in the post–World War II period, it is the United States (Russett 1985; Oneal 1989). Consequently, we use the proportion of the major powers' capabilities held by the United Kingdom as the measure of the hegemon's power in the first sixty years analyzed and that held by the United States for the years after 1945.

This systemic indicator (HEGPOWER) dropped from 33 percent in 1885 to 14 percent in 1913; it fell below 11 percent by 1938. America's hegemony is evident immediately following World War II when it controlled 52 percent of the major powers' capabilities. The U.S. share fell to 26 percent by the early 1980s but rose to 29 percent with the collapse of the Soviet Union in 1992. These movements are consistent with the judgment of historians, so our measure seems valid.

A related perspective on the international system is known as power transition theory. Originally developed by A. F. K. Organski (1968), it, too, draws attention to the power of the hegemon to constrain other states from resorting to military force. When many others believed an equal balance of power led to peace, Organski stressed the argument that it was an imbalance of power (or power preponderance) that made the use of force either unnecessary (for the strong) or impractical (for the weak). Power transition theory has also emphasized the role that states' satisfaction with the status quo plays in explaining who resorts to violence. It predicts that states rising in power will challenge a hegemon only if they are dissatisfied with the international system the hegemon dominates. Lemke and Reed (1996) recently extended this argument in an effort to subsume the democratic peace within power transition theory. Democracies have historically fought less, they contend, because the hegemonic power has been a democracy since the end of the Napoleonic Wars. First Britain, and then the United States, they argue, used its power to structure the international system so that benefits accrued disproportionately to itself and to its mostly democratic allies. Thus, democracies' satisfaction with the status quo created by the most powerful state (a democracy) and reinforced by its system of alliances is said to account for the peace among democratic dyads.

Lemke and Reed assess their argument by creating a measure of each state's satisfaction with the status quo based on the correspondence between its portfolio of allies and that of the hegemon. They do this with a statistical measure of association (tau-b). The more similar the list of one state's allies is to the list of the hegemon's allies, the more that state will share the hegemon's preferences for the management of the international system, the more it will assist the leading state in this effort, and the more it will be rewarded by the hegemon. Like Lemke and Reed, we also created a measure of the satisfaction each pair of states feels for the status quo. This measure of joint satisfaction (SATISFIED) indicates the degree to which each dyad is content with the distribution of benefits achieved under the leadership of the dominant state.[17] If power transition theory is correct, the more satisfied two states are, the less likely they are to fight. Furthermore, if it is satisfaction with the status quo and not democracy per se that accounts for the democratic peace, then the variable SATIS-FIED will be significant when added to our model of conflict and, in its presence, our measures of democracy will not be.

Both hegemonic stability theory and power transition theory hold that the international system will be more peaceful when the hegemon is strong relative to its chief rivals. There is another way in which the hegemon might affect the level of conflict in the system. It might transmit tensions to other states. When the most powerful state is concerned about its own security, there are likely to be consequences for its allies, its rivals, its rivals' allies, and even neutral states. The adage "When elephants fight it is the grass that suffers" captures this phenomenon. It is also possible, to continue the metaphor, that when small animals fight, big ones will be drawn in. Large states, including the hegemon, may intervene in ongoing conflicts involving smaller states because they see an opportunity to achieve gains or avoid losses. In either way, international tensions may be contagious.

We assess this view by creating a measure of the hegemon's sense of its own security. We divide the leading state's defense expenditures by its gross domestic product. Thus, the variable HEGDEFENSE is the share of GDP the hegemon devotes to defense spending. The burden it bears to maintain its military establishment indicates the hegemon's concern with the state of the international system: the ratio of military expenditures to GDP will rise when the hegemon perceives greater dangers and fall when its interests seem less threatened.[18] Our hypothesis is that the global system will experience more numerous disputes when the hegemon is committing more of its resources to the military. We can also determine just

[17]To create the variable SATISFIED, we added 1 to the tau-b score for each state in a dyad, to make this measure positive, and then multiplied the two scores together.

[18]Information on military expenditures is available from the Correlates of War Project. Changes in the hegemon's defense burden are highly correlated with changes in the average defense burden for all the major powers. The great powers seem to agree when tensions are high in the international system. Of course, this may in part be a manifestation of the security dilemma, which was discussed earlier.

how widespread this phenomenon is. Is the effect largely confined to relations between the hegemon and other states in the system, or does the leader's sense of its security also significantly influence the likelihood of dyadic conflict for its allies or even for states unallied with the hegemon?

In the next analysis, we assess the central claim of both hegemonic stability and power preponderance theory: that conflict becomes more likely as the power of the leading state declines relative to the capabilities of its chief rivals.[19] We also test Lemke and Reed's suggestion that it has been the power of the (democratic) hegemon to reward its allies that accounts for the democratic peace. To do this, we add to the systemic analysis discussed earlier two new variables. One is our indicator of the power of the hegemon relative to the capabilities of all the major powers (HEG-POWER); the second is our measure of the joint satisfaction of the two states in each dyad with the international system (SATISFIED). It is appropriate theoretically to include both in the same equation. If the hegemon can regulate the level of conflict in the international system, then its influence should be greatest with those states with which it is most closely allied. Also, the advantages for a state of aligning itself closely with the hegemon should be greatest when the leading state's power is large relative to its chief rivals. It is then that the hegemon should be most able to confer benefits on its supporters.

The first column of Table 5.3 shows clearly that the relative power of the leading state has no effect on the likelihood of dyadic disputes. The measure of hegemonic power has but a trivial effect and is far from being statistically significant (.50 level). A powerful hegemony does not reduce the resort to violence in the international system. Even this essentially neutral effect, however, reflects the inability of a weakened hegemon (Britain) to prevent the outbreak of systemwide wars, World Wars I and II. In an analysis not reported in the table, the effect of hegmonic power became strongly positive when the first year of each of the world wars was dropped from the data set. Then, hegemony was *positively* related to the incidence of disputes in the system, and the relationship was statistically very significant (.001 level). Great hegemonic power does not dampen conflict in the system during these more normal periods of international relations, when there are no big wars among the major powers. *Rather, the*

[19]See Organski 1968; Modelski 1966; Gilpin 1981; Kugler and Lemke 2000; Spiezio 1990.

**Table 5.3: Percentage Change in Risk for Annual Involvement
in a Militarized Dispute, 1886–1992:
Contiguous Dyads, Dyadic and Systemic Influences**

All variables at baseline values except:	*(1)* Systemic Kantian, Hegemonic Power, Satisfaction	*(2)* Systemic Kantian, Hegemon's Defense Burden
Dyadic variables:		
POWER RATIO increased by one standard deviation	−42%	−44%
ALLIES increased by one standard deviation	−43	−45
RELATIVEDEMOC$_L$ increased by one standard deviation	−25	−27
RELATIVEDEPEND$_L$ increased by one standard deviation	−29	−27
RELATIVEIGO increased by one standard deviation	−34	−34
Kantian systemic variables:		
AVGDEMOC increased by one standard deviation	−24	−25
AVGDEPEND increased by one standard deviation	−36	−30
AVGIGO increased by one standard deviation	−10	−20
Realist systemic variables:		
Hegemonic power increased by one standard deviation (HEGPOWER)	+0.1	
Joint satisfaction increased by one standard deviation (SATISFIED)	−2	
Hegemon's defense burden increased by one standard deviation (HEGDEFENSE)		+36

level of dyadic conflict rises. There is no evidence in these results of a Pax Britannica or Pax Americana, contrary to both hegemonic stability and power transition theories.

Nor does the hegemon itself avoid conflict. The United States, for example, fought twelve international wars during its 217 years of independence, from 1783 to 1999. But one-third (four) of those came during the fifty-five years when it could be described as a hegemon. Two (in Korea and Vietnam) occurred during the cold war era, and two (with Iraq and Serbia) came during the single decade, from 1990 to 1999, when the United States was the only superpower.

Neither is there any evidence that states' satisfaction with the status quo accounts for the democratic peace. The measure of joint satisfaction is statistically insignificant (.39 level), while the strong effects of democracy, through both the relative and systemic measures, are still very powerful and significant influences on the likelihood of conflict. It seems clear that the character of their political institutions and culture accounts for the separate peace among democracies, not the satisfaction they are said to have with the international system. It appears that power transition theory exaggerates the ability of even the strongest state to shape the international system for its benefit and the benefit of its allies. As in the previous analysis (reported in Table 5.2), the relative and average trade dependence variables and a high average and especially a high relative level of IGO membership are still closely related to the probability of conflict, as are alliances and the bilateral balance of power.[20]

Finally, we ask whether the hegemon's sense of its own security, as indicated by the proportion of its GDP devoted to defense expenditures (HEGDEFENSE), is associated with a heightened danger of conflict globally. As shown in the second column of Table 5.3, the defense burden of the leading state is closely associated with the risk of disputes. Indeed, the effect is quite large: an increase of one standard deviation in the ratio of the hegemon's defense expenditures to its GDP raises the risk of a dyadic dispute by 36 percent. When the hegemon feels endangered and increases its military spending, there are wide-ranging consequences for states throughout the international system. And the heightened danger of conflict is not limited to the world wars, as was the influence of hegemonic power, or significant only for the hegemon or its allies. In a separate analysis, not reported in the table, we confirmed that other states, too, experience more disputes when the hegemon is concerned with its own security and is devoting a large portion of its wealth to military preparations. Apparently, it is true, as the African proverb suggests, that the grass suffers when elephants fight.

[20]Alternative specifications for evaluating the role that states' satisfaction with the status quo plays made little difference.

Again, the dyadic realist variables—relative power and alliances—have substantial effects, and all the systemic and relative Kantian variables remain substantively important and statistically significant at the .001 level or better. In fact, in this last test, even the systemic measure of states' participation in international organizations makes a substantial difference (a 20 percent cut) in the likelihood that a pair of states will become involved in a dispute. Controlling for the hegemon's defense spending makes this systemic variable significant. Perhaps the effectiveness of IGOs depends in part on the major powers' not feeling a need to develop—and presumably use—large, independent military means for protecting and promoting their interests.

The analyses reported in this section provide consistent, clear evidence that the power of the leading state, the so-called hegemon, has little effect on the incidence of dyadic conflict. There is in our results, then, no support for hegemonic stability theory. Power transition theory is correct that a preponderance of power leads to peaceful dyadic relations; our results repeatedly show that an *imbalance* of power within a dyad increases the prospects for peace. But power transition theory, too, errs in believing that this dyadic effect has important systemic consequences, that a powerful state will be able or willing to pacify interstate relations throughout the system. In short, the benefits of having a hegemon to keep peace in the system appear to be hugely overrated—or even perverse. As noted earlier, except for the onset of the world wars, the incidence of disputes was actually higher in the period 1885–1992 when the hegemon was strong. Having more democracies and more trading states in the system, on the other hand, significantly reduces the probability of conflict, even for states that are not democratic or dependent upon trade.

Coercion or Persuasion?

Just how the Kantian systemic effects work—whether and when they are due more to coercion, persuasion, or example—is not something that can be established by the kind of statistical analysis we are using. A clue to this important inquiry is provided by the work of Antonio Gramsci (Hoare and Smith 1971), who developed the concept of "cultural hegemony" many years ago. Gramsci recognized that even the most powerful do not get their way solely (or even primarily) by means of force. This is true whether we are thinking of individuals in a small group, groups in society, or states in the international system. Instead of resorting to force, the powerful, in Gramsci's view, maintain their position by shaping the desires and perceptions of others so that they conform to their own. The weak eventually come to accept the material and cultural artifacts preferred by the hegemon. Democracy and capitalism are important instances. With the demise of communism and the state that sponsored it, these liberal institutions no longer need to contend with coherent universalistic alternatives. Their influence operates directly by example: by having established in a great historical competition their superiority over autocracy and the state domination of markets. They also indirectly affect the preferences, perceptions, and choices of states throughout the system through the network of international institutions that support and extend democracy and the globalized economy. Thus, both norms and institutions are involved, and as noted before, their separate effects cannot readily be separated.

The importance of Gramsci's insight has been widely recognized by contemporary scholars. Joseph Nye (1990) calls this phenomena "soft power," and John Ruggie (1982) encompassed Gramsci's insight in his theory of "embedded liberalism." Francis Fukuyama (1992) may have exaggerated it, in proclaiming "the end of history," but his fundamental insight is sound: there is no longer significant debate over the relative merits of liberal democracy vis-à-vis either communism or fascism. Surely, many important questions remain to be decided about how politics and economics can best be organized, but a broad verdict of history at this time has been recorded. Boutros Boutros-Ghali, too, understood the power and potential of democracy and markets as part of a Kantian system of peace. When he was UN secretary general he did his best to promote their universal acceptance. As Gramsci and others have recognized, there are real limits to what naked force can accomplish, but we are convinced that power backed by insight can achieve great things—even transform the anarchic international system. A powerful Kantian state in concert with like-minded allies can encourage the formation of a zone of peace, but our empirical results provide powerful evidence that democracy, economic interdependence, and coordinating international organizations are more important to the success of this monumental task than are military capabilities. We return to the uses and limits of hegemony in future chapters.

The Three Kantian Legs

The analyses of this chapter, combined with those of previous chapters, indicate that each of the three elements of the Kantian peace makes a statistically significant, independent contribution to peaceful interstate relations. These pacific benefits are evident even when the influences of other theoretically interesting, potentially confounding factors—geographical contiguity, alliances, relative capabilities, economic growth, etc.—are held constant. More important than the statistical significance of the Kantian variables is their substantive importance. Increasing any one of the dyadic measures by a standard deviation, as shown in Table 5.1, reduces the likelihood of a militarized dispute by more than 20 percent. Even with the addition of our measure of states' participation in IGOs, there continue to be important pacific benefits from democracy and economically important trade. The independent contributions of the Kantian factors are sufficiently great that they are not masked by the correlations among these variables. Democracy, interdependence, and international law and organizations are mutually reinforcing, as we have noted, but to a degree, one element can compensate for weakness in the others. The magnitude of their combined effect is, however, particularly striking. The likelihood of a dispute falls by 71 percent if all three variables are increased simultaneously above their baseline rates.

The pacific benefits of the Kantian factors are most clearly exemplified in the contemporary international system by the experience of Western Europe. There, all three elements have become progressively stronger since the end of World War II. Consequently, a region that was frequently at war now is a stable zone of peace. Yet the contributions of the Kantian forces are not limited to that area, although their relative importance varies across time as well as across regions. The ten states of Southeast Asia are attempting, through ASEAN and other regional organizations, to build a network of economic interdependence and IGOs (Acharya 1998). This may, in time, establish at least a rudimentary security community despite continuing differences in their political systems, which range from quite democratic (Philippines, Thailand, and possibly Indonesia) through mixed regimes (Cambodia, Malaysia, and Singapore) to autocratic ones (Brunei, Laos, Vietnam, and Myanmar).

The Kantian elements certainly support each other, so to some degree, one element may be able to compensate for the weakness of another. No single element, however, should be expected to carry all the burden. India and Pakistan, for example, share a long border and a territorial dispute over Kashmir of more than fifty years duration. They are not allied and have always obtained military assistance from different quarters (India from the Soviet Union, Pakistan from China and the United States). Although India is stronger, the power imbalance between them is not great (1.75 to 1 in 1990). Their level of mutual trade to GDP was less than one-tenth the median for contiguous states, and they shared membership in just thirteen IGOs, as compared with an average of thirty-one for contiguous states. Under these circumstances, even when Pakistan was relatively democratic, it would have been foolhardy to depend on joint democracy as the sole means to prevent war or other forms of militarized dispute.

Historically, the benefits of the Kantian principles are most evident in the post–World War II era, when all three made important contributions to the peacefulness of interstate relations. The peace-inducing effect of democracy was weak before about 1895, but it was even stronger in the interwar years than it was during the cold war era. Interdependence has had the most consistent benefits over the three periods—pre–World War I, the interwar years, and post–World War II. Its effect in reducing conflict was greatest during the cold war and interwar years and somewhat less before World War I. Data for the early post–cold war years indicate that the benefits of democracy especially have continued past the end of the cold war. The benefit of IGOs was greatest prior to World War I, when, however, their small number limited their effect. International organizations did not decrease the likelihood of conflict in the interwar years but have been an important force for peace in the years after 1945. International organizations have broadened their functions and deepened their powers. The supranational aspects of the EU and the powers of the WTO for resolving trade disputes are new. Even the often derided UN is a far more influential organization than was the earlier League of Nations. IGOs today are more complex and effective than were their predecessors. Perhaps the real strength of international organizations as a force for peace is only emerging. There is, then, some variation in the strength of the Kantian effects over time, although the overall picture is one of consistency rather than differences.

Distinguishing the influences of the Kantian systemic averages from the standings of each dyad relative to the annual averages makes the benefits of democracy and trade evident cross-nationally and through time. The international system is more peaceful when there are more democracies and when trade is more important economically. *All* pairs of states— even those not democratic or interdependent—become less dispute-prone at these times. The systemic effects of IGOs are discernible but weaker. Our results suggest that the pacific benefit of international organizations apply largely to their members, though this measure is probably the least satisfactory of our three Kantian variables. There have been fewer social scientific studies of the contribution of IGOs to peace than of the benefits of democracy or interdependence. Our measure of their importance, a simple count of joint memberships, ignores obvious differences in the importance of intergovernmental organizations. Also, we do not examine the contribution of nongovernmental organizations. Much more theoretical work and empirical study is needed in this area.

Some realist influences also significantly affect the likelihood of dyadic disputes. Greater distance between two states, a preponderance of power by one, and minor power status are all consistently related to a reduced chance of conflict. This is not surprising. The Kantian influences have not abolished power politics. Alliances were influential in the post–World War II period but only then. Their failure to have a significant conflict-reducing effect prior to the cold war is perhaps our most surprising finding. Realist influences at the level of the international system also make a difference. Both world wars occurred when Britain, the hegemonic state, was weakened. Yet hegemony does not work consistently, as the hegemonic stability and power transition theories suggest. In more normal periods of international relations, there were more militarized disputes when the hegemon was powerful than when it was weak. On the other hand, when the hegemon feels threatened (as evidenced by higher military spending), the likelihood of disputes rise throughout the system. Peace seems to owe less to the systemic effects of hegemony than it does to strengthened Kantian influences.

Some of these results may displease political ideologues of either the left or the right. Both may feel comfortable with our results linking democracy to peace. The benefits of either free trade or international organizations may be more unsettling to one side or the other. Modern-day liberals may applaud the role of IGOs but, aware of the economic dislocations and inequalities associated with capitalist competition, hesitate to accept that markets, too, can encourage peace. Conservatives, prone to downplay the importance of international organizations, are apt to have the opposite bias. Nonetheless, in this chapter, we have considered the roles intergovernmental organizations can play to promote peace. In earlier chapters, we explored theories linking democracy and economic interdependence to a reduction in international conflict. Now a variety of empirical analyses support those theoretical expectations.

Our effort to understand the complex influences that shape interstate relations is far from complete. It is important to develop a more complete understanding of the ways many of the influences we have considered, including such realist factors as alliances, interact with one another. We will explore some of those interactions in the next chapter. There is a great need for theoretically informed case studies to expand our understanding. Crises like the one that preceded World War I need to be examined in detail, but other situations where the use of force was avoided or not even considered must also be studied. Understanding the causes of war requires not only an appreciation of situations where violence erupted, or was narrowly avoided, but of situations where violence was not an option that political decision makers seriously considered. We need to understand not just the circumstances that have led to particular wars, but also how countries with important differences on serious matters have avoided military action.

For many years, Americans, British, and Canadians, like Swedes and Norwegians, have had conflicts of interest, but the threat of military force has not played a role in their relations. For half a century now, this has been true also of Western Europe, despite its horrible experiences in the preceding decades. The United States and Japan have significant disagreements, especially over trade issues, but the Americans do not expect Japan to bomb Pearl Harbor again, and the Japanese do not expect the United States to drop nuclear weapons on their cities. Both countries have absorbed painful lessons from the past. A Kantian system has been built in these and other spots on the globe. It can be the base for further expansion of democracy, interdependence, and cooperation in international organizations. We explore some of the paths and hurdles to expanding and consolidating the Kantian system in the following chapters.

Virtuous Circles and Indirect Influences

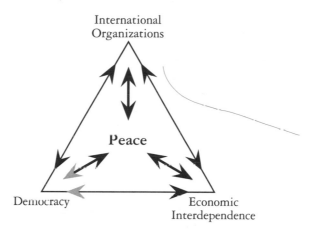

Chapter 1 discussed a system of Kantian influences that were indirect as well as direct. For instance, if democracies and states with economically important trade join the same IGOs, and if IGOs promote both democracy and trade, then we have a set of feedback loops that result in virtuous circles. Or if democracies are especially likely to trade with each other and trade reduces disputes, democracy is having a beneficial indirect impact on the reduction of conflict—through promoting trade—as well as the direct effect we have already considered. Another possibility, mentioned in Chapter 4, is that militarized conflict hampers trade between states, so the evidence we have presented indicating that trade reduces conflict might be capturing the reverse causal relation. A similar question arises if peace promotes the growth of IGOs as well as growing contacts in IGOs increasing the likelihood of peace. Indeed, we expect in the last two cases that causal relations are strong in both directions, producing another set of feedbacks in a true Kantian system.

In this chapter, we explore other links in our system. Four sets of questions correspond to the newly darkened arrowheads in the diagram at the start of the chapter.

1. Do international organizations promote democracy?
2. Why do states join international organizations with one another? Do states engaged in militarized disputes participate in IGOs with their adversaries? Are democracies and important trading partners more likely to participate in the same IGOs?
3. Why, beyond the economic principles of comparative advantage, do states trade with each other? To what degree do states engaged in military disputes avoid trading with their adversaries? Do democracies and IGO partners trade more heavily with each other?
4. Are liberal states at peace with one another because shared democracy and trade produce peaceful relations, as the evidence thus far indicates, or are these states at peace simply because they happen to share common strategic interests not directly tied to their political institutions and economic relations?

Our answers to these questions are necessarily tentative, but the evidence we present indicates that the Kantian system we have outlined is indeed a significant force for peace.

Two Questions We Cannot Settle Here

The arrows highlighted at the start of this chapter do not exhaust all the remaining relations that should be investigated. Two others are represented graphically, with small arrowheads indicating their uncertain status. One possible link runs from economic interdependence to democracy. If trade and free markets (internationally as well as within countries) promote prosperity and if prosperous countries are more likely to be democratic, then there is an indirect benefit to interdependence: trade improves the prospects for democracy and democracies are more peaceful (Weede 1996). There also may be a virtuous circle connecting interdependence to democracy because, as we suggested earlier, trade can transmit ideas. Thus, authoritarian countries trading with democracies may be encouraged to democratize. U.S. trade with China is often justified on these grounds.

One more virtuous circle may be the influence of conflict on democracy. Writers have long asserted that international conflict, or an intense threat of conflict, is inimical to democracy. Harold Lasswell (1941) expressed this fear in a famous article on what he called the "garrison state," and a condition of permanent war against shifting enemies supports the totalitarian state in George Orwell's apocalyptic novel *1984*. Certainly, governments sometimes use threats to national security as a basis for suppressing free thought and expression. Conversely, peace can promote and strengthen democratic institutions, which further improves the prospects for peace. But that would be in addition to, not instead of, the causal arrow from democracy to peace.

However important these two possible relationships may be, they share a common characteristic. Unlike the questions we subject to empirical investigation in this book, they are not best studied at the dyadic level of analysis. Trade may well promote prosperity and enhance democracy, but this is a proposition about individual states, not pairs of states. We expect a country pursuing a policy of free trade policy, one that is economically "open" to use the term defined in Chapter 4, to grow faster than a state that has cut itself off from international markets, but we do not expect a state's particular bilateral trade relations to have much influence on its economy. And trade with a stable democracy may well have beneficial political effects on its less democratic trading partners. The United States entered into the North American Free Trade Agreement (NAFTA) with the intention of promoting democracy in Mexico as well as prosperity in all three members. But, again, the effect of trade should be studied by analyzing the political institutions of individual countries. It is not very helpful to look for this kind of effect in dyadic relationships.

Similarly, it is one thing to contend that a country at peace with all states is apt to be more democratic than a country engaged in serious hostilities with even one powerful adversary. But to assume that peace within any single dyad is likely to make both members of the dyad more democratic, regardless of their relations with all others, is quite another, and is unsupported. We developed this argument in detail (Oneal and Russett 2000b) in response to the research of James, Solberg, and Wolfson

(1999).[1] Here it is sufficient to note that there is no substantial evidence that the influence of peace on states' political character renders the democratic peace, one of the principal elements of our Kantian system, insubstantial.

Questions that are unpromising at the dyadic level of analysis may be more interesting and plausible at the level of the nation-state. Is a country more likely to become autocratic before the onset of a war? Mousseau and Shi (1999) find that there is no significant effect. Other questions may be explored by considering the international system as a whole. Since democracies usually win their wars against authoritarian states and leaders who lose wars are often deposed from office, wars between autocracies and democracies can actually work—though at high cost—to expand the proportion of democracies in the international system. Do wars increase the number of democracies globally by weeding out losing autocrats? When there are more democracies in the system, is the system more peaceful? Mitchell, Gates, and Hegre (1999) report that the answer is yes to both questions. This is, of course, consistent with the systemic analyses we presented in the last chapter. A regional focus may also be appropriate. For example, peace and trade with neighboring states may have a great impact on a country's political development (Maoz 1996; Shin and Ward 1999). These are important questions. But they require different kinds of analyses than those we employ in this book. Consequently, we note the plausibility of these two additional linkages but leave them to others to investigate.

United Nations Peace-Building through Democracy

We do want to address the possibility that international organizations can encourage democracy. This topic is important and has not received the at-

---

[1]We share little common ground with James, Solberg, and Wolfson, as indicated by our recent exchange that now includes James, Solberg, and Wolfson 2000, but we do agree that future work should address further the reciprocal effects between democracy and interstate conflict. At this moment, however, the claim that peace promotes democracy is little more than an interesting hypothesis and certainly not a refutation of the voluminous work indicating that democracy increases the prospects for peace. In addition to the research at the national level of analysis discussed next in the text, Diehl and Goertz (2000, chap. 6) report that whereas long-term rivalries became peaceful after both states were democratic, the end of a rivalry had little effect in promoting democracy.

tention that it is due given the growing number of internal conflicts in the world today. Although the topic is not suitable for dyadic analysis, by reviewing activities of the United Nations, we can suggest some answers to the question of whether international organizations can encourage democracy. We focus, in the discussion that follows, on the role of IGOs in the aftermath of civil wars.

Some IGOs provide important support for democracy among their members, and sometimes even in nonmember countries. (Pastor 1999). One important example is the Organization for Security and Cooperation in Europe (OSCE, formerly the CSCE), an IGO that supervises elections and supports democratic movements and institutions in central and Eastern Europe (Flynn and Farrell 1999). The European Union has similar programs. Indeed, IGOs sometimes exercise greater legitimacy in carrying out programs in support of democracy within sovereign states than individual governments can. It is far more acceptable, for example, for the Organization of American States (OAS) to send observers to monitor elections in Latin American countries than for the U.S. government to do so.[2] In recent years, the role of the OAS in supporting democratization in the Western Hemisphere has grown. For instance, in 1996, General Lino Oviedo, the army commander in Paraguay, was about to stage a coup against his country's democratically elected government. The OAS quickly warned Oviedo that if he did so, his country would be punished by diplomatic and economic sanctions. The general backed off.

The International Monetary Fund and the World Bank do not explicitly make democracy a condition for receiving a loan, but increasingly they stress the need for "good government" and "transparency," terms that strongly imply democratic accountability. In Chapter 5, we mentioned the activities of the United Nations in monitoring free elections. Security Council Resolution 940, adopted in 1994, called on UN members to restore the democratically elected government of Haiti, which had been toppled by a coup. For the first time, the UN had defined the interruption of democracy as a threat to international peace and had authorized the use of force in response.

Freed from the ideological rivalries between East and West, the United Nations has emerged over the past decade as a serious player in efforts

---

[2]For a balance sheet on recent U.S. efforts to promote democracy, see Carothers 1999.

to establish stable democracies. UN peacekeeping was once almost exclusively a response to interstate conflicts. It was limited to monitoring cease-fires with lightly armed troops that operated with the consent of the parties involved and was permitted to use military force only in self-defense. The post–cold war expansion of peacekeeping, however, evolved into "peace-building" in the aftermath of civil wars. Now, after establishing a ceasefire, the UN may disarm the warring factions, restore the civilian economy; and integrate demobilized troops into society. This involves rebuilding (or even building for the first time) an effective civil administration and system of justice and other institutions that permit peaceful contests for political power. The creation of stable representative government is critical to the effective resolution of armed conflict.

In countries where violence had been the dominant means to political power, the UN has helped to block old paths to power while providing alternate means for political competition—namely, the practices and institutions of democratic governance. Some of these activities differ little from the programs to support economic development that have been common for many years. But an important element has been added. The UN explicitly promotes democracy. In this way, a stable peace may be created, one that is not dependent on continuous external enforcement. The UN's political activities certainly include monitoring elections, but they go well beyond this: "United Nations support for democratization helps . . . foster the construction and maintenance of viable and independent States as the basic guarantors of human rights . . . and the basic elements of a peaceful and cooperative international system" (Boutros-Ghali 1996, 23–24). Democratization, in other words, is an important means to durable peace. The UN intervenes politically in order to be an effective peacemaker.[3]

A cease-fire is just the first step toward peace. For it to endure, groups in society must expect that political competition will replace the resort to arms for resolving conflict. The UN has tried to apply this understanding

---

[3]For general information, see *Support by the United Nations System of the efforts of Governments to promote and consolidate new or restored democracies,* A/50/332 and A/51/512, two reports presented to the General Assembly on August 7, 1995, and October 18, 1996. Academic contributions include Daniel and Hayes 1995; Thakur and Thayer 1995; Weiss 1995; Durch 1996; Snow 1995, 1996; Zacarias 1996; Chopra 1998; and Kumar 1998. For a cautionary view, see Paris 1997.

in a number of substantial operations. They include efforts, with very disparate results, in Namibia (UNTAG, 1989–90), Nicaragua (ONUCA/ONUVEN, 1989–92), El Salvador (ONUSAL, 1991–95), Cambodia (UNTAC, 1992–93), Mozambique (ONUMOZ, 1992–94), and Angola (UNAVEM II, 1991–95).

Efforts to build peace in a country divided by civil war can focus on the political elite, the people, or governmental and social institutions. To be effective, they must fulfill two purposes: reduce the capacity of factions to wage war and build participation in democratic institutions. To eliminate the parties' ability to resort to force, the UN has often proceeded to:

- Disarm and demobilize the warring forces.
- Provide ex-combatants with the land, relocation, or training needed to reintegrate them into the civilian economy.
- Restructure and reform the armed forces to include integrating elements of both sides' forces under a single, responsible civilian command.

These activities *reduce the capacity of the former combatants* to muster the troops and equipment necessary to renew armed conflict. Unable to resort to force, they will have greater incentives to turn to peaceful political competition and cooperation. To facilitate this, the UN must undertake programs to *build new capacities* for an effective domestic political process:

- Form transition governments composed of representatives from the warring parties in order to involve local leaders in discussing differences and making compromises. A kind of national council may be created as a consultative body or interim government.
- Build new political parties by providing financial help and technical assistance to individuals and groups with little experience in peaceful political competition.
- Construct new political institutions or reform existing ones. Attention must be given to the electoral system and to the judiciary. Judges, prosecutors, and the police force must be selected in a way that establishes the rule of law.
- Revise political behavior by ensuring that voters and political activists are free from violence and intimidation, securing conditions of free

speech and assembly and access to the mass media, and publicizing violations of civil rights.
- Provide for fair elections by guaranteeing that voters have access to the
polls and that their votes are honestly counted. In the end, elections
must be certified as being free and fair.

By these means, elites are given the opportunity and incentives to pursue peaceful electoral competition, rather than resorting to force. Finally,
the population needs to be empowered in such a way as to remove their incentives to follow the elites in any renewal of violence. To do this, civil society must be reconstituted. The public must be educated and enabled to
use the new political institutions. This can be done in several ways:

- Return and resettle displaced persons, including refugees and political
prisoners.
- Provide humanitarian and economic assistance.
- Educate people about human rights and provide the means for individ-
uals to assert their rights for free political expression.
- Investigate past human rights abuses to prevent their repetition and re-
move those guilty of abuse from positions of power.
- Register voters.

Democratization is possible in deadlocked civil wars because it prom-
ises new avenues of competition where the old way—war—has, by
definition, become ineffective. The organizations from which local leaders draw their power need not be dismantled, but they must be transformed. Armed conflict must be replaced by a competition for votes.
Leaders may then have a chance to achieve high offices that may previously have appeared out of reach. Creating democracy is not an easy task,
nor a cheap one. The UN's operations in Cambodia cost about $1.7 bil-
lion. Typically the parties to a conflict have little experience with democracy, and old habits are not readily broken. But democracy may work in
some states that have not yet achieved much economic development. Indeed, it may be cheaper and easier to achieve significant levels of democracy than to achieve significant levels of wealth.

Table 6.1 lists these various activities, noting those that were carried
out by the UN—including through its various programs and specialized
agencies—in each of the six cases noted above. (Several of the relevant ac-

Table 6.1: The UN as Peacekeeper and Democratizer

UN Action	Namibia UNTAG	Nicaragua ONUCA/ONUVEN	El Salvador ONUSAL	Cambodia UNTAC	Mozambique ONUMUZ	Angola UNAVEM II
Reducing Capacity						
Monitoring of the cease-fire	•			•	•	•
Disarmament, cantonment, and demobilization	•	•	•	•	•	•
Reintegration of ex-combatants			•	•	•	
Reform of the armed forces	•	•	•		•	
Building Capacity						
Creation of transition governments	•		•	•	•	
Assistance to political parties			•		•	
Reform of governmental institutions						
Reform of the electoral and legal systems	•	•		•	•	
Reform of the police force	•		•	•	•	•
Reform of political behavior			•			•
Ensuring a fair electoral campaign	•	•	•	•	•	•
Ensuring fair elections	•	•	•	•	•	•
Empowering the Populace						
Return of displaced persons	•			•	•	
Humanitarian or economic assistance				•	•	
Protection of human rights			•	•		
Investigation of past human rights abuses			•			
Civic education on elections and human rights	•		•	•	•	
Voter registration	•			•	•	

tivities were carried out in Nicaragua by other institutions.) All of the more successful peace-building operations—in Namibia, El Salvador, and Mozambique—used most of these techniques; the worst failure, in Angola, employed fewer than half.

The Effort in Mozambique

Democratization, whether promoted by the UN or not, will not always succeed in establishing democracy, nor in securing peace within a country. Nevertheless, an examination of the UN's operations in Mozambique[4] illustrates how, when used together as a comprehensive program, the steps in Table 6.1 reinforce one another to promote internal peace and democracy.

Reducing capacity: Cease-fire, disarmament, demobilization, reintegration, and reform

In 1992, more than 7,000 peacekeepers were deployed as part of the United Nations Operation in Mozambique (ONUMOZ). They had a mandate to establish law and order and to create an environment in which the government of Mozambique (FRELIMO) and the Mozambique National Resistance (RENAMO) could feel secure enough to demobilize their armies. The demobilization process involved the co-ordinated efforts of several agencies affiliated with the UN that were working with ONUMOZ. UNICEF, for instance, provided equipment for potable water supplies while World Food Programme provided daily food rations. The World Health Organization (WHO) supplied medicines and operated medical clinics. During the transition, demobilized soldiers were given civic and health education, provided with recreational facilities, and taught to read and write. Finally, the International Organization for Migration (IOM) transported demobilized soldiers and their dependents to their preferred destinations.

[4]See Chan and Venancio 1998; Berman 1996; and two UN documents: *Final Report of the Secretary-General on ONUMOZ, S/1994/1449*, December 1994, and in the UN Blue Book Series of documentation, *The United Nations and Mozambique, 1992–95* (New York: United Nations, 1995).

The links between political leaders and their soldiers can be broken by altering the opportunities and incentives faced by soldiers in the process of demobilization. Programs designed to reintegrate ex-combatants into civilian life do just this. In Mozambique, former combatants were paid three months back wages to facilitate their return to society. After reaching the areas where they planned to settle, they remained salaried for an additional three months. Government troops got pensions and disability programs as well. Each demobilizing soldier was entitled to a package of clothing, a two-week food ration, and an agricultural tool kit (with seeds) provided by ONUMOZ. Eventually, this scheme was extended and ex-combatants received another eighteen months of pay from funds provided by both the government and the international community. The United Nations Development Programme (UNDP) had overall responsibility for disbursing these additional funds. The UNDP also ran an occupational skills development program, and the IOM provided basic information about jobs.

By demobilizing large numbers of soldiers and restructuring remaining forces, the potential for a return to violence on a large scale is dramatically reduced. Creating an integrated army out of components of the former warring factions significantly neutralizes the potential for a renewal of the civil war. In Mozambique, both sides retained forces outside the demobilization process—approximately 5,000 government and 2,000 RENAMO troops—as a hedge against postelectoral crises that would undermine their agreement (Alden 1998). Yet these numbers pale in comparison to the original troop levels: 64,000 for the government and 23,000 for RENAMO.

Building capacity: Political parties and governmental institutions

The initial conduits for political action are committees set up to oversee the transition to peace. These are composed of representatives from the various parties to the conflict. Their task is to ease the transition from the polarized political environment of civil war to the more integrated environment of a unified democratic polity. They give local leaders a chance to voice their views, discuss their differences, and reach compromise solutions. Some of the committees may be merged into a transition government with wide-ranging political responsibility for the entire country. For societies where, prior to the transition toward peace, there was only divided political authority over limited segments of the country (both geographical and social), inclusive institutions through which the political future of a unified country can be addressed are an innovation.

In Mozambique, this came in the form of the Supervision and Control Commission (CSC) and the Cease-Fire Commission. UN officials chaired both bodies. Composed of representatives from the government of Mozambique and RENAMO as well as from Italy, Portugal, France, Britain, and the United States, the CSC had the central authority to oversee implementation of the peace agreement, including the tasks of settling disputes and interpreting the provisions of the agreement. The Cease-Fire Commission had a mandate to investigate allegations of cease-fire violations. If a consensus among the representatives of the UN, the government, and RENAMO could not be reached, ONUMOZ teams went out to the field to pass judgment. A national election commission was created to administer the electoral process.

These consultative bodies—transitional power-sharing structures with limited jurisdictions—represent only the precursors to democratic political institutions. In the final analysis, political authority must be derived from free and fair electoral competition. In a country with a history of civil war, autocratic regimes, and little experience in electoral competition, it is naive to expect leaders to understand from the outset what is required by nonviolent political competition. Competing factions must be educated in this process. The General Peace Agreement for Mozambique explicitly entitled RENAMO to financial assistance to convert itself from a military organization into a political party. "It was apparent from the outset that RENAMO was nowhere near prepared to engage in the responsibilities incumbent upon it as partner in the peace process, from politicking on committee structures to the complexities of conducting an electoral campaign" (Alden 1998, 80). When RENAMO declared that the funds made available to it by the government were insufficient and threatened to derail the peace process, the UN created the United Nations Trust Fund for Implementation of the Peace Agreement in Mozambique and, following an appeal to the international community, made additional sums available to RENAMO. In addition, ONUMOZ pressured the government to provide funds and resources to other opposition parties while similar trust funds were being created. Aside from providing financial assistance, ONUMOZ also coordinated the effort to train new political parties in the ways of electoral competition.

Another element in the transition from civil war to civil society is the creation of laws and legal institutions. UNDP personnel assigned to the National Election Commission in Mozambique served as technical advisors and monitors to promote fairness in developing the legal framework for electioneering and a system for giving media access to the political parties. Reforms of the organizational structure, training, composition, and behavior of the existing police force further aided the goal of creating an ordered political environment. Along with a reduction in the local parties' capacity to resort to force and a restructuring of the polity's legal institutions, a strictly civilian police force capable of enforcing the laws of the country impartially becomes an instrument through which peace and fair political competition can be promoted. Development of such a police force requires severing links between the police and any one party to the conflict and training or retraining police officers.

Reforming laws and political institutions is fruitless unless political behavior is changed. To tighten the legal and institutional reforms accompanying the transition, the UN involved itself extensively in the electoral campaign and election in Mozambique. By monitoring political activities actively—censuring those who deviated from the agreed code of conduct and publicizing violations—and giving technical assistance to those who sought to use the opportunities made available through the peace process, it encouraged local parties to conform to democratic norms. UN civilian police monitored the electioneering, while the UNDP trained 52,000 polling officers. Disputes concerning the registration of political parties were brought to ONUMOZ for settlement. In addition to the 1,200 UN observers it provided, ONUMOZ coordinated efforts by various nongovernmental organizations to monitor the polling and counting of ballots. The UN certified the results, and RENAMO accepted defeat.

Reconstituting, educating, and empowering the populace

Severe physical, economic, and social displacement caused by prolonged civil war stands as the immediate impediment to popular participation in the political process. People's immediate needs must be met before they can be asked to become an electorate. An unfolding humanitarian disaster arising from the combined dynamics of war-induced population displacement and widespread drought amplified the challenges in Mozambique. To meet them, the UN Department of Humanitarian Assistance created the Office for the Coordination of Humanitarian Activities. UNOCHA was a novel attempt to integrate the work of NGOs and specialized UN agencies while minimizing redundancy in the assistance provided and enhancing cooperation among the various organizations. The World Food Programme and the International Committee of the Red Cross delivered food and other emergency aid. The UN High Commission on Human Rights (UNHCR) headed the effort to repatriate refugees and return internally displaced people. In his final report on ONUMOZ, the secretary general estimated that 4.3 million people (3 million internally displaced persons, 1.1 million returnees, 200,000 ex-combatants and their dependents) were returned to their original areas of residence, out of a target population of 6.5 million. UNHCR built schools and health clinics. UNICEF and the Programme for Rural Water Supply provided wells and other sources of clean water. The World Food Programme disbursed seeds, and the UNDP coordinated a project to clear land mines left by the war.

Civil war and its social and economic turmoil leave a country's population unprepared for the duties of citizenship in a democratic polity. Even more than the political elite, the vast majority of the populace requires assistance to participate in democratic politics. The UN was instrumental in providing this to the people of Mozambique. It created programs through which people could return safely to their homes and begin to rebuild their lives. It publicized the conditions of the peace agreement and the process of democratization and educated people about their rights and registered them to vote. Although these programs were aimed at the populace, they also increased the options available to the elite. Without programs to mobilize the public politically, democratic competition is not a viable option and cannot be presented to the leaders as an alternative to armed conflict. Without voter registration, an electorate fails to emerge. In addition, a politically aware and mobilized electorate becomes an effective counterbalance to the elite. This is, after all, the essence of democracy.

UN missions have often gone beyond merely training electoral officials and supervising elections in their efforts to resurrect nations torn by civil war. In Mozambique, the UNDP trained 2,600 electoral officials at the national, provincial, and district levels, but it also prepared 8,000 individuals to take a census that could be used as the basis for establishing lists of voters and districting. UN volunteers provided logistical and technical support for registering voters. The UN organized 1,600 individuals into teams that were sent into the countryside to educate people about basic civic rights and responsibilities. With United Nations assistance, more than 80 percent of the eligible population was registered to vote.

To sum up, leadership from the UN can be crucial in reconstructing states after a civil war. Typically these conflicts are waged by parties that receive external support. Since impartiality is critical, international organizations may be more effective than individual governments that may have been allied with one side or the other. Regional organizations such as the OAS and the OSCE may be perceived as impartial but may not have the combination of resources, mandate, and universal acceptance that the UN possesses. And the UN now has a level of experience that other organizations lack.

How successful was the United Nations in its efforts to reconstruct Mozambique? It depends on the standard applied.[5] There is still politically motivated violence, but it is not near the epidemic levels that prompted the UN to intervene. Some political violence is, unfortunately, common in many developing countries. The country remains very poor, but until the terrible floods of the year 2000, its economy was growing rapidly. Its elections have been marred by some abuses, but they have been competitive, and international observers have certified them as reasonably free and fair. Mozambique is far from being an ideal democracy, but certainly conditions are better than before the UN became involved. Does one judge success by the aspirations of those who intervened or by the realities of the civil war and slaughter that preceded it? Democratization is difficult under *any* circumstances, so our standards must be realistic. In that light, much was accomplished, though much remains to be done. Will the UN be successful elsewhere? Not always, but universal success is the wrong standard. The UN frequently is given the tough jobs, for which member states do not want to devote the needed resources and do not want to take responsibility. If the UN carries out a comprehensive package of complementary programs, success often, even sometimes, may be enough.

---

[5]On multiple critera of success, see Kleibocr 1996; Druckman and Stern 1997; and Jett 2000.

Do IGOs Promote Peace, or Vice Versa?[6]

We return now to build on the quantitative analyses of earlier chapters. We want to reconsider one of the conclusions reached in the last chapter, where we said that the prospects for peace improve when states are members of the same international organizations. Joint memberships in IGOs are beneficial, we argued, because they provide opportunities for states to resolve conflict nonviolently. Relations between states are never so harmonious that problems do not arise. Witness the disputes over trade involving the United States and Canada within NAFTA or the United States and the European Union or Japan. These are America's closest allies, but periodically they have significant disagreements over how the economic gains from trade are to be divided. These disagreements do not escalate to violence in part because these countries participate in IGOs that can assist in the disagreements' nonviolent resolution.

Here we examine the link connecting peace (or conflict) to states' participation in IGOs. Our conclusion that IGOs causally affect the likelihood of war or peace is plausible, even likely, but not conclusive. One possibility is that we have the causal arrow reversed, that the number of joint memberships in IGOs is more a consequence of the character of interstate relations than a cause. Actually, it is most likely that a reciprocal relationship exists, with peace and IGO memberships forming a mutually reinforcing feedback loop or virtuous circle (Jervis 1997, chap. 4). In principle, we could look for reverse causality or a reciprocal relationship by constructing a system of two simultaneous equations. This task is extremely demanding, however, and reliable methods for doing it are still being developed. But we can conduct a preliminary exploration by estimating another single equation to explain common IGO memberships. This will give us an initial insight into whether there is an important reverse effect of disputes on the density of states' IGO linkages. It can also tell us whether democracies and trading partners tend to form and join international organizations together. Doing so will expand our knowledge about the three causal arrows going up to the peak of the Kantian triangle.

With a good model for explaining peace in hand, we can build a paral-

---

[6]David R. Davis participated in an earlier version of this analysis (Russett, Oneal, and Davis 1998).

lel one for explaining shared IGO memberships. Many of the same influences are important in both cases, but there are also some important differences. The model that we will use to explain joint IGO memberships must include disputes, of course, since our chief purpose is to find out whether we are right to infer that IGOs reduce the frequency of militarized disputes. Here DISPUTE becomes the first independent variable, testing the hypothesis that two states will be less likely to join the same IGOs or to remain in them if they have recently experienced a military dispute. As before, to give plausibility to our causal inference, we lag this and all the other explanatory variables one year behind IGO memberships.

We noted earlier that democracies should be more likely than other states to join IGOs. Kant expected that representative democracies, sharing common principles of law and political morality, would form "federations" (international organizations) with other democracies. From there, it is an easy step to hypothesize that democracies may be especially likely to join IGOs populated by other democracies. As with the newest members of NATO, they may in part do so with the express purpose of strengthening their democratic institutions. This is the reciprocal relation we considered above: IGOs affecting the political character of their members. To determine empirically whether democracies are apt to share memberships in the same international organizations, we include $DEMOC_L$ as the second independent variable in the regression analysis we are using to explain the variable IGO. Again we assume that the level of democracy of the less democratic member of the pair will most affect the likelihood that the two states will share many IGO memberships. This variable will tell us whether democracies join IGOs with each other. Since autocracies come in diverse ideological and institutional forms, it makes little sense to hypothesize that autocracies in general are more likely to join IGOs with each other than with democracies.

Similarly, we have noted on several occasions that many IGOs are organized to manage economic interdependence among their members. High volumes of international trade demand reliable commitments by states to limiting or eliminating tariffs and nontariff barriers. These commitments are generally negotiated within and enforced by IGOs. As trade increases, there are important implications for the flow of capital and labor and for controlling environmental degradation. This spillover of activities from one area to another as relations grow is clearly illustrated in the development of the European Union. Information must be gathered and disseminated; rules and procedures must be put in place and monitored; systems for mediating, adjudicating, or otherwise resolving disputes must be created.[7] All these require collaborative institutions, frequently IGOs. This is why we hypothesize that the density of IGO memberships will depend in part on the degree to which two states are economically interdependent. To test this, we include the variable $DEPEND_L$ in the equation explaining IGOs as well. Once again, the "weak-link" assumption is appropriate: the greater the trade-to-GDP ratio for the bigger and thus less dependent state, the more IGOs it will join with the smaller state.

States sharing national security interests are likely to form and join IGOs together, too. This leads to the hypothesis that states that are joined in military alliances will share other international organizations as well; often these are designed to build on or to strengthen their military ties. The NATO alliance, for example, encourages cultural contacts between the citizens of member countries on the theory that these will encourage support for the military links. So we include ALLIES as the fourth independent variable in our explanation of dyads' IGO memberships. This allows us to ask whether the widespread alliance system of the United States and the more limited regional system of the Soviet Union largely accounted for the pattern of IGO memberships during the cold war.

Many IGOs are explicitly regional in character. This is hardly surprising. States in the same geographical area of the world generally share common security, commercial, and environmental concerns. IGOs help them address these issues. From the hypothesis that distant states are less likely to have both common interests and common problems, our indicator identifying noncontiguous pairs of states is an obvious control variable to include in the model of IGOs. But in addition to joining IGOs with bordering countries, states often also need organizations to address interests and problems they share with states that, though not contiguous, are still reasonably near. Remember, too, that in measuring contiguity we consider whether imperial states have colonies that are adjacent. Before World War II, for example, some British colonies bordered on Italian

---

[7]The frequency with which national judges in EU countries refer cases to the European Court of Justice is strongly related to the level of their countries' trade with other EU states. See Stone Sweet and Brunell 1998b.

ones, although Italy and Britain themselves were not contiguous. The fact that they had a common colonial boundary created some issues of joint concern to Britain and Italy, but the effect was probably much less than if the home countries themselves had been close together. Our measure of the distance between capitals is the best one to capture this effect: joint memberships in IGOs should increase the closer two states are geographically.

One new influence seems important to an adequate explanation of why states share common IGO memberships. Per capita income is moderately correlated with the number of IGOs to which a state belongs (Jacobson, Reisinger, and Mathers 1986).[8] Rich states tend to have complementary economies and to form IGOs to facilitate their economic relations, so interdependence may be particularly influential in the case of the economically advanced states. Rich countries have widespread interests in international health, environmental, and educational conditions; and they share a concern for global political as well as economic stability. In addition, they can better afford the costs of membership in many IGOs than can poor states. For these reasons, we expect that two wealthy countries will be especially likely to share memberships in IGOs and that poor countries will have fewer joint memberships. To test this hypothesis, we add to our equation a measure of the GDP per capita of the poorer country in each dyad. This is the variable $GDPPerCap_L$. We assume that the income level of the less wealthy state is the effective constraint on the pair's participation in many IGOs.

The six variables we have just discussed are all included in our model to explain the joint membership of states in intergovernmental organizations. Table 6.2 displays the results of estimating this equation in the customary manner. As before, we identify the influence of the variables subject to policy intervention by seeing what difference a comparable change (one standard deviation) in each one has on states' participation in IGOs. As before, we first calculated a baseline rate against which to make these comparisons, assuming this "typical" dyad is contiguous, not allied, and has average levels of trade, democracy, etc. Such a dyad shares membership in just over nineteen IGOs on average. The percentages in Table 6.2 refer to the increase or decrease in the number of shared IGOs

[8]Milanovic (1996) finds that both per capita wealth and democracy promote the integration of economic institutions between states.

resulting from a change in each variable. Unlike most of our earlier analyses, however, we limit our examination of IGOs to the period after World War I. Before World War I, the number of IGOs in the world was too small to give us meaningful results.

Table 6.2: Identifying Influences on Joint IGO Memberships, 1921–92

All variables at baseline levels except:

DISPUTE equals 1	−28%
ALLIES equals 1	+40
GDPPerCap$_L$ increased by one standard deviation	+14
DEMOC$_L$ increased by one standard deviation	+7
DEPEND$_L$ increased by one standard deviation	+20

The effects of geography on states' participation in IGOs are strong, just as they were for explaining disputes, but we do not list them in the table because they are not amenable to policy interventions. The other influences are all statistically significant at the .001 level except for trade (.02 level), so the relationships we observe are unlikely to have occurred by chance. First, consider the impact of the variable DISPUTE on IGO membership. It is negative, as one would expect. If states become involved in a military dispute, they will not share as many contacts in IGOs as pairs of states that have been at peace. On the other hand, states that were not involved in a dispute in the previous year share more IGO memberships. Substantively, this effect is strong. A dyad will share 28 percent fewer memberships if there has been a militarized dispute; that is, there will be fourteen joint memberships instead of nineteen. This suggests that there is an important feedback loop in the Kantian system: IGOs promote peace, and peace promotes joint IGO memberships. Each can reinforce the other in a virtuous circle. Peace encourages states to increase their contacts in international organizations, which strengthens the prospects for continued peaceful relations. There is, however, also the danger of a vicious circle. Disputes cause states to reduce their association in IGOs, which increases the likelihood of more disputes. The reciprocal relations between peace/conflict and states participation in IGOs merit further investigation to clarify their relative importance.

Military allies have a strong propensity to join IGOs with each other: allies on average share twenty-seven international organizations, 40 percent more than a dyad composed of states that are not allied. Wealth also has an effect. Richer countries, with high per capita GDPs, tend to belong to twenty-two common IGOs instead of the baseline nineteen. There is also evidence for a Kantian influence from democracy, independent of the other influences in our model. Shared democracy is associated with a 7 percent higher density of IGO memberships: twenty-one such organizations. The other Kantian variable, $DEPEND_L$, has a stronger impact, with economically interdependent states sharing twenty-three IGOs on average, holding all the other variables at their baseline levels. This is a good indication that increasing levels of economically important trade do lead states to participate in more international organizations together. In the next section, we will consider the influence of IGOs on trade. Those results indicate that there is also a virtuous circle in the Kantian system linking trade and international organizations: each encourages the other.

We have not tried to develop a complete theory of why states join IGOs. Our primary purpose has been to determine whether there is reverse causation from militarized disputes to lower levels of joint participation in IGOs and to assess the effects of democracy and interdependence on joint IGO memberships. In other analyses (Russett, Oneal, and Davis 1998), we considered additional hypotheses about IGOs using other variables. For example, we examined the effect of the more democratic state and the more economically dependent trading partner on the number of joint IGO memberships, and we asked whether open economies promote greater involvement in international organizations. These additional variables often were statistically significant, but they did not notably change the substantive effects or significance levels of the variables we have considered here. Nor did the inclusion of these other influences increase the explanatory power of our model of IGOs much. Since the variables we have used here do quite a good job, explaining almost half of the variance in IGO memberships (R^2 = .48), these strong and parsimonious results will suffice.[9]

In sum, we now have strong evidence for three new loops in the Kantian system. Peace increases IGO memberships, and IGO memberships

[9]Here and in the next chapter, we used ordinary least squares regression analysis, rather than the GEE, to compute the R^2.

increase the prospects for peace. Democracies are more likely to join IGOs with each other than are other states. And states with economically important trade are more likely to share IGO memberships. Additional research is needed to clarify the relative strengths of the reciprocal relations between IGOs and peace and between IGOs and trade.

Who Trades with Whom?[10]

In this section, we address two issues. The first is the effect of conflict on trade. States may reduce their trade with each other in response to conflict. Indeed, the danger of such disruptions is thought to encourage states with economically important commercial relations to avoid militarized disputes. Second is the question of whether democracies trade more with one another than would otherwise be expected. In his January 1994 State of the Union address, President Clinton first expressed his belief in the democratic peace and then his acceptance of the economic corollary: "The best strategy to ensure our security and to build a durable peace is to support the advance of democracy elsewhere. Democracies don't attack each other. They make better trading partners and partners in diplomacy." If democracies do carry on more trade, this trade provides an indirect link to peace, adding to the direct effect of democracy we previously reported. We expect that democracies do have higher than expected levels of trade, even when other influences on the volume of trade are considered. In assessing this hypothesis, we investigate whether alliances, a general openness to trade, and common IGO memberships are also associated with increased trade between states. The last would constitute another important link in the Kantian system.

No one doubts that economic considerations influence international trade. Obviously, a state with a big economy will generally have greater exports and imports than a state with a small economy, though small economies may trade more proportionate to their size in order to take advantage of the international division of labor. (That is, they will not try to produce the complete range of products, from food to high-tech industrial goods, they wish to consume. They will specialize according to their

[10]Harry Bliss coauthored an earlier version of this analysis (Bliss and Russett 1998).

comparative advantage, export these products, and import what they do not produce.) Nonetheless, economics is not everything. It is impossible to explain the preferential trade within the Eastern and Western political blocs during the cold war or the still discernible trading preferences within parts of the former British and French colonial empires (Brams 1966; Louis and Robinson 1994) simply by considering the invisible hand of the market. Political and cultural influences are also apparent.

Mercantilists, Marxists, and imperialists have always been aware that foreign trade can be an instrument of national power. Albert Hirschman (1945), for example, carefully considered how trade could lead to economic dependence and a loss of national autonomy. He showed that the Nazis had sought explicitly to make several smaller states dependent on commercial relations with Germany as a way of extending Germany's power in central Europe. Hirschman's seminal study prepared the way for a generation of Latin American scholars to analyze the influences that made underdeveloped countries economically dependent on larger, more developed economies. With the rapid expansion of foreign trade shortly after World War II, the influence of the state on levels and patterns of trade may well have increased. The power of government became widespread and far-reaching. Many countries reduced their tariffs, but in some cases, they replaced them with myriad and subtle nontariff barriers. To some degree, all states try to influence patterns of trade to the benefit of their own nationals and in accordance with perceptions of their national interests (Krasner 1978). They promote trade with states deemed reliable sources of key products like food, raw materials, and militarily important technology, and they discourage it, by various barriers, with adversaries and potential enemies. Diaz-Alejandro (1975, 214) nicely summed up the situation some time ago: "Which markets are allowed to operate and how, which are encouraged and which are repressed— these are political decisions, both nationally and internationally."

Realists fear that one state may use the economic gains derived from trade to threaten the survival of its trading partner. Unless the benefits of trade are exactly equal, one side gains more resources, relative to its partner, to devote to its military. Because of these security concerns, states must be concerned with the relative gains from trade, not just with their own absolute gains. As a consequence, they will be reluctant to trade with states that may become their adversaries (Grieco 1988; Gowa 1994; Gowa and Mansfield 1993). This was certainly true during the cold war, for the members of NATO, on the one hand, and of the Warsaw Pact, on the other. But liberal thinkers have argued that under less adversarial conditions it is the absolute gains accruing to each trading partner that motivates their behavior (Snidal 1991; Morrow 1997). Thus, we should not be surprised to find that trade between democratic partners is typically greater than when one or both partners are not democracies.

Several arguments support such an expectation. Because democracies are likely to be at peace with one another, a democratic trading partner will feel its security less threatened by another democratic state than by many autocracies. American and British leaders do not worry that the other will use its relative gains from trade to threaten their own security. Their countries can enter into relationships of economic interdependence for the absolute benefits of trade, particularly an improvement in the standard of living, without worrying much about which state gains more. In Powell's terms (1991, 1313), "If the use of force is no longer at issue, then a state's relative loss will not be turned against the state. Relative gains no longer matter, and cooperation now becomes feasible." In addition, the absolute gains that result from trade between two democracies increase their security vis-à-vis potentially hostile third parties. Political leaders may try to regulate trade accordingly. Democratic states may construct policies to encourage their private economic actors to trade with those in other democracies, with whom political relations are stable and peaceful.

Certainly, private actors have their own incentives to restrict trade with countries with whom relations are not reliably peaceful. Since entrepreneurs in democratic countries have reason to believe that shared democracy promotes peace, they can anticipate less risk of interference in their business from war or threats of war when dealing with economic agents in a democratic country. Traders and investors are likely to be more confident in the business practices and laws in another democracy than in those in an autocracy, where expropriations and capricious taxation may threaten their physical or intellectual property. Russia's new and imperfect democracy, without a stable rule of law, has discouraged many foreigners from putting money into the country. It is partly for this reason, as well as the EU's commitment to democracy in principle, that the European Union insists its members must be liberal democracies. Mercosur—the preferential trade zone in South America—adopted the same policy in

1996. It is hard to distinguish the relative strength of the various mechanisms by which public and private actors preferentially promote trade between democracies, because their motives are related and are often complementary. In this case, institutional arrangements reinforce private preferences.

There is some evidence that democracies do trade more with one other. Remmer (1998) shows that democratic governments concluded more agreements for cooperation in the Mercosur region even before Mercosur was founded. Morrow, Siverson, and Tabares (1998) find more trade between democratic great powers. Dixon and Moon (1993) show that U.S. exports were higher to countries that were democratic. Bliss and Russett (1998), in an analysis like that to be reported here but more limited in scope, find that democracies trade more with each other. Mansfield, Milner, and Rosendorff (2000) argue that democracies are much more likely to conclude preferential trading agreements with each other and show that pairs of democracies traded more with each other from 1960 to 1990 than did other kinds of states. But the evidence is not unanimous,[11] and the question warrants a new analysis, over a long time period and for many countries.

Several analyses have found that allies are likely to trade more than nonallied states (Gowa and Mansfield 1993; Mansfield and Bronson 1997a, 1997b). International systems with large blocs of opposing allies, as during the cold war, have distinctive patterns of trade. Many international organizations are designed specifically to facilitate and promote trade among their members. Not surprisingly, trade within the European Union expanded and deepened along with the institutional structure to promote it (Pollins 1989b). There is a long list of regional and other preferential IGOs, on all continents. Many of these are relatively recent creations, but others (like the British Commonwealth) have a long history. Thus, the influences of alliances and international organizations, too, must be considered in explaining bilateral trade.

We now look at the effect of a number of political, institutional, and economic variables on states' trading patterns. We examine relations

[11]Gowa and Mansfield (1993) and Mansfield and Bronson (1997b) did not find more trade between democratic powers, and Verdier (1998) contends that democracy promotes trade only between industrialized countries.

among the same countries—namely, the conflict-prone, politically relevant dyads—we have considered throughout the book.[12] The dependent variable is derived from the trade data used previously: we seek to explain the level of bilateral trade (TRADE). As we noted before, imports and exports between two countries are equivalent; so, for example, Italy's exports to Spain are, save for transportation costs and reporting errors, the same as Spain's imports from Italy. Consequently, the variable to be accounted for is the natural logarithm of the sum of one country's exports to and imports from the other in a year, where trade is measured in millions of constant dollars. Using the logarithm is advisable because of the great differences in the value of trade for the smallest and largest countries. Because the logarithm of zero is undefined, we imputed a value of $100,000—one-tenth the minimum value of trade reported by the IMF—to dyads that had no commercial relations. As we show elsewhere (Oneal and Russett 2001), this is a reasonable assumption that does not unduly influence the results of our analysis. We do not divide trade by either state's GDP. Instead, we use their GDPs as independent variables to explain the level of trade they will have: two large countries will have more trade than one large and one small and, of course, more than two small states.

Economic size is one of the essential components of what economists call the "gravity" model of trade. The theory underlying the gravity model was set forth by Tinbergen (1962) and recently reviewed by Deardorff (1995). The argument is straightforward: the level of trade between two states is primarily a function of the economic size of the trading states and the distance separating them. Shipping costs increase with distance, and greater costs reduce the incentive to trade. The GDPs of the two trading partners are often combined (e.g., Deardorff 1995; Helpman and Krugman 1985, chap. 6) rather than considered separately, so after taking the logarithm, we add the GDPs of the members of each dyad. This creates the variable GDP. Another element of the gravity model is the sum of the

---

[12]Bliss and Russett (1998), in the earlier version of this analysis, added some states, which, though not necessarily global political actors, were major trading states with global economic ties. They included, for the post–World War II era, Germany, Italy, the Netherlands, Belgium (including Luxembourg), Canada, Sweden, Switzerland, and South Korea. The results were not materially different from what we report here.

logarithms of the two countries' populations. If population increases and GDP is held constant, GDP per capita declines. In other words, average income goes down. Consequently, in the gravity model, larger populations will be associated with lower levels of trade, controlling for the GDPs of the countries, because poorer countries trade less than wealthy ones. To account for this, we add the variable POPULATION to our model. The last essential component of the gravity model is distance. Since our measure of the distance between states is the number of miles between capitals (or between major ports for a few large countries) and since even neighboring countries may have their capitals far apart, our measure of noncontiguity is a useful additional indicator of geographical distance to include in our model (Frankel and Romer 1999).

The effects of openness and democracy should be analyzed separately, though the two measures are correlated. Democracies vary to some degree in their commitment to market economics, but virtually all leave a fairly wide scope for free enterprise. The Communist dictatorships did not, at least until China began to open its economy in the 1980s. Many fascist regimes and military dictatorships have also followed autarkic policies, forbidding foreign investment and discouraging trade. Myanmar (formerly Burma) was once the richest country in Southeast Asia, but when General Ne Win took control in 1962, he socialized much of the economy and cut most of the country's ties with the world. Under his policy of "national self-sufficiency," the economy went downhill fast. Myanmar became one of the poorest and most isolated nations in the world.

The experience of Brazil illustrates how democratic governments may pursue more or less open policies in different circumstances. During the 1950s, the elected government followed a policy of protecting industry to encourage substituting domestic manufactures for foreign ones. But by 1964, the economy had stagnated, and a military junta seized power and adopted a more free-market policy. They tried to attract foreign investors and promoted new export industries so the country could afford more imports. For a while the economy grew rapidly, but in 1973, world oil prices rose sharply when the Organization of Petroleum Exporting Countries restricted petroleum output. The higher cost of oil put a tremendous burden on the country's international balance of payments. Brazil tried to cope by obtaining loans from foreign banks and international lending organizations, but by the middle of 1983, its foreign debts hit $90 billion, about four times its annual export earnings. Per capita income fell 12 per-

cent between 1980 and 1983, unemployment skyrocketed, income inequality widened, and the military dictatorship was discredited. The new
civilian government that then took power moved slowly, but in the
decade of the 1990s, President Fernando Henrique Cardoso opened the
economy considerably. This was striking, because in his previous career as
an academic, Cardoso had advocated protecting domestic industry and
limiting foreign investment (Cardoso and Faletto 1979). The government
sharply cut tariffs, and imports more than doubled. Many state-owned
industries were privatized, and new foreign investment in Brazil went
from virtually nothing to almost $30 billion. Real GDP per capita rose
40 percent. Because economic openness and democracy are only moderately correlated and each may be important, we include both in our
model of trade.

Openness is also inversely correlated with economic size. In the contemporary world, a country with a small gross domestic product cannot
be self-sufficient and prosperous, so it is apt to be more dependent on
trade than is a country with a larger GDP. Because the gravity model includes a measure of the economic size of the two states, it would capture
some of this effect even without including a measure of openness, but
states that make a greater political commitment to the liberal principles of
free trade and comparative advantage can be expected to trade more with
other states, so including our measure of openness is, again, appropriate.
Consistent with our previous analyses, we assume that the less open economy will have the greater influence on how much trade flows between the
pair, so again we use the variable $OPEN_L$.

Since a major purpose of this section is to discover whether militarized
disputes significantly diminish trade, we must use DISPUTE as an explanatory variable. As before, this variable equals 1 in a year when a pair
of states have been involved in conflict, and it equals 0 if it was a year of
peace. We lag DISPUTE and all other explanatory variables one year
behind the dependent variable, TRADE, to provide the right causal inference.

Democracy and international organizations constitute the other corners of the Kantian triangle, and they are potentially important for understanding trading patterns. We again use the variable $DEMOC_L$, on
the assumption that the degree of democracy of the less democratic partner will most influence relations between the two states of a dyad. The
more democratic it is, the more willing its even more democratic coun-

terpart will be to trade with it, on the grounds that it will make a stable trading partner and will not pose a military threat. Our hypothesis, then, is that democracies will trade more with other democracies. We do not expect autocracies, because they are an institutionally and ideologically diverse set of countries, to have any particular trade preference for one another, but they may be forced to trade with other autocracies because democracies shun them.

To measure the influence of international organizations on the level of trade, we add to the analysis our standard measure of the number of shared international organization memberships (IGO). Since many international organizations are created to promote trade among their members, lagging the variable IGO a year behind trade gives us an opportunity to compare the variables' relationship with the one we found in the preceding analysis, where we used the opposite lag and the analytical emphasis was on IGOs' managing high levels of trade.

Finally, we include in this trade model the variable ALLIES, because we anticipate that trade will be more common between states that have concluded a mutual defense treaty, an entente, or a nonaggression pact. Although we assume here that allies will trade more because they share security interests (as is reflected in our decision to lag the variable ALLIES one year behind TRADE), it is also possible that states may become allied in order to protect their existing joint commercial interests.

Table 6.3: Identifying Influences on Trade Patterns, 1886–1992

All variables at baseline levels except:

GDP increased by one standard deviation	+683%
POPULATION increased by one standard deviation	−24
DISPUTE equals 1	−8
$OPEN_L$ increased by one standard deviation	+14
ALLIES equals 1	+8
IGO increased by one standard deviation	+15
$DEMOC_L$ increased by one standard deviation	+6

Table 6.3 shows our results. The analysis proves very good overall, predicting 49 percent of the variation in trade patterns. Most of the variables

are very significant statistically. Contiguity is not, but the distance between states is significant at the .001 level. The variable ALLIES is not significant (at only .15), and the variable for the population of the two states (POPULATION) is significant at .01. As indicated at the top of the table, two variables from the gravity model, GDP and POPULATION, have a substantial effect on the level of bilateral trade. The impact of economic size is especially powerful. When the two economies of a dyad are a standard deviation larger than the baseline value, their trade is nearly seven times greater, but note that this increase is the result of a large increment in GDP. As expected, holding GDP constant, larger populations are associated with lower levels of trade. Increasing population lowers trade by 24 percent. Poor countries trade less than wealthy ones.

Though the economists' basic gravity model performs as expected, politics also influences the pattern of trade. The effect of a militarized dispute between members of a dyad is modest. While disputes are followed by lower trade, as expected, the reduction is only 8 percent. Because we include in our analyses only the first year of the world wars, we are not capturing the severe commerce-disrupting consequences of very large wars, but even during wartime, some trade may continue between adversaries (Barbieri and Levy 1999). The important point, however, is that for the cases that we do analyze, the effect of conflict on trade is substantially weaker than is the lagged effect of trade on disputes that we reported in Chapter 4. This is evidence that economically important trade really does reduce conflict and is not just a consequence of previous peaceful interstate relations. This analysis does not decisively settle all questions regarding the direction of causality, but along with several other corroborating analyses (Mansfield 1994; Kim 1998; Oneal and Russett 2000a, 2001), it adds to the evidence that for the full range of militarized disputes, the effect of trade in reducing conflict is at least as strong as the effect of conflict in reducing trade.[13]

[13]One check would be to include a lagged value of the dependent variable TRADE on the right-hand side of the regression equation because trade flows tend to be highly correlated over time. That would, however, beg the theoretical question whether political variables influence trade. A large coefficient for previous trade would simply subsume previous and contemporary political effects. Instead, we have used a Granger model, which includes past values of both trade and the political influences, and this, too, supports our causal inferences (Oneal and Russett 2000a). The results of our test here are also substantially unchanged using a fixed-effects model.

Openness, the ratio of a state's trade with all other countries to its GDP, has both economic and political import. The greater the total trade of the state in each dyad that is less dependent on trade, the higher the level of trade within the dyad. The state less dependent on trade is the limiting factor (or the weak link) influencing the dyad's commercial relations. The relationship is strong: greater openness raises the level of bilateral trade by 14 percent. In part, this effect comes from the need for small economies, whatever their political preferences, to carry on a relatively large amount of foreign trade for reasons of economic efficiency. But this is only a small part of the explanation for the influence of openness, because openness is only modestly correlated with GDP. Most of the effect seems to be a result of political decisions about whether to encourage or discourage foreign trade above or below the level that purely economic influences might indicate. States that deliberately follow policies of economic liberalism toward the world generally trade heavily with one another.

Alliances have a moderate effect on trade; two allies trade 8 percent more with each other than do nonallies. IGOs, however, exert a more substantial impact, contributing a 15 percent increase in trade within the dyad when the number of joint memberships increases. As we have noted, many IGOs promote trade among their members. Combined with the evidence from the preceding analysis that trade influences states' involvement in IGOs, we now have strong evidence of an important feedback loop in the Kantian system: trade and IGOs are mutually reinforcing.

Finally, democracy does promote trade, by 6 percent. Democratic states and their private entrepreneurs do have a preference for trading with one another. Thus, democratic institutions and culture not only have a direct impact on reducing international conflict, which we found in Chapter 3, they also have an indirect benefit through the promotion of trade.[14]

Two very different dyads can illustrate the results of this statistical analysis: Belgium and the Netherlands, and the USSR and the United

---

[14]We checked to see whether dropping OPEN (our variable for openness) would materially change the effects of the remaining variables. It did not. On theoretical grounds, we prefer the more complete model, which shows the independent effect of economically liberal trade-friendly policies.

States. For the first dyad, all the political variables lean in the direction hypothesized to increase dyadic trade: both are democratic, share a very dense web of international organizations, have no experience of militarized disputes, are allied, have very open economies integrated into the world system, and share a common territorial boundary. In 1989, their dyadic trade amounted to $30 billion, 8.1 percent of their combined GDPs. For the latter dyad, with all the variables much less favorable according to our hypotheses, dyadic trade amounted to $5.1 billion, only .07 percent of their combined GDPs. The Soviet-American relationship during the cold war well illustrates the vicious circle connecting political differences, low interdependence, exclusive and competitive regional IGOs, and military threat. Only deliberate and powerful acts of policy making could break these links and move the world back from the brink of a devastating nuclear war.

With these analyses of states' memberships in international organizations and their interdependence, we begin to fill in the arrows at the sides of the triangle that we have used to illustrate the Kantian system. They have also clarified the influence of peace and conflict on trade and IGOs. The vision of peaceful international relations associated with Kant, Wilson, and the founders of the European Union—of peace built on the tripod of shared democracy, economic interdependence, and international law and organization—develops increasing solidity. This set of mutually reinforcing relations shows how after World War II, the mostly democratic, mostly free-market countries of the West constructed a firm basis for peace among themselves (Ikenberry 1996). Democracy, trade, and IGOs produce virtuous circles that reinforce one another and increase the prospects for peace.

Interests, Preferences, and Alliances

One question that has vexed research on the liberal peace concerns the matter of national interests. The term "national interest" is almost as common in realists' writings as is the word "power." What constitute the interests of a nation, and how do they arise? Have democracies and interdependent states avoided substantial conflict among themselves because they were democratic and interdependent, or did they experience little conflict merely because they shared a common enemy? During the cold war, the liberal states of the West formed NATO and other alliances to safeguard their security against the threat they perceived from the Communist countries. Was it coincidental that these alliances were composed primarily of interdependent democracies, or was participation in the Western security system inherently related to their common political institutions and culture and the strength of their economic ties? It was certainly in their strategic interests, faced with a dangerous adversary, to suppress conflicts among themselves—and they did so. But if common security interests were the primary motive for the peacefulness among the Western states during the cold war and these interests were not themselves a consequence of their being interdependent and democratic, then the liberal peace emphasizes the wrong causal relation: it would be a concern for security that limited conflict in the West, not democracy and trade. If this were so, there would be important implications for the future. The end of the cold war might be the end of the peace among liberal states.

Erik Gartzke (1998) has argued that the liberal peace of the post–World War II years did arise primarily from shared interests, as expressed in patterns of voting in the United Nations General Assembly, rather than from democracy and interdependence per se. Henry Farber and Joanne Gowa (1995, 1997a, 1997b; Gowa 1999), too, contend that strategic preferences and interests related to the cold war, only partially expressed in the pattern of explicit alliances, can account for the democratic peace. These critiques must be carefully considered because some of the strongest evidence for the Kantian peace comes from the cold war era. The results reported in Chapter 5 show that states bound together by democracy, interdependence, and IGOs were peaceful throughout the twentieth century, but the strength of these relationships did change somewhat over the years, and the pattern of cold war disputes was undoubtedly conditioned by the bipolar configuration of power. Security interests did substantially shape the policies and behavior of the Western democracies.

The causal connections linking interests, institutions, and behavior are inherently complex. To the degree that the Western system of alliances in the cold war was the result of their common political and economic interests, peace among the interdependent democracies would have pre-

vailed even without the confrontation with the Soviet bloc.[15] Still, the
possibility that the liberal peace was, at least to some degree, a product of
cold war tensions cannot be rejected without analyzing international relations in other historical periods (as we have regularly done throughout
this book) *and* considering the role that states' preferences played in shaping their actions during the cold war era itself. It is that second task we
assume now.

In our new analyses of the cold war period, we use Gartzke's broad-
based measure of states' preferences (1998), derived from countries' voting patterns in the United Nations. This should allay concerns raised by
Farber and Gowa regarding the suitability of alliances as indicators of
national security interests. The analyses we report below show that
democracy and interdependence reduced the likelihood of dyadic conflict during the cold war, even when controlling for states' interests
and preferences, as indicated by their votes in the UN. Furthermore, we
contend that states' interests and preferences are not independent of
the nature of their governments and their economic relations. Instead,
they arise in large part from these very influences. Rather than indicating the independent importance of preferences in shaping interstate
relations, voting in the UN General Assembly can be explained by
the same theoretical variables we use to explain militarized disputes.
Thus, the analyses below show that democracy and interdependence
reduce the risk of conflict directly and independently, when controlling for states' interests, and indirectly, through their influence on those
interests.

In this book, we have assumed that interstate conflict is inherent in the
anarchic international system but that it is constrained by various influences. In contrast, Gartzke (1998) emphasizes inducements for conflict;
for example, he argues that Communist and democratic states fight
largely because they have different preferences, but that if states share interests and preferences, they have an affinity for one another and have little incentive to fight. He proposes that in the post–World War II period,
states' affinities were most clearly manifested by their votes in the UN
General Assembly. He concludes that states' preferences have greater

[15]Many realists acknowledge that states' preferences or interests are derived in part
from domestic politics; see Legro and Moravcsik 1999.

influence on the chances of conflict than do constraints imposed on the use of force by democracy or economic interdependence. Gartzke (1998, 11) acknowledges, however, that this finding would not undermine the democratic peace "if regime type similarity actually leads to similar preferences." If this is so, then democratic institutions or norms would still play a causal role in producing the separate peace among democracies.

Gartzke's analysis is a refinement of Farber and Gowa's argument that national security interests, essentially unrelated to the character of states' political regimes, account for the democratic peace. In fact, the principal reason that we always include an indicator of alliances in our analyses of military conflict is to show that democracy, trade, and IGOs have effects that are independent of states' security interests. Indeed, we have seen that the pacific benefits of the Kantian variables are more consistent than the pacific benefits of alliances. Although Gowa (1999, chap. 6) acknowledges that alliances can serve as a proxy for shared security interests, in their earlier work, Farber and Gowa (1995, 1997a, 1997b) say that merely controlling for alliances is not an adequate test of the democratic peace. States, such as the United States and Japan during the cold war, may cooperate because of common security interests without concluding a formal alliance. In addition, interstate conflict is apt to influence the formation of alliances, so they are not independent indications of preferences. Gartzke's measure of affinity based on UN votes is valuable because it offers an alternative indicator of preferences that is only moderately correlated with alliances (r = .49).

We therefore want to reevaluate the liberal peace while controlling independently for preferences, which are strongly influenced by states' understanding of their national security interests. We begin with the basic Kantian equation used in Chapter 5. It is designed to identify the relative effects of different influences on the risk of a dyadic dispute. To this model, we then add Gartzke's measure of states' interests and preferences, which he called AFFINITY. It is the rank order correlation of states' voting in the United Nations General Assembly; thus, it is a measure of the similarity between two states' preferences as expressed by their diplomats' voting on a variety of topics. As the variable AFFINITY increases, two states are thought to share more interests in common. Consequently, the risk of a dispute should go down. Our analysis is limited to the period

1950–85. These are the cold war years for which Gartzke's data are available.[16]

The first column of Table 6.4 shows the results of estimating the standard Kantian model for just the years 1950–85. There are no surprises. The reductions in risk are roughly in line with what we have regularly seen, and the effects for all but the variable IGO are statistically significant. These results confirm that as our theory leads us to expect, democracy and interdependence have important pacific benefits. We tested Gartzke's thesis by adding the variable AFFINITY to the Kantian model. If AFFINITY captures much of the effect of democracy on disputes during the cold war era, then the separate peace among democratic countries after World War II could have been more the result of congruent preferences regarding national security than of democratic institutions or norms. The results of estimating the Kantian model plus AFFINITY confirm that states' preferences do influence the likelihood of conflict independently of the character of their regime, level of interdependence, etc. Gartzke's measure of the similarity of states' preferences is very significant (.001 level), as shown in the appendix in Table A6.4.

---

[16]Since we are using the same data and theoretical model throughout the book, this analysis differs from one reported earlier (Oneal and Russett 1999b), but the basic results and conclusions are not materially different. As usual, we included controls for distance, contiguity, and major power status but do not show their effects in the table. The analyses reported in Table 6.4 and those in previous chapters differ not only in the time period covered but also to some degree in the states that are included. Switzerland, for example has never been a member of the UN. Japan and many European states that were neutral or fought on the Axis side in World War II were admitted only in the 1950s, East and West Germany became members only in 1973, and North and South Korea only after 1985. Indonesia withdrew for a period, and South Africa was for some time denied the vote. In addition, some small states do not vote regularly. Consequently, the AFFINITY measure is missing for some dyads. Finally, we do not entirely endorse using votes in the General Assembly to assess preferences. They reflect preferences only on the issues states choose to bring before that body. Some issues are put to repeated votes just to embarrass particular states (e.g., Israel, South Africa). Issues currently under consideration by the Security Council are off-limits to the assembly. The specific mix of issues actually voted on can shift dramatically from year to year, and the similarity of states' votes varies across issues (see Kim and Russett 1996). Voting is also often strategic; for example, a state may vote differently if it expects a measure to pass or fail than if it believes the outcome is truly in the balance.

Table 6.4: Percentage Change in Risk for Annual Involvement in a Militarized Dispute and Change in the Affinity of States, 1950–85: Contiguous Dyads, the Liberal Peace and States' Interests

	(1) DISPUTE *Standard Analysis*	(2) AFFINITY	(3) DISPUTE *Direct Effects plus Indirect Effects through AFFINITY*
All variables at baseline values except:			
$DEMOC_L$ increased by one standard deviation	−19%	+26%	−17%
$DEPEND_L$ increased by one standard deviation	−47	+17	−47
IGO increased by one standard deviation	−12	+5	−13
ALLIES equals 1	−47	+88	−47
POWER RATIO increased by one standard deviation	−31	+5	−31

Clearly, UN voting patterns do help predict disputes. A country's votes provide valuable information about its preferences on a variety of international issues, including national security. But what causes UN voting and, ultimately, the preferences for which these votes are an indicator? Any claim that it is preferences, rather than democracy per se, that explain the democratic peace is valid only if states' preferences are not themselves much influenced by the character of political regimes. We argue, instead, that states will have similar interests and preferences, and will vote alike in the General Assembly, if they have similar political systems and are economically interdependent. Logic and evidence suggest this extension of the liberal-peace perspective (Kim and Russett 1996). As we have already seen in this chapter, pairs of democracies are not only more peaceful, they also trade more and share more memberships in international organizations. Accordingly, we expect two states' voting records in the UN to be more alike the more democratic and interdependent they are. Allies are also likely to vote similarly because of their shared security interests.

To find out if UN voting patterns are influenced by the same factors that affect militarized disputes, we substitute AFFINITY for DISPUTE as the dependent variable (the outcome we seek to explain) in the basic Kantian model. The results for this analysis are reported in column 2 of Table 6.4. The model does well in accounting for states' preferences. Democracy, trade, alliances, and power predominance all are strongly and significantly related to the similarity of states' preferences, and the effect of IGOs is nearly significant (.11 level). All the effects are in the opposite direction from what they were in predicting disputes, so the signs in columns 1 and 2 are exactly reversed: democracies, interdependent states, and so forth fight less but cooperate more in the UN. Note the strong effect of an alliance on the variable AFFINITY: the average AFFINITY score of allied states is 88 percent larger than for nonallies. This confirms that security interests are strongly reflected in states' votes in the United Nations. All in all, the simple analysis in column 2 represents a productive start to explaining states' affinities and preferences.

The equation predicting disputes that includes AFFINITY (Table A6.4, col. 3, in the appendix) and the equation predicting AFFINITY (Table A6.4, col. 2) together can be used to estimate the complete effects of political regimes, interdependence, IGO memberships, and common security interests on the frequency of disputes.[17] Using the two equations in combination reveals the net effect of the Kantian variables. There are two causal paths from each Kantian variable to conflict. One indicates the direct effect of democracy, trade, and IGOs on the likelihood of a militarized dispute, controlling for AFFINITY; the other indicates the indirect effect of each of the Kantian variables on the likelihood of conflict through its influence on AFFINITY. The net effects, direct plus indirect, of the Kantian variables, alliances, and the balance of power are shown in column 3 of Table 6.4.

The results in column 3 confirm that the Kantian variables have substantial benefits for interstate relations. Comparing column 3 to column 1 reveals only trivial differences. The direct effects of the Kantian variables on the likelihood of conflict are no different whether these are estimated without considering the independent influence of preferences, as revealed in UN voting, or are estimated by taking into account the direct effects of the Kantian variables, controlling for AFFINITY, and their indirect effects on the incidence of disputes through their influence on this measure of preferences. Gartzke's analysis does not refute the pacific benefits of democracy. It only suggests that the peacefulness of the liberal states is in part a result of their sharing similar preferences and interests derived from their common political regimes and interdependence and in part a result of the constraints on the use of force imposed by their democratic institutions and norms and their economic interests. In short, democracies are constrained from fighting, and they have little to fight about.

Our understanding of the role that preferences play in motivating states to use force or to settle their differences peacefully is still underde-

---

[17]If disputes do not substantially affect the affinity of states, we can ignore this feedback loop and avoid methodological problems caused by simultaneous effects (Kmenta 1986). To see whether there is an important feedback loop from DISPUTE to AFFINITY, we added DISPUTE to the right-hand side of the equation explaining AFFINITY and reestimated the coefficients. DISPUTE added little new information. The coefficient of DISPUTE was significant ($p < .02$), but its substantive impact was modest (a dispute decreased AFFINITY by 8 percent), and it added little to the overall explanatory power of the model. Moreover, the risk reductions and significance levels of the other variables were virtually identical to those in column 3. So it is reasonable to use the equations in columns 2 and 3 to assess the complete effects of the liberal variables on the likelihood of conflict.

veloped. The concept of "preferences" is abstract. National leaders can directly observe other states' institutions, and they have reliable economic indicators regarding the importance of their economic relations. Voting in the United Nations, as recorded in AFFINITY, is certainly observable, but we doubt that in deciding for war or peace, decision makers focus on the pattern of UN voting. Instead, they are more apt to look at prominent general indicators of preferences, such as states' political regimes, the congruence of their economic interests, and, of course, particular contested interests, such as disputed borders.

The results we have reported in this section corroborate our earlier findings: the Kantian variables provide important pacific benefits. Although UN voting can serve as a useful indicator of states' interests, it is not, as we have seen, independent of states' regimes or their economic interdependence.[18] Nor are alliances. Kant anticipated that commercial republics would create an expanding network of defensive alliances (Cederman 2000). In the first half of the twentieth century, democracies, along with some autocracies, fought two great wars side by side. Was the common cause of these democratic states purely a result of their common strategic interests, or did shared interests in democracy and economic freedom play a role even then? And for the post-1945 era, the only period in which a strong and consistent pacific benefit for the variable ALLIES is evident, it strains belief to attribute that effect to strategic interests independent of states' political regimes and economic interdependence. After all, the cold war was a clash of two fundamentally different political and

---

[18]Gartzke (2000) has recently argued that democracy, like a state's preferences, is a product of antecedent conditions, such as economic development. Consequently, it may not be democracy that produces peace so much as it is development. His model of democracy is not realistic, merely predictive, as he notes (204): it includes variables, notably ALLIES but also POWER RATIO and DEPEND, that are more plausibly consequences, rather than causes, of states' being democratic. This dilutes the influence of democracy on interstate conflict in his tests. We argue, on the other hand, that the character of states' political institutions causally affects their preferences as expressed in UN voting. The weight of the evidence indicates that institutional and normative constraints are important, but we agree that democracies also do not fight because they have little to fight about. The individual contributions of economic and political liberalism to peace remain subject to research, but it is important to note that democracy, development, and economic openness are mutually related and reinforcing.

economic systems. The governments, elites, dominant classes, and people of the free-market democracies feared not just for their physical security and national independence but also for their prosperity and their political and economic liberties. They formed strong alliances in order to preserve their way of life, and they succeeded.

The post–cold war era is full of affirmations about the importance of democracy, human rights, and prosperity built upon interdependent world markets. Doubtless some of this is empty rhetoric, but it is also the appeal of sophisticated global economic actors who understand the role of interdependence in their prosperity. In 1999, the democratic countries of NATO fought a war in the name of democracy and maintaining human rights in Europe against a dictatorial government in Serbia that posed no strategic threat. In time, we shall see whether peace among democracies and interdependent states holds. But to claim that "there is no reason to believe the democratic peace . . . will survive the erosion of the East-West split" and that it was "a byproduct of a now extinct period in world politics" (Gowa 1999, 3–4, 114) seems a very premature report of its death.

7

Clash of Civilizations, or Realism and

Liberalism Déjà Vu?[1]

His book conveys a challenge, like he wants us to refute him,
Daring us, by scaring us, to doubt him or dispute him.
Which is fine for academic-argument-displaying
As long as someone powerful won't act on what he's saying.

(Tipson 1997, 168–69)

Samuel Huntington's *The Clash of Civilizations and the Remaking of World Order* (1996) has proven to be one of the most influential recent books on international relations. The responses range from laudatory to scathing.[2] The quotation above is from one of the more perceptive cri-

---

[1]This chapter draws on Russett, Oneal, and Cox 2000.

[2]Huntington 1996 expands and slightly modifies the analysis presented in Huntington 1993a, 1993b. All page references to Huntington are to the 1996 book, unless otherwise noted. As of 1999, the *Social Science Citation Index* reported a total of more than five hundred citations of the book and articles. Kurth 1998 strikes a laudatory note; scathing attacks include Holmes 1997 and most of the responses by

tiques as well as the most amusing. Such a range of reactions is not surprising. Like Huntington's other work, this contribution is smart and
provocative. It is intended to offer "a more meaningful and useful lens
through which to interpret international developments than any alternative" perspective (14). It demands attention. It seems to make sense of
some very important current conflicts, such as those between the United
States and Iraq. But it does not explain the wide coalition—containing
Islamic as well as Western states—that forced Iraq to withdraw from
Kuwait in 1991. It can account for the war between Serbia and NATO,
but at the same time, its argument is inconsistent with NATO's aligning
itself with Serbia's Muslim Albanian minority. Even for those conflicts
that it seems to fit, there may be better explanations, and being right on
occasion does not mean that an argument is correct as a general thesis.
Consequently, Huntington's thesis of a clash of civilizations deserves to be
examined systematically using social scientific methods, and it should be
compared with the explanations of conflict offered in this book.

Huntington's core claim is that "clashes of civilizations are the greatest
threat to world peace" (321) and that "In the post–Cold War world the
most important distinctions among peoples are not ideological, political,
or economic. They are cultural" (21). Huntington's thesis is all too plausible. Fear and hatred of those who are different is familiar, within societies as well as internationally. Yet his theory is not obviously right.
Nations with different ethnic populations coexist peacefully in many regions of the world, and many countries include diverse groups that mix
freely. Indeed, before the mid-twentieth century, interstate conflict was
particularly prevalent *within* the Western world. This was most dramatically the case during the two world wars when tens of millions died. Conflict among the Western states declined during the cold war, when so
much of the world was caught in the tensions between the Communist
bloc and the West. The once popular classification of states into the first,
second, and third worlds also indicates that hostilities in the post–World
War II period involved diverse groups, the North versus the South as well
as East versus West. But this characterization, appropriate for an era in
which conflicts were based primarily on ideology or differences in eco-

---

Ajami, Bartley, Binyan, Kirkpatrick, and Mahbubani in *Foreign Affairs* 72 (4): 2–21
(1993). Other contemporary and widely read books on the alleged power of cultural
differences in promoting conflict include Kaplan 1993 and Moynihan 1993.

nomic development, became less relevant with the end of the cold war. Huntington proposes to replace it with a perspective based on differences between cultures or civilizations.

His central theme is that "culture and cultural identities, which at the broadest level are civilizational identities, are shaping patterns of cohesion, disintegration, and conflict in the post–Cold War world" (20). Thus, his argument is not about the distant past and applies only partially to the early decades of the cold war. He asserts that after the Iranian revolution of 1979, "an intercivilizational quasi-war between Islam and the West" opened up (216, also 185), and that in the 1980s, conflicts across the boundaries of the world's great civilizations increasingly replaced those between Communists and capitalists. In the future, Huntington believes, many of the most violent, prolonged international conflicts will occur across civilizational cleavages or fault lines (253). Recently he declared, "The interplay of power and culture will *decisively* mold patterns of alliance and antagonism among states in the coming years" (Huntington 1999, 46; italics added).

If Huntington's characterization of the recent past were correct, then his understanding of the present and his predictions of the future would have to be taken seriously. His perspective is probably the most prominent alternative theoretical perspective to the realist and Kantian ones explored in this book. A test of it, against realist and Kantian understandings, is thus essential.

The clash of civilizations perspective represents a big idea, with immense implications for policy. Like other big ideas, it has the potential to become not just an analytical interpretation of events, but—if widely believed—a shaper of events. Huntington's theory could become a self-fulfilling prophecy, intensifying conflicts or bringing about some that otherwise would not have occurred. After a century wracked by great wars and now deep into an era of weapons of mass destruction, "Nothing would be more dangerous for the nations of the West and East than to prepare for a supposed confrontation between Christianity and Islam" (Herzog 1999; also see Holmes 1997; Walt 1997). But, if its fundamental thesis is correct, Huntington's book provides an early warning that policy makers could use to defuse the coming conflicts. That is probably what Huntington intended. But is it correct? Is there evidence that civilizations clash?

In this chapter, we use the best scientific methods to assess the validity of Huntington's idea.[3] We conclude that there was not a general "clash of civilizations" in the past and that its application to current events has been selective. Civilizational differences add little to existing realist and Kantian explanations of interstate conflict. Consequently, the theory does not offer a sound guide to the future.

Civilizations and Identity

Huntington's thesis—that cultural differences produce conflict—has deep roots. The philosophers Oswald Spengler and Arnold Toynbee emphasized the historical importance of cultural aspects of civilization. Huntington's argument is also linked to social psychological theories (67). At its heart is the distinction between the in-group and the outsider, where in-group cohesion is attained by nurturing conflict with those who are different. Huntington himself asserts that "identity at any level—personal, tribal, racial, civilizational—can only be defined in relation to an 'other,' a different person, tribe, race, or civilization" (129). The sociological version of this view is commonly associated with Georg Simmel ([1908] 1955); it was interpreted and expanded by Lewis Coser (1956). The in-group/out-group distinction has been extensively applied—with mixed results—to international relations since the 1960s.[4] The focus of this earlier body of research was on the conditions under which intra-group cohesion is enhanced (or fractured) by confrontation with others. One version asserts that humans are essentially hardwired for social conflict based on an in-group/out-group orientation. Shaw and Wong (1988, 207) express the view that "Humanity's propensity for war is the outcome of thousands of years of evolution during which cognition and intolerance of out-group members have been shaped by priorities of gene-culture coevolution."

---

[3]Huntington differentiates his "framework" for "interpretation" from "a work of social science" (13). Yet his goals to "order and generalize about reality" and to "understand causal relationships among phenomena" (30) are surely grounds to employ social scientific methods.

[4]Simmel 1898 was the initial presentation to an English-language audience. Stein 1976 offers a nuanced perspective. Levy 1989b and Heldt 1997b review applications to international relations.

Social psychologists are interested in how people form their social identities (Tajfel and Turner 1986),[5] and their theories have been applied to international relations by the constructivist school. The constructivist turn is intriguing, because as Jonathan Mercer (1995) notes, these theorists foresee the broadening of group identities to include a variety of others with whom it is possible to identify and live in peace. Yet theories of social identity postulate that this broader identity can only be achieved vis-à-vis some newly defined "other."[6] In this view, then, the vision of a pluralistic community "of mutual sympathy and loyalties; of 'we-feeling,' trust, and mutual consideration; of partial identification in terms of self-images and interests; of mutually successful predictions of behavior" (Deutsch et al. 1957, 36; also Adler and Barnett 1998) implicitly leaves some people on the outside.

For Mercer, the construction of identity against an "other" exposes a critical flaw in the constructivist project. Thomas Risse-Kappen (1995b) also notes that the sense of mutual identity among democrats, based in part on a political culture of peaceful conflict resolution, may give rise to a perception of otherness and threat regarding those (nondemocrats) who do not share that culture. Similarly, autocrats may see democrats as culturally "other" and threatening.[7] A concern with the clash of civilizations is, therefore, part of a larger intellectual effort to understand the implications of people's conceptions of identity for international relations. It is important to note that Risse-Kappen's concern—that democracies, united by a common political culture, may demonize nondemocratic states—can be allayed by the importance of democratic institutions: institutional explanations of the democratic peace do not depend on people's sense of identity. And we found in Chapter 3 that democracies are no more likely to fight autocracies than autocracies are to fight each other.

The Clash of Civilizations opens a window onto questions about the effect of culture on politics. Huntington proposes that civilizational differences lead to conflict. It may also be that the character of different civilizations, rather than directly influencing the likelihood of interstate

---

[5]A good review of this and related theories is Sidanius 1993.

[6]Mercer also gives a good review of this literature. For major constructivist applications, see Onuf 1989 and Wendt 1999.

[7]Also see Doyle 1986, 116: "Fellow liberals benefit from a presumption of amity; non-liberals suffer from a presumption of enmity."

violence, shapes the political institutions, economic practices, and security arrangements we have highlighted in our discussion of the Kantian
and realist theories. As we have repeatedly seen, the type of national government, the level of interdependence, and the pattern of alliances influence the incidence of dyadic conflict. The effect of culture, then, might
be an indirect one acting through these important intermediary influences.

This possibility is evident in Huntington's work. His greatest worry
regards the great civilizational divide between the West and all other civilizations—"the West and the rest," as he puts it—that can be traced
largely to the West's acceptance of the principles of democracy and human rights and these principles' more precarious standing elsewhere.
Huntington sees particular danger for the West from Islamic states. In his
view, fundamental differences between the Western and Islamic cultures
concerning the source of governmental legitimacy—whether it is the will
of the people or of scripture and religious authority—are largely insur-
mountable. If, however, Islamic societies are capable of becoming democratic, then the division between the West and Islam would not be so
dangerous.[8] Much the same would be true in regard to the West's other
major potential adversary in Huntington's crystal ball: China and the
Sinic civilization with which it is associated (238).

Do civilizations define the characteristics of states that we have found
to be such important influences on international relations? This possibility, too, is not self-evident. For example, as Huntington acknowledges,
the political cultures of Germany and Japan changed radically after 1945,
from national socialist and fascist to liberal and antimilitarist. Yet German
and Japanese political institutions remain deeply rooted in the distinctive
cultures of these two countries (Berger 1996). States, and their citizens,
can learn from history and their own experience that international conflict costs more than it is worth (Bennett and Stam 1998).[9] But, clearly, in

[8]Midlarsky (1998a) suggests that cultural barriers to full-scale liberal democracy
in Islamic societies are formidable, but that an Islamic version of democracy that includes political rights is possible and could diminish the gap separating Islam from
the West. This would diminish the likelihood of conflict, as we have shown. On this
same theme, see also Weede 1998; Esposito and Voll 1996; and several of the chapters in Garnham and Tessler 1995.

[9]On learning in international relations, see Tetlock 1991; Levy 1994; Reiter
1996.

assessing Huntington's thesis, we must consider the effect of civilizational differences on political regimes, interdependence, and alliances.

A subordinate theme in Huntington's work is the importance of "core" or dominant states within civilizations and their ability to attract countries of similar culture and to repulse those that are culturally dissimilar (155). This may be important to the effectiveness of collective security arrangements within a civilization. When integrated around such a pole, countries in a civilization may develop a more cohesive identity that minimizes their potentially antagonistic relations; those without such a stabilizing influence may experience greater intracivilizational conflict. Core states are thought to foster harmony and reduce violence within their civilizations because they are able to maintain control within spheres of influence.[10] Through negotiations with the core states of other civilizations, they may also provide a degree of order between civilizations (208). Thus, Huntington believes that a strong core will be more capable of maintaining peace within its civilization than a weak one because it can suppress conflict within the civilization and deter conflict from outside. He declares, "The components of order in today's more complex and heterogeneous world are found within and between civilizations. The world will be ordered on the basis of civilizations, or not at all" (156).

The argument that a big state can dominate the relations of smaller states under its hegemony—both pacifying relations among them and controlling their relations with outsiders—is found in many realist discussions. It is central, as we noted in Chapter 5, to hegemonic stability theory and power transition theory.[11] It is also important in Charles Kupchan's prescription (1998) for order in a multipolar international system. Kupchan, like Huntington, regards a multipolar international system as potentially peaceful, provided that each of the major regional poles is itself ordered by benign hegemony based on mutual consent. In his view, peace within the regions cannot be secured by empire, unfettered power, or exploitative behavior. Instead, a region organized on sounder bases can extend the peaceful character of its own internal relations to

[10]Note also Huntington 1999, 49: "For the reasons I set forth in my book, the core state of a civilization can better maintain order among the members of its extended family than can someone outside the family."

[11]Hegemonic stability theory is commonly associated with Gilpin 1981 and Krasner 1985 and is also approvingly cited by Kurth 1998.

other benignly organized regions: "Securing peace within regions is an essential first step toward securing peace globally" (Kupchan 1998, 42). According to Kupchan, a modern hegemon, to be effective, must moderate its realist impulses and exert its influence by first securing mutual consent based on the institutional and normative constraints characteristic of democracy.

Exploring the Effects of Civilizational Differences

To evaluate Huntington's thesis, it is critical—but not always simple—to identify the world's major civilizations and their boundaries. Although Huntington sometimes uses the terms "culture" and "civilization" interchangeably, he also calls attention to their differences. He argues that cultures and civilizations share common elements, such as religion, language, customs, history, and institutions, but that "civilization" is the key to understanding interstate conflict because it is "the highest cultural grouping of people and the broadest level of cultural identity people have" (43). Despite his admonitions that civilizations are dynamic and have no permanent boundaries, Huntington believes that most states can be grouped into eight civilizations: the Western, Sinic, Islamic, Hindu, Slavic-Orthodox, Latin American, Buddhist, and African. The composition of these groups may change over time, but slowly.

Huntington's view that the world is divided into identifiable civilizations is open to a variety of objections. His list of civilizations is to some degree arbitrary, and there are significant differences within each of these groups. Moreover, the criteria for assigning states to civilizations are not always clear. Huntington privileges broad loyalties to civilizations over more specific cultural or ethnic identities, including those that operate at the level of the nation-state. Huntington claims in effect that civilizational identities are more decisive than nationalism in accounting for sources of conflict. This is particularly doubtful in the case of the Islamic civilization, where interests tied to particular states have repeatedly triumphed over Islamic or Pan-Arab sentiments. Also, his discussion of the malleability and evolution of civilizations, along axes of Westernization and modernization (72 ff.), is quite simplified.

These criticisms of Huntington's theory have been extensively developed elsewhere, but despite the attention *The Clash of Civilizations* has received, systematic statistical analyses of the theory are rare. The most substantial work on the role of culture in interstate conflict finds only modest support for the view that cultural differences contribute to conflict. Errol Henderson (1997, 1998) does not specifically consider civilizations, but he carefully assesses whether religious, ethnic, and linguistic similarities reduced the frequency of interstate wars during the period 1950–89. He finds that religious similarity contributes to peaceful relations and, conversely, that differences in religion increase the incidence of war. But he also reports that ethnic and linguistic similarities *increase* the likelihood of war between states—just the opposite of what a cultural or civilizational perspective predicts. Indeed, the harmful effects of ethnic and linguistic similarities roughly counterbalance the peace-promoting effects of a common religion. Moreover, even the peace-promoting effect of religion is far less powerful than the benefits of democracy.

In his "Minorities at Risk" project, Ted Robert Gurr (1994) asks whether Huntington's perspective helps explain violence within states. Are conflicts between people from different civilizations common or becoming so? Gurr's answer is no. Of the fifty most serious ethnopolitical conflicts being fought in 1993–94, only eighteen fell across Huntington's civilizational divides.[12] In the Middle East, for instance, only one active conflict (involving Palestinians in the occupied territories) was waged between peoples from different civilizations, while five (two in Iraq and one each in Iran, Morocco, and Turkey) were fought within a single civilization. The proportion of internal conflicts involving groups from different civilizations was virtually identical before and after the end of the cold war. Moreover, while internal conflicts involving civilizational differences were typically more severe than other internal conflicts begun during the cold war, this was not true of those that began after 1987. Gurr shows that what many imagine to be a recent increase in ethnically based civil wars actually began in the 1960s—and has dropped precipitously from its

---

[12]Huntington (256–57) correctly cites Gurr's evidence that Muslim versus non-Muslim conflicts were common and intense, but he misreads the table in Gurr's appendix as listing thirty intercivilizational conflicts (C:C and C:Is) rather than eighteen (or nineteen with one recoding by Huntington) and does not discuss Gurr's other findings. Other research summarized in this paragraph is from Gurr 1993, 2000; Sadowski 1998; Ayers 2000, 116–17; Wallensteen and Sollenberg 1999; Lian and Oneal 1997; Fearon and Laitin 1996; Licklider 1998.

peak in the early 1990s. Cultural conflicts have also become less intense, and most that have occurred were more "fratricidal," occurring within rather than across civilizations. Violent intrastate nationalist conflicts did not become more intense or inflict more casualties from 1989 to 1996 than before, and while seventeen new conflicts began during that period, twenty-one ended. Most ethnic, linguistic, and religious diversity is not politically destabilizing. Few of the many contacts between people of different ethnic groups escalate to violence. Those that do, as in Africa and the former Soviet Union, are prominently reported, giving us an exaggerated sense of their frequency. Nor are conflicts involving ethnic differences less likely than other kinds of conflict to end with a negotiated settlement. In sum, recent social scientific research raises serious doubts about the utility of cultural and civilizational explanations of conflict, especially of that within states.

In this chapter, we examine the effect of civilizations on conflict between states. We use a variety of tests to determine whether there is a clash of civilizations. First, we evaluate Huntington's thesis in isolation. We ask simply: Does a difference in civilization increase the likelihood that a pair of states will become involved in a militarized interstate dispute? Second, we add key influences from the realist tradition to the model, assessing the effect of cultural differences while controlling for the balance of power and alliances. This test tells us whether Huntington's hypothesis makes a contribution beyond realist theory in predicting the frequency of militarized conflict. Third, we add to our model of interstate conflict the Kantian variables: democracy, economic interdependence, and international organizations. We have shown that both the Kantian and realist factors have substantial power in explaining international conflict. Thus we confront Huntington's theory of world politics with the alternatives we have emphasized. Do civilizational differences explain conflicts that are not accounted for by liberalism or realism? Is the clash of civilizations distinguishable from the account of international politics these older traditions offer?[13]

---

[13]Huntington also compares his perspective with alternatives, notably on pages 31–35. The "184 States, More or Less" and "Sheer Chaos" alternatives focus on the realist state-centric system of power and alliances. "Open World: Euphoria and Harmony" and "Two Worlds: Us and Them" represent versions of liberal arguments about the role of democracy and differences in economic development. His critique

We conduct several other tests of Huntington's thesis as well. We estimate the peacefulness of pairs of states within each of the eight civilizations and the peacefulness of pairs of states split across civilizational lines. If Huntington is right, dyads within each one of the civilizations will be more peaceful than dyads split across a civilizational boundary. Next, we evaluate his West versus the rest hypothesis. To do this, we identify those pairs of states that are composed of one Western state and one state from any other civilization. We then estimate the incidence of conflict for these dyads relative to all other pairs of states. Similarly, we test whether there is particular animosity between Western and Islamic states or between the West and the Sinic civilization. Then, we assess two propositions about the effect of core states within civilizations: (1) that civilizations with a strong core (or hegemon) are more peaceful than civilizations with a weak core, and (2) that democratic core states are particularly able to promote peaceful relations within their civilizational sphere of influence.

We perform these tests using our data for the 1950–92 period. Limiting our analyses to the years after World War II seems appropriate since Huntington addressed events in these years when he first presented his argument in 1993. Huntington does not believe that the effects of civilizational differences are limited to the post–cold war era, but he does argue that they have recently gained added importance. Consequently, we consider whether the intensity of the cold war affected the likelihood of militarized disputes across civilizational boundaries. First, we ask if the incidence of conflict between civilizations increased from 1950 to 1992. Then, we assess the intensity of civilizational conflicts while controlling explicitly for the intensity of the East-West confrontation as indicated by the level of U.S. defense expenditures. Next, we determine whether the clash of civilizations increased after the Iranian revolution or since the end of the cold war in 1989.

Finally, we consider the possibility that civilizational differences have significant indirect effects on the likelihood of conflict through important

---

of the liberal argument concentrates on the widespread absence of democracy, but he notes that shared democratic institutions, where they exist, diminish conflict. He does not consider the conflict-reducing effect of trade in this section, but on page 67, he explicitly rejects this view. Our purpose is to confront the hypothesis of civilization-based conflict directly with specific hypotheses central to other perspectives.

realist and liberal variables. If civilizational identities can substantially predict which states become allied, which have high levels of trade, which share memberships in IGOs, and which govern themselves similarly, then it could be argued that civilizations are the prime movers behind these political and economic factors and account for their influence on international conflict. If, however, civilizational identities do not well predict alliances, trade, IGO memberships, or political systems, then this argument fails.

As in previous chapters, we evaluate Huntington's theory by analyzing the behavior of pairs of states observed annually. A focus on dyads is essential for any theory, such as Huntington's, that posits that the probability two states will come into conflict varies with their military, political, or cultural characteristics. Huntington, however, is concerned not only with the frequency of disputes but also with the "most pervasive, important, and dangerous conflicts" (28) and those which have the potential to engulf others: "Violence between states and groups from different civilizations . . . carries with it the potential for escalation as other states and groups from these civilizations rally to the support of their 'kin countries' " (28). According to his theory, fault line wars are apt to be "protracted conflicts" (253). It is not clear, though, how "pervasiveness," "importance," and "danger" are to be assessed. Since Huntington's theory has not been subjected to systematic empirical testing, it is not always precisely specified. With the dyad as the unit of analysis, however, our tests give due weight to broad, spatially extended conflicts. A dispute limited to a single pair of states in one year is registered once in our data; that is, the variable DISPUTE would equal 1 only for that dyad-year. Conflicts involving two states on either side in one year, however, lead to four dyad-years being coded positively. And counting each year of a temporally extended dispute or series of disputes, as we do, gives greater weight to protracted conflicts, as Huntington's perspective requires. Furthermore, disputes that last for several years often involve many casualties.

Designing a Simple Test

We start our assessment of *The Clash of Civilizations* with the simplest test. We created a new variable, labeled SPLIT, that indicates whether the two states in a dyad come from different civilizations or not. It is coded 1 if the dyad is culturally heterogeneous; it equals 0 if the two states are from the same civilization. To make this determination, we relied primarily on the map Huntington provided (26–27). Knowing to which of the eight civilizations a state belongs allows us to determine if the dyad is split across a civilizational boundary or belongs to the Western, Sinic, Islamic, Hindu, Slavic-Orthodox, Latin American, Buddhist, or African civiliation. Classifying the states of the world is usually straightforward, but not always. Huntington does not put three "lone states" into any of his civilizations, and he identifies a few states as "cleft" or "torn" between more than one civilization.[14]

[14]The criteria underlying Huntington's classificatory scheme are not perfectly clear. In most cases, religion seems to be the primary criterion, but geographical location plays a major part in a few civilizations, notably the African and the Latin American. We relied primarily on Huntington's map but also consulted the text to clarify difficult choices. The Buddhist civilization was not in his 1993 article, and in the book he says Buddhism is "not the basis of a major civilization" (e.g., 48). Nevertheless, the map identifies the Buddhist as one of the eight civilizations. The three "lone states" are Japan, Ethiopia ("culturally isolated" [136]), and Haiti ("truly a kinless country" [137]). Japan is identifiably separate on Huntington's map; Ethiopia and Haiti are not, but we regard the text as more accurately reflecting his intentions. The map suggests that all the former British Caribbean states are Latin American, but that is inconsistent with his text: "The single civilization Caribbean Community (CARICOM) . . . has created an extensive variety of cooperative arrangements, with more intensive cooperation among some sub-groupings. Efforts to create broader Caribbean organizations bridging the Anglo-Hispanic fault line in the Caribbean have, however, consistently failed" (131). This is the only point at which he refers to any multistate civilization that is not identified as such on his map. Considering their parliamentary political systems and predominantly protestant Christian religious identity, we coded most of these island states as being in the Western civilization. Four countries are "torn," home to two or more civilizations in which leaders of one predominant culture want to shift to another (139–54): Russia (Orthodox to Western), Mexico (Latin to Western), Turkey (Islamic to Western), and Australia (Western to "Asian"). On the map, however, all are unambiguously identified with the first civilization listed for each, and we so classified them. The civilizations of several states in Africa cannot be determined definitively from the map, nor are they clearly indicated in the text. When in doubt, we consulted USCIA 1994 on religious composition and allotted those with greater than 50 percent Muslim population to the Islamic group and the rest to the African group. Accordingly, we assigned Nigeria to the African civilization, though it is identified as a "cleft country" in the text and is split on the map. India is another divided, cleft country, but surely it must be identi-

There are also inconsistencies between his map and the text of his book. The most curious case is Israel. In the text, Huntington is sometimes ambivalent (e.g., 48); often he labels it non-Western (90, 156, 186), and on page 188, he calls it a civilization of "Zionism and politicized Judaism." On the map, it appears to be part of the Islamic civilization. In light of its history as a stable parliamentary democracy and the predominance of Jewish immigration from Europe and America (Eisenstadt 1985, 296), we coded it as Western. Because the vast majority of Israel's disputes have been with Islamic states, this coding increases the evidence in support of Huntington's hypothesis, though in general the coding of the ambiguous cases affects only a small fraction of the total number of observations we analyze.

As we have done with each analysis throughout this book, we evaluate Huntington's theory while holding the essential realist variables constant: the distance separating the two states in each dyad; whether they are contiguous, either directly or through colonial possessions; and whether the dyad contains a major power. It is especially important in this analysis to hold geographical proximity and the influence of shared boundaries constant because many of the conflicts Huntington identifies at the fault lines of civilizations are between neighboring states, where conflict would be expected whether or not there were civilizational or cultural differences. Therefore, we first determine if being split by a civilizational boundary adds to the explanation of conflict provided by the essential realist controls. Then, we add the other realist constraints we have considered: the balance of relative power within each dyad (POWER RATIO) and whether the pair of states is allied (ALLIES). Next, we introduce the three Kantian variables. As before, we determine the influence of democratic institutions and norms using the democracy score of the less democratic state in the dyad (DEMOC$_L$), because it is the state that is less constrained by democracy. Interdependence is measured by the bilateral

---

fied with the Hindu civilization. Sri Lanka's identification is unclear on the map and sometimes in the text, but Huntington identifies it as Buddhist (48), consistent with the CIA's estimate that the country is 69 percent Buddhist. On the basis of its largest religious group (41 percent), we assigned the former Yugoslavia to the Orthodox civilization. The Philippines is also cleft in the text and on the map, but on the basis of its 92 percent Christian population, we assigned it to the West. South Africa is difficult, and ambiguous in the text; we followed the map and coded it as African.

trade-to-GDP ratio for the state that is less dependent on the pair's bilateral trade (DEPEND$_L$). The number of common memberships in international organizations shared by both members of the dyad (IGO) is the final Kantian influence.

Civilizational, Realist, and Liberal Influences on Conflict

Our first analysis of Huntington's thesis treats the likelihood of a dispute as a consequence only of civilizational differences, indicated by the variable SPLIT, and the essential realist influences: contiguity, distance, and whether the dyad contains a major power. In this test, the measures of geographical proximity were, as usual, very important determinants of the likelihood of conflict. SPLIT, too, was important. If a dyad is split between civilizations, the risk of a dispute is 84 percent greater than for a pair of states that is not divided across a civilizational boundary. All three of these influences were statistically significant at the .001 level.

Table 7.1: Percentage Change in Risk for Annual Involvement in a Militarized Dispute, 1951–92: Contiguous Dyads, Hypotheses from *Clash of Civilizations* and Realist and Kantian Theories

All variables at baseline values except:	(1)	(2)	(3)
SPLIT equals 1	+49%	+34%	+12%
ALLIES equals 1	−56		−50
POWER RATIO increased by one standard deviation	−28		−38
DEMOC$_L$ increased by one standard deviation		−27	−26
DEMOC$_L$ decreased by one standard deviation		+35	+34
DEPEND$_L$ increased by one standard deviation		−22	−36
IGO increased by one standard deviation		−30	−34

Support for Huntington's theory declines, however, as the other realist and the Kantian variables are added to the equation. In column 1 of Table 7.1, we show the results after adding to the initial specification two other realist variables, identifying allies and the relative power of the two states.[15] Both of these are very significant statistically (.001 level) and substantively important. Making the states allied reduces the probability of a militarized dispute by 56 percent; increasing the balance of power by one standard deviation lowers it by 28 percent. Allies are less likely to fight, and a preponderance of power inhibits conflict. There is still evidence in this specification that states split across civilizations are prone to conflict. The measure for SPLIT is not so significant statistically as before (.03 level), but it nonetheless is associated with a 49 percent increase in the likelihood of conflict. For the "clash of civilizations," so far so good.

In column 2, we evaluate Huntington's thesis in the presence of just the Kantian variables and the three essential controls. We do not include our measures of alliances or the balance of power in this test. The variable SPLIT still brings a 34 percent increase in the risk of conflict, but its effect is not quite statistically significant (.11 level). This suggests that civilizational difference matters a lot in some cases, but not in others: the average effect (increasing conflict by 34 percent) is not trivial, but the effect is variable (hence, the lack of statistical significance). By contrast, democracy is highly significant (.001 level). If we increase the lower democracy score so that both states are very democratic, the risk of a dispute drops by 27 percent; if we decrease the lower democracy score so that at least one state is highly autocratic, the danger of a dispute is 35 percent above the baseline rate. If the number of IGO memberships shared by the two states is high, the risk of a dispute drops by 30 percent (also significant at the .001 level). The effect of trade is somewhat smaller (a 22 percent reduction in the risk of conflict) but still substantial and significant (.05 level). In the presence of the Kantian variables, then, the contribution of civilizational differences to explaining the incidence of militarized disputes declines.

Finally, in column 3, we report the independent effect of civilizational differences on the likelihood of dyadic conflict in the period 1950–92 in the presence of all the realist and Kantian influences. All the variables in the table except SPLIT are highly significant (at the .001 level for all but economic interdependence, which reaches the .03 level). Alliances and relative power make big differences, as usual, in the annual likelihood that an otherwise average dyad will experience a dispute (in this case, 50 percent and 38 percent reductions, respectively). So, too, do democracy (a

---

[15]As usual, we do not show the risk-reducing percentages for the influences not subject to policy control: distance, contiguity, and major power status.

26 percent reduction in the risk of conflict if both states are democracies, or a 34 percent increase if one is autocratic), economic interdependence (36 percent reduction), and international organizations (34 percent risk reduction). In competition with all the realist and liberal influences, the variable SPLIT is associated with just a 12 percent increase in risk, and it is far from statistical significance (.30 level).[16] Thus, any one of the realist or Kantian variables has a far greater impact on interstate conflict than does the clash of civilizations.

Although we believe Huntington's theory mostly applies to recent decades of international relations, to be sure we were not stacking the deck against it, we also performed an analysis like that in column 3 for the full period 1885–1992, to see if there was evidence for the hypothesis if the years before the cold war were included. SPLIT still was not statistically significant. These analyses show that, while incomplete, the realist and Kantian traditions provide a far better explanation for international conflict than do civilizational differences. This conclusion is reinforced by the additional tests of the "clash" perspective that we report next.

What Are the Patterns of Conflict within and between Particular Civilizations?

One important test of the thesis advanced in *The Clash of Civilizations* is to ask whether interstate disputes are less common within particular civilizations than they are among dyads that are split across civilizational lines. Huntington has argued that conflict is more likely between states from different civilizations than it is for states from the same cultural

---

[16]We conducted several additional tests of Huntington's basic hypothesis. First, we assessed whether the variable SPLIT had a greater effect for contiguous pairs of states, which are particularly prone to conflict and might be more subject to this influence, by including an interactive term, SPLIT*CONTIG, in the analysis reported in the third column of Table 7.1; but the coefficient of the interactive term was not statistically significant. Thus, there is no evidence that states that are split across civilizational boundaries, whether they are contiguous or not, are more likely to become involved in a dispute once the realist and liberal influences are taken into account. In an earlier analysis (Russett, Oneal, and Cox 2000; see also Henderson and Tucker 1999), we assessed Huntington's theory using all pairs of states for which we had data, not just the politically relevant dyads. These results are even less supportive of the theory.

group. In the tests we have reported thus far, we compared the incidence of conflict for split dyads to the average for all eight civilizations. But with a test only slightly more complex, we can compare the likelihood of conflict for a pair of states from any one particular civilization to the risk for a pair of states from each of the other civilizations and for a pair of states that are split.

To conduct this test, we created a variable for each civilization that distinguishes dyads from that civilization from all other pairs. Thus, the variable WESTERN equals 1 if both states in a dyad are from the Western civilization; it is 0 for all other pairs. The variable SINIC equals 1 if two states are from the civilization associated with the Chinese culture, and it equals 0 for all others. This procedure was followed for each of the eight civilizations. We added these eight indicators to all the realist and Kantian variables. If Huntington is right that dyads within the same civilization are more peaceful, the risk of conflict should be less for dyads in any one of the civilizations than for the split pairs of states.

Table 7.2 shows our results. There is little evidence that civilizations

Table 7.2: Percentage Change in Risk for Annual Involvement in a Militarized Dispute within Civilizations, 1951–92

All variables at baseline values except:

ALLIES equals 1	−48%
POWER RATIO increased by one standard deviation	−37
DEMOC$_L$ increased by one standard deviation	−18
DEPEND$_L$ increased by one standard deviation	−20
IGO increased by one standard deviation	−23
WESTERN equals 1	−74
SINIC equals 1	+179
ISLAMIC equals 1	+9
HINDU equals 1	+55
ORTHODOX equals 1	−71
LATIN equals 1	−8
AFRICAN equals 1	−14
BUDDHIST equals 1	+184

clash. First, notice that the realist and Kantian variables perform much as they did in column 3 of Table 7.1. All are statistically significant at the .04 level or better. The risk factor for each civilization reported in Table 7.2 indicates the change in the likelihood of conflict for a dyad within that civilization relative to the pairs of states that are split across some civilizational line. If Huntington were right, each of the influences would be negative, indicating that the risk of conflict is reduced within that civilization. The percentages reported allow us to compare the peacefulness of the eight civilizations one to another: the most peaceful civilization has the greatest risk reduction. In fact, only two of the eight civilizational effects are negative and statistically significant.

The West has been the most peaceful of the eight civilizations. There was 74 percent less conflict for Western pairs of states than for split states that otherwise had identical characteristics. This reflects the regularization of peaceful relations among the industrialized democracies since the bloodletting of World War II. It also undoubtedly indicates the influence of the cold war. The internal peacefulness of the West does not mean that it is especially dispute-prone toward other civilizations. We shall see below that it is not. The Orthodox civilization also was significantly more peaceful (71 percent) than split pairs of states; again the consequences of the cold war are manifest. A common Eastern Christian culture could help explain the peacefulness of Huntington's Orthodox civilization, but it is also true that the Soviet Union kept a peace of sorts in the region until 1989. Given events since then, it is apparent that the countries of Eastern Europe prefer the peace conferred by democracy and free trade. Both of these findings are highly significant statistically as well as being very impressive substantively.

The risk reductions reported for Latin America and Africa also indicate slightly less conflict for the dyads located in these regions when compared to split pairs, but neither effect is remotely significant: the probability that these results would have occurred purely by chance is .44 and .32, respectively. The other four civilizations, however, actually had *greater* conflict among their members than the dyads split across civilizational boundaries. For the Sinic and Buddhist groups, this effect is very significant statistically and huge substantively (179 percent and 184 percent increases in risk). Huntington characterizes the Islamic civilization as being in conflict with "its Orthodox, Hindu, African, and Western Christian neighbors" (183)—a region with "bloody borders" (244). If so, it also has a bloody interior: pairs of Islamic states were more dispute-prone than the split dyads as a group, though this difference is not statistically significant.

In sum, the evidence from looking at the incidence of conflict within the eight civilizations individually provides little support for Huntington's thesis. Only two of the eight groups are clearly more pacific internally than the split pairs of states that he expects to be conflict-prone. Half of the civilizations were actually more conflictual internally than this reference group during the post–World War II period, and two of these were significantly so. This spread—ranging from a statistically significant benefit for two civilizations, to a statistically insignificant reduction in conflict for two others, to a statistically insignificant increase in conflict for two others, and finally to a statistically significant increase for two other civilizations—is just what would be expected if there were in fact no relationship between civilizations and interstate violence. These dramatic differences among the eight groups also explain why the variable SPLIT was not statistically significant in the test reported in column 3 of Table 7.1.

What about the contention that the sharpest and most dangerous division is between the "West and the rest"? Column 1 of Table 7.3 provides

Table 7.3: Percentage Change in Risk for Annual Involvement in a Militarized Dispute, 1951–92: The West versus Others

All variables at baseline values except:	(1)	(2)	(3)	(4)	(5)
WEST vs. REST equals 1	+27%				
WEST vs. ISLAM equals 1		+19%	−15%		
ISRAEL vs. ISLAM equals 1			+246		
WEST vs. ORTHODOX equals 1				+96%	
WEST vs. SINIC equals 1					+150%
ALLIES equals 1	−48	−50	−46	−50	−51
POWER RATIO increased by one standard deviation	−37	−37	−37	−39	−33
$DEMOC_L$ increased by one standard deviation	−27	−26	−28	−26	−25
$DEPEND_L$ increased by one standard deviation	−35	−35	−31	−36	−40
IGO increased by one standard deviation	−35	−35	−34	−37	−30

an initial answer. All the realist and Kantian variables continue to do well in predicting the pattern of conflict (all are significant at the .001 level except for DEPEND$_1$, which is at the .04 level). There also is some support for Huntington's view that the West is confronted by states from other civilizations. The risk of a militarized dispute for dyads that contain one Western state and one state from any other civilization is 27 percent greater than for all other dyads, though the effect is only marginally significant (.10).

In the remaining columns of Table 7.3, we break down this general "West versus the rest" distinction. In column 2, we use an indicator to assess the risk of violence between the West and Islam. There is a tendency for Western and Islamic states to fight more often, all other things being equal, but the impact—only 19 percent—is weaker than might be expected given the prominence with which these incidents have been reported. The West-versus-Islam effect, in any event, is weaker than any of the other influences in the model, and it is not statistically significant (.22 level). With a closer look, even this effect fades. For the reasons explained earlier, we included Israel in the West, though Huntington did not. In column 3 of Table 7.3, we show what happens when we remove from the West-versus-Islam group all the dyads that include Israel and reestimate the level of conflict between the West and Islam, controlling for the Arab-Israeli conflict separately. The risk of military conflict for pairs of states (excluding Israel) split between the West and Islam is actually less than for other pairs of states, though the effect is not statistically significant (.23 level). The effect reported in column 2 is, therefore, the result of the animosity between Israel and its Arab neighbors throughout the post–World War II period. Not surprisingly, the risk of conflict between Israel and an Islamic state is much higher than for other dyads: a 246 percent increase. The essence of the purported clash between the West and Islam is simply the familiar Arab-Israeli conflict. For other Western countries, there is no effect.

We did find two groups with which the West experienced significantly more frequent disputes. Column 4 in Table 7.4 shows that there was great conflict between the Western and Orthodox groups during the 1950–92 years, and column 5 indicates significantly greater interstate violence between the Western and Sinic countries. This is what the "West versus the rest" hypothesis reduces to. Rather than link either of these results to civilizational differences, however, it is much more plausible to interpret them as evidence of cold war conflict across the old iron curtain in Europe and the bamboo curtain in Asia.

Do Regional Hegemonies Reduce the Likelihood of Conflict?

Can a strong core state, or hegemon, keep the peace within its own civilization? Some civilizations have powerful cores—single states with the vast majority of economic strength and military capabilities. These include India, with about 99 percent of the resources of the tiny Hindu group; the Soviet Union, with 86 to 90 percent of the Orthodox group's capabilities during the cold war years; and China, usually with 70 percent or more of the Sinic group's capabilities. In the middle is the West, which might be characterized as having two cores, the United States and a Franco-German one. The U.S. core is much stronger than the continental one, usually possessing more than 40 percent of all Western capabilities.

The other four civilizations cannot be characterized as having strong cores. Thailand is the strongest member of the rather small Buddhist group; its capabilities as a fraction of those of the whole civilization were usually in the 40–65 percent range. But Thailand is not a strong state, and it is geographically situated at the intersection of two much more powerful civilizational hegemonies, those of China and India. The Thais, consequently, are in no position to be hegemonic. Brazil is by far the strongest power in the Latin American group, but it held only a modest amount (usually about 30 percent) of the capabilities of the region, confirming Huntington's view that the group lacks a strong core. He also characterizes the Islamic and African groups as lacking a core. Our simple measure of the capabilities held by the largest state in each civilization reflects that conclusion, too.

South Africa held more than 85 percent of the capabilities of all independent African states during the 1950s, but with the subsequent decolonization of Africa, that dropped quickly to about 40 percent. During the apartheid years, South Africa tried unsuccessfully to be a regional hegemon and to impose peace in its part of the continent. Turkey was the strongest Islamic country in most years, with about 20 percent of that group's capabilities, though occasionally Egypt or Iran slipped ahead. But with its internal cultural divisions, South Africa was hardly in a good position to lead the African states; nor, as a "torn" country, divided between two civilizations, was Turkey. Consequently, the share of militarily relevant capabilities held by South Africa or Turkey may exaggerate their strength as core states; in any case, they were already toward the low end of the scale. Using the share of capabilities held by the largest state seems, therefore, a reasonable way to gauge how strong any civilization's core is.

The idea that a strong state is able (and willing) to pacify interstate relations within its civilization can be assessed with a test similar to that reported in Table 7.2. To do this, we used the variables identifying each of the eight civilizations and the eight measures of each of the leading state's share of a civilization's total capabilities. For just three of the eight civilizations did we find any support at all for the proposition that a strong core reduces conflict, and the result was statistically significant for only the African group. For the other five civilizations, the strength of the hegemon was related to greater conflict, not less, and for three of them, the result was statistically significant. In short, a strong core state is not associated with more peaceful regional politics. If anything, the domination of a civilization by a strong core state makes the group more prone to internal conflict. This result is consistent with our discovery in Chapter 5 that hegemony in the international system as a whole does not reduce international conflict.

A related hypothesis, which we noted above, is that a democratic core state, acting as a benign sort of hegemon, can pacify relationships within its own civilization. Of the four civilizations that might be characterized as regional hegemonies, only two were led by states that were consistently democratic. America's leadership of NATO during the cold war, which relied fairly heavily on persuasion and consensus-building (Chernoff 1995), seems to fit Kupchan's hypothesis, accounting in part for peaceful relations within the West, but India's domination of the Hindu group had no peace-inducing effects. Of the two autocratic hegemonies, one—China's—produced a high rate of conflict within the civilization, and the other—the Soviet Union's influence over the Orthodox group—produced internal peace, though one would not describe the Soviet's influence as terribly benign. Thus, there seems to be no relationship between the democratic character of the largest state and its success in maintaining peace in its group. It is not that democracy is unimportant, but that hegemony is.

Does the Clash of Civilizations Grow over Time?

As noted earlier, Huntington's thesis is meant to apply more to recent times than to the more distant past.[17] In fact, he has suggested that the cold war suppressed civilizational conflicts: the East-West conflict was so crucial, involving the threat of a nuclear world war, that all other rivalries were forced into the background. It is possible, therefore, that our analyses of the years from 1950 through 1992 are distorted by the effects of the cold war and do not represent the pattern of conflict that should be expected as the cold war faded. To assess this possibility, we conducted four tests, each designed to reveal in a different way whether the effect of civilizational differences on the likelihood of dyadic conflict grew as the cold war ended.

Our first test involved simply noting the passage of time from 1950 to 1992 and determining statistically whether the effect of being split across a civilizational boundary, as indicated by the variable SPLIT in the specification in column 3 of Table 7.1, increased as the cold war waned.[18] In this test, we assumed that the intensity of the cold war declined steadily in the post–World War II period. What we found when we estimated this model, however, was that the danger of a dispute for a split dyad *decreased*, not increased, as time passed.

In our second test, we used the same basic technique but with a better measure of the intensity of the cold war. We know that the cold war did not decline uniformly from year to year. The end of the Korean War and the death of Stalin in 1953 had very big effects; in other years, there was little change in the status quo. And in some years, the intensity of the East-West confrontation increased. This occurred notably with the escalation of U.S. involvement in the war in Southeast Asia in the late 1960s and during the Reagan years, when the U.S. re-confronted the "evil empire." What we needed, therefore, was a measure that more accurately reflects the hostility of the Western and Soviet blocs. One measure that has

---

[17]Huntington says (14) that while a civilizational approach may help us understand global politics in the late twentieth century, that does not mean it would have been equally helpful in the mid-twentieth century. This does not identify a breakpoint or transition.

[18]We created an interactive variable consisting of the variable YEAR, which marks the passage of time from 1950 to 1992, times the variable SPLIT.

proved useful is the size of the United States' defense burden in each year: the United States' military expenditures divided by its gross domestic product. We used the same variable in Chapter 5 to measure the hegemon's sense of its own security. The rationale for using it to assess the intensity of the cold war is straightforward. When U.S. policy makers and the American people devoted more resources to the military, it was because they felt insecure due to the increased level of international tensions and increased risk of war. During the cold war, the source of that insecurity was primarily the Soviet bloc, of course. Consistent with subjective interpretations, the trend in the defense burden was downward over time, but there were dramatic rises as the wars in Korea and Vietnam escalated and in the 1980s. In the post–cold war era, the U.S. defense burden has declined sharply precisely because the military-political tensions associated with the East-West division have diminished so dramatically.

In our second test, then, we determined whether the effect of civilizational differences increased as the U.S. defense burden declined. We assumed in this test that the ratio of military expenditures to GDP is a good measure of the intensity of the cold war. The test is the same as the first one described above except that the U.S. defense burden replaces the simple indicator of time. Again the answer proved contrary to expectations: conflicts among split dyads became less common as the intensity of the cold war diminished. The cold war seems to have fanned interstate rivalries, not suppressed them.

Next, we determined whether the effect of civilizational differences was greater after two great transitional events, either of which may have demarcated the cold war period, when East-West rivalries prevailed, from a period when the clash of civilizations became important. The first possible turning point is 1979, the year of the Iranian revolution. Huntington marks this dramatic event, which was immediately followed by the seizure of the American embassy in Teheran and the onset of the hostage crisis, as a point when civilizational conflicts became more prominent. Iran was the first state to be ruled by Islamic fundamentalists, and the revolution there was quickly followed by strong fundamentalist movements throughout the region, most notably in Afghanistan and Algeria. Although the second event, the end of the cold war, did not occur until nearly a decade later, the rise of Islamic fundamentalism reduced the significance of the East-West divide, as the Soviets found out in the course of their war in Afghanistan in the early 1980s.

We started again with the basic specification indicated in column 3 of Table 7.1; that is, all of the realist and Kantian variables were included in our model of interstate conflict. First, we distinguished disputes that occurred in the years 1950–78 from those that came afterward in order to determine if the frequency of conflict for split dyads was greater after the Iranian revolution, as Huntington has suggested. In fact, the frequency of conflicts across civilizational boundaries dropped rather than rose after the Iranian revolution. Finally, we asked whether the dispute-inducing effect of the variable SPLIT became stronger after the cold war was effectively over. We used 1988 as the last year of the cold war, as in earlier chapters, and distinguished disputes that occurred in the years 1950–88 from those in the post–cold war period. Once again, disputes between civilizations became less common over time, dropping after the cold war ended. Many old conflicts were resolved or reduced—notably in Afghanistan, El Salvador, Cambodia, the Middle East, and Namibia—when the cold war ended and the superpowers no longer had an incentive to meddle in regional conflicts.

However one asks the question, the answer is the same: disputes across civilizational boundaries did not increase over time as the cold war waned. Quite the opposite is true. They became more infrequent. Our assessment of Huntington's thesis is consistent with the evidence from Chapter 5: during the cold war, the superpowers often instigated or magnified what would otherwise have been localized disputes. The cold war did not suppress conflict between civilizations. It exacerbated regional violence.

Are Civilizations the Prime Mover?

We consider one more question in this chapter. If civilizational differences are not an important cause of conflict directly, do they have important indirect effects through the variables that we have repeatedly found to be significant? Perhaps civilizational identity is the prime mover behind the important realist and Kantian influences in our analyses, explaining who allies with whom, who trades with whom, which countries share many common IGO memberships, and which have democratic political systems.

We used four paired sets of equations to explore this possibility, one set for each of the four variables that could plausibly be influenced by civilizational differences. The first equation in each pair was used to predict dyads' alliances, political systems, trade, or IGO memberships from our collection of variables: whether they were part of different civilizations (SPLIT), what distance they were from each other, whether they were contiguous, and whether one state was a major power, plus the three other variables (from among ALLIES, DEPEND, IGO, and $DEMOC_L$) not being predicted by that equation. Thus, allies, interdependence, IGOs, and democracy were explained one by one by all the other variables in the model in column 3 of Table 7.1. This tells how much of the variation in each variable can be accounted for by the bundle of other variables. The second equation in each pair used only SPLIT as a predictor, to see how much it could account for by itself. By comparing these two measures of the variance explained, we get an indication of how important civilizations are in accounting for each of the predicted variables. If civilizational differences can account for much of the variance in alliances, trade, IGOs, and political institutions, they might have important indirect influences on the likelihood of conflict. This test is very generous to the civilization hypothesis, because SPLIT is the only variable tested alone; therefore, it receives credit for any predictive power it really shares with all the other variables in the full specification.[19]

Alliances prove easiest to predict this way. The full equation explained 32 percent of the variance; or to state this in the usual terms, the R^2 was .32, meaning that all the variables together accounted for just under a third of the total variation in the incidence of alliances across all dyads. Pairs of states split by civilizations were less likely to become allied, and this effect was significant at the .001 level. Alliances are most common within Huntington's civilizational boundaries, but there are many exceptions. The Arab League is composed entirely of Islamic states, but the Warsaw Pact included states from both the Western and Orthodox civilizations. Most NATO members are Western, but Greece is Orthodox and Turkey is Islamic. Contiguity and IGO memberships were also strongly associated with the pattern of alliances. States are more apt to ally with neighbors than with more distant states, and alliances are often themselves IGOs and are often associated with other international organi-

---

[19]The variable SPLIT is rather strongly correlated with some of these variables, notably alliances and IGOs (.52 and .46, respectively).

zations. Shared democracy and the level of trade had little effect on the propensity of states to ally with one another. For the equation predicting alliances from SPLIT alone, the R^2 was .22. Comparing this to the .32 with the complete set of variables shows that civilizational identities are important in shaping states' alliance commitments, but most of the variation in alliance patterns remains unexplained.

Civilizational differences are much less successful in explaining the Kantian variables. The attempt to predict IGO memberships using all other variables worked well (producing an R^2 of .45), as would be expected from the analysis in Chapter 6. But the strongest contributions to the prediction were by, in order, democracy, alliances, and distance, with SPLIT in fourth place. With only SPLIT as a predictor, the R^2 dropped by more than half, to .21.

The full equation for explaining bilateral interdependence showed an R^2 of .26; this was accounted for primarily by IGOs, distance, and states' political systems, in that order. This, too, is broadly consistent with our more elaborate effort, in Chapter 6, to explain the pattern of bilateral trade. SPLIT was not significantly related to the economic importance of dyadic trade, and when it was the only variable in the equation, the R^2 was just .07. Interdependence, as manifested in decisions by states and entrepreneurs, does not closely correspond to the boundaries of civilizations.

The equations predicting shared democratic political systems explained even less of the variance. The R^2 for the equation with all the variables was only .03, mostly attributable to their joint IGO memberships. With SPLIT alone as the predictor, the R^2 was .00. Civilizational differences are not useful at all in predicting joint democracy. There can be no indirect effect, therefore, on the incidence of disputes through this variable.[20] Democracies can be found in all of Huntington's civilizations.

To summarize this set of results, civilizational borders do play a substantial, though limited, role in shaping the pattern of alliances: SPLIT alone accounts for more than a fifth of the variance in the variable ALLIES. Many allies are from the same cultural group, but there are also numerous exceptions. Civilizational boundaries also affect memberships in international organizations but less significantly. They have little im-

---

[20]Earlier evidence that culture is little related to political similarities, trade, and IGO memberships can be found in Russett 1967.

pact on interdependence or democracy. Overall, being split between civilizations does not exert enough influence on the Kantian variables to support a claim that it is a major indirect influence on who engages in militarized disputes. Civilizations do not make the difference; the Kantian and realist influences do.

The Insignificance of Civilizational Differences

In *The Clash of Civilizations*, Huntington argues plausibly that fundamental cultural identities play an important role in shaping interstate relations. He bolsters his argument with illustrative historical examples but does not subject it to scientific tests. In this chapter, we assessed the clash of civilizations systematically, using a variety of empirical tests with data over the period 1950–92. These analyses of states' involvement in militarized disputes during the post–World War II era show that differences in civilization tell us little about the likelihood that two states will become involved in conflict. Knowing whether a pair of states is split across civilizational boundaries does not improve our ability to predict whether their relations will be marked by violence beyond what we know on the basis of the realist and Kantian influences. In our complete model, each of these variables is significantly related to the likelihood of a dispute, but civilizational differences are not. Moreover, states within four of the eight civilizations fought more among themselves than did states split across civilizations.

Nor is Huntington's warning of impending conflict between the West and the rest of the world supported by the evidence. Conflicts involving the West and other states in the post–World War II years primarily reflect the cold war rivalry between East and West across the iron curtain in Europe and the bamboo curtain in Asia. There is no evidence of a clash between the Western states and Islam except as it involves Israel and the Islamic, particularly Arab, states. The dominance of a civilization by a strong core state, democratic or not, does not inhibit conflict within a civilization. Conflicts between civilizations became relatively less common, not more so, as the cold war waned. The evidence clearly indicates that the cold war exacerbated regional disputes, rather than suppressing them. Thus, there is reason to hope that the violence that worried Huntington will become less common as the cold war recedes into history.

Finally, civilizational similarities and differences help predict alliance patterns and states' joint memberships in IGOs, but they make little contribution to understanding countries' political institutions or their commercial interactions. Consequently, there is no reason to believe that they have major indirect effects on the likelihood of conflict through these variables.[21]

In *The Clash of Civilizations*, Huntington challenged policy makers and scholars to consider the role that basic cultural identity plays in international relations. We can be grateful that it is more benign than he suggested, because civilizations represent a highly aggregated form of human cultural characteristics that would be difficult to alter. Policies adopted over the course of a few years could not be expected to change the nature of civilizations that have evolved over centuries. Fortunately, the evidence we have assembled strongly indicates that national leaders need not attempt such a Herculean task. Civilizations do not define the fault lines along which international conflict occurs. More relevant are the Kantian and realist influences. Common bonds of democracy, economic interdependence, and international organizations unite many states, but separate them from others. The realist influences are more important for states that do not share Kantian ties. For them, realpolitik still determines the incidence of conflict. Consequently, policy makers should focus on what they can do: peacefully extending democracy, economic interdependence, and IGOs to the parts of the world still excluded. These are the more important and more malleable determinants of interstate relations. Strengthening them can mitigate what might otherwise appear to be clashes of civilizations.

The absence of significant cultural conflict is encouraging for another reason. A sense of shared identity among peoples who govern themselves democratically constitutes a form of in-group feeling, one that might fos-

[21]It is important to identify some of what is not explored here. The empirical analyses necessarily end with 1992. We do not address whether some kinds of conflicts are more intense with more casualties, although we do take into account the duration of disputes by including all years in which there was conflict and the breadth of disputes by identifying all dyads in multistate conflicts. We do not consider acts of terrorism by nonstate actors, a subject to which Huntington devotes great attention. Nor do we systematically investigate the role of civilizational factors in conflicts wholly within states, though we do discuss others analysts' findings. These and other matters await further research.

ter animosity toward those who govern themselves differently. International commerce and free-market institutions might have similar effects. This is the potentially dangerous aspect of the Kantian prescription for peace. But if such a strong cultural factor as civilizational identity has so little impact on the probability of conflict between pairs of states, perhaps the sense of identity that emerges from a shared political system or important economic relations will not be threatening either. What we have in common with others need not be a threat to peaceful relations with those outside the group.

Nor is Kant's prescription for "perpetual peace" justified only by shared liberal values of tolerance and the nonviolent resolution of conflict. Cultural explanations of the liberal peace are but part of the justification for confidence that democracy, interdependence, and consultation in IGOs can bring about a more peaceful world. Rather, the Kantian view is promising precisely because it does not depend solely on intangible values, norms, and shared identity. It is equally supported by the self-interest of citizens and policy makers alike. If it is in the interest of political elites not to fight unnecessary wars so that they may retain political office, and if commercial interests have a stake in maintaining and promoting the ties that make them richer, they will do so. Peace does not depend upon moral conversion, therefore, but is ultimately derived from calculations of self-interest. Civilizations play little role in this.

We close with another verse from the poetic review quoted at the beginning of the chapter (Tipson 1997, 166):

> Networks and computing make the difference fundamental,
> By skewing and redoing social bonds—and governmental.
> Since entity identity is much more problematic,
> Crash-courses in world politics should not be so dogmatic.

8

The Kantian Peace in the

Twenty-First Century

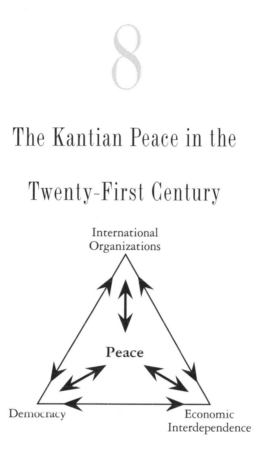

In 1795, Immanuel Kant contended that international peace could be established on a foundation of three elements: republican constitutions, "cosmopolitan law" embodied in free trade and economic interdependence, and international law and organizations. Kant's vision is remarkable for several reasons. There were very few democracies in the world in the late 1700s and no international organizations as we now know them. There was trade, of course, but most countries followed mercantilist principles, subordinating the economy to the interests of the state and seeking economic independence when possible. Kant's interest in the problem of war is in itself noteworthy, because he believed that peace—a "perpetual peace," not just a lull in the fighting between wars—was possible. Most people then, as many do now, thought that war was inherent in human nature, but Kant proposed that a stable, long-lasting peace could be achieved. He believed the world would eventually become weary of war and that democracy, interdependence, and international organizations could constrain states from resorting to military force. Kant and the other classical liberals were not idealists. They accepted that not all wars could be eliminated but believed the frequency of violence between states could be substantially reduced. Nor did they think that peace depended upon a great moral conversion. Peace was possible not because people everywhere would finally begin to love their neighbors as themselves, but because emerging institutions made war contrary to people's self-interest.

Kant's bold theory was largely deductive and speculative. But in this book, we have presented a great deal of evidence that he was right: democracy, interdependence, and intergovernmental organizations sharply reduce the likelihood of militarized disputes and increase the prospects for peaceful interstate relations. We have tested Kant's theses using social scientific methods, something that has only recently become possible. Kant's theses can now be evaluated systematically because the triangle of institutions that Kant discussed has come into existence in substantial parts of the world. History, specifically the years 1885–1992, can be used as a laboratory to assess the peacefulness of democratic, interdependent states linked by IGOs. Our research is also made possible because voluminous information about this historical period has become available in a form necessary for statistical analysis. In addition, the statistical procedures, software, and computing capacity necessary for analyzing this massive amount of information have been developed. Our data would be useless were it not for the technological revolution that has made computers so prodigious and so cheap. For these reasons, it is only now possible, 205 years after Kant published *Perpetual Peace*, to evaluate his theory scientifically.

In this final chapter, we review our principal findings and present our prognosis for international relations in the twenty-first century. We believe that the chances for peace are good, probably better than at any time in history. The likelihood of war between two great powers in the near future is small. How many other times during past centuries could one have said that? Powerful historical forces are pushing the world away from the brink of war. Yet peace is hardly inevitable. Rather, our findings and their implications for the future should encourage us to do what we can today to insure that the Kantian peace is strengthened where it now operates and spread to areas still gripped by realpolitik.

Success in widening further the zone of stable peace depends significantly on the successful integration of Russia and China into the Kantian system. Looking to the future requires, therefore, that we consider how the West should deal with these powerful states. Imagination will be required to meet the challenges posed by Russia's recovery from its current weakness and China's continued growth, but already elements of democracy and interdependent economic relations are being extended to these states, and their involvement in international organizations with the West is increasing. These processes are likely to continue for the same reasons that liberalism has spread to so many other countries in the post–World War II period. Integrating Russia and China into the Kantian system would not only reduce further the danger of war among the major powers—a conflict that would inevitably engulf many other states as well—but also would allow for the extension of the zone of peace to developing countries. It is in the so-called third world where the specter of interstate conflict is greatest now and in the foreseeable future.

The Evidence for a Kantian Peace

Kant began his theorizing with attention to democracy. It is in many ways the linchpin of his analysis. He was confident that democracies would be more peaceful than autocracies for a simple reason: in a democracy, those who would bear the costs of a war are the ones who decide whether it shall be fought. As Kant put it in *Perpetual Peace* ([1795] 1970, 100):

> If . . . consent of the citizens is required to decide whether or not war is to be declared, it is very natural that they will have great hesitation in embarking on so dangerous an enterprise. For this would mean calling down on themselves all the miseries of war, such as doing the fighting themselves, supplying the costs of the war from their own resources, painfully making good the ensuing devastation, and, as the crowning evil, having to take upon themselves a burden of debt which will embitter peace itself and which can never be paid off on account of the constant threat of new wars.

It is evident from this passage that Kant did not believe that the citizens of democratic states were necessarily more moral than other people, just that they had greater control over the policies of their country and would make careful, self-interested calculations in deciding whether to fight. He was confident that many wars that otherwise would occur would not withstand the careful scrutiny of citizens in a democracy.

On the other hand, when a state is not democratic,

it is the simplest thing in the world to go to war. For the head of state is not a fellow citizen, but the owner of the state, and a war will not force him to make the slightest sacrifice so far as his banquets, hunts, pleasure palaces and court festivals are concerned. He can thus decide on war, without any significant reason, as a kind of amusement, and unconcernedly leave it to the diplomatic corps (who are always ready for such purposes) to justify the war for the sake of propriety. (Kant [1795] 1970, 100)

Kant's description of the contrast between democracies and autocracies brings the experience of Iraq vividly to mind. While Iraqi citizens suffer tremendous deprivation, Saddam Hussein continues to live in luxury, even building new palaces for his enjoyment despite the disastrous war with Iran in the 1980s and his defeat in the 1991 Gulf War.

Kant emphasized the importance of the sovereignty of the people in reducing the incidence of war. Citizens in a democratic state can influence governmental policy directly, through public opinion, or indirectly, through their representatives. The regular occurrence of elections is obviously important in this process. It is the mechanism that forces government to consider the will of the people. A division of responsibility in the declaration and prosecution of war is also beneficial. That is why the U.S. Constitution gives Congress the power to declare war and the authority to fund the military. It is also why Congress in 1973, following the Vietnam War, passed the War Powers Act. This law was intended to strengthen congressional influence over the president when military means short of war are being considered.

The existence of a loyal but independent political opposition not only limits the ability of a democratic government to wage a capricious, ill-advised war, it also enhances the ability of the state to signal that it is really willing to use force when important interests are truly threatened. When the opposition expresses a widespread popular belief that fundamental interests are at stake, its support for any threat to use the military means that the government cannot then easily retreat. Democratic leaders will not lightly risk the political consequences of backing down or fighting a losing battle, and they cannot override the wishes of the people once a line in the sand has been drawn. The existence of a vocal opposition thus reduces the danger of war by miscalculation. If, however, the opposition rallies against the use of force, any threat by the government loses credibility in the eyes of the opposing country—it is apt to be only a bluff

(Schultz 2000). The limited ability of a president or prime minister to determine policy not only constrains him or her from using military force, it also makes a commitment to maintain the peace more credible, because this policy, too, once adopted by popular sanction and the action of diverse governmental bodies, is not easily reversed.

In addition to structural or institutional constraints, recent theories call attention to the cultural basis for the democratic peace and to the ability of democracies to commit themselves to international agreements. A culture that emphasizes the nonviolent resolution of domestic conflict encourages a state to employ such methods in its external relations, and indeed, there is empirical evidence that governments that use force against their own people are more likely to use the military against their neighbors (Rummel 1997). All these forces for peace operate most effectively in relations between democratic states. Kant did not believe that democracies would never fight, only that they would avoid unnecessary conflict. In their relations with nondemocratic states willing to use force, democracies, too, will resort to the older, more terrible logic of realism.

The evidence we have presented indicates clearly that there is a separate peace among democratic states. Even controlling for the pacifying effects of interdependence and joint memberships in intergovernmental organizations, we found that two democracies are 33 percent less likely than the average dyad to become involved in a militarized dispute. This is a conservative estimate of the pacific benefits of democracy, because we have also shown that democracies are more likely to trade with one another and to join the same international organizations. Democracy has, therefore, important indirect benefits through these other Kantian elements. We have also seen that the risk of conflict declines as the proportion of democracies in the international system increases. As their number grows, democracies seem able to influence international norms and institutions, thereby affecting the probability that force will be used even by states that are not themselves particularly democratic. This influence is also plausible because democracies are more likely to win their wars than autocracies are. Consequently, autocracies must be concerned about the security implications of weakening themselves in war, whether the war is with democracies or other autocracies. They must become increasingly careful as the number of democracies in the system grows. This systemic influence is another indirect benefit of democracy for peace.

The strong support we have reported for the democratic peace is consistent with our previous work and with the great majority of research done in recent years, some of which we reviewed in Chapter 2. Over the years, the peacefulness of democracies has been subjected to a great variety of tests. In an important recent article, Bennett and Stam (2000) estimate the effect of democracy on the likelihood of militarized disputes using twenty-four different statistical models. The results are consistent with the democratic peace in all of them. Our analyses show not only that democracies do not fight other democracies but that they are more peaceful on average, as individual states, than are autocracies. This contravenes the conventional wisdom that, individually, democracies fight as often as nondemocracies do. But the greater peacefulness of democracies in general follows from the fact that the risk of conflict goes down or remains constant if an autocracy is replaced by a democracy. A democracy's relations with other democratic states are dramatically more peaceful, while the danger of war with autocracies is unchanged. Previous efforts to measure the peacefulness of democracies missed this finding because they failed to consider adequately other influences on the probability of conflict.

Democracies act according to realist principles in their dealings with autocracies, but they are no more likely to fight with an autocracy than is another autocratic state. This is important. It means that a newly established democracy will be at peace with its democratic neighbors, and being democratic will not make it more prone to fight autocratic neighbors than if it had remained nondemocratic. We reported additional evidence in Chapter 3 that the process of democratization does not generally increase the likelihood of conflict, as some have feared. It is the *level* of democracy that influences the likelihood of conflict, not how recently these political institutions were established. Thus, if policies designed to promote democracy around the world lead promptly to the consolidation of democratic institutions and practices, there is no reason, even in the short term, to expect an increase in the frequency of violence between countries.

Interest in the pacific benefits of economic interdependence preceded even Kant's treatise on perpetual peace. In the early seventeenth century, the French philosopher Emeric Crucé argued that wars arose from international misunderstandings and the domination of society by the warrior class but that both causes of interstate violence could be ameliorated by commerce: trade and investment create common interests for commercial partners; increase the prosperity and political power of the peaceful, productive members of society; and encourage mutual understanding. Though over the years many philosophers, historians, economists, and politicians have expressed confidence in the conflict-reducing consequences of international commerce, the British liberals deserve particular credit for developing and promoting this argument. David Ricardo, for example, wrote in 1817:

> Under a system of perfectly free (international) commerce, each country naturally devotes its capital and labour to such employments as are most beneficial to each. This pursuit of individual advantage is admirably connected with the universal good of the whole. By stimulating industry, by rewarding ingenuity, and by using most efficaciously the peculiar powers bestowed by nature, it distributes labour most effectively and most economically while, by increasing the general mass of production, it diffuses general benefit, and binds together, by one common tie of interest and intercourse, the universal society of nations. (Quoted in Cole 1999, 185)

As with democracy, the pacific benefits of interdependence do not depend on people everywhere becoming convinced that war is immoral. Instead, the classical liberals emphasized that the "pursuit of individual advantage," as Ricardo put it, leads to actions that link individuals and nations by interdependent ties of mutual benefit. Interdependence increases the prospects for peace because individuals can generally be expected to pursue their interests rationally, and it is not in the interest of one state to fight another with which it has important economic relations.

While liberals emphasize the role of reason and self-interest in explaining the pacific benefits of interdependence, the constructivist school of international relations calls attention to the collateral benefits of commerce for people's understanding of one another. Trade and foreign investment serve as media for communication between nations on a broad range of matters beyond their specific commercial relations, thereby exposing people to the ideas and perspectives of others on a range of issues. These communications, too, are apt to be important channels for averting interstate conflict. As interdependence grows, it contributes to the creation of a security community (Deutsch et al. 1957), in which shared values make a resort to force unimaginable. As we saw in Chapter 6, trade also encourages the development of international law and organizations. This occurs for the same reason that such institutions arise in domestic societies: they are needed to regulate and manage commercial relations. In a variety of ways, then, international trade and investment are expected to increase the likelihood of peace.

While Crucé advocated free trade as a means to promote peace long before any state had become truly democratic, contemporary social scientists have paid much more attention to the pacific benefits of democracy. They have been relatively slow to appreciate the important role that interstate commerce, too, can play. Much of the explanation for this can be traced to the effect of World War I on the liberal view. Just before that war, Sir Norman Angell published a book called *The Great Illusion* (1911). He argued that the most important states of Europe had become so interdependent that war could no longer serve their economic interests. Angell's book was well received, especially because many feared there might be a war between England and Germany. Indeed, the two countries were engaged in a dangerous naval arms race. *The Great Illusion* was translated into seventeen languages and sold over a million copies. Many came to believe that Angell had proven that war was impossible. He had not, as the events of 1914–18 soon demonstrated. Although the states of Europe were more interdependent than they had ever been, a terrible war still erupted. It was not a limited war of the type Europe had experienced on several occasions since the defeat of Napoleon in 1815; it was the "Great War."

Angell did *not* argue that interdependence made war impossible. It was not war that was the great illusion. Rather, it was the belief, then common, that war could serve national economic interests: that a state, by successful military action, could secure new sources of raw materials or access to new markets, or could seize territory from a bordering state and incorporate its wealth. The tremendous financial cost of World War I—not to mention the loss of ten million lives—and the collapse of the international economy in the Great Depression proved that Angell had not been mistaken. It *is* an illusion to believe that when states are interdependent, force can be used without incurring economic loss: the more interdependent the states, the greater the cost of military conflict. That was what Angell had tried to say. He published *The Great Illusion* to educate Europeans regarding the nature of their interdependence. Angell hoped to show that war in the modern world was unprofitable and, thereby, to avert the war that so many feared. For his efforts, Angell was awarded the Nobel Peace Prize for 1933.[1]

Our analyses show that Kant, Ricardo, Angell, and the other classical liberals were correct. The use of military force does adversely affect states' commercial relations. We showed in Chapter 6 that military disputes reduce the level of bilateral trade. Interstate conflict does have economic costs. Some of the gains of trade are lost even at low levels of violence. The logical consequence is that states will try to avoid conflict when their commercial relations are economically important. Our analyses show consistently that this, too, is true. As we saw in Chapter 5, two states with a relatively high level of bilateral trade are 33 percent less likely to become involved in a dispute than are states with an average level of interdependence, all other things being equal. The results we report in Chapter 4 show that this benefit is not limited to states of roughly equal size. Asymmetry in the economic importance of trade, as is characteristic of the commercial relations of a large and a small country, does not reduce the benefits of trade or provoke military conflict, as many have feared. Furthermore, states that are open to the global economy are more peaceful than average, even controlling for the level of their bilateral interdependence. A state that trades a lot with any country or group of countries—that is open economically—is constrained from using force, even against states with which its commercial ties are limited. Indeed, as shown in Chapter 4, the total trade-to-GDP ratio has nearly as large a beneficial effect on the prospects for peace as the bilateral trade-to-GDP ratio does.

The results we have reported regarding the pacific benefits of economic interdependence are consistent with the consensus that is now emerging (Rosecrance 1986; Mueller 1989; McMillan 1997; Barbieri and Schneider 1999). Bennett and Stam (2000), in their independent examination of the Kantian peace, report that economically important trade is more frequently related to a reduction in dyadic conflict than is any other variable in their analyses except democracy and geographical contiguity. Interdependence is significantly related to the incidence of conflict, as often as is the realists' favorite variable, the balance of power, and more often than is being allied. The substantive benefits of interdependence are among the largest in Bennett and Stam's analyses.

After surveying the consequences of World War I, many concluded that

---

[1]Our discussion of Angell benefited from reading Miller 1986.

Angell was right in believing that wars are costly but wrong in concluding that these costs would have a significant deterrent effect on the use of military force. Alfred Thayer Mahan (quoted in Miller 1986, 38–39, also 79), an American admiral and military strategist of the early twentieth century, argued that nations fight for "ambition, self-respect, resentment of injustice, sympathy with the oppressed, hatred of oppression," even if substantial economic losses are apt to be incurred. Certainly, it is true that nations fight for a variety of reasons and sometimes knowingly accept a high price in treasure and human life in pursuit of their objectives. Economic interdependence (like democracy) will not prevent all conflicts. No one believes they will. But our results indicate clearly that the skeptics are wrong: the likelihood of conflict declines as its economic cost increases. This important finding will have to withstand the sort of detailed examination to which the democratic peace has been subjected over the past twenty years, but the results thus far are very encouraging.

Finally, we considered the consequences of shared memberships in intergovernmental organizations on the risk that two states will become involved in a militarized dispute. States that are in close and frequent contact, like individuals, inevitably disagree on what should be done, who should bear costs incurred in mutually beneficial enterprises, or what is the fair division of joint gains. They experience conflict in the broadest meaning of that word. This is true of the United States and Canada, the United States and Japan or Europe, and among the states of the European Union. What is needed are nonviolent means of resolving conflict when it does arise. Kant suggested that a loose federation of sovereign (but interdependent) states could aid in preserving the peace.

The literature on the contribution of particular international organizations to world peace is vast, but there are few social scientific studies of how IGOs in general affect interstate relations. Do dense networks of intergovernmental organizations reduce the incidence of interstate violence? Many international relations scholars believe that international organizations are relatively unimportant because they lack the means of enforcing their decisions. Whatever authority IGOs have, they argue, is simply derivative of the power of their members. In fact, few international organizations can force compliance with their directives or with international law by coercive means; nevertheless, they frequently perform many other functions associated with governments. They may encourage cooperation by facilitating consultation and coordination among their members. They may create norms that make noncompliance with their decisions politically difficult. More centralized IGOs can impose various economic sanctions: allow states to impose countervailing tariffs, freeze assets, refuse to grant loans, prohibit commercial aviation or shipping, for instance. In Chapter 5, we briefly discussed six functions international organizations can perform that aid states in resolving their disagreements peacefully.

Our analyses indicate that a dense network of IGOs does reduce the incidence of conflict. A pair of states that shares membership in a substantial number of international organizations is 24 percent less likely than average to have a dispute, holding other influences constant. Other research we have conducted (Oneal and Russett 1999c), as well as the recent analyses of Bennett and Stam (2000), shows that the pacific benefits of intergovernmental organizations are smaller than those of democracy or economic interdependence. And the estimated effect of IGOs is more dependent on the precise form of the test. It is important to note, however, that evidence for the constraining effect of IGOs is strongest for what we have called the politically relevant dyads—contiguous pairs of states and pairs that include at least one major power—and that these dyads account for the great majority of interstate disputes. It may be, too, that the constructive role played by IGOs is captured in some statistical analyses by the measures of democracy and trade. We know that democracies and economically interdependent states are involved together in more IGOs: cooperation seems to grow naturally out of the affinity liberal states have for one another. The pacific benefits of international organizations may be largely derivative of these more fundamental liberal factors. This does not mean IGOs are unimportant. If they were, liberal states would not create and join them, but the contribution of intergovernmental organizations to maintaining the peace in some tests may largely be subsumed by the measures of democracy and interdependence.

The summary of our findings thus far understates the pacific contribution of the Kantian system because we have emphasized the independent contributions of each of its three elements. In the real world, one Kantian influence does not usually increase while the others are held constant. Rather, as Kant anticipated, democracies tend to be interdependent and members of the same IGOs. There are also important feedback loops connecting trade and international organizations. And it may be that economically important trade opens up societies to external influences, making it hard to sustain autocratic rule. This last possible link is outside the scope of our current research, but it does seem consistent with the experiences of Eastern Europe and even China. Good things do often go together. It is important, therefore, to recall that the likelihood of a dispute drops by 71 percent if all the Kantian influences are increased simultaneously. This clearly shows that, as Kant was bold to say, peace is possible.

In our view, peace is not only possible, it is becoming more and more likely. The prognosis for the future of international relations is good because democracy is likely to spread and interdependence to increase. The reasons are simple: people prefer self-government to authoritarian rule, and they would rather enjoy the prosperity that comes from interdependence than remain isolated and poor. But if these long-term influences are to have the opportunity to have their beneficial effects, the West and other members of the Kantian system will need to deal successfully with the challenge posed by the inevitable recovery of Russia and the continued growth of China. These countries will have to be integrated into the Kantian system. We now turn our attention to this challenge.

Incorporating Russia and China into the Kantian System

The prospects for peace in the coming decades depend upon the success of the West in maintaining good relations with Russia and China. How can the Kantian community manage the demise of a cold war superpower—the Soviet Union—and the resurrection of a smaller but still powerful Russia, a state that has been a major power for centuries? And how can the Kantian states cope with the rise of a new power, China, whose population of over a billion people gives it enormous potential? The short answer to both questions is that the West must do what it can to promote democracy in these countries, engage them in mutually beneficial ties of interdependence, and involve them in a network of intergovernmental organizations that can aid in resolving nonviolently the disagreements that will inevitably arise. These general prescriptions for policy follow obviously from the theories we have discussed and the evidence presented for them. Here we take an unconventional look at the role NATO could play in this process.[2] We argue that the decision to ex-

---

[2]The middle sections of this chapter draw heavily on an earlier article (Russett and Stam 1998).

pand the North Atlantic alliance into Eastern Europe makes it desirable eventually to include Russia as well, finally ending the division of Europe created by the cold war. Further expansion of collective security arrangements must eventually include China. This can increase the prospects for liberal reform there, reduce the risk of conflict among the major powers, and aid in extending the zone of stable peace to developing countries, particularly in Africa and Asia.

For a combination of reasons, including domestic politics, organization inertia, and sloppy strategic analysis (Goldgeier 1998), NATO has expanded up to, but not yet beyond, the boundaries of the former Soviet Union. NATO members now are considering another increase in its membership, but any expansion that excludes Russia endangers liberal reforms there and ignores the West's biggest future security problem: the possibility of a global power transition with China later in this century. In that context, Russia matters because of the potential power of a Russian-Chinese alliance. The need to prevent such an alignment should be central to all thinking about the long-term future of NATO.

Russia needs to be integrated into the Kantian community in the short run, and in the longer run, the community's web of transactions and institutions should also include the countries of Asia, especially China. The European Union can play a role in this process, but neither Russia nor China for the foreseeable future will meet the EU's high standards for membership. It will be some time before democracy and free markets are firmly established in these countries. Even if they were, the size of Russia and China, their low per capita incomes, and their backward economic sectors would make the cost of admitting them into the EU prohibitive. NATO offers an alternative means of drawing these powers into the Kantian system. Admittedly, expanding the Western security system to incorporate Russia, and then using it to create a collective security system in which China is integrally involved, faces formidable obstacles. It is nevertheless worthwhile, as a thought experiment at least, to consider whether these suggestions are as fanciful as they may at first seem.

Despite powerful objections to the first round of NATO expansion in 1999,[3] the Czech Republic, Hungary, and Poland are now members of the North Atlantic alliance. Despite the official statements of Western governments, that expansion was directed against the danger of a resur-

[3]See Mandelbaum 1995; Brown 1995; Kugler 1996; Dean 1997; McGwire 1997.

gent, nationalist Russia. It had no compelling purpose otherwise, and it created significant new dangers: reviving Russian fears of Western intentions, strengthening Russian militarists and nationalists, and inducing greater instability in Russian domestic politics and foreign policy. The immediate result was greater Russian intransigence on arms control issues. Implementation of the START treaty, designed to make dramatic reductions in strategic nuclear arsenals, has been delayed indefinitely, and the Russian military has reversed its long-standing commitment not to be the first to use nuclear weapons against conventional attack.

Further expansion by NATO into Eastern Europe without a satisfactory agreement with Russia may actually create a threat that is now absent (Arbatov 1996; Kitfield 1996). If that happens, the West could find itself confronted by a hostile and isolated Russia. Even worse, Russia might form an alliance with China. Such an alliance could be attractive if these two powers see themselves as excluded from a Western community seeking to establish hegemony over the international system. If Russia can make continued progress in democratization and in building a market economy, further NATO expansion should not take place without it. This would play an important role in the larger strategy of drawing Russia into the Kantian system.

NATO could secure the integrity of the boundaries of the East European states by incorporating Russia within the alliance, rather than by keeping this important country out and making an implicit military threat. NATO secures its members' borders from possible challenge within the alliance as well as from external threats. From a longer perspective, one must ask not only what the Russians might contribute to NATO but also what NATO could do for Russia, and what the Russians would then not do for the Chinese. A future round of NATO expansion that incorporated Russia into NATO and other Western institutions would eliminate Russian concern about encirclement and address the long-term problem of growing Chinese power. It would also facilitate Russia's becoming a normal democratic state within the Euro-Atlantic community (Goodby 1998). That would in itself contribute substantially to the prospects for peace.

Russia's Options

Continued expansion of NATO without Russia runs the risk of creating a severe security dilemma. What choices are available to Russia as it faces an alliance that is far stronger than Russia itself is or can hope to be? One possible reaction would be *bandwagoning*.[4] A state may try to cooperate with those that might threaten it. This is, in essence, the policy that Mikhail Gorbachev began and that led to the end of the cold war. To date, Russia's leaders have largely followed Gorbachev's precedent of co-operating with the West. If Russia were integrated into NATO, this process would be reinforced; if it is not, other more dangerous alternatives become more likely. Russia's second option would be to *hide*, to withdraw into heavily armed isolation. An isolated Russia would be highly dependent on its nuclear weapons and is apt to perceive itself as being surrounded by enemies: Western, Islamic, and Asian. A xenophobic Russia with an economy once again autarkic and burdened by militarism would almost certainly revert to autocracy. This outcome is surely not in the interests of the West. Russians are not likely to see isolation as a viable option for the long run, however.

If NATO will not take Russia in, Russia's third choice would be to look eastward for a partner with which to *balance* the West. Expanding NATO without Russia could lead to a rapprochement between Russia and China and even to a formal military alliance. True, there is a long history of trouble in Russian-Chinese relations, and the Chinese leadership is not confident that Russia has the power or political stability to be an effective ally (Repko 1996; Rozman 1999). Such an alliance would experience real friction, but to protect their interests, states will find allies where they can, when they must. Russian leaders have never liked to face adversaries on two fronts. To avoid this, they might turn to China. A China-Russia alliance would recreate the bipolar world that Richard Nixon deftly shattered with his opening to China in 1972.

An alliance would bring major benefits to both sides. For Russia, China's vast population and expanding economy would provide a weighty counterbalance to NATO. For China, a Russian partner with industry and great natural resources would be a big catch. Russia's military tech-

[4]Snyder 1990, 1994; Christensen and Snyder 1990; Schweller 1994; Schroeder 1994.

nology, while inferior to that of the West, remains the most modern part of the Russian economy and a potential catalyst for military development. In virtually every category, Russia's capabilities are superior to China's. In submarines and surface ships, missiles and aircraft, communications and nuclear weapons, the Russians have much to offer a large and increasingly wealthy state. Easy access to Russian technology would hasten Chinese military modernization.

Warning signs of Sino-Russian military cooperation have already appeared. In the late 1990s, for the first time since the 1960s Russia exported advanced military technologies to China. It began by agreeing to sell China advanced SU-27 fighter planes and to build a production line in Shenyang to make more. This signals warmer relations because the SU-27 is a transcontinental fighter, and if China were hostile, Moscow would be within its range. Russia later announced the sale of two advanced cruise missile warships and opened talks on the possible sale of ballistic missiles. On the diplomatic front, Russia has flirted on and off with Beijing. In December 1996, President Yeltsin and Chinese prime minister Li Peng announced a package of large troop cuts on their borders, trade agreements, and arms deals. In an April 1997 meeting, Yeltsin and Chinese president Jiang Zemin called for a "multipolar" world in contrast to a unipolar one where, in Yeltsin's terms, "someone else is going to dictate conditions" (Joint Statement 1997; also Shinkarenko and Malkina 1996). In December 1998, then Russian prime minister Yevgeny Primakov called for a Russia-China-India triangle to counteract NATO (BBC Summary 1998).

How to Avoid the Dangers of a Russia-China Alliance

Neither Russia nor China constitutes a serious threat to the West at present. In the long run, it is China, not Russia, that presents the greatest challenge to the Kantian community. We do not mean to imply that the Chinese government's intentions are other than defensive: to secure the country's territorial integrity, including but not exceeding its historic claims. But the period of transition in global leadership from one great power to another is marked by the potential for instability. If the rising power is dissatisfied with its place in the international system, there is the danger of a great war (Kugler and Lemke 2000; Lemke and Kugler 1996;

DiCicco and Levy 1999). As we saw in the analyses presented in Chapter 5, the two world wars occurred as Great Britain's power relative to its rivals declined. The rise of a dissatisfied challenger creates dangers even if the challenger is not expansionist. Fears, uncertainties, and miscalculations provide danger enough.

Two complementary strategies—one realist and one Kantian—can together manage the rising power of China. The realist element is for the United States and its allies to maintain a favorable balance of power for as long as possible. A preponderance of power deters the initiation of conflict, as we have seen. Deterrence can work, as long as the West's capabilities exceed China's by a substantial margin. Integrating Russia into NATO would augment the power of the alliance. In the long term, the greatest constraint on a state's power is population (Organski and Organski 1961). With 146 million people, Russia poses no fundamental danger to NATO's nearly 800 million population, but it would help balance China's 1.3 billion citizens. The challenge posed by China arises not just from its size but also from the rapidity of its economic growth. Until recently, its per capita gross domestic product is reported to have grown by 8 percent per year. If this were to continue and NATO grew at only 2 percent per year, the Chinese would reach parity in 2030.[5] A power transition within thirty years is unlikely, however. There is no historical precedent—Japan included—for a country to sustain economic growth as high as 8 percent over so long a period, and China's growth has slowed every year since 1996. Certainly, China will suffer huge environmental problems at its current rate of growth (Esty 1997; Smil 1997; Wen-Yuan and Harris 1996). Economic growth in the West may exceed 2 percent as well. Nevertheless, China's economic potential in the long run is great. Whether it will approach the West in thirty years or only after a longer period is not the real issue. China is destined to pose a challenge to the Western-dominated international system. If the situation is not managed properly, it could have as much mischievous leverage in world politics as the conflict with the Soviet Union did at the height of the cold war. A China aligned with Russia would increase this risk.

A pure strategy of deterrence, necessitating at least implicit threats and

[5]These estimates are at purchasing power parity; calculations based on exchange rates show the Chinese economy to be much smaller. The 8 percent growth rate for China may be exaggerated (Segal 2000).

military containment, is fraught with danger. It can intensify underlying disagreements and increase China's commitment eventually to force fundamental change in the international system (Huth and Russett 1993). Deterrence—especially nuclear deterrence—simply cannot be relied upon indefinitely. It can, however, buy valuable time, during which other means of ensuring the peace can be brought to bear. A realist would also endorse the principle of building an alliance of strong, neighboring states as part of a strategy of containment. Realism's recommendations for preponderant power and alliance have found support in this book. The results presented in Chapter 5, however, caution us not to place too much faith in the effectiveness of hegemony.

The Kantian way of managing the rise of China is to ensure that the rising power accepts the fundamental nature of the international order. Transitions involving major powers have resulted in great wars only when at least one was authoritarian and followed an economic policy of autarky (Houweling and Siccama 1993). A peaceful transition occurred in the late nineteenth century when the United States passed Britain as a world power. America did not question the basic organizing principles of international relations and shared many common economic, political, and security interests with Britain. Consequently, Britain did not fight to maintain its preeminence. Deterrence remained in the background for a while, but both the United States and Britain knew that they had powerful incentives to settle their differences peacefully. And, in contrast to Britain and Germany, they did (Campbell 1974; Perkins 1968; Rock 1989). In the long run, the Kantian approach of integration and accommodation provides the only practical solution for the challenge posed by the ascendance of China.

Why Not Bring Russia into NATO?

The standard objections to admitting Russia into NATO are not trivial, but the reasons for admitting it outweigh these concerns. We have argued that there are three reasons to include Russia in the course of continued expansion of the alliance: (1) it is a way of preventing the alienation of Russia and preserving the peace between this major power and the West, (2) it is a better means of guaranteeing the security of the Eastern European countries, and (3) it provides a margin of safety in the West's future relations with China. A number of objections have been raised to this idea. We consider three of the most important in this section.

Murky motives: We could not trust Russia to behave as a loyal ally

Did Americans and Europeans trust the Germans forty-five years ago? A major reason for bringing West Germany into NATO in 1955 was the fear that German nationalism would be revived. In the words of Lord Ismay, the first secretary general of NATO, the North Atlantic alliance would serve "to keep the Germans down . . . and the Russians out." The way to contain German expansionism was to include Germany in the Western security system.[6] Similar concerns brought West Germany into the whole range of European institutions, led to Gorbachev's acceptance of a united Germany in NATO (Zelikow and Rice 1995; Maier 1997), and continue to motivate French and German policy. We should include Russia in NATO in part because we do not fully trust its intentions. Integrating Russian and NATO military forces would require a convergence of doctrine, command, training, and equipment, opening the Russian military to outside influence to a degree impossible to obtain otherwise. Just as NATO bound Germany to Europe and the United States, Russia's integration into the alliance would reduce the risk of a dangerous rise of nationalism by strengthening civilian control of its military.

Many fear that if Russia were admitted into NATO it would inhibit the alliance's ability to act decisively, especially reducing its capacity to intervene on its periphery in places like Bosnia and Kosovo. Russia could veto or obstruct NATO's already limited capacity for out-of-area operations.[7] This has undoubtedly been an important consideration. Russia's greatest fear from NATO's operations in Kosovo was that they would serve as a precedent for overriding Russian sovereignty in the event of a revolt by one of its ethnic minorities. Indeed, if Russia were a member of the alliance, there would have been greater opportunity for the West to monitor Russia's military action to suppress rebel forces in Chechnya. As

[6]Useful reviews of NATO's early years include Artner 1985; Park 1986; Baylis 1992; and Kirchner and Sperling 1992.

[7]This is the view of Art (1998), who prefers a looser, less institutionalized "concert of Europe," but Art's prescription is based on much the same analysis as presented here.

for Russia's preventing the West from acting along its periphery, it is important to recognize that such operations are likely to be limited in number anyway by their inherent difficulty. The coercive enforcement of human rights is, under the best of circumstances, a difficult task and one to be undertaken only rarely. In any event, should Russia prove obstructive, other members of NATO could cooperate on an ad hoc basis to meet the problem, as they did in 1991 in response to Iraq's invasion of Kuwait.

A paper bear: The Russians cannot meet NATO's high military standards

Certainly, Russia cannot meet NATO's military standards at the moment. Yet NATO has repeatedly admitted countries whose militaries needed substantial restructuring and modernization. Greece, Turkey, Spain, the new Eastern European members were all judged not by their existing military capabilities but by their potential once integrated into the alliance. In making this determination, a variety of political as well as military contributions were considered. On these grounds, Russia's admission would not be exceptional. With reorganization, Russia could substantially add to the military capabilities of the alliance. Integrating Russia into NATO would also reduce some costs for the West. Being able to integrate Russian nuclear weapons into NATO's nuclear command and control system would be extremely valuable. One of the greatest fears about Russia concerns the loss of control of its nuclear weapons. Admitting it into NATO would provide greater means to limit this risk. Leaving Russia out of the alliance encourages it to continue relying on nuclear deterrence, with thousands of warheads. The decision to expand NATO without including Russia has greatly complicated all arms control efforts to reduce nuclear weaponry (Turner 1997; Steinbruner 2000).

Hollow political and economic institutions: Russia's economy is not sufficiently market-oriented, and its political system is unstable and not truly democratic

These political and economic objections are well taken, but the problems will only worsen if NATO expands but excludes Russia. Including Russia as a full partner in the alliance would defuse Russian perceptions of an external threat that strengthen the hands of the radical nationalists. And much has been accomplished in Russia since the Soviet Union was peace-fully disbanded in 1991, in what was the greatest voluntary act of politi-cal decentralization and decolonization in history. Russia has now held three parliamentary elections and three presidential elections with wide-spread popular participation. All were vigorously contested with guaran-tees of free speech and a lively press. Furthermore, vast portions of the old Soviet economic system have been sold to private investors, much of the market is competitive, and the economy has again begun to grow.

Much remains to be done in reforming both the political and eco-nomic systems. The governing parties control much of the mass media; elections are inordinately influenced by those with the money to advertise and conduct polls; many of the new capitalists who dominate the govern-ment and economy are former Soviet bureaucrats who enriched them-selves with corrupt deals; and the economy is a mix of freedom, central control, bribery, and chaos. Yet, are Russian democracy and market eco-nomics less well developed than those of Romania, where hopes for in-clusion in the next round of NATO expansion have been encouraged? Remember that Portugal joined the alliance under the Salazar dictator-ship, and neither Greece nor Turkey was expelled during its period of mil-itary rule (Bosgra and van Krimpen 1969; Hart 1990).

If we expect the Russians to continue to develop open political and economic institutions, it is necessary to address their security fears. In the long run, the best way to solidify the process of reform is to integrate Russia into Western institutions as rapidly as feasible, with the prospect of further integration when democracy and a free market become firmly es-tablished. NATO can play a leading role in this process. NATO is not just another military alliance, but an international organization with a strong track record of institutionalized coordination of its members' military forces and an ability to shape their preferences and international behavior. When its three new Eastern European members joined, Secretary of State Madeleine Albright stated: "The purpose of NATO enlargement is to do for Europe's east what NATO did 50 years ago for Europe's west: to inte-grate new democracies, defeat old hatreds, provide confidence in eco-nomic recovery and deter conflict," (Albright and Obey 1997).[8] The

---

[8]Secretary Albright's comments reflect her testimony before the U.S. Senate on April 23, 1997, and her comments to the House of Representatives on March 5, 1997.

same objectives can be served by eventually extending membership to Russia.

Russian entry into NATO will not happen immediately. It would take years of preparation by the Russians and the Western community (Baranovsky and Spanger 1992). NATO's secretary general recently suggested that Russia might join NATO within twenty years. The point is to start the process. It is something the Russians have said they want. In 1991, Boris Yeltsin repeatedly requested that Russia be allowed to join NATO. He even endorsed the membership of central European states in 1993, provided that Russia had the same opportunity.[9] Certainly much has changed in Russia since then. The political standing of those Russians who advocated close and rapid integration with the West has declined to some degree, but in March 2000, then Prime Minister (now President) Vladimir Putin again urged that Russia be admitted to the North Atlantic alliance. Substantial political forces in Russia oppose this and, indeed, the whole process of rapprochement between Russia and the West. Nevertheless, if Russia were to decline an invitation to join, it would be its own choice, not the result of exclusion by NATO.

Bringing Russia into NATO would complete what Peter the Great and others tried to do from the eighteenth century onward: integrate Russia with the West, to their mutual benefit. It would enhance the security of the West, including the East Europeans, and address concerns over the power of the military in Russia. For these reasons, the inclusion of Russia in the North Atlantic alliance seems the way finally to end the cold war. It would also help NATO balance the rise of China.

How Would the Chinese React?

Both the United States and the Soviet Union exacerbated the cold war by being insensitive to the other's fears. Would including Russia in NATO simply recreate a bipolar confrontation, this time with an adversary that, in the long term, is potentially even more powerful, or make the clash of civilizations into a self-fulfilling prophecy? It should not, and it need not.

---

[9]Yeltsin insisted it was inevitable that Eastern and Western Europe would become more unified, and he predicted that NATO would evolve into a single armed force for one free Europe (*Current Digest* 1992). Also see Crow 1993.

The Chinese have adequate deterrents against either Russian or Western aggression. An invasion and occupation of China's vast territory is simply unimaginable. China also possesses the world's third largest stockpile of nuclear weapons, which are increasingly sophisticated. It is vital, however, that China, as well as Russia, not depend on nuclear deterrence. Russia, China, and the West all need to develop a long-term solution for insuring their security.[10] That will require a convergence of both preferences and interests, in the web of a Kantian system.

The rise of China does not recreate a danger like the cold war conflict between NATO and the Warsaw Pact because China is no longer driven by an ideology that is incompatible with good, mutually beneficial relations with the West. After World War II ideological differences made conflict between East and West virtually inevitable. The Soviet Union did not just offer different domestic policies. It was fundamentally opposed to the continued existence of capitalism anywhere in the world. Marxist-Leninist doctrine, which provided the theoretical underpinnings of the Soviet system, was a revolutionary ideology (Gaddis 1997). Soviet leaders believed that the world was to be transformed from a capitalist system into one of international communism and that the class struggle between a growing urban proletariat and the bourgeois owners of capital made this inevitable. This class-based dichotomy was reflected in the split between East and West. Soviet doctrine claimed that the Communist system would win in the end because the Soviets had the superior economic system.

China's recent leaders have largely abandoned Marxist economics and vigorously embraced capitalism and more open markets in an attempt to modernize. In China, the West confronts not an expansionist regime driven by a fundamentally different ideology but a growing power governed by a variant of Asian authoritarianism. This does pose a political challenge to Western liberalism (Mahbubani 1993), but not one that is comparable to that which fueled the cold war. Asian authoritarianism is not inevitably subversive the way Marxism-Leninism was. It is not advanced by the Chinese as a political and economic model for other states, particularly the advanced countries of the West, and no one in the West

---

[10]The two contrasting policies for managing relations with China are known as containment and engagement, represented respectively by Bernstein and Munro (1996) and Nathan and Ross (1997). Also see Nye 1998; Saunders 1999.

thinks it is a system worth emulation. Certainly, the Chinese have given no indication that they seek to export their particular form of government by force. Indeed, they seem prepared to learn from the West in the economic realm, and despite the best efforts of the Chinese Communist party, that is bound to shape their political system. The Western democracies should continue to engage China on human rights, not abandoning the advocates of democracy within China. Those advocates will gain influence over time. Meanwhile, the capitalist democracies will be able to demonstrate the advantages of liberal economic and political theory.

Confronted with an expanding NATO, China will have the same three basic strategic options that are available to Russia. It can try to balance NATO, hide, or get on the bandwagon. A Chinese effort to balance an expanded Western alliance by securing allies is unlikely to work. If NATO brings Russia in, it is hard to see what other powerful state could be enlisted in this effort. China might conceivably try to strike an accord with India or Japan, but neither option is really plausible. India has long been China's greatest regional rival. In any event, an alliance with India would not bring China the advanced industrial and technological support it needs. It is equally hard to imagine Japan, ever more integrated economically and politically with the West, throwing its weight to the Chinese. Indeed the future growth of China is likely to raise concern in both India and Japan and bring them into closer strategic cooperation with NATO. Chinese balancing against an expanding NATO is unlikely to work.

The West must pay careful attention to the issue of Taiwan. This is probably the one problem that could force a confrontation with China. It is apt to become an increasingly thorny issue as the regional balance of power shifts toward China. Taiwan cannot afford to incite Beijing by a declaration of independence. Such an act might provoke an attack by the mainland and endanger the support the United States and its allies extend to Taiwan. The United States has committed itself to the policy of "one China, two systems" that proved successful in the case of Hong Kong. It is hard to imagine the United States abandoning a democracy and important commercial partner if China makes an unprovoked mainland attack on its province, but Taiwan, too, has a responsibility to resolve this danger. Deterrence by the West has a role to play in allowing this situation to be settled peacefully, but only in combination with a policy of engagement and respect for China's territorial integrity.

Beijing's second possible response to the inclusion of Russia in NATO is to hide. China could conceivably follow a policy of isolation, but this strategy, too, is unlikely to succeed. China's leaders will have to face tough choices with big economic and political consequences. They will have to make trade-offs involving the high cost of military modernization, the requirements of continued economic growth, and the difficulty of maintaining an autarkic regime as the Chinese middle class grows. A huge increase in military spending would be necessary if China tried to compete on its own with the West militarily. This would threaten the Chinese economy and create real political dangers for the ruling elite. The legitimacy of the Chinese Communist party depends on its ability to continue to deliver economic growth.

Armed isolation would be very costly. In the long term, the prospects for the Chinese economy are good, if the country continues to adopt sound economic policies. But in the short term, China's leaders would have to devote proportionally more resources to the military than the United States and NATO do if they wanted to match the military strength of the West. China's military expenditures amounted to about 2.3 percent of its gross domestic product in 1995. In the same year, the United States spent 3.8 percent of its GDP on the military.[11] The U.S. economy is about two and half times the size of China's, so China would have to spend nearly 10 percent of its GDP on defense to match the U.S. level and nearly 18 percent to keep pace with the combined capabilities of all of NATO and Russia. Although the Chinese army is huge, the war in the Persian Gulf in 1991 and against Serbia in 1999 demonstrate that sheer numbers no longer carry the weight in conventional war that they did during the conflict in Korea in 1950–53,[12] and China's military is in far worse condition today than the Soviet Union's was before its collapse.

To try to match the West's overwhelming capability, therefore, China would be forced to spend even more on modernization than the comparisons above indicate. The Chinese leadership would have to forego either

[11]USACDA 1997. Other economic and demographic data come from the 1997 *CIA World Fact Book* available on-line at www.odci.gov/cia/publications/nsolo/wfb-all.htm.

[12]Technology alone cannot guarantee victory, but the combination of skilled personnel and technical superiority brings stunning defeat to unprepared states (Biddle 1996).

domestic consumption or investment, creating domestic political dangers. China cannot have it all—economic gains, political autocracy, and a huge army.[13] An isolated China bent on achieving strategic parity with the West could not long expect continued Western investment and trade in technologically sophisticated goods. The West demonstrated during the cold war its ability and willingness to restrict the flow of material that might be diverted to the military. To maintain interest from Western investors and traders, China will have to remain a part of the global economy, with the constraining links of interdependence that entails, and not become a military threat to others. In short, diverting massive new resources to the military is probably not a viable alternative for the leaders of China. The history of the Soviet Union suggests what could happen if they tried simultaneously to catch up with the West militarily and to satisfy the rising expectations of the Chinese people. China's growing dependence on foreign commercial relations puts it on the path of cooperative relations. Foreign trade already amounts to over 25 percent of China's GDP, and 40 percent of its exports go to the United States. Taiwanese investment on the mainland amounts to $40 billion. The more interdependent with the world China becomes, the harder it will be to reverse direction. This makes it unlikely that China will choose either confrontation or isolation.

China's final alternative in response to the expansion of NATO would be to get on the bandwagon, to bind its security interests with those of the West and Russia. This would be consistent with past Chinese policies. China turned westward in response to Nixon's initiative in 1972 and was not deterred from this by the West's military advantage (Qingshan 1992). Chinese leaders could have interpreted the Western presence in South Korea, South Vietnam, and Taiwan, as well as the existence of the Southeast Asia Treaty Organization, as a threat that required confrontation or isolation. Instead, they saw improved relations with the United States as a way to improve their economy and strengthen their security in the long term. Today, new efforts should be made to engage China in a dense network of economic interdependence and international organizations (Brzezinski 1996; Shambaugh 1996; Segal 1996). Engagement will reward major elements of the Chinese leadership and discourage conflict

[13]Nolan 1996; Ward, Davis, and Chan 1993; Ward, Davis, and Lofdahl 1995; Chan 1995.

with the West. China's entry into the World Trade Organization can be an important step. Because China is already more integrated into the global economy than Russia is, a formal security arrangement linking China to the West is not so pressing as it is for Russia. In any event, expanding NATO to include Russia could be a step toward establishing a truly global security system that includes not just the European countries but China and other Asian ones as well.

If democratization, economic interdependence, and association in international organizations continue to draw the major powers together, the next few decades may see a historic opportunity to strengthen the role of the UN Security Council in world politics. It might then play the role that was intended when the United Nations was established in 1945. The inclusion of Russia in NATO would be the final step in repairing the divisions created by fifty years of the cold war. The association of many of the major Western powers (the United States, Britain, and France) with Russia, China, and others in a revitalized Security Council could not only strengthen the prospects for peace among the major powers but also be a way of extending peace into the periphery. This is not a call for a new age of imperialism or the establishment of a global condominium. It is simply a recognition that the world should no longer stand by while hundreds of thousands are massacred, as happened in Rwanda, just because the violence occurs outside NATO's area of operations. Increased cooperation in the Security Council would make significant peacekeeping or peacemaking operations more feasible. Even though the Security Council is dominated by the great powers that are its permanent members, it will be more widely acceptable to have these actions taken by the UN rather than NATO. The UN is a universal organization, there are representatives of all the world's regions on the Security Council, and in the General Assembly even small states have their voices heard on most issues. The cooperation of the West, Russia, and China in a collective security system based in the United Nations would mark a new era in international politics.

The False Hope of Hegemony

Henry Luce, founder of the *Time, Life,* and *Fortune* publishing empire, hoped that the United States would assert its leadership in international relations. In 1941, he predicted that the twentieth century would be "The American Century." And so, at times, it seemed to be. The United States provided the margin of victory in World War II, though the Soviet Union, fighting alone on the eastern front and sustaining twenty to twenty-five million casualties, was the most important contributor to the defeat of Germany. The United States was also the strongest power in the Western coalition that won the cold war. Indeed, Luce might have been surprised at how often Americans underestimated the degree to which the United States and its allies dominated international relations during the cold war era. The collapse of the Soviet Union finally made clear, however, how great the Western advantage really was.

The Soviet Union was bested on every major dimension of the competition between East and West. Militarily, it could not match American technology; Soviet weapons were rarely equal to their American counterparts. Economically, it began from too small a productive base and was unable ultimately to match the growth rates of dynamic Western economies. For a while, its economic performance seemed impressive. Reconstruction after World War II was vigorous, and the Soviet economy benefited from moving rural labor to the cities, where they were more effectively employed, and from copying Western technology. Eventually, however, the Soviet economy exhausted the economic potential of state socialism. The perverse structure of incentives did not reward private initiative, and centralized control of the economy lacked the flexibility of markets. The Soviet Union was particularly unable to adopt the technologies associated with the information revolution because its autocratic political system was inconsistent with the proliferation of computers, E-mail, and the World Wide Web. Consequently, growth rates in the East fell precipitously in the Brezhnev era and afterwards, and the environmental and human costs of forced industrialization became apparent. The Soviet system lost ideological legitimacy as its citizens and those of Eastern Europe compared their living standards and political fetters with the conditions of their Western neighbors. As diplomat and historian George Kennan anticipated in a famous telegram and article (Kennan ["X"] 1947), the West would eventually triumph in its competition with communism because of the superiority of its political and economic system. It needed only to contain the Soviet military threat and allow its advantage to become manifest.

Today, the international system contains several states that can reasonably be characterized as major powers, but there is only one superpower: the United States. The collapse of the Soviet Union starkly exposed the absence of any challenger to U.S. dominance (Wohlforth 1999). The United States maintains by far the largest and most effective military establishment in the world. It spends more than all the rest of NATO on defense, and 75 percent more than China, Russia, Iran, Iraq, North Korea, and Serbia combined (USACDA 1997). We found in our empirical analyses that a preponderance of power, not a balance, was associated with a low probability of a militarized dispute. While the United States is not able to impose peace everywhere in the world, it can certainly overwhelm any state or group of states that tries to challenge its security or vital interests. Memories of the Gulf War and the air campaign against Serbia are still vivid.

Nor is America's power limited to the military realm. It has great economic leverage. The dollar is the preferred storehouse of wealth for national reserves around the world and the most important currency for international trade and investment. It is no accident that oil and many other basic commodities are priced in U.S. dollars. The North American Free Trade Area contains the world's largest market, bigger even than the European Union. It is a market to which other states simply must export and from which they get key imports. The United States is very influential in the International Monetary Fund, the World Trade Organization, the World Bank, and other international economic institutions. Consequently, it has enormous power to affect monetary affairs and trade practices, combat financial and copyright offenses, and compel observance of environmental and safety conditions. Japanese and German challenges to American economic predominance, so prominent a decade or so ago, have faded. The United States also benefits from its position in the world of culture. English is the most widely used international language and the principal medium of communication in many areas of science and high technology. American universities are among the world's most respected, though the United States probably exercises even greater influence abroad through its popular music, television, and film. Thus, American might is importantly supplemented by its economic and cultural prominence (Brzezinski 1996).

The strength of the United States today gives no cause for complacency, however. Nor does its military preeminence constitute a permanent solution to the danger of international anarchy. An attempt to maintain peace by the threat of force is a dangerous strategy, especially in the nuclear era. Ten million people died in World War I; fifty million or so died in World War II. It is not hard to imagine a nuclear war that would claim many more lives. Nuclear weapons do not make war impossible. Indeed, they can only serve as a deterrent if there is a chance that they will be used, and over a long period of time, the cumulative effect of many small, individual risks makes catastrophe all too likely.[14] In the second half of the cold war, the victory of the West was more threatened by the danger of stumbling into a nuclear war than by the Warsaw Pact per se. Such a fate was avoided more by good luck than we like to acknowledge.

The importance of U.S. hegemony is also easily exaggerated. It is true that the incidence of war has declined since the end of the cold war. From 1950 to 1989, there were almost eight major wars per decade on average, each with at least 1,000 battle deaths. In the 1990s, there were five.[15] And the number of civil wars—that seeming bane of post–cold war flux—dropped precipitously after peaking in 1992 (Wallensteen and Sollenberg 1999; Gurr 2000; Marshall 2001), thanks in part to peace agreements made effective by the great expansion, in numbers and sophistication, of UN peace-building operations. In the 1990s, three times more peace treaties were signed than in the three previous decades combined (Annan 2000, 43). Our analyses strongly suggest that the greater peacefulness of the 1990s is due less to America's new hegemonic power than to a decline in the tensions associated with the cold war rivalry. The world wars of the twentieth century erupted after British hegemony had declined, but our tests in Chapter 5 show that hegemonic power is not a consistent force for international peace.

Much more important for global peace than the strength of the hegemon is its sense of security. When it feels secure, peace is likely not just

[14]If there is only one chance in a hundred of a nuclear war in a year, there is better than a fifty-fifty chance that *at least one* nuclear war will have occurred after sixty-nine years. Even much smaller dangers of nuclear war are unacceptable when compared to historically meaningful lengths of time. The Egyptians were building pyramids more than 5,000 years ago. Projecting our thoughts forward for such a period reveals the ultimate inadequacy of deterrence given the destructiveness of modern weaponry.

[15]Wallensteen and Sollenberg (1999) report three international wars through 1998, to which must be added NATO-Serbia and probably India-Pakistan in 1999.

for the strongest state and its allies but for others in the system as well. The decline in the ratio of U.S. military expenditures to its GDP from its cold war high of 13.6 percent to 3.2 percent in 1999 indicates clearly that the United States today perceives less danger in the international system. Even as recently as 1983, it devoted 6.4 percent of its gross domestic product to defense. We also saw in Chapter 7 that ethnic conflicts were more frequent when the cold war was intense, not after it ended. Many international and domestic wars, fanned by the superpowers, were concluded when the cold war adversaries lost interest in regional rivalries. Nostalgia for the bipolar era (Mearsheimer 1990) is therefore misplaced. The superpowers may occasionally have restrained others from fighting, but they more often encouraged conflict as part of their competition for global influence. It may still be a dangerous world, but it is much less so with the end of the cold war.

The story of Damocles illustrates the danger of seeking peace through military strength and deterrence alone. According to Greek legend, Damocles envied the wealth and happiness of Dionysius, the autocratic ruler of Syracuse. To show Damocles the perilous nature of a life sustained by power, Dionysius invited him to a banquet where he was seated under a sword hanging by a single hair. Today we live under a threat not of swords but of weapons of mass destruction. If peace is to be sustained in this century and beyond, it must be established on more sure foundations. In any event, the current dominance of the United States will not last forever. It will eventually give way, not just because of the rise of China but also as a result of the growth and continuing process of integration in Europe, Asia, Latin America, and elsewhere. This does not portend a "clash of civilizations." Our analyses in Chapter 7 show little danger of that. Therefore, the diffusion of power need not give rise to a fragmented and competitive world, but it would surely help in avoiding such a fate if the United States and its allies were to encourage the spread of the Kantian peace by promoting democracy, interdependence, and the rule of international law.

There are good reasons for optimism. We have seen that the three Kantian elements substantially reduce the danger of war, and we can reasonably expect that the number of democracies and their economic interdependence will increase. People naturally desire to be free, to govern themselves in order that they may enjoy liberty. As a consequence, democracy will be preferred to authoritarianism. People also desire prosperity. They would rather be rich than poor. The collapse of the Soviet bloc is evidence that this entails capitalism in some form (Fukuyama 1992). Free markets lead to specialization according to comparative advantage and international trade, a tendency that seems bound to increase as the costs of communication and transportation continue to decline. In turn, the growth of democracy and interdependence encourages the rise of international organizations and law to facilitate interstate relations.

Peace does not depend, therefore, on people being transformed into angels, but on constructing a system of incentives whereby even self-seeking devils would be well behaved "so long as they possess understanding" (Kant [1795] 1970, 112). For Kant, a philosopher of the Enlightenment, the causal sequence leading to perpetual peace was evidence of an ordered universe and, perhaps, of providential design. Yet he did not think that the process was determined or the outcome certain (Bohman and Lutz-Bachmann 1997; Williams and Booth 1999). Reason will not inevitably prevail because individuals do not always act in ways that are consistent with their long-term interests. Human affairs are not governed by mechanistic laws like those that regulate the tides: People must learn from experience, including the experience of war, and choose to change their behavior. The outcome is not certain, but there is hope because

> states find themselves compelled to promote the noble cause of peace, though not exactly from motives of morality. . . . Nature guarantees perpetual peace by the actual mechanism of human inclinations. And while the likelihood of its being attained is not sufficient to enable us to *prophesy* the future theoretically, it is enough for practical purposes. It makes it our duty to work our way towards this goal, which is more than an empty chimera. (Kant [1795] 1970, 114; italics in original)

For the foreseeable future, military force will remain an important tool for preventing and rebuffing aggression. Some states remain outside the Kantian system and can be dangerous. But force no longer needs to be the chief means of maintaining peace—nor, because of the risks created by modern weapons, can it continue to be. Deterrence is unnecessary in most situations because international politics is not an unending violent struggle. Assuming that everyone is a potential enemy is a mistake, and a poor guide to action. It risks becoming a self-fulfilling prophecy that is ultimately self-defeating.

A different kind of world can be nurtured, one in which most conflicts of interests are not managed primarily by the threat of violence. Democracy and free enterprise already govern much of the global polity and economy. Those—whether Asian authoritarians, religious fundamentalists, or Western postmodernists—who reject one or the other do so in tones more defensive than confident. The Kantian conditions for peace should be enhanced by Western economic and political assistance to countries willing to liberalize their political and economic systems. It is important to help them achieve a high level of democracy smoothly and rapidly. This is cheaper than building the arms necessary for survival in a world governed by realist principles. Chapter 3 showed that transitions to democracy do not make international conflict more likely, and Chapter 4 found that the pacific benefits of international commerce are not confined to states of similar size: neither democratization nor asymmetric interdependence increases the likelihood of interstate violence. The benefits of liberalism need not be confined, therefore, to the powerful. Nor should the powerful seek to impose liberalism on others.[16]

Extending the Kantian system will require cooperation. Multilateralism will be crucial. The United States has a major role to play, but if it is to lead effectively, it cannot do so through the unilateral exercise of power. It will have to appeal to shared beliefs and perceptions about what actions are legitimate. The less the disparity in capabilities between the leading state and others, the more the leading state must articulate and respect the common principles that unite them. In many cases, the specific means by which these principles are to be advanced is subject to debate; nevertheless, agreement is often possible, as the recent interventions in Iraq, Somalia, Haiti, Bosnia, and Kosovo indicate. Power provides an opportunity for leadership, but it also creates the danger of oppression. It behooves the United States to be constrained by other states' perceptions of what is just and proper. Multilateralists understand that. In 1990, President George Bush used that understanding to assemble, under UN auspices, the coalition that fought the Gulf War.

---

[16]Accepted principles of sovereignty prohibit fighting a war for the purpose of changing another state's form of government. Kant ([1797] 1970, 168–70) accepted war to resist blatant aggression, never to punish or subjugate. In a just postwar settlement, however, he thought the victor might require a defeated aggressor to adopt a republican constitution so as to discourage its warlike inclinations. See Orend 1998.

If multilateralism is to be effective, international organizations will have to play an important role. The United Nations in particular deserves support. Other countries must believe, however, that the UN and other international institutions serve their interests as well as those of the United States. Those institutions need to be enhanced, not gutted. In the longer term, the composition and procedures of key organizations, such as the UN Security Council, will have to be critically and imaginatively reconsidered and constructive reforms undertaken (Hurd 1999; Russett 1997). The United States will be in a stronger position to lead if it supports the United Nations. Its leadership and its ability to promote democracy in other countries will suffer if it behaves undemocratically with its allies and in international organizations.

The United States has undermined its moral authority in recent years by refusing to sign or to ratify a long list of multilateral treaties, covering just about the full spectrum of international issues. These include the Comprehensive Test Ban Treaty, the Land Mines Convention, the Law of the Sea Convention, the International Convention on the Rights of the Child, the treaty to establish a permanent International Criminal Court, and the Kyoto Protocol on global warming. None of these agreements is flawless, and they should be improved, but most other countries have ratified them or will do so. The war over Kosovo should have been brought to the UN Security Council at an early stage for its approval. Washington is still grudging about fulfilling its legal obligations to pay its United Nations dues, threatens to abrogate the Anti-Ballistic Missile Treaty if Russia will not accept a U.S. system of missile defense, and moves ever more overtly toward making nuclear threats to deter the use of biological and chemical weapons, thereby violating its pledge in support of the Nuclear Non-Proliferation Treaty. Watching all this, even some of America's friends perceive the United States as a state that invokes international law to bind others but ignores it when it seems in its immediate self-interest to do so.

A country with only 4 percent of the world's population cannot indefinitely act unilaterally with impunity. If the world is to escape the sword hanging over it, the United States will need not just the approval but the active support of the allies that stood with it during the cold war as well as of those that can be brought into the Kantian community in the future. Some Americans might prefer a different kind of world. Isolationists want to avoid exercising power abroad, but they are not always ready to live with the consequences of inaction. Unilateralists are prepared to use military force in pursuit of important national interests without much concern for international support and to expand the military budget while cutting support for international institutions. But the unipolar character of our world is inevitably transitory. It does provide, however, an opportunity to create a more peaceful world, one based not so much on military force as on the principles of democracy, interdependence, and international cooperation. Kant would say it is a moral imperative.

Appendix: Methods and Tables

A Note Regarding Our Methodology

Many people are initially attracted to quantitative analysis because it seems to offer a greater degree of certainty than historical studies. It is really political *science*. Traditional students of international relations, who work with case studies of important events, must often weigh the relative importance of alternative pieces of evidence. Was the memo that President Truman received from the State Department on July 1 more influential in his thinking about the outbreak of the Korean War in 1950 than the cable from the U.S. embassy the night before? Instead of dealing with such imponderables, the novice thinks, I will rely on numbers. After all, 6 is indisputably bigger than 5. Similarly, an estimated coefficient in a statistical regression analysis either is or is not significant at the .05 level.

In reality, things are not nearly so simple. Quantitative analysis requires a researcher to make a lot of difficult decisions. He or she must decide which data to use, and sometimes the data are known not to be entirely reliable. Is it better to use flawed information in a precise statistical test, or not to make a test at all? Social scientists must also decide about which cases to consider, how to measure key variables, and which statistical tests to perform. Sometimes the best choice is clear, but often it is not.

One approach to such dilemmas is to perform a test in all the possible ways that seem reasonable. For example, we report throughout this book the results of tests using a subset of all pairs of states: the politically relevant dyads, those that are either contiguous or contain one of the major powers. Some political scientists, however, prefer to analyze all dyads and urge us to do the same. Our response has often been to estimate the same regression equation with both sets of cases and report two sets of results. Others recommend accounting for temporal dependence in the time series with a control for the years of peace since the last dispute, not with a correction for autoregression using the General Estimating Equation. Both methods are reasonable, and each has its advantages, so we have reported tests with both techniques (Oneal and Russett 1999a, 1999b, 1999c).

If one were to use all possible combinations regarding the two sets of cases and the two corrections for temporal dependence, there would be four separate tests for each equation—with just these two choices. But should these four tests be done only with data for which we have the greatest confidence, or should we replace missing data for, say, trade using secondary sources and interpolation between known values? Now, there are eight possible tests for each equation, and this does not exhaust by any means, as we will see, the methodological decisions to be made. Because we take the advice of our colleagues seriously, especially when they are reviewers and editors of journals, our practice has been to conduct *lots* of statistical tests. Others have, too. Bennett and Stam (2000) have conducted independent tests of the Kantian peace and report twenty-four analyses of one basic specification. That is a lot, but even so, none was limited to the politically relevant dyads, as we prefer. If they took our advice, they would have had to estimate forty-eight equations!

Though we like to look at lots of alternative tests, our editors assure us that most people find columns and columns of numbers boring. We have, therefore, simplified whenever possible by presenting what in our view are the results of the single best specification. We have offered justifications at the relevant places in the book for most of the methodological choices we have made. Here we would like briefly to bring together some of the most important and state or restate our position on them.

First, we have limited our analyses to the politically relevant dyads because some pairs of states really do seem irrelevant to a study of the causes of war. Studying only contiguous pairs of states and those that contain at least one major power excludes dyads that, in the great majority of cases, had no reasonable opportunity to engage in armed conflict. They were either too weak militarily or had few serious interests at stake or, in most cases, both. Including all possible pairs of states, especially if care is not taken to control properly for the substantial effect of geographical distance, can, for example, mask the pacific benefits of trade by sharply increasing the number of peaceful dyads with a low level of interdependence. It seems certain that the absence of conflict between Mali and Argentina is unrelated to their negligible economic ties, so to include this dyad in a test of the liberal theory may just muddy the waters. As noted above, we have conducted analyses with both sets of cases and still found support for the Kantian peace.

A second choice is whether to examine all years for each dispute between a pair of states, as we have done, or to examine only the first year. Many quantitative analysts prefer to study the onset of disputes and to exclude subsequent years. They argue that the use of force in later years is qualitatively different from the decision to become engaged in conflict, but all our theories of the causes of war begin with the assumption that national leaders are rational. This implies that they frequently reevaluate a decision to use force. Unsophisticated decision makers may not review past decisions, and sophisticated people may not reconsider unimportant choices, but the decision to threaten, display, or use force is manifestly consequential, and all nations have established procedures designed to select leaders who are thought to have exceptional decision-making abilities.

Consequently, we agree with Blainey (1988, x) that "the beginning of wars, the prolonging of wars, the ending of wars and the prolonging or shortening of periods of peace all share the same causal framework. The same explanatory framework and the same factors are vital in understanding each stage in the sequel of war and peace." Decision makers do frequently reevaluate their positions, escalating, de-escalating, or maintaining a conflict contingent on changes in domestic politics, economic and military resources, and international alignments. Our research assistant Jake Sullivan examined 167 multiyear disputes from the period 1950–92 and found that slightly more than half either involved a change in the level of force employed from one year to another or that in the second or subsequent year of a dispute, a new dispute arose. This is a clear indication that policy makers do not relinquish control of events. Including subsequent years of each dispute is also a way of weighting more heavily in our analyses the most serious conflicts, that is, real wars and the disputes that had the greatest potential to become wars; otherwise, these very serious events are indistinguishable from a threat of minor military action. We have examined the effect of distinguishing between the onset of a dispute and all the years of involvement (Oneal and Russett 1999a, 1999c), as have Bennett and Stam (2000). Analyses with the different measures of conflict do not produce substantially different results.

Some analysts go further, recommending that we look only at the first year of a dispute and only at pairs of states that were involved at its inception. They want to exclude what they call "joiners." In considering this suggestion, too, it is important to recall our basic assumption: that states are sovereign and decision makers are rational. The diffusion of war to include other dyads, as Blainey argues, involves the same sorts of choices as the initiation of conflict: to honor an alliance or not, to attack another state or not, or to avoid being attacked by making concessions. Militarized disputes are (fortunately) rare events anyway. Excluding joiners reduces further the number of uses of military force available for analysis, making detection of statistically significant patterns all the more difficult. It especially reduces the effects of multistate and multiyear disputes—those that are most violent and of greatest concern. World War II involved seventy-eight different dyads, but if only the original participants are considered, this great global conflict becomes just a dispute between Germany and Poland, with the same statistical weight as Peru's seizure of a U.S. fishing vessel.

We did drop subsequent years of the two world wars because we lack data on economic interdependence for these years, but in general, using all dyads involved in a dispute, including joiners, and using subsequent years of disputes are probably the best ways to factor the severity of disputes into our testing. Because there are so few disputes, using the number of fatalities, information available in the Correlates of War Project's data, produces results that are virtually indistinguishable from a binary indicator of disputes. With so many dyadic years of peace (zeros in the data), anything else (1, 2, 3, 4, etc. on the COW fatality scale) just looks like not-zero in a statistical test.

Researchers using logistic regression must address the problem of temporal dependence in the time series. The observations for a dyad in one year are not independent of observations in previous years, and the solution for this violation of the assumptions of regression analysis is not as well developed when the dependent variable is binary, as it is with continuous measures. One common approach to this problem is to estimate logistic regressions while controlling for the number of years that have elapsed from the most recent occurrence of a dispute, as we have done on several occasions. This solution for temporal dependence is problematic, however, because it rests on the assumption that the effects of the theoretical variables and of time are separable, that the number of years elapsed since the last dispute is independent of the influences of the theoretical variables (Beck, Katz, and Tucker 1998). This seems very unlikely, particularly in the case of trade. Trade falls with the occurrence of a dispute, which is why states are thought to avoid conflict when trade is economically important. It rises over time after a dispute has ended, as traders' confidence in the durability of peaceful relations increases.

To guard against the danger of wrongly rejecting a true hypothesis, we have most often estimated the coefficients in our equations using the General Estimating Equation (GEE) (Diggle, Liang, and Zeger 1994). GEE is a quasi-likelihood method developed specifically for pooled time-series, cross-sectional analyses. A great virtue is its flexibility. It can be used to estimate general linear models, including analyses of dependent variables that are binary, continuous, or counts of events. Researchers can specify the function linking the independent variables to the variable to be explained and the correlational structure of the error terms. We have assumed that our time series exhibit an autoregressive process of the first order (AR1). Thus, we allow for temporal dependence in the time series but do so in a way that gives the variables in our theoretically specified model primacy in accounting for interstate conflict.

We should also note the recent critique of pooled cross-sectional and time-series analysis by Green, Kim, and Yoon (2001). They recommend that we evaluate our theories while taking into account differences among dyads in the frequency with which they experience conflict. They favor estimating a regression equation that includes indicators for the individual pairs of states. Thus, there would not be a single constant in the regression equation, but a separate constant for each dyad. A fixed-effects model loses a great deal of information when used to explain militarized disputes, however, because many dyads have not experienced any armed conflict. Consequently, their experience does not enter into the estimation. In the analysis reported by Green, Kim, and Yoon, for example, the number of cases drops by 93 percent when fixed effects are taken into account. This statistical technique increases our confidence that our results describe the effects of theoretical variables through time rather than only cross-sectionally, but we do not believe it is generally a good method for testing our theories of interstate conflict. It would be like restricting epidemiological studies of cancer to those who have had the disease, as if the continued health of those who eat healthy foods, exercise, do not smoke, and do not have cancer is irrelevant. In any event, analysis of data for the period 1885–1992 indicates that democracy and trade are robustly related to peaceful outcomes even when fixed effects are considered (Oneal and Russett 2001).

If we are to have confidence in encouraging policy makers to promote liberal institutions and values globally, we must be as sure as science will allow that the Kantian influences actually *cause* a reduction in interstate conflict. Of course, we can never establish causal relations beyond doubt, but we must do what we can to guard against the possibility that causality runs only from peace to the Kantian factors and not vice versa. Lasswell (1941), for example, worried that peace was crucial in sustaining democracy. He was concerned that a history of conflict might cause a democracy to restrict personal liberties or suspend elections such that it became a "garrison state." Indeed, as we have frequently noted, it is very likely that there are important reciprocal relations between the Kantian variables and peace. This is most evident in the case of interdependence. Commerce is thought to promote peace precisely because conflict endangers trade and foreign investment. Examination of such reciprocal relations is an important area for further research. Kim's work (1998) is the best thus far. She sought to disentangle the feedback between trade and interstate conflict in the period 1950–85, with a system of two simultaneous equations. Using rich models to account for both bilateral trade and the likelihood of a dyadic dispute, she concludes that the effect of trade on conflict is stronger than the effect of conflict on trade.

Vector autoregression (VAR) or Granger-causality testing is another way to address the issue of endogeneity, and one that we are exploring

(Oneal and Russett 2000a, 2001). This approach has several advantages. First, it does not assume that reciprocal effects are simultaneous. Past values of both conflict and the Kantian variables can affect the likelihood of a current conflict over a period of years. Second, it controls for temporal dependence in the time series in a manner that is substantially richer and more complete than a count of the time elapsed since the last dispute. In estimating the current likelihood of conflict, it would distinguish, for example, between a dyad that enjoyed nineteen years of peace and then suffered a military dispute from a pair of states that was involved in a dispute every year for twenty years. Our preliminary results using VAR analyses are very encouraging: democracy, economically important trade, and cooperation in intergovernmental organizations reduce the likelihood of conflict substantially, even when the history of dyadic disputes is held constant.

Support for the Kantian peace, especially the benefits of democracy and economic interdependence, is extremely robust, as we have tried to show in this book. No variable is significant in every possible test, but if the weight of the evidence is considered, there is little doubt that the liberals were right: democracy, economic interdependence, and cooperation in international organizations reduce the incidence of war. But scientific investigation is never final, and there are many interesting questions still to ask and to answer. Science is also very much a cooperative enterprise. That is why we have made the data set used in this book (and those in a number of earlier studies) publicly available. We hope some of our readers will take the opportunity to conduct statistical tests just the way they think it should be done, using a different set of variables, a different statistical technique, and so forth. Let us know what you find!

Meanwhile, here are tables presenting, in fuller detail and in customary fashion, the analyses we summarized in the simplified tables embedded in the chapters.

Table A3.1: Logistic Regression of Democracy and Other Influences on Involvement in a Militarized Dispute, 1886–1992

Variable	Coefficient (Standard Error)	Significance Level (One-Tailed Tests)
Alliances (ALLIES)	−.650 (.152)	<.001
Power ratio (POWER RATIO)	−.258 (.042)	<.001
Lower democracy (DEMOC$_L$)	−.0811 (.0098)	<.001
Noncontiguity (NONCONTIG)	−.939 (.173)	<.001
Log distance (DISTANCE)	−.316 (.067)	<.001
Only minor powers (MINORPWRS)	−.533 (.182)	<.002
Constant	−1.11 (.538)	<.02
Wald Chi^2	198	
P of Chi^2	<.001	
N	39,988	

Table A4.1: Logistic Regression of Democracy, Trade, and Other Influences on Involvement in a Militarized Dispute, 1886–1992

Variable	*(1) With Dyadic Liberal Variables*		*(2) Adding Openness*	
	Coefficient (Standard Error)	*Significance Level (One-Tailed Tests)*	*Coefficient (Standard Error)*	*Significance Level (One-Tailed Tests)*
Alliances (ALLIES)	-.677 (.152)	<.001	-.562 (.160)	<.001
Power ratio (POWER RATIO)	-.296 (.043)	<.001	-.290 (.047)	<.001
Lower democracy (DEMOC$_L$)	-.0670 (.0098)	<.001	-.0564 (.0099)	<.001
Lower dependence (DEPEND$_L$)	-56.3 (14.3)	<.001	-40.6 (12.5)	<.001
Lower openness (OPEN$_L$)			-1.83 (.51)	<.001
Noncontiguity (NONCONTIG)	-1.04 (.168)	<.001	-1.00 (.17)	<.001
Log distance (DISTANCE)	-.373 (.067)	<.001	-.376 (.068)	<.001
Only minor powers (MINORPWRS)	-.698 (.182)	<.001	-.473 (.182)	<.005
Constant	-.580 (.533)	<.14	-.189 (.572)	<.38
Wald Chi^2	221		232	
P of Chi^2	<.001		<.001	
N	39,988		36,621	

Table A5.1: Logistic Regression of Democracy, Trade, IGO Membership, and Other Influences on Involvement in a Militarized Dispute, 1886–1992

Variable	Coefficient (Standard Error)	Significance Level (One-Tailed Tests)
Alliances (ALLIES)	−.539 (.159)	<.001
Power ratio (POWER RATIO)	−.318 (.043)	<.001
Lower democracy ($DEMOC_L$)	−.0608 (.0094)	<.001
Lower dependence ($DEPEND_L$)	−52.9 (13.4)	<.001
International organizations (IGO)	−.0135 (.0043)	<.001
Noncontiguity (NONCONTIG)	−.989 (.168)	<.001
Log distance (DISTANCE)	−.376 (.065)	<.001
Only minor powers (MINORPWRS)	−.647 (.178)	<.001
Constant	−.128 (.536)	<.41
Wald Chi^2	228	
P of Chi^2	<.001	
N	39,988	

Table A5.2: Logistic Regression of Systemic and Relative Kantian Measures and Other Influences on Involvement in a Militarized Dispute, 1886–1992

Variable	Coefficient (Standard Error)	Significance Level (One-Tailed Tests)
Alliances (ALLIES)	−.590 (.157)	<.001
Power ratio (POWER RATIO)	−.395 (.046)	<.001
Relative lower democracy (RELATIVEDEMOC$_L$)	−.330 (.066)	<.001
Relative lower dependence (RELATIVEDEPEND$_L$)	−1.13 (.33)	<.001
Relative international organizations (RELATIVEIGO)	−.400 (.070)	<.001
Average democracy (AVGDEMOC)	−.234 (.038)	<.001
Average dependence (AVGDEPEND)	−89.8 (11.8)	<.001
Average international organizations (AVGIGO)	−.0116 (.0071)	<.06
Noncontiguity (NONCONTIG)	−1.06 (.16)	<.001
Log distance (DISTANCE)	−.425 (.063)	<.001
Only minor powers (MINORPWRS)	−.983 (.190)	<.001
Constant	.701 (.538)	<.10
Wald Chi^2	305	
P of Chi^2	<.001	
N	39,988	

Table A5.3: Logistic Regression of Kantian and Realist Systemic and Relative Measures and Other Influences on Involvement in a Militarized Dispute, 1886–1992

Variable	(1) Systemic Kantian Hegemonic Power, Satisfaction		(2) Systemic Kantian, Hegemon's Defense Burden	
	Coefficient (Standard Error)	Significance Level (One-Tailed Tests)	Coefficient (Standard Error)	Significance Level (One-Tailed)
Power ratio (POWER RATIO)	−.394 (.046)	<.001	−.408 (.047)	<.001
Alliances (ALLIES)	−.589 (.159)	<.001	−.619 (.157)	<.001
Relative lower democracy (RELATIVEDEMOC$_L$)	−.326 (.067)	<.001	−.342 (.068)	<.001
Relative lower dependence (RELATIVEDEPEND$_L$)	−1.12 (.329)	<.001	−1.04 (.323)	<.001
Relative international organizations (RELATIVEIGO)	−.394 (.073)	<.001	−.389 (.070)	<.001
Average democracy (AVGDEMOC)	−.231 (.038)	<.001	−.245 (.041)	<.001
Average dependence (AVGDEPEND)	−90.5 (12.8)	<.001	−72.3 (11.8)	<.001

	Model 1		Model 2	
Average international organizations (AVGIGO)	-.0122 (.0078)	<.06	-.0259 (.0083)	<.001
Hegemonic power (HEGPOWER)	.168 (.696)	<.50		
Joint satisfaction (SATISFIED)	-.0282 (.0961)	<.39		
Hegemon's defense burden (HEGDEFENSE)			11.3 (1.4)	<.001
Noncontiguity (NONCONTIG)	-1.06 (.164)	<.001	-1.03 (.16)	<.001
Log distance (DISTANCE)	-.423 (.063)	<.001	-.442 (.062)	<.001
Only minor powers (MINORPWRS)	-.990 (.194)	<.001	-1.05 (.20)	<.001
Constant	.739 (.560)	<.10	.317 (.527)	<.28
Wald Chi^2	318		355	
P of Chi^2	<.001		<.001	
N	39,936		39,988	

Table A6.2: Regression of Influences on Joint IGO Memberships, 1921–92

Variable	Coefficient (Standard Error)	Significance Level (One-Tailed Tests)
Dispute (DISPUTE)	−5.47 (1.54)	<.001
Alliances (ALLIES)	7.65 (1.22)	<.001
Lower per capita GDP (GDPPerCap$_L$)	.000841 (.000186)	<.001
Lower democracy (DEMOC$_L$)	.180 (.051)	<.001
Lower dependence (DEPEND$_L$)	352 (171)	<.02
Noncontiguity (NONCONTIG)	−1.22 (.82)	<.07
Log distance (DISTANCE)	−1.59 (.34)	<.001
Constant	25.7 (2.9)	<.001
Wald Chi^2	203	
P of Chi^2	<.001	
N	29,984	

Table A6.3: Regression of Influences on Trade Patterns, 1886–1992

Variable	Coefficient (Standard Error)	Significance Level (One-Tailed Tests)
Gross domestic product (GDP)	.624 (.037)	<.001
Population (POPULATION)	−.119 (.051)	<.01
Dispute (DISPUTE)	−.084 (.037)	<.02
Lower openness ($OPEN_L$)	.753 (.137)	<.001
Alliances (ALLIES)	.0719 (.0672)	<.15
International organizations (IGO)	.00692 (.00174)	<.001
Lower democracy ($DEMOC_L$)	.00869 (.00245)	<.001
Noncontiguity (NONCONTIG)	−.0534 (.1268)	<.34
Log distance (DISTANCE)	−.611 (.074)	<.001
Constant	−11.8 (1.0)	<.001
Wald Chi^2	692	
P of Chi^2	<.001	
N	33,185	

Table A6.4: The Liberal Peace and States' Interests: Logistic Regression of Influences on Involvement in a Militarized Dispute and Linear Regression of Influences on Affinity, 1951–85

Variable	(1) DISPUTE Standard Equation		(2) AFFINITY		(3) DISPUTE Standard Equation plus AFFINITY	
	Coefficient (Standard Error)	Significance Level (One-Tailed Tests)	Coefficient (Standard Error)	Significance Level (One-Tailed Tests)	Coefficient (Standard Error)	Significance Level (One-Tailed Tests)
Lower democracy ($DEMOC_L$)	−.0328 (.0143)	<.02	.0105 (.0010)	<.001	−.0220 (.0143)	<.07
Lower dependence ($DEPEND_L$)	−61.4 (23.9)	<.005	4.37 (1.19)	<.001	−57.7 (25.2)	<.02
International organizations (IGO)	−.00725 (.00659)	<.14	.000611 (.000483)	<.11	−.00714 (.00673)	<.15
Alliances (ALLIES)	−.686 (.243)	<.003	.247 (.018)	<.001	−.495 (.251)	<.03
Power ratio (POWER RATIO)	−.274 (.079)	<.001	.00919 (.00460)	<.03	−.262 (.077)	<.001
Noncontiguity (NONCONTIG)	−1.30 (.31)	<.001	−.101 (.025)	<.001	−1.38 (.30)	<.001

	Coeff. (SE)	p	Coeff. (SE)	p	Coeff. (SE)	p
Log distance (DISTANCE)	-.385 (.102)	<.001	.00811 (.01054)	<.23	-.368 (.098)	<.001
Only minor powers (MINORPWRS)	-.550 (.367)	<.07	.111 (.032)	<.001	-.420 (.346)	<.13
States' preferences (AFFINITY)					-.711 (.166)	<.001
Constant	-.300 (.937)	<.38	.0855 (.0836)	<.16	-.335 (.906)	<.36
Wald Chi²	111		962		136	
P of Chi²	<.001		<.001		<.001	
N	19,497		19,497		19,497	

Table A7.1: Logistic Regression of Clash of Civilizations, Realist, and Liberal Influences on Involvement in a Militarized Dispute, 1951–92

	(1)		(2)		(3)	
Variable	Coefficient (Standard Error)	Significance Level (One-Tailed Tests)	Coefficient (Standard Error)	Significance Level (One-Tailed Tests)	Coefficient (Standard Error)	Significance Level (One-Tailed Tests)
Split (SPLIT)	.448 (.224)	<.03	.310 (.244)	<.11	.123 (.228)	<.30
Alliances (ALLIES)	-.868 (.212)	<.001			-.729 (.199)	<.001
Power ratio (POWER RATIO)	-.245 (.055)	<.001			-.345 (.060)	<.001
Lower democracy (DEMOC$_L$)			-.0471 (.0121)	<.001	-.0458 (.0126)	<.001
Lower dependence (DEPEND$_L$)			-24.1 (14.6)	<.05	-42.2 (21.8)	<.03
International organizations (IGO)			-.0189 (.0054)	<.001	-.0224 (.0058)	<.001
Noncontiguity (NONCONTIG)	-.978 (.273)	<.001	-1.16 (.28)	<.001	-1.17 (.25)	<.001

	Model 1		Model 2		Model 3	
Log distance (DISTANCE)	-.400 (.095)	<.001	-.496 (.101)	<.001	-.453 (.089)	<.001
Only minor powers (MINORPWRS)	-.296 (.280)	<.15	-.355 (.291)	<.12	-.822 (.280)	<.002
Constant	-.167 (.702)		-.0499 (.8263)	<.48	.690 (.696)	<.17
Wald Chi²	112		146		188	
P of Chi²	<.001		<.001		<.001	
N	28,071		28,071		28,071	

**Table A7.2: Logistic Regression of Influences on Involvement in a
Militarized Dispute within Civilizations, 1951–92**

Variable	Coefficient (Standard Error)	Significance Level (One-Tailed Tests)
Alliances (ALLIES)	−.710 (.228)	<.001
Power ratio (POWER RATIO)	−.344 (.064)	<.001
Lower democracy (DEMOC$_L$)	−.0308 (.0126)	<.008
Lower dependence (DEPEND$_L$)	−22.5 (12.5)	<.04
International organizations (IGO)	−.0146 (.0063)	<.02
(WESTERN)	−1.41 (.35)	<.001
(SINIC)	1.23 (.42)	<.002
(ISLAMIC)	.0916 (.2957)	<.38
(HINDU)	.492 (.492)	<.16
(ORTHODOX)	−1.30 (.46)	<.003
(LATIN)	−.0913 (.4376)	<.42
(AFRICAN)	−.169 (.354)	<.32
(BUDDHIST)	1.25 (.54)	<.01
Noncontiguity (NONCONTIG)	−1.00 (.26)	<.001
Log distance (DISTANCE)	−.446 (.100)	<.001

Table A7.2 (*continued*)

Variable	Coefficient (Standard Error)	Significance Level (One-Tailed Tests)
Only minor powers (MINORPWRS)	−.780 (.327)	<.01
Constant	.765 (.835)	<.18
Wald Chi^2	256	
P of Chi^2	<.001	
N	28,177	

Table A7.3: Logistic Regression of Influences on Involvement in Militarized Disputes between the West and Others, 1951–92

Variable	(1) Coefficient (Standard Error)	(1) Significance Level (One-Tailed Tests)	(2) Coefficient (Standard Error)	(2) Significance Level (One-Tailed Tests)
(WEST vs. REST)	.261 (.196)	<.10		
(WEST vs. ISLAM)			.186 (.236)	<.22
(ISRAEL vs. ISLAM)				
(WEST vs. ORTHODOX)				
(WEST vs. SINIC)				
Alliances (ALLIES)	−.693 (.202)	<.001	−.728 (.193)	<.001
Power ratio (POWER RATIO)	−.336 (.059)	<.001	−.343 (.061)	<.001
Lower democracy ($DEMOC_L$)	−.0473 (.0122)	<.001	−.0461 (.0122)	<.001
Lower dependence ($DEPEND_L$)	−41.299 (22.307)	<.04	−42.017 (22.089)	<.03
International organizations (IGO)	−.0233 (.0059)	<.001	−.0227 (.0057)	<.001
Noncontiguity (NONCONTIG)	−1.183 (.248)	<.001	−1.170 (.250)	<.001
Log distance (DISTANCE)	−.461 (.083)	<.001	−.435 (.083)	<.001
Only minor powers (MINORPWRS)	−.794 (.282)	<.003	−.832 (.277)	<.002
Constant	.713 (.681)	<.15	.616 (.678)	<.19
Wald Chi^2	192		189	
P of Chi^2	<.001		<.001	
N	28,134		28,071	

Table A7.3 (*continued*)

	(3)		(4)		(5)
Coefficient (Standard Error)	Significance Level (One-Tailed Tests)	Coefficient (Standard Error)	Significance Level (One-Tailed Tests)	Coefficient (Standard Error)	Significance Level (One-Tailed Tests)
−.180 (.234)	<.23				
1.455 (.573)	<.006	.761 (.340)	<.02	1.060 (.386)	<.003
−.655 (.198)	<.001	−.728 (.196)	<.001	−.763 (.198)	<.001
−.334 (.060)	<.001	−.348 (.059)	<.001	−.292 (.060)	<.001
−.0497 (.0125)	<.001	−.0458 (.0122)	<.001	−.0433 (.0121)	<.001
−34.894 (19.604)	<.04	−43.279 (23.493)	<.04	−48.241 (24.012)	<.03
−.0219 (.0057)	<.001	−.0249 (.0059)	<.001	−.0192 (.0055)	<.001
−1.186 (.250)	<.001	−1.202 (.242)	<.001	−1.260 (.250)	<.001
−.384 (.086)	<.001	−.415 (.088)	<.001	−.496 (.086)	<.001
−.878 (.280)	<.001	−.766 (.265)	<.002	−.781 (.285)	<.003
.134 (.698)	<.43	.532 (.711)	<.23	.786 (.716)	<.14
202 <.001		191 <.001		197 <.001	
28,071		28,177		28,071	

References

Abbott, Kenneth W., and Duncan Snidal. 1998. Why States Act through Formal International Organizations. *Journal of Conflict Resolution* 52 (1): 3–32.

Acharya, Amitav. 1998. Collective Identity and Conflict Management in Southeast Asia. In *Security Communities in Comparative Perspective*, edited by Emanuel Adler and Michael N. Barnett. Cambridge: Cambridge University Press.

Adler, Emanuel. 1998. Seeds of Peaceful Change: The OSCE as a Pluralistic Security Community–Building Organization. In *Security Communities in Comparative Perspective*, edited by Emanuel Adler and Michael N. Barnett. Cambridge: Cambridge University Press.

Adler, Emanuel, and Michael N. Barnett, eds. 1998. *Security Communities in Comparative Perspective*. Cambridge: Cambridge University Press.

Albright, Madeleine, and David Obey. 1997. Does NATO Enlargement Serve U.S. Interests? *CQ Researcher* 7 (19): 449.

Alden, Chris. 1998. The United Nations, Elections, and the Resolution of Conflict in Mozambique. In *War and Peace in Mozambique* by Stephen Chan and Moises Venancio with contributions from Chris Alden and Sam Barnes. New York: St. Martin's.

Almond, Gabriel. 1950. *The American People and Foreign Policy.* New Haven, CT: Yale University Press.

Alworth, J. S. 1988. *The Finance, Investment, and Taxation Decisions of Multinationals.* Oxford: Blackwell.

Angell, Norman. 1911. *The Great Illusion: A Study of the Relation of Military Power in Nations to Their Economic and Social Advantage.* New York: Putnam.

Annan, Kofi. 2000. *We the People: The Role of the United Nations in the 21st Century.* New York: United Nations.

Arat, Zehra F. 1991. *Democracy and Human Rights in Developing Countries.* Boulder, CO: Lynne Rienner.

Arbatov, Alexei. 1996. Eurasia Letter: A Russian-U.S. Security Agenda. *Foreign Policy* 104 (fall): 102–17.

Archer, Clive. 1994. *The Institutions of Integration.* London: Arnold.

Armstrong, K., and S. Bulmer. 1998. *The Governance of the Single European Market.* Manchester: University of Manchester Press.

Art, Robert J. 1998. Creating a Disaster: NATO's Open Door Policy. *Political Science Quarterly* 113 (3): 383–405.

Artner, Stephen J. 1985. *A Change of Course: The West German Social Democrats and NATO, 1957–1961.* Westport, CT: Greenwood Press.

Ayers, R. William. 2000. A World Flying Apart? Violent Nationalist Conflict and the End of the Cold War. *Journal of Peace Research* 37 (1): 105–17.

Bachteler, Tobias. 1997. Explaining the Democratic Peace: The Evidence from Ancient Greece Reviewed. *Journal of Peace Research* 34 (3): 315–22.

Baker, James A. 1995. *The Politics of Diplomacy: Revolution, War and Peace, 1989–1992.* New York: Putman.

Baranovsky, Vladimir, and Hans-Joachim Spanger, eds. 1992. *In from the Cold: Germany, Russia, and the Future of Europe.* Boulder, CO: Westview.

Barbieri, Katherine. 1996. Economic Interdependence: A Path to Peace or a Source of Interstate Conflict? *Journal of Peace Research* 33 (7): 29–49.

Barbieri, Katherine, and Jack Levy. 1999. Sleeping with the Enemy: The Impact of War on Trade. *Journal of Peace Research* 36 (4): 463–79.

Barbieri, Katherine, and Gerald Schneider. 1999. Globalization and Peace: Assessing New Directions in the Study of Trade and Conflict. *Journal of Peace Research* 36 (4): 387–404.

Barnett, Michael N., and Martha Finnemore. 1999. The Politics, Power, and Pathologies of International Organizations. *International Organization* 53 (4): 699–732.

Baylis, John. 1992. *The Diplomacy of Pragmatism: Britain and the Formation of NATO, 1942–1949.* Hampshire: Macmillan.

BBC Summary of World Broadcasts. 1998. Primakov Threatens Former USSR Republics with "Measures" If They Join NATO. *Tass.* British Broadcasting Company, December 24.

Beck, Nathaniel, and Jonathan Katz. 2001. Throwing the Baby Out with the Bathwater: A Comment on Green, Kim, and Yoon. *International Organization* 55 (2). Forthcoming.

Beck, Nathaniel, Jonathan N. Katz, and Richard Tucker. 1998. Beyond Ordinary Logit: Taking Time Seriously in Binary-Time-Series-Cross-Section Models. *American Journal of Political Science* 42 (4): 1260–88.

Beck, Nathaniel, Gary King, and Langche Zeng. 2000. Improving Quantitative Studies of International Conflict: A Conjecture. *American Political Science Review* 94 (1): 21–36.

Bennett, D. Scott. 1997a. Democracy, Regime Change, and Rivalry Termination. *International Interactions* 22 (4): 367–97.

———. 1997b. Testing Alternative Models of Alliance Duration, 1816–1985. *American Journal of Political Science* 41 (3): 846–78.

———. 1998. Integrating and Testing Models of Rivalry Termination. *American Journal of Political Science* 42 (4): 1200–1232.

Bennett, D. Scott, and Allan Stam, III. 1996. The Duration of Interstate Wars, 1816–1985. *American Political Science Review* 90 (2): 239–57.

———. 1998. A Combined Model of War Outcomes and Duration: Modeling the Declining Advantages of Democracy. *Journal of Conflict Resolution* 42 (3): 344–66.

———. 2000. Research Design and Estimator Choices for Analyzing Interstate Dyads: When Decisions Matter. *Journal of Conflict Resolution* 44 (5): 653–85.

Benoit, Kenneth. 1996. Democracies Really Are More Pacific (in General). *Journal of Conflict Resolution* 40 (4): 636–57.

Benson, Michelle, and Jacek Kugler. 1998. Power Parity, Democracy, and the Severity of Internal Violence. *Journal of Conflict Resolution* 42 (2): 196–209.

Bercovitch, Jacob. 1991. International Mediation and Dispute Settlement: Evaluating the Conditions for Successful Mediation. *Negotiation Journal* 7 (January): 17–30.

Bercovitch, Jacob, and Jeffrey Langley. 1993. The Nature of Dispute and the Effectiveness of International Mediation. *Journal of Conflict Resolution* 37 (4): 670–91.

Berger, Thomas U. 1996. Norms, Identity, and National Security in Germany and Japan. In *The Culture of National Security: Norms and Identity in World Politics*, edited by Peter J. Katzenstein. New York: Columbia University Press.

Berman, Eric. 1996. *Managing Arms in Peace Processes: Mozambique.* New York: United Nations, Institute for Disarmament Research.

Bernstein, Richard, and Ross H. Munro. 1996. *The Coming Conflict with China.* New York: Knopf.

Bertram, Eva. 1995. Reinventing Governments: The Promise and Perils of United Nations Peacebuilding. *Journal of Conflict Resolution* 39 (3): 387–418.

Biddle, Stephen. 1996. Victory Misunderstood: What the Gulf War Tells Us about the Future of Conflict. *International Security* 21 (2): 139–79.

Blainey, Geoffrey. 1988. *The Causes of War.* 3d ed. New York: Free Press.

Blanton, Shannon Lindsey. 2000. Promoting Human Rights and Democracy in the Developing World: U.S. Rhetoric versus U.S. Arms Exports. *American Journal of Political Science* 44 (1): 123–31.

Bliss, Harry, and Bruce Russett. 1998. Democratic Trading Partners: The Liberal Connection. *Journal of Politics* 60 (4): 1126–47.

Bohman, James, and Matthias Lutz-Bachmann, eds. 1997. *Perpetual Peace: Essays on Kant's Cosmopolitan Ideal.* Cambridge, MA: MIT Press.

Bollen, Kenneth. 1993. Liberal Democracy: Validity and Method Factors in Cross-National Measures. *American Journal of Political Science* 37 (4): 1207–30.

Bosgra, S. J., and C. van Krimpen. 1969. *Portugal and NATO.* Amsterdam: Angola Committee.

Boutros-Ghali, Boutros. 1992. *An Agenda for Peace.* New York: United Nations.

———. 1993. *Report on the Work of the Organization from the Forty-Seventh to the Forty-Eighth Session of the General Assembly.* New York: United Nations.

———. 1995a. *An Agenda for Development.* New York: United Nations.

————. 1995b. *Support by the United Nations System to Promote and Consolidate New or Restored Democracies.* New York: United Nations, A/50/150.

————. 1996. *An Agenda for Democratization.* New York: United Nations.

Brams, Steven J. 1996. Transaction Flows in the International System. *American Political Science Review* 60 (4): 880–98.

Braumoeller, Bear. 1997. Deadly Doves: Liberal Nationalism and the Democratic Peace in the Soviet Successor States. *International Studies Quarterly* 41 (3): 375–402.

Brawley, Mark R. 1993a. *Liberal Leadership: Great Powers and Their Challengers in Peace and War.* Ithaca, NY: Cornell University Press.

————. 1993b. Regime Types, Markets and War: The Importance of Pervasive Rents in Foreign Policy. *Comparative Political Studies* 26 (2): 178–97.

Bremer, Stuart A. 1992. Dangerous Dyads: Conditions Affecting the Likelihood of Interstate War, 1816–1965. *Journal of Conflict Resolution* 36 (2): 309–41.

————. 1993. Democracy and Militarized Interstate Conflict, 1816–1965. *International Interactions* 18 (3): 231–49.

————. 1996. Advancing the Scientific Study of War. In *The Process of War,* edited by Stuart A. Bremer and Thomas R. Cusack. Philadelphia: Gordon and Breach.

Brilmayer, Lea. 1994. *American Hegemony: Political Morality in a One-Superpower World.* New Haven, CT: Yale University Press.

Brooks, Stephen G. 1997. Dueling Realisms. *International Organization* 51 (3): 445–78.

————. 2000. *The Globalization of Production and International Security.* Ph.D. diss., Yale University.

Brown, Archie. 1996. *The Gorbachev Factor.* Oxford: Oxford University Press.

Brown, Michael E. 1995. The Flawed Logic of NATO Expansion. *Survival* 37 (1): 34–52.

Brzezinski, Zbigniev. 1996. Geopolitical Pivot Points. *Washington Quarterly* 19 (4): 209–16.

Bueno de Mesquita, Bruce, and David Lalman. 1992. *War and Reason.* New Haven, CT: Yale University Press.

Bueno de Mesquita, Bruce, James Morrow, Randolph Siverson, and Alastair Smith. 1999. An Institutional Explanation of the Democratic Peace. *American Political Science Review* 93 (4): 791–807.

Bueno de Mesquita, Bruce, and Randolph Siverson. 1995. War and the Survival of Political Leaders: A Comparative Study of Regime Types and Political Accountability. *American Political Science Review* 89 (4): 841–53.

———. 1997. Nasty or Nice: Political Systems, Endogenous Norms, and the Treatment of Adversaries. *Journal of Conflict Resolution* 41 (1): 175–99.

Bueno de Mesquita, Bruce Randolph Siverson, and Gary Woller. 1992. War and the Fate of Regimes: A Comparative Analysis. *American Political Science Review* 86 (3): 638–46.

Bull, Hedley. 1977. *The Anarchical Society.* London: Macmillan.

Burkhart, Ross E., and Michael S. Lewis-Beck. 1994. Comparative Democracy: The Economic Development Thesis. *American Political Science Review* 88 (4): 903–10.

Campbell, C. S. 1974. *From Revolution to Rapprochement: The United States and Great Britain, 1783–1900.* New York: Wiley.

Caporaso, James. 1992. International Relations Theory and Multilateralism: The Search for Foundations. *International Organization* 46 (3): 599–632.

Cardoso, Fernando Henrique, and Enzo Faletto. 1979. *Dependency and Development in Latin America.* Berkeley and Los Angeles: University of California Press.

Carothers, Thomas. 1999. *Aiding Democracy Abroad: The Learning Curve.* Washington, DC: Carnegie Endowment for International Peace.

Cederman, Lars Erik. 2000. Back to Kant: Reinterpreting the Democratic Peace as a Collective Learning Process. *American Political Science Review* 94 (4). Forthcoming.

Chan, Stephen, and Moises Vanancio. 1998. *War and Peace in Mozambique.* New York: St. Martin's.

Chan, Steve. 1995. Grasping the Peace Dividend: Some Propositions on the Conversion of Swords into Plowshares. *Mershon International Review* 39 (1): 53–95.

———. 1997. In Search of Democratic Peace: Problems and Promise. *Mershon International Studies Review* 41 (2): 59–91.

Chaney, Carole Kennedy, R. Michael Alvarez, and Jonathan Nagler. 1998. Explaining the Gender Gap in U.S. Presidential Elections. *Political Research Quarterly* 51 (2): 311–39.

Chernoff, Fred. 1995. *After Bipolarity: The Vanishing Threat, Theories of Cooperation, and the Future of the Atlantic Alliance.* Ann Arbor: University of Michigan Press.

Chopra, Jarat, ed. 1998. *The Politics of Peace-Maintenance.* Boulder, CO: Lynne Rienner.

Choucri, Nazli, and Robert North. 1975. *Nations in Conflict: National Growth and International Violence.* New York: Freeman.

Christensen, Thomas, and Jack Snyder. 1990. Chain Gangs and Passed Bucks: Predicting Alliance Patterns in Multipolarity. *International Organization* 44 (2): 137–68.

Cioffi-Revilla, Claudio. 1998. *Politics and Uncertainty: Theory, Models, and Application.* New York: Cambridge University Press.

Claude, Inis. 1984. *Swords into Plowshares: The Problems and Progress of International Organizations,* 4th ed. New York: Random House.

Coase, Ronald H. 1937. The Nature of the Firm. *Economica* 4. Reprinted in *The Firm, the Market, and the Law.* (Chicago: University of Chicago Press, 1988).

Cobden, Richard. 1886. *The Political Writings of Richard Cobden.* London: Cassell.

Cole, Matthew A. 1999. Examining the Environmental Case against Free Trade. *Journal of World Trade* 33: 183–96.

Copeland, Dale. 1996. Economic Interdependence and War: A Theory of Trade Expectations. *International Security* 20 (4): 5–41.

Coplin, William, and J. Martin Rochester. 1972. The Permanent Court of International Justice, the International Court of Justice, the League of Nations and the United Nations: A Comparative Empirical Survey. *American Political Science Review* 66 (2): 529–50.

Coser, Lewis. 1956. *The Function of Social Conflict.* New York: Free Press.

Crow, Suzanne. 1993. Russian Views on an Eastward Expansion of NATO. *Radio Free Europe/Radio Liberty Research Report* 15 (October): 21–22.

Cullather, Nick. 1999. *Secret History: The CIA's Classified Account of Its Operations in Guatemala, 1952–1954.* Stanford, CA: Stanford University Press.

Cupitt, Richard, Rodney Whitlock, and Lynn Williams Whitlock. 1996. The [Im]mortality of Intergovernmental Organizations. *International Interactions* 21 (4): 389–404.

Current Digest of the Soviet Press 1992. 43 (51): 21–2; 43 (52): 19.

Dahl, Robert A. 1971. *Polyarchy.* New Haven, CT: Yale University Press.

Daniel, Donald, and Brad Hayes, eds. 1995. *Beyond Traditional Peacekeeping.* New York: St. Martin's.

Dean, Jonathan. 1997. The NATO Mistake: Expansion for All the Wrong Reasons, *Washington Monthly* 29 (7): 35–38.

Deardorff, Alan V. 1995. Determinants of Bilateral Trade: Does Gravity Work in a Neoclassical World? Working paper, National Bureau of Economic Research, Cambridge, MA, December.

de Soysa, Indra, and John R. Oneal. 1999. Boon or Bane? Reassessing the Productivity of Foreign Direct Investment. *American Sociological Review* 64 (5): 766–82.

Deutsch, Karl W. 1953. *Nationalism and Social Communication.* Cambridge, MA: MIT Press.

Deutsch, Karl W., Sidney Burrell, Robert Kahn, Maurice Lee, Martin Lichterman, Raymond Lindgren, Francis Loewenheim, and Richard Van Wagenen. 1957. *Political Community and the North Atlantic Area.* Princeton, NJ: Princeton University Press.

Diaz-Alejandro, Carlos. 1975. North-South Relations: The Economic Component. *International Organization* 29 (2): 213–41.

DiCicco, Jonathan, and Jack S. Levy. 1999. Power Shifts and Problem Shifts: The Evolution of the Power Transition Research Program. *Journal of Conflict Resolution* 44 (6): 675–704.

Diggle, Peter J., Jung-Yee Liang, and Scott L. Zeger. 1994. *Analysis of Longitudinal Data.* Oxford: Clarendon Press.

Diehl, Paul, and Gary Goertz. 2000. *War and Peace in International Rivalry.* Ann Arbor: University of Michigan Press.

Dixon, William J. 1993. Democracy and the Management of International Conflict. *Journal of Conflict Resolution* 37 (1): 42–68.

———. 1994. Democracy and the Peaceful Settlement of International Conflict. *American Political Science Review* 88 (1): 14–32.

———. 1998. Dyads, Disputes and the Democratic Peace. In *The Political Economy of War and Peace*, edited by Murray Wolfson. Boston: Kluwer.

Dixon, William J., and Stephen Gaarder. 1992. Presidential Succession and the Cold War: An Analysis of Soviet-American Relations, 1948–1992. *Journal of Politics* 54 (1): 156–76.

Dixon, William J., and Bruce E. Moon. 1993. Political Similarity and

American Foreign Trade Patterns. *Political Research Quarterly* 46 (1): 5–25.

Domke, William. 1988. *War and the Changing Global System.* New Haven, CT: Yale University Press.

Doorenspleet, Renske. 2000. Reassessing Three Waves of Democratization. *World Politics* 52 (3): 384–406.

Doran, Charles F. 1991. *Systems in Crisis: New Imperatives of High Politics at Century's End.* New York: Cambridge University Press.

dos Santos, Theotonio. 1970. The Structure of Dependence. *American Economic Review* 60 (2): 231–36.

Doyle, Michael W. 1986. Liberalism and World Politics. *American Political Science Review* 80: 1151–61.

———. 1992. An International Liberal Community. In *Rethinking America's Security: Beyond Cold War to New World Order,* edited by Graham Allison and Gregory Treverton. New York: Norton.

———. 1995. Liberalism and World Politics Revisited. In *Controversies in International Relations Theory,* edited by Charles W. Kegley, Jr. New York: St. Martin's.

———. 1997. *Ways of War and Peace.* New York: Norton.

Druckman, Daniel, and Paul C. Stern. 1997. Evaluating Peacekeeping Missions. *Mershon International Studies Review* 41 (1): 151–65.

Durch, William J., ed. 1996. *UN Peacekeeping, American Policy, and the Uncivil Wars of the 1990s.* New York: St. Martin's.

The Economist. 1997. One World? October 18, 79–80.

Eisenstadt, S. N. 1985. *The Transformation of Israeli Society.* London: Weidenfeld and Nicholson.

Ellingsen, Tanja. 2000. Colorful Community or Ethnic Witches Brew? Multiethnicity and Domestic Conflict during and after the Cold War. *Journal of Conflict Resolution* 43 (2): 228–49.

Ellingsen, Tanja, and Nils Petter Gleditsch. 1996. Democracy and Armed Conflict in the Third World. In *Causes of Conflict in the Third World,* edited by Dan Smith and K. Volden. Oslo: North-South Coalition and International Peace Research Institute.

Elman, Miriam, ed. 1997. *Paths to Peace: Is Democracy the Answer?* Cambridge, MA: MIT Press.

Enterline, Andrew. 1996. Driving While Democratizing. *International Security* 20 (4): 183–96.

————. 1998a. Regime Changes and Interstate Conflict, 1816–1992. *Political Research Quarterly* 51 (2): 385–409.

————. 1998b. Regime Changes, Neighborhoods, and Interstate Conflict, 1816–1992. *Journal of Conflict Resolution* 42 (6): 804–29.

Epstein, Martin, ed. 1913. *The Statesman's Yearbook, 1913.* London: Macmillan.

Esposito, John L., and John O. Voll. 1996. *Islam and Democracy.* New York: Oxford University Press.

Esty, Daniel. 1997. *Sustaining the Asia Pacific Miracle: Environmental Protection and Economic Integration.* Washington, DC: Institute for International Economics.

Esty, Daniel, Jack Goldstone, Ted Robert Gurr, Barbara Harff, Marc Levy, Gepffreu Dabelko, Pamela Surko, and Alan Unger. 1998. *State Failure Task Force Report: Phase II Findings.* McLean, VA: Science Applications International Corporation.

European Commission. 1996. *Eurobarometer: Public Opinion in the European Union.* Report no. 45. Brussels: European Commission.

Eyerman, Joe, and Robert A. Hart. 1996. An Empirical Test of the Audience Cost Proposition: Democracy Speaks Louder than Words. *Journal of Conflict Resolution* 40 (4): 597–616.

Farber, Henry, and Joanne Gowa. 1995. Polities and Peace. *International Security* 20 (2): 123–46.

————. 1997a. Building Bridges Abroad. *Journal of Conflict Resolution* 41 (3): 455–56.

————. 1997b. Common Interests or Common Polities? *Journal of Politics* 57 (3): 393–417.

Fay, Sidney Bradshaw. 1928. *The Origins of the World War.* 2 vols. New York: Macmillan.

Fearon, James D. 1994a. Domestic Political Audiences and the Escalation of International Disputes. *American Political Science Review* 88 (3): 577–92.

————. 1994b. Signaling versus the Balance of Power and Interests: An Empirical Test of a Crisis Bargaining Model. *Journal of Conflict Resolution* 38 (2): 236–69.

Fearon, James D., and David D. Laitin. 1996. Explaining Interethnic Cooperation. *American Political Science Review* 90 (4): 715–35.

Feld, Werner, and Robert Jordan, with Leon Hurwitz. 1994. *International Organizations: A Comparative Approach.* 3rd ed. Westport, CT: Praeger.

Feng, Yi. 1997. Democracy, Political Stability, and Economic Growth. *British Journal of Political Science* 27 (3): 391–418.

Ferguson, Niall. 1999. *The Pity of War.* New York: Basic Books.

Finnemore, Martha. 1993. International Organizations as Teachers of Norms: The United Nations Educational, Scientific, and Cultural Organization and Science Policy. *International Organization* 47 (4): 565–97.

Finnemore, Martha, and Kathryn Sikkink. 1998. International Norm Dynamics and Political Change. *International Organization* 52 (4): 887–17.

Flynn, Gregory, and Henry Farrell. 1999. Piecing Together the Democratic Peace: The CSCE, Norms and the "Construction" of Security in Post–Cold War Europe. *International Organization* 53 (3): 505–35.

Forsythe, David P. 1992. Democracy, War, and Covert Action. *Journal of Peace Research* 29 (4): 385–95.

Frankel, Jeffrey A., and David Romer. 1999. Does Trade Cause Growth? *American Economic Review* 89 (3): 379–99.

Freedom House. 1998. *Freedom in the World: The Annual Survey of Political Rights and Civil Liberties, 1997–1998.* Piscataway, NJ: Transaction Books.

Friedman, Thomas L. 1999. *The Lexus and the Olive Tree.* New York: Farrar, Straus, and Giroux.

Fukuyama, Francis. 1992. *The End of History and the Last Man.* New York: Free Press.

Gaddis, John Lewis. 1987. *The Long Peace: Inquiries into the History of the Cold War.* New York: Oxford University Press.

———. 1997. *We Now Know: Rethinking Cold War History.* New York: Oxford University Press.

Galilei, Galileo. [1590] 1960. *De Motu.* Translated by I. E. Drabkin and Stillman Drake in *On Motion and Mechanics.* Madison, WI: University of Wisconsin Press.

Gardner, Richard. 1980. *Sterling Dollar Diplomacy in Current Perspective.* New York: Columbia University Press.

Garfinkel, Michelle R. 1994. Domestic Politics and International Conflict. *American Economic Review* 84: 1294–309.

Garnham, David, and Mark Tessler, eds. 1995. *Democracy, War, and Peace in the Middle East.* Bloomington: Indiana University Press.

Garrett, Geoffrey. 1998. Global Markets and National Politics: Collision Course or Virtuous Circle? *International Organization* 52 (4): 787–824.

Gartner, Scott, and Gary Segura. 1998. War, Casualties, and Public Opinion. *Journal of Conflict Resolution* 42 (3): 278–300.

Gartzke, Erik. 1998. Kant We All Just Get Along? Opportunity, Willingness and the Origins of the Democratic Peace. *American Journal of Political Science* 42 (1): 1–27.

———. 1999. War Is in the Error Term. *International Organization* 53 (3): 567–87.

———. 2000. Preferences and the Democratic Peace. *International Studies Quarterly* 44 (1): 191–212.

Gasiorowski, Mark J. 1986. Economic Interdependence and International Conflict: Some Cross-National Evidence. *International Studies Quarterly* 30 (1): 23–38.

Gasiorowski, Mark J., and Solomon W. Polachek. 1982. Conflict and Interdependence: East-West Trade and Linkages in the Era of Detente. *Journal of Conflict Resolution* 26 (4): 709–29.

Gastil, Raymond. 1978. *Freedom in the World.* New York: Freedom House.

Gaubatz, Kurt T. 1996. Democratic States and Commitment in International Relations. *International Organization* 50 (1): 109–39.

———. 1999. *Elections and War: The Electoral Incentive in the Democratic Politics of War and Peace.* Stanford, CA: Stanford University Press.

Geller, Daniel, and J. David Singer. 1998. *Nations at War: A Scientific Study of International Conflict.* New York: Cambridge University Press.

Gelpi, Christopher, and Michael Griesdorf. 1997. Winners or Losers: Democracies in International Crisis, 1918–1988. Paper presented at the annual meeting of the American Political Science Association, Washington, DC.

Geva, Nehemia, Karl DeRouen, and Alex Mintz. 1993. The Political Incentive Explanation of "Democratic Peace": Evidence from Experimental Research. *International Interactions* 18 (3): 215–29.

Gilpin, Robert. 1981. *War and Change in World Politics.* New York: Cambridge University Press.

Gleditsch, Kristian, and Michael D. Ward. 2000. War and Peace in Space and Time: The Role of Democratization. *International Studies Quarterly* 44 (1): 1–29.

Gleditsch, Nils Petter. 1997. Environmental Conflict and the Democratic Peace. In *Conflict and the Environment,* edited by Nils Petter Gleditsch. The Hague: Kluwer Academic.

Gleditsch, Nils Petter, and Håvard Hegre. 1997. Peace and Democracy: Three Levels of Analysis. *Journal of Conflict Resolution* 41 (2): 283–310.

Goertz, Gary. 1994. *Contexts of International Politics.* Cambridge: Cambridge University Press.

Goldgeier, James. 1998. NATO Expansion: The Anatomy of a Decision. *Washington Quarterly* 21 (1): 85–112.

Goldstein, Joshua. 1988. *Long Cycles: Prosperity and War in the Modern Age.* New Haven, CT: Yale University Press.

Goodby, James E. 1998. *Europe Undivided: The New Logic of Peace in U.S.-Russian Relations.* Washington, DC: U.S. Institute of Peace.

Gowa, Joanne. 1994. *Allies, Adversaries, and International Trade.* Princeton, NJ: Princeton University Press.

———. 1999. *Ballots and Bullets: The Elusive Democratic Peace.* Princeton, NJ: Princeton University Press.

Gowa, Joanne, and Edward D. Mansfield. 1993. Power Politics and International Trade. *American Political Science Review* 87 (2): 408–420.

Graham, Thomas W. 1988. The Pattern and Importance of Public Awareness and Knowledge in the Nuclear Age. *Journal of Conflict Resolution* 32 (2): 319–33.

Green, Daniel M. 1999. The Lingering Liberal Moment: An Historical Perspective on the Global Durability of Democracy after 1989. *Democratization* 6 (2): 1–41.

Green, Donald, Soo Yeon Kim, and David Yoon. 2001. Dirty Pool. *International Organization* 55 (2). Forthcoming.

Grieco, Joseph M. 1988. Realist Theory and the Problem of International Cooperation: Analysis with an Amended Prisoners' Dilemma Model. *Journal of Politics* 50 (3): 600–624.

Gurr, Ted Robert. 1993. *Minorities at Risk: A Global View of Ethnopolitical Conflicts.* Washington, DC: U.S. Institute of Peace.

———. 1994. Peoples against States: Ethnopolitical Conflict and the Changing World System. *International Studies Quarterly* 3 (38): 347–77.

———. 2000. *Peoples vs. States: Ethnopolitical Conflict and Accommodation at the End of the Twentieth Century.* Washington, DC: U.S. Institute of Peace.

Haas, Ernst. 1958. *The Uniting of Europe.* Stanford, CA: Stanford University Press.

————. 1964. *Beyond the Nation-State: Functionalism and International Organization.* Stanford: Stanford University Press.

————. 1990. *When Knowledge Is Power: Three Models of Change in International Organizations.* Berkeley: University of California Press.

————. 1993. Collective Conflict Management: Evidence for a New World Order. In *Collective Security in a Changing World Order,* edited by Thomas G. Weiss. Boulder, CO: Lynne Rienner.

Hart, Parker T. 1990. *Two NATO Allies at the Threshold of War: Cyprus, a Firsthand Account of Crisis Management, 1965–1968.* Durham, NC: Duke University Press.

Hart, Robert A., and William Reed. 1999. Selection Effects and Dispute Escalation: Democracy and Status Quo Evaluations. *International Interactions* 25 (3): 243–63.

Hegre, Håvard. 2000. Development and the Liberal Peace: What Does It Take to Be a Trading State? *Journal of Peace Research* 37 (1): 5–30.

Hegre, Håvard, Tanja Ellingsen, Monica Jakobsen, Arvid Raknerud, and Nils Petter Gleditsch. 1997. Towards a Democratic Civil Peace? Democracy, Democratization and Civil War, 1834–1992. Paper presented at the annual meeting of the International Studies Association, Toronto.

Heldt, Birger. 1997a. The Dependent Variable of the Domestic-External Conflict Relationship: Anecdotes, Theories, and Systematic Studies. *Journal of Peace Research* 34 (1): 101–6.

————. 1997b. Reconstructing Kant: Propositions and Methodological Considerations. Yale University Political Science Department, New Haven, CT. Typescript.

————. 1999. Domestic Politics, Absolute Deprivation, and the Use of Armed Force in Interstate Territorial Disputes. *Journal of Conflict Resolution* 43 (4): 451–78.

Helpman, Elhanan, and Paul Krugman. 1985. *Market Structure and Foreign Trade: Increasing Returns, Imperfect Competition, and the International Economy.* Cambridge, MA: MIT Press.

Henderson, Errol. 1997. Culture or Contiguity? Ethnic Conflict, the Similarity of States, and the Onset of Interstate War, 1829–1989. *Journal of Conflict Resolution* 41 (5): 649–68.

————. 1998. The Democratic Peace through the Lens of Culture, 1820–1989. *International Studies Quarterly* 42 (3): 461–84.

Henderson, Errol, and J. David Singer. 2000. Civil War in the Post-Colonial World. 1946–92. *Journal of Peace Research* 37 (3): 275–99.

Henderson, Errol, and Richard Tucker. 1999. Clear and Present Strangers: The Clash of Civilizations and International Conflict. Paper presented to the annual meeting of the International Studies Association, Washington, DC.

Hermann, Margaret G., and Charles W. Kegley. 1996. Ballots: A Barrier against the Use of Bullets and Bombs. *Journal of Conflict Resolution* 40 (3): 436–60.

———. 1998. The U.S. Use of Military Intervention to Promote Democracy: Evaluating the Record. *International Interactions* 24 (2): 91–114.

Herzog, Roman. 1999. *Preventing the Clash of Civilizations: A Peace Strategy for the Twentieth Century.* New York: St. Martin's.

Hewitt, J. Joseph, and Jonathan Wilkenfeld. 1996. Democracies in International Crisis. *International Interactions* 22 (2): 123–42.

Hirschman, Albert O. 1945. *National Power and the Structure of Foreign Trade.* Berkeley and Los Angeles: University of California Press.

Hoare, Quintin, and Geoffrey Newell Smith, eds. 1971. *Selections from the Prison Diaries of Antonio Gramsci.* New York: International Publishers.

Hobson, J. A. 1902. *Imperialism: A Study.* London: Allen and Unwin.

Hoffmann, Stanley. 1995. *The European Sisyphus: Essays on Europe, 1964–1994.* Boulder, CO: Westview.

Holmes, Stephen. 1997. In Search of New Enemies. *London Review of Books,* April 24, 3–10.

Holsti, Ole. 1972. *Crisis Escalation War.* Montreal: McGill University Press.

Houweling, Henk, and Jan Siccama. 1993. The Neo-Functionalist Explanation of World Wars: A Critique and an Alternative. *International Interactions* 18 (4): 387–408.

Howard, Michael. 1978. *War and the Liberal Conscience.* New Brunswick, NJ: Rutgers University Press.

Huntington, Samuel P. 1991. *The Third Wave: Democratization in the Late Twentieth Century.* Norman: University of Oklahoma Press.

———. 1993a. The Clash of Civilizations? *Foreign Affairs* 72 (3): 22–49.

———. 1993b. If Not Civilizations, What? *Foreign Affairs* 72 (4): 186–94.

———. 1996. *The Clash of Civilizations and the Remaking of World Order.* New York: Simon and Schuster.

————. 1999. The Lonely Superpower: The New Dimension of Power. *Foreign Affairs* 78 (2): 35–50.

Huntley, Wade. 1996. Kant's Third Image: Systemic Sources of the Liberal Peace. *International Studies Quarterly.* 40 (1): 45–76.

Hurd, Ian. 1999. Legitimacy and Authority in International Politics. *International Organization* 53 (2): 379–408.

Hurrell, Andrew. 1998. An Emerging Security Community in South America? In *Security Communities,* edited by Emmanuel Adler and Michael Barnett. Cambridge: Cambridge Community Press.

Huth, Paul. 1996. *Standing Your Ground.* Ann Arbor: University of Michigan Press.

Huth, Paul, and Bruce Russett. 1993. General Deterrence between Enduring Rivals: Testing Three Competing Models. *American Political Science Review* 87 (1): 61–73.

Ikenberry, G. John. 1996. The Myth of Post–Cold War Chaos. *Foreign Affairs* 75 (3): 79–91.

International Monetary Fund (IMF). 1997. *Direction of Trade.* Washington, DC: International Monetary Fund; distributed by Inter-University Consortium for Political and Social Research, Ann Arbor, MI.

Jackman, Robert. 1993. *Power without Force.* Ann Arbor: University of Michigan Press.

Jacobson, Harold K. 1984. *Networks of Interdependence: International Organizations and the Global Political System.* 2d ed. New York: Knopf.

Jacobson, Harold K., William Reisinger, and Todd Mathers. 1986. National Entanglements in International Organizations. *American Political Science Review* 80 (1): 141–59.

Jaggers, Keith, and Ted Robert Gurr. 1995. Tracking Democracy's Third Wave with the Polity III Data. *Journal of Peace Research* 32 (4): 469–82.

James, Patrick, and Glenn Mitchell. 1995. Targets of Covert Pressure: The Hidden Victims of the Democratic Peace. *International Interactions* 21 (1): 85–107.

James, Patrick, and John R. Oneal. 1991. The Influence of Domestic and International Politics on the President's Use of Force. *Journal of Conflict Resolution* 35 (2): 307–32.

James, Patrick, and Jean Sebastien Rioux. 1998. International Crises and Linkage Politics: The Experiences of the United States, 1953–1994. *Political Research Quarterly* 51 (3): 781–812.

James, Patrick, Eric Solberg, and Murray Wolfson. 1999. An Identified

Systemic Analysis of the Democracy-Peace Nexus. *Defence and Peace Economics* 10 (1): 1–37.

———. 2000. Democracy and Peace: Reply to Oneal and Russett. *Defence and Peace Economics* 11 (2): 215–29.

Jervis, Robert. 1976. *Perception and Misperception in International Politics.* Princeton, NJ: Princeton University Press.

———. 1997. *System Effects: Complexity in Political and Social Life.* Princeton, NJ: Princeton University Press.

Jett, Douglas C. 2000. *Why Peacekeeping Fails.* New York: St. Martin's.

Joint Statement by the People's Republic of China and the Russian Federation. 1997. *Beijing Review* 39 (20): 6–8.

Joyner, Christopher. 1999. The United Nations and Democracy. *Global Governance* 5 (3): 333–57.

Kacowicz, Arie M. 1998. *Zones of Peace in the Third World: South America and West Africa in Comparative Perspective.* Albany: State University of New York Press.

Kant, Immanuel. [1795] 1970. *Perpetual Peace: A Philosophical Sketch.* Reprinted in *Kant's Political Writings*, edited by Hans Reiss. Cambridge: Cambridge University Press.

———. [1797] 1970. The Metaphysics of Morals. Reprinted in *Kant's Political Writings*, edited by Hans Reiss. Cambridge: Cambridge University Press.

Kaplan, Robert D. 1993. *Balkan Ghosts: A Journey through History.* New York: Vintage.

Kegley, Charles W., and Margaret Hermann. 1995. Military Intervention and the Democratic Peace. *International Interactions* 21 (1): 1–21.

———. 1997. Putting Military Intervention into the Democratic Peace. *Comparative Political Studies* 30: 78–107.

Kennan, George F. ["X"]. 1947. The Sources of Soviet Conduct. *Foreign Affairs* 25 (4): 566–82.

Keohane, Robert O. 1984. *After Hegemony: Cooperation and Discord in the World Political Economy.* Princeton, NJ: Princeton University Press.

———. 1986. Reciprocity in International Relations. *International Organization* 40 (1): 1–27.

———. 1990. Multilateralism: An Agenda for Research. *International Journal* 45 (4): 731–64.

Keohane, Robert O., and Lisa Martin. 1995. The Promise of Institutionalist Theory. *International Security* 20 (3): 39–51.

Keohane, Robert O., and Joseph S. Nye, eds. 1977. *Power and Interdependence: World Politics in Transition.* Boston, MA: Little Brown.

Keohane, Robert O., Joseph S. Nye, and Stanley Hoffmann, eds. 1993. *After the Cold War: International Institutions and State Strategies in Europe, 1989–1991.* Cambridge, MA: Harvard University Press.

Kim, Soo Yeon. 1998. Ties That Bind: The Role of Trade in International Conflict Processes, 1950–1992. Ph.D. diss. Yale University.

Kim, Soo Yeon, and Bruce Russett. 1996. The New Politics of Voting Alignments in the United Nations. *International Organization* 50 (4): 629–52.

Kindleberger, Charles. 1973. *The World in Depression, 1929–1939.* Berkeley: University of California Press.

King, Gary. 2001. Proper Nouns and Methodological Propriety: Pooling Dyads in International Relations Data. *International Organization* 55 (2). Forthcoming.

Kirchner, Emil J., and James Sperling. 1992. *The Federal Republic of Germany and NATO: Forty Years After.* London: Macmillan.

Kitfield, James. 1996. A Larger NATO Means Bigger Headaches? In *NATO and the Changing World Order: An Appraisal by Scholars and Policymakers,* edited by Kenneth W. Thompson. Lanham, MD: University Press of America.

Kleiboer, Marieke. 1996. Understanding Success and Failure of International Mediation. *Journal of Conflict Resolution* 40 (2): 360–89.

Kmenta, Jan. 1986. *Elements of Econometrics.* 2d ed. New York: Macmillan.

Kozhemiakin, Alexander. 1998. *Expanding the Zone of Peace? Democratization and International Security.* Houndmills: Macmillan.

Krain, Matthew. 1997. State-Sponsored Mass Murder. *Journal of Conflict Resolution* 41 (3): 331–60.

Krain, Matthew, and Marissa Edson Myers. 1997. Democracy and Civil War: A Note on the Democratic Peace Proposition. *International Interactions* 23 (1): 109–18.

Krasner, Stephen. 1978. *In Defence of the National Interest: Raw Materials, Investments, and U.S. Foreign Policy.* Princeton, NJ: Princeton University Press.

———. 1985. *Structural Conflict: The Third World against Global Liberalism.* Berkeley: University of California Press.

Kroll, J. A. 1993. The Complexity of Interdependence. *International Studies Quarterly* 37 (2): 321–48.

Kugler, Jacek, and Douglas Lemke. 2000. The Power Transition. In *Handbook of War Studies*, 2d ed., edited by Manus I. Midlarsky. Ann Arbor: University of Michigan Press.

Kugler, Richard L. 1996. *Enlarging NATO: The Russia Factor*. Santa Monica, CA: RAND.

Kumar, Krishna, ed. 1998. *Postconflict Elections, Democratization, and International Assistance*. Boulder, CO: Lynne Rienner.

Kupchan, Charles A. 1998. After Pax Americana: Benign Power, Regional Integration, and the Sources of a Stable Multipolarity. *International Security* 23 (2): 40–79.

Kupchan, Charles A., and Clifford A. Kupchan. 1991. Concerts, Collective Security, and the Future of Europe. *International Security* 16 (1): 114–61.

Kurth, James. 1998. Inside the Cave: The Banality of I.R. Studies. *The National Interest* 53: 29–40.

Lai, Brian, and Dan Reiter. 2000. Democracy, Political Similarity, and International Alliances, 1816–1992. *Journal of Conflict Resolution* 43 (2): 203–27.

Lakatos, Imre. 1970. Falsification and the Methodology of Scientific Research Programmes. In *Criticism and the Growth of Knowledge*, edited by I. Lakatos and A. Musgrave. Cambridge: Cambridge University Press.

———. 1978. *The Methodology of Scientific Research Programmes*. Cambridge: Cambridge University Press.

Lake, David. 1992. Powerful Pacifists: Democratic States and War. *American Political Science Review* 86 (1): 24–37.

Lasswell, Harold D. 1941. The Garrison State. *American Journal of Sociology* 46 (4): 455–68.

League of Nations. Various issues. *International Trade Statistics*. Geneva: League of Nations.

Leblang, David. 1997. Political Democracy and Economic Growth: Pooled Cross-Sectional and Time Series Evidence. *British Journal of Political Science* 27 (3): 453–72.

Leeds, Brett Ashley. 1999. Domestic Political Institutions, Credible Commitments, and International Cooperation. *American Journal of Political Science* 43 (4): 979–1002.

Leeds, Brett Ashley, and David R. Davis. 1997. Domestic Political Vulnerability and International Disputes. *Journal of Conflict Resolution* 41 (6): 814–34.

———. 1999. Beneath the Surface: Regime Type and International Interaction, 1953–78. *Journal of Peace Research* 36 (1): 5–22.

Legro, Jeffrey, and Andrew Moravcsik. 1999. Is Anybody Still a Realist? *International Security* 24 (2): 5–55.

Lemke, Douglas, and Jacek Kugler, eds. 1996. *Parity and War*. Ann Arbor: University of Michigan Press.

Lemke, Douglas, and William Reed. 1996. Regime Types and Status Quo Evaluations: Power Transition Theory and the Democratic Peace. *International Interactions* 22 (2): 143–64.

Lenin, V. I. [1916] 1929. *Imperialism*. Reprint, New York: Vanguard.

Lerner, Daniel. 1956. French Business Leaders Look at EDC. *Public Opinion Quarterly* 20 (1): 212–21.

Levy, Jack. 1989a. The Causes of War: A Review of Theories and Evidence. In *Behavior, Society, and Nuclear War*, edited by P. E. Tetlock et al. New York: Oxford University Press.

———. 1989b. The Diversionary Theory of War: A Critique. In *Handbook of War Studies*, edited by Manus Midlarsky. Boston: Unwin Hyman.

———. 1994. Learning and Foreign Policy: Sweeping a Conceptual Minefield. *International Organization* 48 (2): 279–312.

Lian, Bradley, and John R. Oneal. 1993. Presidents, the Use of Military Force, and Public Opinion. *Journal of Conflict Resolution* 37 (2): 277–300.

———. 1997. Cultural Diversity and Economic Development: A Cross-National Study of Ninety-eight Countries, 1960–1985. *Economic Development and Cultural Change* 46 (1): 61–78.

Licklider, Roy E. 1998. Early Returns: Results of the First Wave of Statistical Studies of Civil War Termination. *Civil Wars* 1 (3): 121–32.

Lindberg, Leon. 1963. *The Political Dynamics of European Economic Integration*. Stanford, CA: Stanford University Press.

Lister, Frederick K. 1999. *The Early Security Confederations: From the Ancient Greeks to the United Colonies of New England*. Westport, CT: Greenwood.

Louis, William Roger, and Ronald Robinson. 1994. The Imperialism of Decolonization. *Journal of Imperial and Commonwealth History* 22 (3): 462–511.

Luttwak, Edward. 1999. *Turbo-Capitalism: Winners and Losers in the Global Economy*. New York: HarperCollins.

MacMillan, John. 1998. *On Liberal Peace: Democracy, War, and the International Order.* London: Tauris.

Maddison, Angus. 1989. *The World Economy in the Twentieth Century.* Paris: Organization for Economic Cooperation and Development.

—————. 1991a. *Dynamic Forces in Capitalist Development: A Long-Run Comparative View.* Oxford: Oxford University Press.

—————. 1991b. A Long Run Perspective on Saving. Institute of Economic Research, University of Groningen. Unpublished manuscript.

—————. 1995. *Monitoring the World Economy: 1820–1992.* Paris: Organization for Economic Cooperation and Development.

Mahbubani, Kishore. 1993. The Dangers of Decadence: What the Rest Can Teach the West. *Foreign Affairs* 72 (4): 10–14.

Maier, Charles S. 1997. *The Crisis of Communism and the Collapse of East Germany.* Princeton, NJ: Princeton University Press.

Mandelbaum, Michael. 1995. Preserving the New Peace: The Case against NATO Expansion. *Foreign Affairs* 74 (3): 9–13.

Mansfield, Edward. 1994. *Power, Trade, and War.* Princeton, NJ: Princeton University Press.

Mansfield, Edward, and Rachel Bronson. 1997a. Alliances, Preferential Trading Arrangements, and International Trade Patterns. *American Political Science Review* 87 (3): 624–38.

—————. 1997b. The Political Economy of Major-Power Trade Flows. In *The Political Economy of Regionalism,* edited by Edward Mansfield and Helen Milner. New York: Columbia University Press.

Mansfield, Edward, Helen Milner, and B. Peter Rosendorff. 2000. Free to Trade: Democracies, Autocracies, and International Trade. *American Political Science Review* 94 (2): 305–22.

Mansfield, Edward, and Jack Snyder. 1995. Democratization and the Danger of War. *International Security* 20 (1): 5–38.

—————. 1996. The Effects of Democratization on War. *International Security* 20 (4): 196–207.

—————. 1997. A Reply to Thompson and Tucker. *Journal of Conflict Resolution* 41 (2): 457–61.

Maoz, Zeev. 1993. The Onset and Initiation of Disputes. *International Interactions* 19 (1): 27–47.

—————. 1996. *Domestic Sources of Global Change.* Ann Arbor: University of Michigan Press.

————. 1997. The Controversy over the Democratic Peace: Rearguard Action or Cracks in the Wall? *International Security* 22 (1): 162–98.

————. 1998. Realist and Cultural Critiques of the Democratic Peace: A Theoretical and Empirical Re-assessment. *International Interactions* 24 (1): 1–89.

Maoz, Zeev, and Nazrin Abdolali. 1989. Regime Types and International Conflict. *Journal of Conflict Resolution* 33 (1): 3–35.

Maoz, Zeev, and Bruce Russett. 1993. Normative and Structural Causes of Democratic Peace, 1946–1986. *American Political Science Review* 87 (3): 624–38.

March, James, and Johan Olsen. 1984. The New Institutionalism: Organizational Factors in Political Life. *American Political Science Review* 78 (3): 734–49.

Marshall, Monty G. 1999. *Third World War.* Lanham, MD: Rowman, Littlefield.

————. 2001. Assessing the Societal and Systemic Impact of Warfare. In *From Reaction to Prevention: Opportunities for the UN System in the New Millennium*, edited by David Malone and Fen Osler Hampson. Boulder, CO: Lynne Rienner.

Martin, Lisa. 2000. *Democratic Commitments.* Princeton, NJ: Princeton University Press.

Martin, Lisa, and Beth Simmons. 1998. Theories and Empirical Studies of International Institutions. *International Organization* 52 (4): 729–57.

Maull, Hanns. 1990–91. Germany and Japan: The New Civilian Powers. *Foreign Affairs* 69 (5): 91–106.

McMillan, Susan M. 1997. Interdependence and Conflict. *Mershon International Studies Review* 41 (Supplement 2): 33–58.

McGwire, Michael. 1997. *NATO Expansion and European Security.* London: Brasseys.

Mearsheimer, John. 1990. Back to the Future: Instability in Europe after the Cold War. *International Security* 15 (1): 5–56.

————. 1992. Disorder Restored. In *Rethinking America's Security: Beyond Cold War to World Order*, edited by Graham Allison and Gregory Treverton. New York: Norton.

————. 1994–95. The False Promise of International Institutions. *International Security* 19 (3): 5–49.

Meernik, James. 1994. Presidential Decision Making and the Political Use of Force. *International Studies Quarterly* 38 (1): 121–38.

————. 1996. United States Military Intervention and the Promotion of Democracy. *Journal of Peace Research* 33 (4): 391–402.

Meernik, James, and Peter Waterman. 1996. The Myth of the Diversionary Use of Force by American Presidents. *Political Research Quarterly* 49 (3): 573–90.

Mercer, Jonathan. 1995. Anarchy and Identity. *International Organization* 49 (2): 229–52.

Miall, Hugh. 1992. *The Peacemakers: Peaceful Settlement of Disputes since 1945.* New York: St. Martin's.

Midlarsky, Manus. 1995. Environmental Influences on Democracy: Aridity, Warfare, and a Reversal of the Causal Arrow. *Journal of Conflict Resolution* 39 (2): 224–62.

————. 1998a. Democracy and Islam: Implications for Civilizational Conflict and the Democratic Peace. *International Studies Quarterly* 42 (3): 485–512.

————. 1998b. Democracy and the Environment: An Empirical Assessment. *Journal of Peace Research* 35 (3): 341–62.

Milanovic, Branko. 1996. *Nations, Conglomerates, and Empires: The Tradeoff between Income and Sovereignty.* Policy Research Working Paper no. 1675. Washington, DC: World Bank.

Miller, J. D. B. 1986. *Norman Angell and the Futility of War: Peace and the Public Mind.* Basingstoke, Hampshire: Macmillan.

Miller, Ross A. 1995. Democratic Structures and the Diversionary Use of Force. *American Journal of Political Science* 39 (3): 760–85.

————. 1999. Regime Type, Strategic Interaction, and the Diversionary Use of Force. *Journal of Conflict Resolution* 43 (3): 388–402.

Milner, Helen. 1991. The Assumption of Anarchy in International Relations Theory. *Review of International Studies* 171 (January): 67–85.

Mintz, Alex, and Nehemiah Geva. 1993. Why Don't Democracies Fight Each Other? An Experimental Study. *Journal of Conflict Resolution* 37 (3): 484–503.

Mitchell, Brian R. 1981. *European Historical Statistics, 1750–1975.* 2d ed. New York: Facts on File.

Mitchell, Sara McLauglin, and Brandon Prins. 1999. Beyond Territorial Contiguity: Issues at Stake in Democratic Militarized Disputes. *International Studies Quarterly* 43 (1): 169–83.

Mitchell, Sara McLaughlin, Scott Gates, and Håvard Hegre. 1999. System Evolution and Dynamic Relationships in International Relations. *Journal of Conflict Resolution* 43 (6): 771–92.

Mitrany, David. 1966. *A Working Peace System.* Pittsburgh, PA: Quadrangle.

Modelski, George. 1966. *Exploring Long Cycles.* Boulder, CO: Lynne Rienner.

Moon, J. Donald. 1975. The Logic of Political Inquiry: A Synthesis of Opposed Perspectives. In *The Handbook of Political Science*, vol. 1, edited by Nelson W. Polsby and Fred I. Greenstein. Reading, MA: Addison-Wesley.

Moravcsik, Andrew. 1997. Taking Preferences Seriously: A Positive Liberal Theory of International Politics. *International Organization* 51 (4): 513–53.

———. 1998. *The Choice for Europe: Social Purpose and State Power from Messina to Maastricht.* Ithaca, NY: Cornell University Press.

Morgenstern, Oskar, Klaus Knorr, and Klaus P. Heiss. 1973. *Long Term Projections of Power: Political, Economic, and Military Forecasting.* Cambridge, MA: Ballinger.

Morrow, James. 1994. Modelling the Forms of International Cooperation: Distribution versus Information. *International Organization* 48 (3): 387–423.

———. 1997. When Do "Relative Gains" Impede Trade? *Journal of Conflict Resolution* 41 (1): 12–37.

Morrow, James, Randolph Siverson, and Tressa Tabares. 1998. The Political Determinants of International Trade: The Major Powers 1907–90. *American Political Science Review* 92 (3): 649–62.

Most, Benjamin A., and Harvey Starr. 1989. *Inquiry, Logic, and International Politics.* Columbia: University of South Carolina Press.

Mousseau, Michael. 1997. Democracy and Militarized Interstate Collaboration. *Journal of Peace Research* 34 (1): 73–87.

———. 1998. Democracy and Compromise in Militarized Interstate Conflicts, 1816–1992. *Journal of Conflict Resolution* 42 (2): 210–30.

———. 2000. Market Prosperity, Democratic Consolidation, and Democratic Peace. *Journal of Conflict Resolution* 42 (4): 472–507.

Mousseau, Michael, and Yuhang Shi. 1999. A Test for Reverse Causality in the Democratic Peace Relationship. *Journal of Peace Research* 36 (6): 639–63.

Moynihan, Daniel Patrick 1993. *Pandaemonium: Ethnicity in International Politics.* New York: Oxford University Press.

Mueller, John E. 1973. *War, Presidents, and Public Opinion.* New York: Wiley.

———. 1989. *Retreat from Doomsday: The Obsolescence of Major War.* New York: Basic Books.

Muller, Edward N., and Erich Weede. 1990. Cross-National Variation in Political Violence: A Rational Action Approach. *Journal of Conflict Resolution* 34 (4): 624–51.

Murphy, Craig. 1994. *International Organizations and Industrial Change: Global Governance since 1850.* New York: Oxford University Press.

Nathan, Andrew J., and Robert S. Ross. 1997. *The Great Wall and the Empty Fortress: China's Search for Security.* New York: Norton.

Nelson, Brent, and Alexander Stubb. 1998. *The European Union: Readings on the Theory and Practice of European Integration.* 2d ed. Boulder, CO: Lynne Rienner.

Nie, Norman H., Jane Junn, and Kenneth Stehlik-Barry. 1996. *Education and Democratic Citizenship in America.* Chicago: University of Chicago Press.

Nierop, Tom. 1994. *Systems and Regions in Global Politics: An Empirical Study of Diplomacy, International Organization and Trade, 1950–1991.* New York: Wiley.

Nincic, Miroslav. 1992. *Democracy and Foreign Policy: The Fallacy of Political Realism.* New York: Columbia University Press.

Niu Wen-Yuan, and William Harris. 1996. China: The Forecast of Its Environmental Situation in the Twenty First Century. *Journal of Environmental Management* 47 (2): 101–15.

Nolan, Peter. 1996. Large Firms and Industrial Reform in Former Planned Economies: The Case of China. *Cambridge Journal of Economics* 20 (1): 1–28.

Nuttall, Simon. 1992. *European Political Cooperation.* New York: Oxford University Press.

Nye, Joseph S. 1990. *Bound to Lead: The Changing Nature of American Power.* New York: Basic Books.

———. 1998. China's Re-emergence and the Future of the Asia Pacific. *Survival* 39 (4): 65–79.

Olson, Mancur. 1971. *The Logic of Collective Action: Public Goods and the Theory of Groups.* Cambridge: Harvard University Press.

————. 1993. Dictatorship, Democracy, and Development. *American Political Science Review* 87 (3): 567–76.

Oneal, John R. 1989. Measuring the Material Base of the East-West Balance of Power. *International Interactions* 15 (2): 177–96.

————. 1990a. Testing the Theory of Collective Action: NATO Defense Burdens, 1950–1984. *Journal of Conflict Resolution* 34 (3): 426–48.

————. 1990b. The Theory of Collective Action and Burden Sharing in NATO. *International Organization* 44 (3): 379–402.

Oneal, John R., and Anna Lillian Bryan. 1995. The Rally 'Round the Flag Effect in U.S. Foreign Policy Crises, 1950–1985. *Political Behavior* 17 (3): 379–401.

Oneal, John R., and Paul F. Diehl. 1994. The Theory of Collective Action and NATO Defense Burdens: New Empirical Tests. *Political Research Quarterly* 48 (2): 373–96.

Oneal, John R., Bradley Lian, and James Joyner. 1996. Are the American People "Pretty Prudent"? Public Responses to U.S. Use of Force. *International Studies Quarterly* 40 (2): 261–80.

Oneal, John. R., Frances Oneal, Zeev Maoz, and Bruce Russett. 1996. The Liberal Peace: Interdependence, Democracy, and International Conflict, 1950–1985. *Journal of Peace Research* 33 (1): 11–38.

Oneal, John R., and Bruce Russett. 1997. The Classical Liberals Were Right: Democracy, Interdependence, and Conflict, 1950–1985. *International Studies Quarterly* 41 (2): 267–94.

————. 1999a. Assessing the Liberal Peace with Alternative Specifications: Trade Still Reduces Conflict. *Journal of Peace Research* 36 (4): 423–32.

————. 1999b. Is the Liberal Peace Just an Artifact of Cold War Interests? Assessing Recent Critiques. *International Interactions* 25 (3): 1–29.

————. 1999c. The Kantian Peace: The Pacific Benefits of Democracy, Interdependence, and International Organizations, 1885–1992. *World Politics* 52 (1): 1–37.

————. 2000a. *Causes* of Peace: Democracy, Interdependence, and International Organizations, 1885–1992. Paper presented at the annual meeting of the Peace Science Society (International), New Haven, CT.

————. 2000b. Why "An Identified Systemic Analysis of the Democracy-Peace Nexus" Does Not Persuade. *Peace and Defense Economics* 11 (2): 197–214.

————. 2001. Clear and Clean: The Fixed Effects of Democracy and

Economic Interdependence. *International Organization* 55 (2). Forthcoming.

O'Neill, Barry. 1999. *Honor, Symbols, and War.* Ann Arbor: University of Michigan Press.

Onuf, Nicholas. 1989. *World of Our Making: Rules and Rule in Social Theory and International Relations.* Columbia: University of South Carolina Press.

Onuf, Nicholas G., and Thomas J. Johnson. 1995. Peace in the Liberal World: Does Democracy Matter? In *Controversies in International Relations Theory,* edited by Charles W. Kegley, Jr. New York: St. Martin's.

Oren, Ido. 1995. The Subjectivity of the "Democratic" Peace. *International Security* 20 (2): 147–84.

Orend, Brian. 1998. Kant on International Law and Armed Conflict. *Canadian Journal of Law and Jurisprudence* 11 (2): 329–81.

Organski, A. F. K. 1968. *World Politics.* New York: Knopf.

Organski, A. F. K., and Jacek Kugler. 1980. *The War Ledger.* Chicago: University of Chicago Press.

Organski, A. F. K., and Catherine Organski. 1961. *Population and World Power.* New York: Knopf.

Owen, John. 1997. *Liberal Peace, Liberal War: American Politics and International Security.* Ithaca, NY: Cornell University Press.

Page, Benjamin, and Robert Shapiro. 1992. *The Rational Public: Fifty Years of Trends in Americans' Policy Preferences.* Chicago: University of Chicago Press.

Papayoanou, Paul. 1996. Interdependence, Institutions, and the Balance of Power: Britain, Germany, and World War I. *International Security* 20 (4): 42–76.

Paris, Roland. 1997. Peacebuilding and the Limits of Liberal Internationalism. *International Security* 22 (2): 54–89.

Park, William. 1986. *Defending the West: A History of NATO.* Boulder, CO: Westview Press.

Partell, Peter, and Glenn Palmer. 1999. Audience Costs and Interstate Crises: An Empirical Assessment of Fearon's Model of Dispute Outcomes. *International Studies Quarterly* 42 (2): 389–405.

Pastor, Robert A. 1999. The Third Dimension of Accountability: The International Community in National Elections. In *The Self-Restraining State: Power and Accountability in New Democracies,* edited by Andreas Schedler, Larry Diamond, and Marc Plattner. Boulder, CO: Lynne Rienner.

Peceny, Mark. 1997. A Constructivist Interpretation of the Liberal Peace: The Ambiguous Case of the Spanish-American War. *Journal of Peace Research* 34 (4): 415–30.

———. 1999. Forcing Them to Be Free. *Political Research Quarterly* 52 (3): 549–82.

Perkins, Bradford. 1968. *The Great Rapprochement: England and the United States, 1985–1914.* New York: Atheneum.

Poe, Steven C., C. Neal Tate, and Linda Camp Keith. 1999. Repression of the Human Rights to Personal Integrity Revisited: A Global Cross-National Study Covering the Years 1976–1993. *International Studies Quarterly* 43 (2): 291–313.

Polachek, Solomon W. 1980. Conflict and Trade. *Journal of Conflict Resolution* 24 (March): 55–78.

———. 1992. Conflict and Trade: An Economics Approach to Political International Interactions. In *Economics of Arms Reduction and the Peace Process,* edited by Walter Isard and Charles H. Anderton. Amsterdam: North Holland.

———. 1997. Why Democracies Cooperate More and Fight Less: The Relationship between Trade and International Cooperation. *Review of International Economics* 5 (August): 295–309.

Polachek, Solomon W., and Judith A. McDonald. 1992. Strategic Trade and the Incentive for Cooperation. In *Disarmament, Economic Conversion, and Management of Peace,* edited by Manas Chatterji and Linda Rennie Forcey. New York: Praeger.

Polanyi, Karl. 1944. *The Great Transformation.* Boston: Beacon Press.

Pollins, Brian. 1989a. Conflict, Cooperation, and Commerce: The Effect of International Political Interactions on Bilateral Trade Flows. *American Journal of Political Science* 33 (3): 737–61.

———. 1989b. Does Trade Still Follow the Flag? *American Political Science Review* 83 (2): 465–80.

Pollins, Brian, and Randall Schweller. 1999. Linking the Levels: The Long Wave and Shifts in U.S. Foreign Policy, 1790–1993. *American Journal of Political Science* 43 (2): 431–64. Boulder, CO: Lynne Rienner.

Powell, Robert. 1991. Absolute and Relative Gains in International Relations Theory. *American Political Science Review* 85 (4): 1305–22.

Przeworski, Adam, Michael Alvarez, Jose Antonio Chebub, and Fernando Limongi. 1996. What Makes Democracies Endure? *Journal of Democracy* 7 (1): 39–55.

Przeworski, Adam, and Fernando Limongi. 1997. Modernization: Theories and Facts. *World Politics* 49 (2): 155–83.

Putnam, Robert D. 1993. *Making Democracy Work: Civic Traditions in Modern Italy.* Princeton, NJ: Princeton University Press.

Qingshan, Tan. 1992. *The Making of U.S. China Policy: From Normalization to the Post–Cold War Era.* Boulder, CO: Lynne Rienner.

Raknerud, Arvid, and Håvard Hegre. 1997. The Hazard of War: Reassessing the Evidence for the Democratic Peace. *Journal of Peace Research* 34 (4): 385–404.

Ratner, Steven. 1995. *The New UN Peacekeeping: Building Peace in Lands of Conflict after the Cold War.* New York: St. Martin's.

Ray, James Lee. 1995. *Democracy and International Politics: An Evaluation of the Democratic Peace Proposition.* Columbia: University of South Carolina Press.

———. 1997. The Democratic Path to Peace. *Journal of Democracy* 8 (1): 49–64.

———. 1998. Does Democracy Cause Peace? In *Annual Review of Political Science, 1998*, edited by Nelson W. Polsby. Palo Alto, CA: Annual Reviews.

Raymond, Gregory A. 1994. Democracies, Disputes, and Third Party Intermediaries. *Journal of Conflict Resolution* 38 (1): 24–42.

———. 1996. Demosthenes and Democracies: Regime-Types and Arbitration Outcomes. *International Interactions* 22 (1): 1–20.

Reed, William. 1997. Alliance Duration and Democracy: An Extension and Cross-Validation of "Democratic States and Commitment in International Relations." *American Journal of Political Science* 41 (4): 1072–78.

———. 2000. A Unified Statistical Model of Conflict Onset and Escalation. *American Journal of Political Science* 44 (1): 84–93.

Reiter, Dan. 1995a. Exploding the Powder Keg Myth: Pre-emptive Wars Almost Never Happen. *International Security* 20 (2): 5–34.

———. 1995b. Political Structure and Foreign Policy Learning: Are Democracies More Likely to Act on the Lessons of History? *International Interactions* 21 (1): 39–62.

———. 1996. *Crucible of Beliefs: Learning, Alliances, and World Wars.* Ithaca, NY: Cornell University Press.

Reiter, Dan, and Curtis Meek. 1999. Determinants of Military Strategy, 1903–1994: A Quantitative Empirical Test. *International Studies Quarterly* 43 (2): 363–87.

Reiter, Dan, and Allan Stam III. 1997. The Soldier's Decision to Surrender: Prisoners of War and World Politics. Paper presented at the annual meeting of the American Political Science Association, Washington, DC.

———. 1998a. Democracy and Battlefield Effectiveness. *Journal of Conflict Resolution* 42 (3): 359–77.

———. 1998b. Democracy, War Initiation and Victory. *American Political Science Review* 92 (2): 377–90.

———. 2000. *Search for Victory: Understanding the Sources of Democratic Military Power.* Forthcoming.

Remmer, Karen. 1998. Does Democracy Promote Interstate Cooperation? Lessons from the Mercosur Region. *International Studies Quarterly* 42 (1): 25–51.

Rengger, N. J., comp., with John Campbell. 1995. *Treaties and Alliances of the World.* 6th ed. New York: Stockton.

Repko, Sergei. 1996. We'll Never Be Allies. *Current Digest of the Post-Soviet Press* 48 (30): 21–22.

Reuveny, Rafael, and Heejoon Kang. 1996. International Trade, Political Conflict/Cooperation, and Granger Causality. *American Journal of Political Science* 40 (3): 943–70.

Rioux, Jean-Sebastien. 1998. A Crisis-Based Evaluation of the Democratic Peace Proposition. *Canadian Journal of Political Science* 31 (2): 263–83.

Risse-Kappen, Thomas. 1995a. *Cooperation among Democracies: The European Influence on U.S. Foreign Policy.* Princeton, NJ: Princeton University Press.

———. 1995b. Democratic Peace—Warlike Democracies? A Social-Constructivist Interpretation of the Liberal Argument. *European Journal of International Relations* 1 (4): 491–518.

———. 1996. Collective Identity in a Democratic Community: The Case of NATO. In *The Culture of National Security: Norms and Identity in World Politics,* edited by Peter Katzenstein. New York: Columbia University Press.

Rock, Stephen R. 1989. *Why Peace Breaks Out: Great Power Rapprochement in Historical Perspective.* Chapel Hill: University of North Carolina Press.

Rosecrance, Richard. 1986. *The Rise of the Trading State: Commerce and Conquest in the Modern World.* New York: Basic Books.

————. 1999. *The Rise of the Virtual State: Wealth and Power in the Coming Century.* New York: Basic Books.

Rosenne, Shabtai. 1995. *The World Court and How It Works.* 5th ed. Dordrecht: Martinus Nijhoff.

Rousseau, David. 1996. *Domestic Institutions and the Evolution of International Conflict.* Ph.D. diss., University of Michigan.

————. 1997. Regime Change and International Conflict: Is Democratization Really So Dangerous? Paper presented at the annual meeting of the American Political Science Association, Washington, DC.

Rousseau, David, Christopher Gelpi, Dan Reiter, and Paul Huth. 1996. Assessing the Dyadic Nature of the Democratic Peace, 1918–1988. *American Political Science Review* 90 (3): 512–33.

Rozman, Gilbert. 1999. China's Quest for Great Power Identity. *Orbis* 43 (3): 383–402.

Rubinson, Richard. 1976. The World Economy and the Distribution of Income within States. *American Sociological Review* 41 (4): 638–59.

Ruggie, John Gerard. 1982. International Regimes, Transactions, and Change: Embedded Liberalism in the Postwar Economic Order. *International Organization* 36 (2): 379–416.

Rummel, R. J. 1985. Libertarian Propositions on Violence within and between Nations: A Test against Published Research Results. *Journal of Conflict Resolution* 29 (3): 419–55.

————. 1991. *China's Bloody Century: Genocide and Mass Murder since 1900.* New Brunswick, NJ: Transaction.

————. 1994. *Death by Government.* New Brunswick, NJ: Transaction.

————. 1995a. Democracies *Are* Less Warlike than Other Regimes. *European Journal of International Relations* 1 (4): 457–79.

————. 1995b. Democracy, Power, Genocide, and Mass Murder. *Journal of Conflict Resolution* 39 (1): 3–26.

————. 1997. *Power Kills: Democracy as a Method of Non-Violence.* New Brunswick, NJ: Transaction.

Russett, Bruce. 1963. *Community and Contention: Britain and the United States in the Twentieth Century.* Cambridge, MA: MIT Press.

————. 1967. *International Regions and the International System: A Study in Political Ecology.* Chicago: Rand McNally.

————. 1985. The Mysterious Decline of American Hegemony, or, Is Mark Twain Really Dead? *International Organization* 32 (2): 207–31.

————. 1990. *Controlling the Sword: The Democratic Governance of National Security.* Cambridge, MA: Harvard University Press.

————. 1993. *Grasping the Democratic Peace: Principles for a Post–Cold War World.* Princeton, NJ: Princeton University Press.

————. 1995. The Democratic Peace: And Yet It Moves. *International Security* 19 (4): 164–75.

————. 1996a. Counterfactuals about War and Its Absence. In *Counterfactual Thought Experiments in World Politics: Logical, Methodological, and Psychological Perspectives,* edited by Philip Tetlock and Aaron Belkin. Princeton, NJ: Princeton University Press.

————. 1996b. Ten Balances for Weighing UN Reform Proposals. *Political Science Quarterly* 111 (2): 259–69.

————. 1998. A Neo-Kantian Perspective: Democracy, Interdependence, and International Organizations in Building Security Communities. In *Security Communities in Comparative and Historical Perspective,* edited by Emanuel Adler and Michael Barnett. Cambridge: Cambridge University Press.

————, ed. 1997. *The Once and Future Security Council.* New York: St. Martin's.

Russett, Bruce, John R. Oneal, and Michaelene Cox. 2000. Clash of Civilizations or Realism and Liberalism Déjà Vu? Some Evidence. *Journal of Peace Research* 36 (6): 583–608.

Russett, Bruce, John R. Oneal, and David Davis. 1998. The Third Leg of the Kantian Tripod for Peace: International Organizations and Militarized Disputes, 1950–1985. *International Organization* 52 (3): 441–48.

Russett, Bruce, J. David Singer, and Melvin Small. 1968. National Political Units in the Twentieth Century: A Standardized list. *American Political Science Review* 62 (3): 932–51.

Russett, Bruce, and Allan C. Stam III. 1998. Courting Disaster: An Expanded NATO vs. Russia and China. *Political Science Quarterly* 113 (3): 361–82.

Russett, Bruce, and Harvey Starr. 2000. From Democratic Peace to Kantian Peace: Democracy and Conflict in the International System. In *Handbook of War Studies,* 2d ed., edited by Manus Midlarsky. Ann Arbor: University of Michigan Press.

Sadowski, Yahya. 1998. *The Myth of Global Chaos.* Washington, DC: Brookings Institution.

Saunders, Phillip C. 1999. A Virtual Alliance for Asian Security? *Orbis* 43 (2): 237–56.

Schroeder, Paul. 1994. Historical Reality vs. Neo-Realist Theory. *International Security* 19 (1): 108–48.

Schultz, Kenneth. 1998. Domestic Opposition and Signaling in International Crises. *American Political Science Review* 92 (4): 829–44.

———. 1999. Do Democratic Institutions Constrain or Inform? Contrasting Two Institutional Perspectives on Democracy and War. *International Organization* 53 (2): 233–66.

———. 2000. *Democracy and Bargaining in International Crises.* Cambridge: Cambridge University Press.

Schultz, Kenneth A., and Barry Weingast. 1997. Limited Governments, Powerful States. In *Strategic Politicians, Institutions, and Foreign Policy,* edited by Randolph Siverson. Ann Arbor: University of Michigan Press.

Schweller, Randall. 1992. Domestic Structure and Preventive War: Are Democracies More Pacific? *World Politics* 44 (2): 235–69.

———. 1994. Bandwagoning for Profit: Bringing the Revisionist State Back In. *International Security* 19 (1): 72–107.

Segal, Gerald. 1996. East Asia and the Constrainment of China. *International Security* 20 (4): 107–35.

———. 2000. Does China Matter? *Foreign Affairs* 78 (5): 24–36.

Semmel, Bernard. 1970. *The Rise of Free Trade Imperialism.* Cambridge: Cambridge University Press.

Sen, Amartya. 1981. *Poverty and Famine.* New York: Oxford University Press.

Senese, Paul. 1997. Between Disputes and War: The Effect of Joint Democracy on Interstate Conflict Escalation. *Journal of Politics* 59 (1): 1–27.

———. 1999. Democracy and Maturity: Deciphering Conditional Effects on Levels of Dispute Intensity. *International Studies Quarterly* 43 (3): 483–502.

Shambaugh, David. 1996. Containment or Engagement of China? Calculating Beijing's Responses. *International Security* 21 (2): 180–209.

Shanks, Cheryl, Harold K. Jacobson, and Jeffrey H. Kaplan. 1996. Inertia and Change in the Constellation of International Governmental Organizations. *International Organization* 50 (4): 593–627.

Shaw, R. Paul, and Yuwa Wong. 1988. *Genetic Seeds of Warfare: Evolution, Nationalism and Patriotism.* Boston: Unwin Hyman.

Shin, Michael, and Michael Don Ward. 1999. Lost in Space: Political Geography and the Defense-Growth Trade-off. *Journal of Conflict Resolution* 43 (6): 793–817.

Shinkarenko, Pavel, and Tatyana Malkina. 1996. Yeltsin Visit Marks Closer Russia-China Ties. *Current Digest of the Post-Soviet Press* 48 (17): 6–9.

Sidanius, James. 1993. The Psychology of Group Conflict and the Dynamics of Aggression. In *Explorations in Political Psychology*, edited by Shanto Iyengar and William McGuire. Durham, NC: Duke University Press.

Simmel, Georg. 1898. The Persistence of Social Groups. *American Journal of Sociology* 4: 662–98, 829–36.

———. [1908] 1955. *Conflict*. Translated by K. H. Wolff. New York: Free Press.

Simon, Michael W., and Erik Gartzke. 1996. Political System Similarity and the Choice of Allies. *Journal of Conflict Resolution* 40 (4): 617–35.

Singer, J. David. 1995. *Alliances, 1816–1984*. Ann Arbor: University of Michigan, Correlates of War Project.

Singer, J. David, Stuart Bremer, and John Stuckey. 1972. Capability Distribution, Uncertainty, and Major Power War, 1820–1965. In *Peace, War, and Numbers*, edited by Bruce Russett. Beverly Hills: Sage.

Singer, Max, and Aaron Wildavsky. 1993. *The Real World Order: Zones of Peace/Zones of Turmoil*. Chatham, NJ: Chatham House.

Siverson, Randolph. 1995. Democracies and War Participation: In Defense of the Institutional Constraints Argument. *European Journal of International Relations* 1 (4): 481–89.

Siverson, Randolph, and Juliann Emmons. 1991. Birds of a Feather: Democratic Political Systems and Alliance Choices. *Journal of Conflict Resolution* 35 (2): 285–306.

Siverson, Randolph, and Harvey Starr. 1991. *Diffusion of War: A Study of Opportunity and Willingness*. Ann Arbor: University of Michigan Press.

Small, Melvin, and J. David Singer. 1976. The War-Proneness of Democratic Regimes. *Jerusalem Journal of International Relations* 1 (1): 50–69.

Smil, Vaclav. 1997. China's Environment and Security: Simple Myths and Complex Realities. *SAIS Review* 17 (1): 107–26.

Smith, Alastair. 1996. Diversionary Foreign Policy in Democratic Systems. *International Studies Quarterly* 40 (1): 133–53.

Smith, Michael J. 1986. *Realist Thought from Weber to Kissinger.* Baton Rouge: Lousiana State University Press.

Snidal, Duncan. 1991. Relative Gains and the Pattern of International Cooperation. *American Political Science Review* 85 (1): 701–27.

———. 1997. International Political Economy Approaches to International Institutions. In *Economic Analysis of International Law*, edited by Jagdeep Bhandari and Alay Sykes. Cambridge: Cambridge University Press.

Snow, Donald M. 1995. *National Security: Defense Policy for a New International Order.* 3d ed. New York: St. Martin's.

———. 1996. *Uncivil Wars: International Security and the New Internal Conflicts.* Boulder, CO: Lynne Rienner.

Snyder, Jack. 1990. Averting Anarchy in the New Europe. *International Security* 14 (4): 5–41.

———. 1994. Russian Backwardness and the Future of Europe. *Daedalus* 123 (2): 179–202.

———. 2000. *From Voting to Violence: Democratization and Nationalist Conflict.* New York: Norton.

Solingen, Etel. 1996. Democracy, Economic Reform and Regional Cooperation. *Journal of Theoretical Politics* 8 (1): 79–114.

Spero, Joan. 1990. *The Politics of International Economic Relations.* 4th ed. New York: St. Martin's.

Spiezio, K. Edward. 1990. British Hegemony and Major Power War, 1815–1939: An Empirical Test of Gilpin's Model of Hegemonic Governance. *International Studies Quarterly* 34 (2): 165–81.

Sraffa, Piero, ed. 1951. *The Works and Correspondence of David Ricardo.* Vol. 5. Cambridge: Cambridge University Press.

Stam, Allan, III. 1996. *Win, Lose, or Draw: Domestic Politics and the Crucible of War.* Ann Arbor: University of Michigan Press.

Starr, Harvey. 1992a. Democracy and War: Choice, Learning, and Security Communities. *Journal of Peace Research* 29 (2): 207–13.

———. 1992b. Why Don't Democracies Fight One Another? Evaluating the Theory-Findings Research Loop. *Jerusalem Journal of International Relations* 14 (1): 41–59.

———. 1995. The Diffusion of Democracy Revisited. Paper presented at the annual meeting of the International Studies Association, Chicago, IL.

———. 1997a. *Anarchy, Order, and Integration: How to Manage Interdependence.* Ann Arbor: University of Michigan Press.

————. 1997b. Democracy and Integration: Why Democracies Don't Fight Each Other. *Journal of Peace Research* 34 (2): 153–62.

Stata Reference Manual. 1999. Release 6. College Station, TX: Stata Press.

Stein, Arthur A. 1976. Conflict and Cohesion. *Journal of Conflict Resolution* 20 (1): 143–72.

Stein, Arthur R. 1993. Governments, Economic Interdependence, and International Cooperation. In *Behavior, Society, and International Conflict*, vol. 3, edited by Philip Tetlock, Jo Husbands, Robert Jervis, P. C. Stern, and Charles Tilly. New York: Oxford University Press.

Steinbruner, John. 2000. *Principles of Global Security.* Washington, DC: Brookings Institution.

Stone Sweet, Alec, and Thomas L. Brunell. 1998a. Constructing a Supranational Constitution: Dispute Resolution and Governance in the European Community. *American Political Science Review* 91 (1): 63–82.

————. 1998b. The European Court and the National Courts: A Statistical Analysis of Preliminary References, 1961–95. *Journal of European Public Policy* 5 (March): 66–97.

Summers, Robert, and Alan Heston. 1991. The Penn World Trade Model (Mark 5): An Expanded Set of International Comparisons, 1950–1988. *Quarterly Journal of Economics* 106 (2): 327–69.

Summers, Robert, Alan Heston, Daniel Nuxoll, and Bettina Aten. 1995. *The Penn World Table (Mark 5.6a).* Cambridge, MA: National Bureau of Economic Research.

Tajfel, Henry, and John C. Turner. 1986. The Social Identity Theory of Intergroup Behavior. In *Psychology of Intergroup Relations*, 2d ed., edited by Stephen Worchel and William G. Austin. Chicago: Nelson Hall.

Taylor, Michael. 1982. *Community, Anarchy, and Liberty.* New York: Cambridge University Press.

Taylor, Michael, and Sara Singleton. 1993. The Communal Resource: Transaction Costs and the Solution of Collective Action Problems. In *Proceedings of a Conference on Linking Local and Global Commons*, edited by Robert O. Keohane, Michael D. McGinnis, and Elinor Ostrom. Cambridge, MA: Harvard University Center for International Affairs.

Tetlock, Philip. 1991. Learning in U.S. and Soviet Foreign Policy: In Search of an Elusive Concept. In *Learning in U.S. and Soviet Foreign Policy*, edited by George Breslauer and Philip Tetlock. Boulder, CO: Westview.

Thakur, Ramesh, and Carlyle Thayer, eds. 1995. *A Crisis of Expectations: UN Peacekeeping in the 1990s.* Boulder, CO: Westview.

Thompson, William R., and Richard Tucker. 1997a. Bewitched, Bothered, and Bewildered: A Reply to Farber and Gowa and to Mansfield and Snyder. *Journal of Conflict Resolution* 41 (2): 462–77.

———. 1997b. A Tale of Two Democratic Peace Critiques. *Journal of Conflict Resolution* 41 (2): 428–54.

Tinbergen, Jan. 1962. *Shaping the World Economy.* New York: Twentieth Century Fund.

Tipson, Frederick. 1997. Culture Clash-ification: A Verse to Huntington's Curse. *Foreign Affairs* 76 (2): 166–69.

Turner, Stansfield. 1997. *Caging the Nuclear Genie: An American Challenge for Global Security.* Boulder, CO: Westview.

Union of International Associations. 1992–93. *Yearbook of International Organizations, 1992/93.* 10th ed. Vol. 2. New York: G. F. Saur. See also other editions.

Urwin, Derek. 1995. *Community of Europe: A History of European Integration since 1945.* 2d ed. New York: Longman.

U.S. Arms Control and Disarmament Agency (USACDA). 1997. *World Military Expenditures and Arms Transfers 1996.* Washington, DC: U.S. Government Printing Office.

U.S. Central Intelligence Agency (USCIA). 1994. *World Factbook 1994–95.* McLean, VA: Brassey's.

Van Belle, Douglas. 1997. Press Freedom and the Democratic Peace. *Journal of Peace Research* 34 (4): 405–14.

Vanhanen, Tatu. 1984. *The Emergence of Democracy: A Comparative Study of 119 States, 1850–1979.* Helsinki: Finnish Society of Sciences and Letters.

———. 1990. *The Process of Democratization: A Comparative Study of 147 States, 1980–88.* New York: Crane Russak.

———. 2000. A New Data Set for Measuring Democracy, 1810–1998. *Journal of Peace Research* 37 (2): 251–65.

Vasquez, John A. 1993. *The War Puzzle.* Cambridge: Cambridge University Press.

Verdier, Daniel. 1994. *Democracy and International Trade: Britain, France, and the United States, 1860–1990.* Princeton, NJ: Princeton University Press.

———. 1998. Democratic Convergence and Free Trade. *International Studies Quarterly* 42 (1): 1–24.

Volgy, Thomas, and John E. Schwarz. 1997. Free Trade, Economic Inequality, and the Stability of Democracies in the Democratic Core of Peace. *European Journal of International Relations* 3 (2): 239–53.

Wallace, Michael, and J. David Singer. 1970. Intergovernmental Organization in the Global System. *International Organization* 24 (2): 239–87.

Wallensteen, Peter, and Margareta Sollenberg. 1998. Armed Conflict and Regional Conflict Complexes, 1989–1997. *Journal of Peace Research* 35 (5): 621–34.

———. 1999. Armed Conflict 1989–1998. *Journal of Peace Research* 36 (5): 593–606.

Walt, Stephen. 1997. Building Up New Bogeymen. *Foreign Policy* 106: 177–89.

Waltz, Kenneth. 1979. *Theory of International Politics.* Reading, MA: Addison-Wesley.

Wang, Kevin. 1996. Presidential Responses to Foreign Policy Crises: Rational Choice and Domestic Politics. *Journal of Conflict Resolution* 40 (1): 68–97.

Ward, Michael D., David R. Davis, and Steve Chan. 1993. Military Spending and Economic Growth in Taiwan. *Armed Forces and Society* 19 (4): 533–50.

Ward, Michael D., David R. Davis, and Corey L. Lofdahl. 1995. A Century of Tradeoffs: Defense and Growth in Japan and the United States. *International Studies Quarterly* 39 (1): 27–50.

Ward, Michael D., and Kristian Gleditsch. 1998. Democratizing for Peace. *American Political Science Review* 92 (1): 51–62.

Watson, Adam. 1992. *The Evolution of International Society: A Comparative Historical Analysis.* London: Routledge.

Way, Christopher. 1997. Manchester Revisited: A Theoretical and Empirical Evaluation of Commercial Liberalism. Ph.D. diss., Stanford University.

Weart, Spencer. 1998. *Never at War: Why Democracies Will Not Fight One Another.* New Haven, CT: Yale University Press.

Weede, Erich. 1996. *Economic Development, Social Order, and World Politics.* Boulder, CO: Lynne Rienner.

———. 1998. Islam and the West: How Likely Is a Clash of These Civilizations? *International Review of Sociology* 8 (2): 183–95.

Weiss, Thomas G., ed. 1995. *The United Nations and Civil Wars.* Boulder, CO: Lynne Rienner.

Wendt, Alexander. 1994. Collective Identity Formation and the International State. *American Political Science Review* 88 (2): 384–98.

———. 1999. *Social Theory of International Politics.* Cambridge: Cambridge University Press.

Wendt, Alexander, and Raymond Duvall. 1989. Institutions and International Order. In *Global Changes and Theoretical Challenges: Approaches to World Politics for the 1990s,* edited by Ernst-Otto Czempiel and James Rosenau. Lexington, MA: Lexington.

Werner, Suzanne, and Douglas Lemke. 1997. Opposites Do Not Attract: The Impact of Domestic Institutions, Power, and Prior Commitments on Alignment Choices. *International Studies Quarterly* 41 (3): 529–46.

Williams, Howard, and Ken Booth. 1999. Kant: Theorist beyond Limits. In *Classical Theories of International Relations,* edited by Ian Clark and Iver Neumann. New York: St. Martin's.

Wohlforth, William. 1993. *The Elusive Balance.* Ithaca, NY: Cornell University Press.

———. 1999. The Stability of a Unipolar World. *International Security* 24 (1): 5–41.

Wright, Quincy. 1965. 2d ed. *A Study of War.* Chicago: University of Chicago Press.

Young, Oran. 1967. *The Intermediaries: Third Parties in International Crises.* Princeton, NJ: Princeton University Press.

Zacarias, Agostinho. 1996. *The United Nations and International Peacekeeping.* London: Tauris.

Zartman, William, ed. 1995. *Collapsed States: The Disintegration and Restoration of Legitimate Authority.* Boulder, CO: Lynne Rienner.

Zelikow, Philip, and Condoleeza Rice. 1995. *Germany Unified and Europe Transformed: A Study in Statecraft.* Cambridge, MA: Harvard University Press.

Zweifel, Thomas D., and Patricio Navia. 2000. Democracy, Dictatorship, and Infant Mortality. *Journal of Democracy* 11 (2): 99–114.

Name Index

Abbott, Kenneth W., 163
Abdolali, Nazrin, 51
Acharya, Amitav, 193
Adler, Emanuel, 33, 74n, 76, 243
Ajami, Fuad, 240n
Albright, Madeleine, 291
Alden, Chris, 207, 208
Almond, Gabriel, 55n
Alvarez, R. Michael, 99
Alworth, J. S., 142
Angell, Sir Norman, 129, 278–80
Annan, Kofi, 167, 300
Arat, Zehra F., 79
Arbatov, Alexei, 284
Arbenz, Jacobo, 142
Archer, Clive, 28n
Armas, Castillo, 142
Armstrong, K., 28n
Art, Robert J., 289n
Artner, Stephen J., 289n
Ayers, R. William, 247n

Bachteler, Tobias, 49n
Baker, James, 15

Baranovsky, Vladimir, 292
Barbieri, Katherine, 133n, 134, 135, 139, 140n, 226, 279
Barnett, Michael N., 74n, 76, 165, 243
Baylis, John, 289n
Beck, Nathaniel, 46, 106n, 122, 311
Bennett, D. Scott, 60, 64, 66, 67, 106n, 172n, 244, 276, 279, 281, 308, 310
Benoit, Kenneth, 49n
Benson, Michelle, 70n
Bercovitch, Jacob, 164n
Berger, Thomas U., 244
Berman, Eric, 206n
Bernstein, Richard, 293n
Bertram, Eva, 168
Biddle, Stephen, 295n
Blainey, Geoffrey, 309, 310
Bliss, Harry, 218n, 221, 222n
Bohman, James, 302
Bollen, Kenneth, 46
Booth, Ken, 302
Bosgra, S. J., 291
Boutros-Ghali, Boutros, 33, 167, 168, 192
Brams, Steven J., 219

Braumoeller, Bear, 52
Brawley, Mark R., 56, 168
Bremer, Stuart A., 46*n*, 49, 53, 103
Brilmayer, Lea, 79
Bronson, Rachel, 221
Brooks, Stephen G., 23, 181
Brosio, Manlio, 164
Brown, Archie, 31
Brown, Michael E., 283*n*
Brunell, Thomas L., 163, 214*n*
Bryan, Anna Lillian, 67*n*, 69
Brzezinski, Zbigniew, 296, 299
Bueno de Mesquita, Bruce, 44*n*, 54, 55, 56, 59,
    66, 74*n*, 115
Bull, Hedley, 17, 23
Bulmer, S., 28*n*
Burkhart, Ross E., 72

Campbell, C. S., 288
Caporaso, James, 165
Cardoso, Fernando Henrique, 224
Carothers, Thomas, 201*n*
Cederman, Lars Erik, 71, 180*n*, 236
Chan, Stephen, 206*n*
Chan, Steve, 44*n*, 48, 296*n*
Chaney, Carole Kennedy, 99
Chernoff, Fred, 261
Chopra, Jarat, 202*n*
Choucri, Nazli, 23, 152
Christensen, Thomas, 285*n*
Cioffi-Revilla, Claudio, 107*n*
Claude, Inis, 163*n*
Coase, Ronald H., 164
Cobden, Richard, 29–30, 34, 36, 128–29
Cole, Matthew A., 277
Copeland, Dale, 135
Coplin, William, 164*n*
Coser, Lewis, 242
Cox, Michaelene, 239*n*, 255*n*
Crow, Suzanne, 292*n*
Crucé, Emeric, 127–28, 276–77, 278
Cullather, Nick, 142
Cupitt, Richard, 160

Dahl, Robert A., 44
Daniel, Donald, 202*n*
Davis, David R., 64, 69, 115, 212*n*, 217, 296*n*
Dean, Jonathan, 283*n*
Deardorff, Alan V., 134, 222
DeRouen, Karl, 62
de Soysa, Indra, 148
Deutsch, Karl W., 74–75, 77, 130, 166, 243, 277
Diaz-Alejandro, Carlos, 219
DiCicco, Jonathan, 287
Diehl, Paul F., 162, 200*n*
Diggle, Peter J., 311
Dixon, William J., 65, 112, 164*n*, 173, 221
Domke, William, 129, 133, 162

Doorenspleet, Renske, 99*n*
Doran, Charles F., 56
dos Santos, Theotonio, 132
Doyle, Michael W., 23, 71, 78, 90, 157, 243*n*
Druckman, Daniel, 211*n*
Dubois, Pierre, 159–60
Durch, William J., 202*n*
Duvall, Raymond, 166

Eisenstadt, S. N., 252
Ellingsen, Tanja, 70*n*
Elman, Miriam, 47*n*
Emmons, Julian, 59*n*
Enterline, Andrew, 51*n*, 52
Epstein, Martin, 140
Esposito, John L., 244*n*
Esty, Daniel, 70*n*, 287
Eyerman, Joe, 64*n*

Faletto, Enzo, 224
Farber, Henry, 60, 61, 229, 230, 231
Farrell, Henry, 201
Fay, Sidney Bradshaw, 176
Fearon, James D., 64*n*, 88, 247*n*
Feld, Werner, 161
Feng, Yi, 73
Finnemore, Martha, 162, 165
Flynn, Gregory, 201
Forsythe, David P., 62
Frankel, Jeffrey A., 72*n*, 223
Friedman, Thomas L., 181
Fukuyama, Francis, 192, 302

Gaarder, Stephen, 112
Gaddis, John Lewis, 134, 293
Galilei, Galileo, 43, 44
Gardner, Richard, 38
Garfinkel, Michelle R., 51
Garnham, David, 244*n*
Garrett, Geoffrey, 78
Gartner, Scott, 67*n*
Gartzke, Erik, 59*n*, 61, 106*n*, 229, 230–32, 236*n*
Gasiorowski, Mark J., 132*n*
Gastil, Raymond, 45*n*
Gates, Scott, 180*n*, 200
Gaubatz, Kurt T., 44*n*, 60, 69
Geller, Daniel, 177*n*
Gelpi, Christopher, 61–62
Geva, Nehemia, 62, 65
Gilpin, Robert, 56, 184, 188*n*, 245*n*
Gleditsch, Kristian, 51, 52
Gleditsch, Nils Petter, 50, 70*n*, 79, 180*n*
Goertz, Gary, 54, 200*n*
Goldgeier, James, 283
Goldstein, Joshua, 152
Goodby, James E., 284
Gowa, Joanne, 60, 61, 69, 114, 136, 219, 221,
    229, 230, 231, 237

Graham, Thomas W., 55*n*
Gramsci, Antonio, 191–92
Green, Daniel M., 123
Green, Donald, 107*n*, 311–12
Grieco, Joseph M., 219
Griesdorf, Michael, 61–62
Grotius, Hugo, 30, 33–34
Gurr, Ted Robert, 45*n*, 46, 48*n*, 70*n*, 97*n*, 110, 247, 300

Haas, Ernst, 27, 76*n*, 164*n*, 165
Harris, William, 287
Hart, Robert A., 46*n*, 64*n*
Hayes, Brad, 202*n*
Hegre, Håvard, 50, 59*n*, 70*n*, 153*n*, 180*n*, 200
Heiss, Klaus R., 141*n*
Heldt, Birger, 68*n*, 153*n*, 242*n*
Helpman, Elhanan, 222
Henderson, Errol, 49, 70*n*, 247, 255*n*
Hermann, Margaret G., 63
Herzog, Roman, 241
Hewitt, J. Joseph, 46*n*, 164*n*
Hirschman, Albert O., 132, 219
Hoare, Quintin, 191
Hobbes, Thomas, 22–23, 30, 33, 41, 42, 90, 179
Hobson, J. A., 131, 152
Hoffmann, Stanley, 28*n*, 77
Holmes, Stephen, 239*n*, 241
Holsti, Ole, 23
Houweling, Henk, 288
Howard, Michael, 128
Huntington, Samuel P., 177, 239–60, 262–64, 267–68
Huntley, Wade, 66, 90, 180*n*
Hurd, Ian, 304
Hurrell, Andrew, 40
Hurwitz, Leon, 161
Huth, Paul, 69, 288

Ikenberry, G. John, 30, 228

Jackman, Robert, 77
Jacobson, Harold K., 160, 162, 173, 179, 215
Jaggers, Keith, 45*n*, 46, 48*n*, 97*n*, 110
James, Patrick, 62, 69, 199, 200*n*
Jefferson, Thomas, 78
Jervis, Robert, 107*n*, 212
Jett, Douglas C., 211*n*
Jiang Zemin, 286
Johnson, Thomas J., 77–78
Jordan, Robert, 161
Joyner, Christopher, 168
Joyner, James, 55*n*, 63
Jung-Yee Liang, 311

Kacowicz, Arie M., 40, 58
Kang, Heejoon, 136

Kant, Immanuel, 10, 29, 30, 33, 41, 53, 71, 76, 78–79, 90, 98, 128, 139, 157, 158, 173, 213, 228, 236, 269, 271–76, 279, 280, 281–82, 302, 303*n*, 305
Kaplan, Jeffrey H., 160*n*, 173*n*
Kaplan, Robert D., 240*n*
Katz, Jonathan N., 46, 106*n*, 311
Kautilya, 34
Kegley, Charles W., 63
Keith, Linda Camp, 79
Kennan, George F. ["X"], 298
Keohane, Robert O., 28*n*, 130, 132, 160, 164, 165, 169
Kim, Soo Yeon, 61, 107*n*, 136, 226, 232*n*, 234, 311–12
Kindleberger, Charles, 25
King, Gary, 106*n*, 122
Kirchner, Emil J., 289*n*
Kitfield, James, 284
Kleiboer, Marieke, 211*n*
Kmenta, Jan, 235*n*
Knorr, Klaus, 141*n*
Kozhemiakin, Alexander, 51
Krain, Matthew, 70
Krasner, Stephen, 219, 245*n*
Kroll, J. A., 132
Krugman, Paul, 222
Kugler, Jacek, 56, 70*n*, 88, 185, 286
Kugler, Richard L., 188*n*, 283*n*
Kumar, Krishna, 202*n*
Kupchan, Charles A., 163*n*, 165, 245–46, 261
Kupchan, Clifford A., 163*n*, 165
Kurth, James, 239*n*, 245*n*

Lai, Brian, 59*n*
Laitin, David D., 247*n*
Lakatos, Imre, 59
Lake, David, 56, 58, 66
Lalman, David, 44*n*, 54, 55, 66, 74*n*, 115
Langley, Jeffrey, 164*n*
Lasswell, Harold, 199, 312
Leblang, David, 73
Leeds, Brett Ashley, 64, 69, 115
Legro, Jeffrey, 230*n*
Lemke, Douglas, 58, 59, 186, 188, 286
Lenin, V. I., 34, 131, 152
Lerner, Daniel, 130
Levy, Jack, 68*n*, 129, 135, 226, 242*n*, 244*n*, 287
Lewis-Beck, Michael S., 72
Lian, Bradley, 55*n*, 63, 67*n*, 69, 247*n*
Liang, Jung-Yee, 311
Licklider, Roy E., 247*n*
Limongi, Fernando, 72
Lindberg, Leon, 27
Li Peng, 286

Lister, Frederick K., 128
Locke, John, 23, 179
Lofdahl, Corey L., 296n
Louis, William Roger, 219
Luce, Henry, 297–98
Luttwak, Edward, 175
Lutz-Bachmann, Matthias, 302

McDonald, Judith A., 132n
McGwire, Michael, 283n
Machiavelli, Niccolò, 33
MacMillan, John, 79
McMillan, Susan M., 78n, 133n, 279
Maddison, Angus, 141n, 175n
Mahan, Alfred Thayer, 280
Mahbubani, Kishore, 240n, 293
Maier, Charles S., 289
Malkina, Tatyana, 286
Mandelbaum, Michael, 283n
Mansfield, Edward, 51, 65, 117, 133, 136, 219, 221, 226
Mao Zedong, 34, 70, 78
Maoz, Zeev, 37, 44n, 46n, 47n, 51, 53, 200
March, James, 160
Marshall, Monty G., 123n, 179, 300
Martin, Lisa, 131, 165, 169
Marx, Karl, 34
Mathers, Todd, 162, 173n, 179, 215
Maull, Hanns, 34
Mearsheimer, John, 132, 162, 301
Meek, Curtis, 67
Meernik, James, 63, 69
Mercer, Jonathan, 243
Miall, Hugh, 164n
Midlarsky, Manus, 79n, 244n
Milanovic, Branko, 215n
Mill, John Stuart, 128
Miller, J.D.B., 279n, 280
Miller, Ross A., 69
Milner, Helen, 65, 162, 221
Mintz, Alex, 62, 65
Mitchell, Brian R., 140n, 144n, 176
Mitchell, Glenn, 62
Mitchell, Sara McLaughlin, 64, 180n, 200
Mitrany, David, 27, 129, 165
Modelski, George, 188n
Moon, Bruce E., 221
Moravcsik, Andrew, 28n, 78n, 230n
Morgenstern, Oskar, 141n
Morrow, James, 220, 221
Most, Benjamin A., 53, 54, 91
Mousseau, Michael, 59, 65, 153n, 200
Moynihan, Daniel Patrick, 240n
Mueller, John E., 67n, 151, 279
Muller, Edward N., 70n
Munro, Ross H., 293n

Murphy, Craig, 38, 168
Myers, Marissa Edson, 70n

Nagler, Jonathan, 99
Nathan, Andrew J., 293n
Navia, Patricio, 79
Nelson, Brent, 28n
Nie, Norman H., 77
Nierop, Tom, 170n
Nincic, Miroslav, 55n
Niu Wen-Yuan, 287
Nixon, Richard, 285
Nobel, Alfred, 39
Nolan, Peter, 296n
North, Robert, 23, 152
Nuttall, Simon, 28n
Nye, Joseph S., 28n, 130, 132, 192, 293n

Obey, David, 291
Olsen, Johan, 160
Olson, Mancur, 56
Oneal, John R., 49, 52, 55n, 63, 67n, 69, 95n, 97n, 103, 106n, 114, 115, 119, 133n, 139n, 141n, 148, 162, 172n, 185, 199, 217, 222, 226, 232n, 239n, 247n, 255n, 281, 308, 310, 312, 313
O'Neill, Barry, 94
Onuf, Nicholas G., 77–78, 243n
Oppenheimer, J. Robert, 10
Oren, Ido, 49n
Orend, Brian, 303n
Organski, A.F.K., 56, 88, 185, 186, 188n, 287
Organski, Catherine, 287
Orwell, George, 199
Owen, John, 44n

Page, Benjamin, 55n
Paine, Thomas, 128
Palmer, Glenn, 64n
Papayoanou, Paul, 131
Paris, Roland, 202n
Park, William, 289n
Partell, Peter, 64n
Pastor, Robert A., 201
Peceny, Mark, 49n, 64
Perkins, Bradford, 288
Poe, Steven C., 79
Polachek, Solomon W., 132n, 136
Polanyi, Karl, 78
Pollins, Brian, 136, 152, 221
Powell, Robert, 220
Prins, Brandon, 64
Przeworski, Adam, 72
Putnam, Robert D., 75

Qingshan, Tan, 296
Quesnay, François, 128

Raknerud, Arvid, 59*n*
Ratner, Steven, 168
Ray, James Lee, 44*n*, 47, 49*n*
Raymond, Gregory A., 65, 164*n*, 173
Reed, William, 46*n*, 58, 186, 188
Reisinger, William, 162, 173*n*, 179, 215
Reiter, Dan, 55, 59, 66, 67, 68, 75, 244*n*
Remmer, Karen, 221
Rengger, N. J., 104*n*
Repko, Sergei, 285
Reuveny, Rafael, 136
Ricardo, David, 128, 138, 277, 279
Rice, Condoleeza, 289
Rioux, Jean-Sebastien, 50, 69
Risse-Kappen, Thomas, 44*n*, 75, 131, 166, 167, 243
Robinson, Ronald, 219
Rochester, J. Martin, 164*n*
Rock, Stephen R., 288
Romer, David, 72*n*, 223
Rosecrance, Richard, 130, 141, 144, 279
Rosendorff, B. Peter, 65, 221
Rosenne, Shabtai, 33
Ross, Robert S., 293*n*
Rousseau, David, 46*n*, 50, 52, 57*n*
Rozman, Gilbert, 285
Rubinson, Richard, 132
Ruggie, John Gerard, 21, 38, 78, 192
Rummel, Rudolph J., 44*n*, 49*n*, 70, 78, 275
Russett, Bruce, 43*n*, 44*n*, 46*n*, 47*n*, 48, 49*n*, 52, 53, 55*n*, 61, 62, 66, 74*n*, 95*n*, 97*n*, 103, 106*n*, 114, 115, 119, 130, 133*n*, 139*n*, 164, 167, 170*n*, 172*n*, 180*n*, 185, 199, 217, 218*n*, 221, 222, 226, 232*n*, 234, 239*n*, 255*n*, 266*n*, 281, 282*n*, 288, 304, 308, 310, 312, 313

Sadowski, Yahya, 247*n*
Saunders, Phillip C., 293*n*
Schneider, Gerald, 133*n*, 279
Schroeder, Paul, 19, 163*n*, 285*n*
Schultz, Kenneth A., 64, 66, 275
Schumpeter, Joseph, 129
Schwarz, John E., 72*n*
Schweller, Randall, 55*n*, 152, 285*n*
Segal, Gerald, 287*n*, 296
Segura, Barry, 67*n*
Semmel, Bernard, 129
Sen, Amartya, 78
Senese, Paul, 46*n*
Shambaugh, David, 296
Shanks, Cheryl, 160*n*, 173*n*
Shapiro, Robert, 55*n*
Shaw, R. Paul, 242
Shi, Yuhang, 200
Shin, Michael, 200
Shinkarenko, Pavel, 286
Siccama, Jan, 288

Sidanius, James, 243*n*
Sikkink, Kathryn, 162
Simmel, Georg, 242
Simmons, Beth, 165
Simon, Michael W., 59*n*
Singer, J. David, 49, 70*n*, 103, 104*n*, 169*n*, 177*n*, 180*n*
Singer, Max, 44*n*
Singleton, Sara, 75
Siverson, Randolph, 55, 59*n*, 66, 67, 221
Small, Melvin, 49, 180*n*
Smil, Vaclav, 287
Smith, Adam, 29, 36, 128
Smith, Alastair, 69
Smith, Geoffrey Newell, 191
Smith, Michael J., 23
Snidal, Duncan, 163, 220
Snow, Donald M., 202*n*
Snyder, Jack, 51, 117, 121, 285*n*
Solberg, Eric, 199, 200*n*
Solingen, Etel, 79
Sollenberg, Margareta, 48*n*, 247*n*, 300
Soo Yeon Kim, 61, 107*n*, 136, 226, 232*n*, 234, 311–12
Spanger, Hans-Joachim, 292
Spengler, Oswald, 242
Sperling, James, 289*n*
Spero, John, 142
Spiezio, K. Edward, 188*n*
Sraffa, Piero, 138
Stalin, Joseph, 70, 262
Stam, Allan C. III, 59, 66, 67, 68, 106*n*, 107*n*, 172*n*, 244, 276, 279, 281, 282*n*, 308, 310
Starr, Harvey, 43*n*, 48, 53, 54, 55, 74*n*, 91
Stein, Arthur A., 242*n*
Steinbruner, John, 290
Stern, Paul C., 211*n*
Stone Sweet, Alec, 163, 214*n*
Stubbs, Alexander, 28*n*
Stuckey, John, 103
Sullivan, Jake, 310
Summers, Robert, 141*n*, 144*n*
Sun Szu, 34

Tabares, Tressa, 221
Tajfel, Henry, 243
Tan Qingshan, 296
Tate, C. Neal, 79
Taylor, Michael, 75, 77
Tessler, Mark, 244*n*
Tetlock, Philip, 244*n*
Thakur, Ramesh, 202*n*
Thayer, Carlyle, 202*n*
Thompson, William R., 51*n*
Thucydides, 85, 88
Tinbergen, Jan, 134, 222
Tipson, Frederick, 239–40, 269
Toynbee, Arnold, 242

Truman, Harry S., 307
Tucker, Richard, 46, 51n, 106n, 255n, 311
Turgot, Anne Robert, 128
Turner, John C., 243
Turner, Stansfield, 290

Urwin, Derek, 28n

Van Belle, Douglas, 62
Vanhanen, Tatu, 45, 46, 99n
van Krimpen, C., 291
Vasquez, John A., 162
Venancio, Moises, 206n
Verdier, Daniel, 56, 131, 221n
Volgy, Thomas, 72n
Voll, John O., 244n

Wallace, Michael, 169n
Wallensteen, Peter, 48n, 247n, 300
Walt, Stephen, 241
Waltz, Kenneth, 88, 92, 112
Wang, Kevin, 69
Ward, Michael Don, 51, 52, 200, 296n
Waterman, Peter, 69
Watson, Adam, 19
Way, Christopher, 132–33
Weart, Spencer, 44n, 71
Weede, Erich, 44n, 70n, 72n, 198, 244n
Weingast, Barry, 66

Weiss, Thomas G., 202n
Wendt, Alexander, 23, 74n, 107n, 166, 168, 179, 243n
Wen-Yuan, Niu, 287
Werner, Suzanne, 59
Whitlock, Lynn Williams, 160
Whitlock, Rodney, 160
Wildavsky, Aaron, 44n
Wilkenfeld, Jonathan, 46n, 164n
Williams, Howard, 302
Wilson, Woodrow, 19–20, 30, 41, 228
Wohlforth, William, 31, 299
Wolfson, Murray, 199, 200n
Woller, Gary, 55, 66
Wong, Yuwa, 242
Wright, Quincy, 85

Yeltsin, Boris, 286, 292n
Yi Feng, 73
Yoon, David, 107n, 311–12
Young, Oran, 164n
Yuhang Shi, 200
Yuwa Wong, 242

Zacarias, Agostonho, 202n
Zartman, William, 168
Zelikow, Philip, 289
Zemin, Jiang, 286
Zeng, Langche, 122
Zweifel, Thomas D., 79

General Index

accountability, of national leaders, 54, 55, 56, 79
Adenauer, Konrad, 24, 25, 228
AFFINITY variable, 231–36
Afghanistan, 68, 263, 264
Africa,
  border disputes in, 86
  colonialism in, 21, 86
  economic growth in, 73
  ethnic disputes in, 248
  in Huntington's civilization grouping, 246,
    251, 252n, 256, 257, 260–61
African Telecommunications Union, 16
Agency for the Prohibition of Nuclear
    Weapons, 165
Algeria, 263
alliances, 50
  after World War II, 113, 173, 195, 231
  against common enemy, 60–61, 173, 229
  before World War II, 113
  between democracies, 60, 229
  collective security and, 89, 163n, 173, 214,
    225, 229–30
  common interests of, 59–62, 103, 136, 173,
    214, 225, 229, 236

  in conflict reduction, 89, 103–4, 151, 172,
    196
  as consequence of international balance of
    power, 60, 214, 229–30
  hegemony and, 188, 288
  peaceful, 48
  polarity and, 92, 112
  states' preferences and, 234, 236
  trade between, 136, 221, 227
  unequal strengths of, 170
  in world wars, 19–20, 92, 104, 173, 176,
    236
ALLIES variable, 104, 109, 173, 189, 214,
    216, 225, 226, 236n, 252, 253, 256,
    265–66
amalgamation, in security communities, 75
America, *see* Canada; Latin America; United
    States
American Children's Institute, 16
anarchy,
  Hobbesian system of, 23, 179
  defined, 18
  as vicious circle, 22–23
  and war, 90, 230

377

Angell, Sir Norman, 129, 278–80
Angola, 203, 205, 206
Anti-Ballistic Missile Treaty, 304
Arab-Israeli conflict, 23, 259
Arab-Israeli trade, 139n, 181
Arab League, 170, 173, 265
Argentina, 40, 72, 151
ASEAN (Association of South East Asian
    States), 16, 193
Asia,
    authoritarianism in, 293–94, 303
    cold war and, 60, 260
    colonies in, 21
    economic growth in, 73
    economic interdependence in, 34, 41, 193,
        301
    international organizations in, 34, 193, 283
    interstate systems in, 34
    realist politics in, 34
    security community in, 193
    see also specific nations
Association of South East Asian States
    (ASEAN), 16, 193
Australia, 251n
Austria, and World War II, 94
Austria-Hungary,
    as great power, 102
    and Thirty Years War, 19
    and World War I, 24, 92, 104, 175–76
autarky (economic isolation), 25, 32, 37, 110,
    223, 257, 285, 288, 304–5
autocracies,
    aggressiveness of, 51, 52
    in conflict reduction, 114–16
    decaying, 70
    famine and, 78
    in IGOs, 213
    prisoners of war and, 67
    regime instability of, 51
    wars and disputes between, 49, 50, 115–16,
        180, 276
    in Warsaw Pact, 111
    wealth extracted from citizens in, 57, 220
autocratization, process of, 51, 117–22
AUT-to-DEM variable, 119
AVGDEMOC variable, 181–83, 189
AVGDEPEND variable, 181–83, 189
AVGIGO variable, 181–83, 189

Bay of Pigs invasion (1961), 132
Belgium, 88, 133–34, 222n, 227–28
bell-shaped ("normal") curve, 108n
Berlin Wall, dismantling of (1989), 93
bipolar systems, 92, 111, 112, 174, 214, 229–
    30, 286
Bonaparte, Napoleon, 19, 87, 118, 184, 278
Bosnia, 289, 303
Boutros-Ghali, Boutros, 33, 167, 168, 192

Brazil, 40, 223–24, 260
Bretton Woods conference, 21, 168
Brezhnev, Leonid, 298
Britain, *see* Great Britain
Brosio, Manlio, 164
Brunei, 193
Buddhist civilization, 246, 251, 252n, 256,
    257, 260
Burma (Myanmar), 193, 223
Burundi, 81
Bush, George, 15, 65, 68, 303

Cambodia, 193, 203, 204, 205, 264
Canada,
    cooperation of U.S. and, 16, 196, 212
    distance computations for, 101n
    IGOs and, 31
    trading patterns of, 222n
capitalism,
    critics of, 131–32
    in Kantian peace, 302
    Marxist-Leninist doctrine vs., 293
Caribbean nations, 251n
Castro, Fidel, 132
Catalonia, 28
cats-and-dogs effect, 115
Central Commission for the Navigation of the
    Rhine, 160, 176
Chad, 65
"cheap talk," 96
Chechnya, 289
Chile, 40, 62
China,
    communism in, 34
    and democracy, 273, 283, 294
    economic growth of, 287, 288, 295–96, 301
    economic isolation of, 25, 135, 295–96
    famines in, 78
    as great power, 102, 282, 293
    and Hong Kong, 294
    and international organizations, 161, 282,
        283, 294–97
    and international trade, 41, 147, 296
    in Kantian peace, 273, 282–88, 292–97
    middle class of, 295
    military capability of, 295–96
    Nixon in, 285, 296
    nuclear weapons of, 293
    options of, 294–97
    population of, 287
    Russian alliance with, 283–89
    Sinic civilization of, 244, 260, 261
    and Taiwan, 137, 294, 296
    and UN Security Council, 20, 297
    warming relations between West and, 16,
        147, 223, 272–73, 293–97
civilizations, Huntington's use of term, 246
civil liberties, in democracies, 44, 65, 176

civil society, 73, 204, 209
civil wars, 70–71, 201, 209, 210, 211
Clash of Civilizations and the Remaking of World Order, The (Huntington), 239–69
  changes over time, 262–64
  civilizations grouped in, 246, 251
  core claim of, 240–41
  effects of cultural differences in, 246–50
  and identity, 242–46
  insignificant differences in, 267–69
  patterns of conflict in, 255–60
  policy implications of, 241
  prime movers in, 264–67
  regional hegemonies in, 260–61
  responses to, 239–40
  social psychology and, 242
  statistical assessment of, 248–69
Clinton, William, 67, 68, 69, 218
Cobden, Richard, 29–30, 34, 36, 128–29
cold war,
  autarky in, 37
  bipolarity in, 92, 111, 112, 174, 214, 229–30, 286
  Communist bloc in, 32, 139n, 229–30, 260, 263
  East-West hostility and rivalry in, 31, 60, 103, 135, 201, 228, 229–30, 240, 241, 262–64, 283, 292, 293, 298–99, 300–301
  end of, 15, 31–32, 37, 60, 92–93, 229, 263, 264, 267, 285, 298, 300, 301
  era of (1950–85), 20, 91, 111
  European integration during, 28
  global balance of power in, 28
  global institutions in, 21–22
  ideological differences in, 60
  international trade in, 219–20, 228
  Kantian peace in, 229–30
  military interventions in, 63, 301
  NATO and, 164, 220, 229, 261, 293
  nuclear threat in, 300
  years previous to (1886–1939), 112
collective goods, 56, 57
"colonialism"
  Africa and, 21, 86
  Asia and, 21
  competition and, 152
  end of, 21, 23, 177, 179
  Europe and, 20, 34, 219
  geographic proximity and, 101, 214–15, 252
commerce, *see* international trade
communication, international, 164
Communist bloc, *see* Eastern Europe; Soviet Union
Communist tradition, 34
community, use of term, 75
Comprehensive Test Ban Treaty, 304
Concert of Europe, 19, 159–60, 163n

Conference on Security and Cooperation in Europe (CSCE), 33, 167, 201
conflict,
  asymmetrical economic relations and, 132, 143, 147
  bilateral vs. multilateral, 95
  causes and constraints on, 85–91, 280, 311
  changes in level of force in, 95n
  channeling of, 77
  civilizations and, 239–69
  contagion of, 102
  costs of, 101n, 135, 137, 151, 181, 244, 278–79
  COW data on, 94–95, 310–11
  cultural differences and, 242–47
  in database, 94–95
  democracy and, 199–200, 249n
  economic effects on third parties, 144
  economic growth and, 151–53
  great powers in, 1–8, 102, 108
  hegemony and, 189–91, 260–61
  intrastate, 247–48
  "joiners" in, 310
  religion and, 248, 303
  risk factors for, 107–9, 280
  trade as source of, 132, 134–38
  see also conflict management; conflict reduction; war
conflict management, 64–66, 91
  choosing which wars to fight, 67
  law applied in, 73
  mediation by third parties in, 65
conflict reduction, 81–123
  alliances and, 89, 103–4, 151, 172, 196
  arms control and, 290
  autocracy and, 114–16
  democracy and, 97–123, 191
  in democratic peace proposition, 61
  economic interdependence and, 145–48
  epidemiology and, 82–85, 91–94
  geography in, 86–87, 100–103
  global experience in, 104–11
  international organizations and, 171–74, 182, 275, 289
  Kantian influences in, 90–91, 174, 179, 181, 312
  over time, 116
  political competition in, 202–3, 204, 274–75
  in political transitions, 116–22, 288
  power and, 87–88, 90, 103, 172, 303
  realism and, 90–91, 100–104, 195, 268, 287–88
  trade and, 133, 145–50, 182, 191, 218–22, 279–80
Congo, Republic of, 86
Congress, U.S., War Powers Act, 274
Congress of Vienna, 159–60

constitutional government, *see* democracy
constructivist school, 243, 277–78
Correlates of War, *see* COW Project
countries, *see* states; *specific countries*
covert action, 62–63
COW (Correlates of War) Project,
    alliances identified in, 104
    composite capabilities index, 103
    data compiled by, 94–95, 310–11
    hegemons identified in, 185
    major powers identified in, 101–2, 149*n*
    military expenditures data from, 187*n*
Croatia, 121
Crucé, Emeric, 127–28, 276–77, 278
Cuba, 34, 132, 136
Cuban missile crisis (1692), 132
cultural clashes, *see* Clash of Civilizations
cultural hegemony, 191–92
cultures, Huntington's use of term, 246
Cyprus, 164
Czechoslovakia, 94, 104, 142
Czech Republic, 73, 121, 283

Damocles, sword of, 301
decision makers, rationality of, 309–10
decision makers' perceptions, exclusion from
    data, 106, 107*n*
Declaration of Independence, U.S., 78
decolonialization, 21, 23, 177, 179
de Gasperi, Alcide, 24, 25, 228
democide, 70
DEMOC measure, 98–100, 109–10, 114–16,
    138, 170–73, 213, 215–16, 223, 224–
    25, 252–53, 256, 265–66
democracy,
    accountability in, 54, 55, 56, 79
    central relationships in, 76–77
    changes over time in, 177–79, 181, 194–
        95
    chaos in, 96
    characteristics of, 97
    civil war and, 70–71
    coherent, 110
    community of, 77
    conflict and, 199–200, 249*n*
    cultural norms in, 65
    defense of, 55
    definitions of, 44
    diplomatic actions of, 96
    domestic stability in, 78
    domestic violence in, 70
    economic development and, 72–73
    in eighteenth century, 29
    elections in, 37, 44, 55, 56, 69, 78
    and end of cold war, 31–32
    and entrepreneurship, 157, 220
    equality in, 29
    EU and, 38, 167, 220

    in former Soviet Union, 15, 31–32, 51–52,
        118, 282
    freedom in, 29, 37, 44, 78
    free markets in, 125, 198
    free press in, 62
    hegemony of, 57, 188, 246, 261
    human rights in, 44, 237
    IGOs and, 38, 40, 164, 179, 218, 234
    imperfect, 98, 121–22
    institutional checks and balances in, 79
    internal political strength of, 63
    international trade and, 38, 131, 157, 179,
        198–99, 218–22, 225–28, 234, 278
    intervention of, 62–64
    in Kant's triangle, 29, 35–42, 174, 193–96,
        271–72
    laws and legal institutions in, 209
    legitimacy and, 70, 77
    and lenders of international capital, 66
    liberalism and, 76–77, 192
    Mercosur and, 40
    military expenditures lower for, 51
    partial, 70
    peace and, *see* democratic peace; Kantian
        peace
    in period 1885–1992, 92, 111, 194
    and political integration, 74–76
    political parties in, 207–9, 274
    preponderance of, 123, 167, 179, 184
    promotion of, 24, 25, 52
    prosperity and, 25, 72
    public opinion in, 68–69
    rating systems for, 45–46
    separation of government powers in, 29, 53
    shared identity of, 268–69
    shift toward vs. level of, 118–20
    society and, 77–79
    and status quo, 56–58, 186–87
    threats to, 52, 176
    transition to, *see* democratization
    transparency of, 54, 64, 65, 79, 168, 201
    and UN, 33, 38, 167–68, 200–206
    in virtuous circles, 29–33
    as winner in war, 66–68, 180, 275
democratic peace, 36, 37, 43–79, 169
    broader phenomena of, 71–74, 276
    civil wars and, 70–71
    common interests and, 59–62
    conflict management and, 64–66, 91
    contextual theories of, 53–54, 58–59
    cultural explanations of, 53–54, 55, 58, 73,
        275
    domestic conflict-foreign conflict and, 68–70
    dyads in, 46, 47–52, 53–58, 66, 95–96,
        275
    internal politics and, 54
    international trade and, 218–22, 278
    interventions and, 62–64

Kant and, *see* Kantian peace
in post-cold war era, 112, 194, 228, 229–37
post-World War II, 112, 194, 228, 229
and power transition theory, 58, 186–87
in pre-cold war era (1886–1939), 112
realist critique of, 60
robust support for, 46, 276
scientific progress and, 59
and security communities, 74–76, 231
status quo and, 56–58, 190
strategic thinking and, 52, 54–58
structural explanations of, 53–54, 55, 58
victories in, 66–68, 275
see also peace
democratic peace proposition, 43–44, 61
democratization,
barriers to, 123
effects of, 52, 116–22, 202
and exclusionary nationalism, 121
increases in, 179, 303
international organizations and, 200–206
process of, 51–52, 206–11
statistical analysis of, 118–22
DEM-to-AUT variable, 119
dependency theorists, 131–32, 143, 147
DEPEND variable, 141, 143, 145–47, 149*n*,
170–73, 214, 216–17, 236*n*, 252–3,
256, 259, 265–66
dictatorships, aggressiveness of, 56
Dionysius, 301
DISPUTE variable, 213, 215–16, 224–25,
233–35, 250
distance,
in conflict reduction, 86–87, 100–103, 195
in gravity model, 223
great-circle, 101
of major ports, 101*n*
natural logarithm of, 101*n*
trade and, 134–35, 226
doves vs. hawks, 54, 55, 66
dyads, 47–52, 74
of autocracies, 49, 50
conflict potentials of, 102, 195
of democracies, 46, 48–50, 100, 110, 116,
122–23, 228, 234
in democratic peace, 46, 53–58, 66, 95–96,
275
distance computations for, 101*n*
economic interdependence of, 126, 134–38,
149
geographic proximity of, 50, 86–87, 100–
103
IGO memberships of, 74, 169–70
imbalance of power in, 48, 51, 191
individual states as distinct from, 49, 50
major and minor powers in, 102, 309
mutual identity of, 107*n*
one autocracy and one democracy in, 114–16

politically relevant, 102, 281, 309
status quo and, 186–87
trade patterns of, 222–28
world wars and, 175
dyad-year, as unit of analysis, 105

East Asia, *see* Asia
Eastern Europe,
autarky in, 32, 110
and breakup of Soviet Union, 32, 51, 92,
167
and cold war, *see* cold war
collective security of, 288
democratization of, 51–52, 118, 121, 201,
257
economic growth in, 73
and international organizations, 33, 167,
282, 283–84, 290, 291
East Germany,
Communist collapse in, 92
merger of West and, 21, 92, 289
UN membership of, 232*n*
Economic and Monetary Union, 27
Economic and Social Council, 30
economic competition, unbridled, 78, 195
economic development, 72–73, 236*n*
economic interdependence, 125–55
analytical problems of, 133–38
changes over time, 177–79, 181, 194
conflict reduction and, 145–48
direction of causation in, 135
and end of cold war, 31–32
in global economy, 25–29
growth and conflict in, 151–53
and IGOs, 213–15
in Kant's triangle, 35–42, 174, 193–96,
271–72
liberal peace of, 127–33
measurement of, 141–45
of open economies, 148–51
and peace, 25, 125–51, 155, 237, 276–80,
312
regional, 34, 193, 301
and security communities, 277–78
trade and, *see* international trade
in virtuous circles, 29–33
and World War I, 174–75, 176
economic sanctions, 37, 135–36, 164, 281
Ecuador, 81
Egypt, 261
elections,
in democracies, 37, 44, 55, 56, 69, 78
UN assistance with, 167–68, 201, 204,
210–11
El Salvador, 203, 205, 206, 264
embedded liberalism, 78, 192
endogeneity, research on, 312–13
energy consumption, in power ratio, 103

English language, predominance of, 299
entrepreneurship, 157, 220
environmental degradation, 79
epidemiology, 82–85, 91–94, 105
Estonia, 121
Ethiopia, 251*n*
ethnic conflicts, 118, 247–48, 289, 301
ethnic minorities, 86, 289
ethnic ties, 86, 247
Europe,
    absence of war in, 158
    and colonial system, 20, 34, 219
    congress system in, 159–60, 163*n*
    democracies in, 24, 44, 150, 201
    dictatorial rule in, 20
    economic interdependence in, 278–79,
        301
    Hanseatic League in, 128
    international organizations in, 33, 158–61,
        289
    interstate systems in, 17, 20–21, 29–33
    Kantian principles in, 31
    postwar years in, 24–33, 40
    principle of sovereignty in, 17–19
    virtuous circles built in, 24–29
    wars in, *see specific wars*
    see also specific nations
European Central Bank, 27
European Coal and Steel Community, 26, 27
European Commission, 27, 166
European Common Market, 27, 158
European Community, 27
European Court of Human Rights, 27
European Court of Justice, 27, 164, 214*n*
European Defense Community, 28
European Parliament, 27
European Union (EU), 27–29, 31, 174–75
    democracy as prerequisite to, 38, 167,
        220
    as IGO, 168–69, 194, 214
    and Kantian peace, 228, 283
    mutual identification in, 166
    as security community, 75–76, 158
    trade patterns of, 221
    U.S. relationship with, 212
external sovereignty, 17

Falkland Islands, 151
fascism, 223
fault line wars, 250, 252
feedback loops, 38, 197, 216, 227, 281
Finland, 93*n*
fixed-effects model, 106*n*, 107*n*, 312
France,
    appeasement policy of, 52
    in cold war, 60
    and democracy, 60
    former colonies of, 20, 219

as great power, 101–2
international trade with, 133–34, 175
and Mozambique, 208
neighboring states and, 50
revolutionary ideology of, 117–18
in security community, 158
and Thirty Years War, 19
and UN Security Council, 20, 297
in world wars, 92, 104, 175–76
freedom, in democracy, 29, 37, 44, 78
French Revolution, 18–19, 117–18

game theory, 54–55, 96
garrison state, 199, 312
GATT (General Agreement on Tariffs and
    Trade), 21, 168
GDP (gross domestic product), 134, 141
    military expenditures-to-GDP ratio, 187–88,
        263–64, 301
    real GDP per capita, 152–53
    size and, 224
    trade-to-GDP ratio, 137, 141, 142, 143,
        145, 147, 154, 179, 183*n*, 214, 253
GDPPerCap variable, 215–17, 223, 226
GEE (general estimating equation), 106*n*,
    311
General Agreement on Tariffs and Trade
    (GATT), 21, 168
Geneva Convention, 67
geography, 50, 86–87, 100–103
    and colonial holdings, 101, 214–15, 252
    distance computations for, 101*n; see also* dis-
        tance
    in Huntington's groupings, 251*n*
    and IGO memberships, 215, 216
    and noncontiguity measure, 101
Germany,
    Allied occupation of, 24
    as autocracy, 50, 118, 144
    Berlin Wall dismantled in, 93
    democracy in, 46
    depression and, 25
    economic strength of, 299
    as great power, 102, 185
    international trade with, 145, 175–76, 219,
        222*n*
    liberal policies in, 34
    and NATO, 89, 289
    quest for power of, 57–58
    radical political change in, 244
    reunification of, 21, 92, 289
    in security community, 158
    sovereignty of, 180*n*
    UN membership of, 232*n*
    Weimar Republic of, 25, 41, 118
    and world wars, 19–20, 22, 24, 25, 31, 92,
        94, 104, 152, 175, 278, 288, 298, 310
glasnost (openness), 32

global economy, 20–22
  economies of scale in, 25
  Great Depression and, 20, 24–25, 41, 78, 150, 278
  interdependence in, 25–29
  investment in, 25–26, 130, 141, 220, 277
  trade in, *see* international trade
  world wars and, 20–21, 150, 174–76, 278–80
global systems, *see* international systems
global warming, 304
Gorbachev, Mikhail, 31–33, 285, 289
government,
  legitimacy of, 77, 78, 244
  responsibilities of, 78
  separation of powers in, 29, 53
  society and, 77–79
Granger model, 226n, 312–13
gravity model of trade, 222–23
Great Britain,
  appeasement policy of, 52
  in cold war, 60
  and democracy, 46, 60, 144
  former colonies of, 20, 44, 131, 214–15, 219, 221
  as great power, 101–2, 185, 288
  hegemony of, 57–58, 87, 185, 186, 188, 195
  and international trade, 20, 29, 129, 137, 175–76
  and Mozambique, 208
  and Thirty Years War, 19
  and UN Security Council, 20, 297
  U.S. relationship with, 81, 196, 220, 288
  in world wars, 92, 104, 175–76, 188, 195, 278, 288
Great Depression, 20, 24–25, 41, 78, 150, 278
Great Illusion, The (Angell), 278–79
great powers,
  conflicts of, 1–8, 102, 108
  constraining effects of, 281
  in COW Project data, 101–2, 149n
  military force of, 87
  networks of, 50
  in pre–cold war era, 112
  in statistical analysis, 102, 309
  trade between, 221
  transitions in, 288
  UN and, 297
Great War, *see* World War I
Greece, 61, 103, 164, 265, 290, 291
Grenada, 63–64
gross domestic product, *see* GDP
Grotius, Hugo, 30, 33–34
GROWTH variable, 153
Guatemala, 62, 142–43, 147
Gulf War (1990–91), 65, 274, 295, 299, 303

Haiti, 201, 251n, 303
Hanseatic League, 128
hawks vs. doves, 54, 55, 66
HEGDEFENSE variable, 187–88, 189, 190
hegemonic stability theory, 184–86, 187, 189, 191, 195, 245
hegemony,
  and alliances, 188, 288
  in civilization groups, 260–61
  and conflict, 189–91, 260–61
  cultural, 191–92, 245
  defense spending by, 187–88, 190, 195, 263–64, 300–301
  democracy and, 57, 188, 246, 261
  identification of, 185
  in Kantian peace, 297–305
  and power transition theory, 58, 186–87, 195
  realist theories of, 22, 159, 184, 195
  statistical analysis of, 184–91
  Thirty Years War and, 19
  world wars and, 184–85, 188, 298
HEGPOWER indicator, 185–86, 188, 189
Helsinki Accords (1975), 33, 167
Hindu civilization, 246, 251, 252n, 256, 257, 260, 261
Hitler, Adolf,
  aggression of, 22, 52, 65, 70, 94
  fall from power of, 56
  rise to power of, 41, 118
  and World War II, 22, 25, 52, 94
Hobbes, Thomas,
  anarchy and, 23, 179
  chaos and, 22
  realist theories of, 22–23, 30, 33, 41, 90
  vicious circle of, 22–23, 42
Hobson, J. A., 131, 152
Honduras, 142
Hong Kong, 294
hostage crisis, 263
human rights,
  in democracies, 44, 237
  of Helsinki Accords, 33, 167
  international law and, 79
  NATO and, 237, 290
  UN and, 30, 33, 202, 204, 210
  West and, 244, 294
Hungary,
  Austria and, 19, 24, 92, 102, 104, 175–76
  conflicts with neighbors of, 118, 121
  NATO and, 283
  prosperity in, 73
  in Warsaw Pact, 104
Huntington, Samuel, *see Clash of Civilizations*
Hussein, Saddam, 56, 65, 69, 117, 274

ideological affinity, 60
IGOs (intergovernmental organizations), 31
  autocracies and, 213

IGOs (*continued*)
  changes over time, 177–84, 194–95, 216
  civil wars and, 201
  democracies and, 38, 40, 164, 179, 218, 234
  early forms of, 159–60
  economic interdependence in, 213–15
  formation of, 16, 38
  functions of, 162–63, 168–69
  indirect effects of, 167–69, 184
  influence of, 161–67, 212–18, 280
  international trade among, 38, 212, 218, 227
  in multilevel systems, 34, 160
  participation in, 31, 158, 159–61, 177, 212, 213
  peaceful interaction in, 38, 272, 280–82
  regional, 164, 193, 214, 221, 228
  reverse causality of, 168–69
  shared memberships in, 215–18
  statistical analysis of, 169–71
  unequal strengths of, 170
  use of term, 16, 160
  see also international organizations
IGO variable, 169–74, 213–18, 225, 232–35, 253, 256, 265–66
IMF, *see* International Monetary Fund
imperialism, wars of, 151, 152
independent effect, use of term, 105
India, 251n–52n, 260, 261, 286, 294
India-Pakistan conflict, 48, 194, 300n
Indonesia, 123, 193, 232n
infant mortality rates, 78–79
information,
  communication of, 164
  free movement of, 54
  restricted access to, 65
INGOs (international nongovernmental organizations), 16–17
  in multilevel systems, 34
  and peace, 38–39
in-group/out-group distinction, 242–43
institutions, defined, 160
interest groups, influence of, 130
intergovernmental organizations, *see* IGOs
internal sovereignty, 17
International Bank for Reconstruction and Development, *see* World Bank
international civil society, elements of, 73
International Court of Justice, 33, 65
International Criminal Court, 30, 304
international exchange, 168
international law,
  on human rights, 79
  in interstate interactions, 73
  in Kant's triangle, 29, 157–58, 193, 271–72
  and organizations, 158, 162
  and peace, 30, 73, 278
  and trade, 129

International Monetary Fund (IMF), 21, 30, 139, 168, 177, 201, 222, 299
international nongovernmental organizations (INGOs), 16–17, 34, 38–39
International Organization for Migration (IOM), 206, 207
international organizations, 16, 157–96
  changes over time, 177–84, 194, 216
  coercion or persuasion in, 163, 191–92
  for collective security, 158
  communication in, 164
  democracy-building by, 200–206
  and end of cold war, 31–32
  IGOs, *see* IGOs
  indirect effects of, 167–69
  in interstate interactions, 73–74, 275
  in Kant's triangle, 29, 35–42, 174, 193–96, 271–72
  legal standing of, 161
  mediation in, 163–64
  mutual identification in, 166
  and peace, 33, 37, 73, 162, 168–69, 191, 217–18, 278, 280–82
  post-World War II networks of, 26–29, 113, 160, 161, 173, 195, 216, 231
  problem-solving in, 165
  reverse causality of, 168–69
  socialization in, 165
  statistical analysis of, 169–74
  and trade, 50, 61, 129, 281–82
  in virtuous circles, 29–33
  and world wars, 19–20, 160, 174–77
international relations,
  central questions of, 15–16
  constructivist school of, 243, 277–78
  liberal theories of, 24, 126n
international systems, 15–42
  anarchy as vicious circle in, 22–23
  bipolar vs. multipolar, 92
  changes over time in, 92, 177–84
  conflict reduction in, 91
  dynamic nature of, 35
  economic interdependence in, 26–29
  European achievement of, 29–33
  hegemony in, 298–301
  Hobbesian, 22–23
  interactions supporting peace in, 33–35, 195
  Kantian triangle and, 35–42
  Lockean, 23, 129
  modern state system in, 16–22
  multipolar, 92, 112, 245–46, 303–5
  nongovernmental influences on, 38–39
  power transition theory in, 186–87, 190
  realist views of, 90–91, 159, 195
  technology and, 20, 21
  use of term, 16
  virtual circles in, 24–29

International Telecommunication Satellite Organization (INTELSAT), 164
International Telecommunication Union, 164
international trade,
  analysis of patterns in, 221–28
  asymmetry and, 279
  barriers to, 25, 150, 213, 219
  between allies, 136, 221, 227
  changing levels of, 150, 177, 195
  communication and, 130–31, 135, 139, 142, 198
  conflict reduction of, 133, 145–50, 182, 191, 218–22, 279–80
  democracy and, 38, 131, 157, 179, 198–99, 218–22, 225–28, 234, 278
  domestic market and, 144
  economically important, 126, 140–41, 218–19
  economic interdependence and, 138–48, 198–99, 276–80
  economic sanctions vs., 37, 135–36, 164, 281
  GATT and, 21, 168
  in global economy, 20–22, 24–26, 41, 281–82
  IGOs and, 38, 212, 218, 227
  IMF data for, 139
  incentives in, 29–30
  in Kant's triangle, 29, 38, 271
  Latin America and, 40, 219
  law and, 129
  measurement of, 133–38, 141–45
  in multinational corporations, 142
  national power and, 219
  national security and, 136, 220
  networks of, 50, 61, 129, 281–82
  in open economics, 148–51, 302
  peace and, 26, 30, 37, 57–58, 70, 72, 126–30, 190, 276–79
  preferential, 65, 221
  realism and, 219–20
  reciprocal relations in, 135, 213
  unequal balance of, 147–48
  WTO and, 21, 38, 168
interventions, 62–64
  cold war and, 63
  covert action, 62–63
  overt action, 63
  promotion of democracy as goal of, 64
  public opinion and, 62–63
  sovereignty violated in, 64
  by U.S., 62–64, 142–43
investment,
  communication and, 130–31, 141
  conflict and, 141
  in global economy, 25–26, 130, 141, 220, 277
  peace and, 26, 126

IOM (International Organization for Migration), 206, 207
Iran, 136, 241, 247, 261, 263, 264, 274
Iran-Contra scandal, 63
Iraq,
  and Saddam Hussein, 56, 65, 69, 117, 274
  and Iran, 117, 247
  and Kuwait (Gulf War), 21, 23, 33, 65, 180*n*, 274, 295, 303
  U.S. relations with, 68, 136, 190, 240
iron and steel production, in power ratio, 103
Islamic civilization, 246, 251, 252, 256, 257–58, 260–61, 265
Islam vs. non-Islam conflicts, 247*n*
Islam vs. the West, 241, 243, 244, 259, 263
isolation, economic (autarky), 25, 32, 37, 110, 223, 257, 285, 288, 304–5
Israel, 23, 81, 136, 139*n*, 170, 181, 252, 259
Italy,
  as autocracy, 50
  colonies of, 214–15
  as great power, 102
  and Mozambique, 208
  trading patterns of, 222
  and world wars, 20, 24, 92, 104, 176

Japan,
  as autocracy, 118
  as democratic state, 110
  economic growth of, 287, 299
  as great power, 102
  in Huntington's thesis, 251*n*
  IGOs and, 31, 232*n*, 294
  and international trade, 41, 145
  liberal policies in, 34
  radical political change in, 244
  sovereignty of, 180*n*
  Taisho democracy in, 31, 41, 150
  U.S. relationship with, 196, 212, 231, 294
  and world wars, 20, 24, 31
Jefferson, Thomas, 78
Jiang Zemin, 286

Kant, Immanuel, 98, 139
  and the Enlightenment, 302
  on international organizations, 213, 228
  on moral imperative, 78–79, 305
  Perpetual Peace by, 29, 53, 90, 128, 269, 271–72, 273–74, 302
  on republicanism, 76
  three principles of, *see* Kantian triangle
  war accepted by, 303*n*
Kantian peace, 231, 236, 271–305
  China in, 273, 282–88, 292–97
  cold war and, 229–30
  elements of, 271, 301
  EU and, 228, 283
  evidence for, 273–82, 301–2

Kantian peace (*continued*)
  hegemony in, 297–305
  multilateralism in, 303–5
  NATO in, 282–97
  Russia in, 273, 282–92
Kantian subsystem of states, 180
Kantian triangle, 35–42, 44
  on conflict reduction, 90–91, 174, 179, 181, 312
  elements of change in, 41
  feedback loops in, 38, 197, 216, 227, 281
  indirect influences in, 197–200
  interrelationships in, 173, 179
  measuring the influence of, 104–11, 182, 191, 212–18, 248, 252–57, 259, 264, 312
  threats to, 41–42
  three new loops in, 217–18
  three principles of, 10, 29–33, 71, 157–58, 173, 193–96, 271–72, 273
Kantian variables,
  average levels through time, 178, 179
  dyadic vs. systemic consequences of, 159, 181–83
  net effects of, 235–36
  pacific benefits of, *see* Kantian peace
Kashmir, 194
Korean War, 139n, 190, 262, 263, 295, 307
Kosovo, 67, 289, 303, 304
Kuwait, 21, 23, 33, 144, 180n, 240, 290
Kyoto Protocol, 304

Land Mines Convention, 304
Laos, 193
Latin America,
  Caribbean nations and, 251n
  cold war and, 60
  democracy in, 40, 201
  economic interdependence in, 301
  in Huntington's civilization grouping, 246, 251, 256, 257, 260
  international organizations in, 161
  international trade with, 40, 219
  interstate disputes in, 40
  Mercosur in, 40, 220–21
  nuclear nonproliferation in, 40, 165
  OAS in, 201, 211
  see also specific nations
Latvia, 121
Law of the Sea Convention, 304
League of Nations, 19–20, 30, 41, 140, 150, 161, 174, 194
legitimacy, 70, 77, 78, 79, 244
Lenin, V. I., 34, 131, 152
Leviathan (Hobbes), 22
Lewinsky, Monica, 68
liberal democracy, 192

liberalism,
  Asian authoritarianism vs., 293–94
  in conflict reduction, 90
  elements in, 79, 277
  embedded, 78, 192
  use of term, 78
  World War I and, 278–79
liberal peace, 127–33, 136–37, 145, 150, 169, 228–31, 234, 269
liberal policies,
  accountability of leaders, 54
  comparative advantage, 144, 302
  free movement of information, 54
  free trade in, 36, 129, 144, 148, 302
  and Kant's triangle, 36, 76–77, 90
  moves toward, 51–52, 273, 303
  opposition groups, 54
  shared among states, 61
  society and, 77–79
Libya, 65, 136
linguistic diversity, and conflict, 248
linguistic similarities, and peace, 247
Lithuania, 121
Locke, John, 23, 179
logistic regression analysis, 105, 138, 311
Luce, Henry, 297–98
Luxembourg, 222n

Maastricht Treaty (1991), 28
Machiavelli, Niccolò, 33
major powers, *see* great powers
Malaysia, 193
Mao Zedong, 34, 70, 78
Marx, Karl, 34
mediation, 128, 163–64
medicine, epidemiology and, 82–85, 91–94, 105
mercantilism, 25
Mercosur, 40, 220–21
Mexico, 31, 199, 251n
Middle East,
  Arab-Israeli relations in, 23, 139n, 181, 259
  Arab League in, 170, 173, 265
  Gulf War in, 65, 274, 295, 299, 303
  hostilities in, 81, 247, 264
  and principle of sovereignty, 23
  see also specific nations
MIDs (militarized interstate disputes), 94–96
military expenditures, in power ratio, 103
military expenditures-to-GDP ratio, 187–88, 263–64, 301
military manpower, in power ratio, 103
Mill, John Stuart, 128
Monnet, Jean, 24, 25, 228
moral imperative, 78–79, 305
Morocco, 247
Mozambique, 203, 205, 206–11

multilateralism, 303–5
multiple regression analysis, 105
multipolar systems, 92, 112, 245–46, 303–5
Muslim vs. non-Muslim conflicts, 247*n*
Muslim populations, 251*n; see also* Islamic civilization
Mussolini, Benito, 56
mutual identification, 166
Myanmar (Burma), 193, 223

NAFTA (North American Free Trade Agreement), 16, 199, 212, 299
Namibia, 203, 205, 206, 264
Napoleonic Wars, 18, 57, 118, 159, 184, 186
national interest,
    broad concept of, 60
    protection of, 81
    realist concept of, 228–30
    states' UN votes and, 229–36
    trade and, 219
nationalism, 77, 121, 246
nations, *see* states; *specific nations*
NATO (North Atlantic Treaty Organization),
    coercive actions of, 163, 237, 240, 290, 300*n*
    in cold war, 164, 220, 229, 261, 293
    in conflict reduction, 89, 103, 289
    expansion of, 283–85, 288–92, 294, 297
    formation of, 61
    as IGO, 16, 164, 170, 173, 213, 214, 265
    in Kantian peace, 282–97
    long-term future of, 283
    as mediator, 164
    military standards of, 290
    trade limitations in, 136
Netherlands, 20, 88, 131, 175, 222*n*, 227–28
Ne Win, General, 223
New Zealand, 48
Nicaragua, 62–63, 142, 203, 205, 206
Nigeria, 73, 123, 251*n*
1984 (Orwell), 199
Nixon, Richard, 285, 296
Nobel, Alfred, 39
noncontiguity measure, 101
Nordic states, cooperation among, 31
North American Free Trade Agreement (NAFTA), 16, 199, 212, 299
North Atlantic Treaty Organization, *see* NATO
North Korea, 34, 41, 136, 232*n*
North Vietnam, 180*n*
Nuclear Non-Proliferation Treaty, 40, 304
nuclear war, threat of, 40, 87, 112, 165, 228, 262, 284, 285, 288, 290, 293, 300–301, 304

OAS (Organization of American States), 201, 211
oligarchic republic, U.S. South as, 71

OPEC (Organization of Petroleum Exporting Countries), 223
OPEN measurement, 144, 148–49, 223, 224, 225, 227
opposition groups, existence of, 54
Organization for Security and Cooperation in Europe (OSCE), 33, 201, 211
Organization of American States (OAS), 201, 211
Orthodox-Slavic civilization, 246, 251, 256, 257, 259, 260, 261, 265
Orwell, George, 199
otherness, culture and, 242–43
Oviedo, Gen. Lino, 201

Paine, Thomas, 128
Pakistan, 48, 110, 119, 194, 300*n*
Palestine, 247
Pan-Arab sentiments, 246
Paraguay, 40, 201
peace,
    balance of power in, 88
    cease-fire in, 202–3, 206
    clashes of civilization vs., 240
    coercion toward, 163, 302–3
    democracy and, *see* democratic peace
    desirability of, 81–82
    economic interdependence and, 25, 126, 154–55, 237, 276–80, 312
    and free trade, 29, 126
    incentives for, 302
    international law and, 30, 73, 278
    international organizations and, 33, 37, 73, 162, 168–69, 191, 217–18, 278, 280–82
    international trade and, 26, 30, 37, 57–58, 70, 72, 126–30, 190, 276–77, 278–79
    and Kant's triangle, 35–42, 312; *see also* Kantian peace
    multiple paths to, 53, 81
    mutual responsiveness and, 58
    Nobel prize for, 39
    participants in, 39
    social, 78
    steps toward, 33–35, 202–3, 302–5
    in twenty-first century, 271–305
peace-years method, 106*n*
per capita income, 215
perestroika (restructuring), 32
Permanent Court of Arbitration, 164
Perpetual Peace (Kant), 29, 53, 90, 128, 269, 271–72, 273–74, 302
Philippines, 193, 252*n*
Poland,
    democracy in, 121
    and NATO, 283
    prosperity in, 73
    sovereignty of, 18
    in world wars, 94, 310

polarity,
  in post-cold war era (1989–1992), 92–93,
    174
  in pre-cold war period (1886–1939),
    112
  use of term, 92
political actors, use of term, 160
Polity III data, 97–99
population,
  in power ratio, 103, 185, 287
  and trade, 223, 225, 226
POPULATION variable, 223, 225, 226
Portugal,
  former colonies of, 20
  and international trade, 20
  and Mozambique, 208
  and NATO, 61, 291
post-cold war era,
  cultural clashes in, 240–41, 249
  democratic peace in, 112, 194, 228, 229–
    37
  democratization in, 179, 303
  international organizations in, 174
  interstate relations in, 93, 111
  period (1989–1992) of, 112
  polarity in, 92–93, 174
power,
  balance of, 88, 103, 109, 138, 229–30
  change over time, 92
  in conflict reduction, 87–88, 90, 103, 172,
    303
  diffusion of, 301
  dimensions of, 103
  imbalance of, 48, 51, 61–62, 103, 109,
    131–32, 184, 186, 191, 287
  insight and, 192
  international trade and, 219
  leadership and, 303, 304
  military, 88, 298, 301
  preponderant, 88, 109, 172, 186, 191, 195,
    287, 299
  soft, 192
  states' preferences and, 234
  see also hegemony
POWER RATIO variable, 103, 109, 146,
    149n, 189, 236n, 252, 253, 256
power transition theory, 58, 186–87, 189, 190,
    191, 195, 245
preferences, of states, 230–36
Primakov, Yevgeny, 286
private goods, 56
prosperity,
  and democracy, 25, 72
  economic interdependence and, 26–29
  and free trade, 29, 198
  post-World War II, 25, 132, 179, 237
Prussia, 19, 128
Putin, Vladimir, 292

quantitative analysis,
  attraction of, 307
  decisions in, 307–8
  methodology of, 307–13
  tables of, 314–29
  see also statistical analysis
Quesnay, François, 128

rational-choice models, 76, 165
real GDP per capita, 152–53
realism,
  and conflict reduction, 90–91, 100–104,
    195, 268, 287–88
  democratic peace and, 60
  in Hobbesian system, 22–23, 33, 41, 90
  and imbalance of power, 48, 61–62, 88,
    103, 109, 184, 287
  and international trade, 219–20
  measuring the influence of, 104–11, 126n,
    145, 159, 182, 191, 248, 252, 253–57,
    259, 264
  and military preparedness, 23
  national interest in, 228–30
  political theories of, 22, 34
  self-fulfilling prophecy of, 23
Red Cross International, 210
refugees, 164, 204
RELATIVEDEMOC variable, 181–83, 189
RELATIVEDEPEND variable, 181–83, 189
RELATIVEIGO variable, 181–83, 189
religion,
  and conflict, 248, 303
  in Huntington's groupings, 251n–52n, 257
  and peaceful relations, 247
  rulers' decisions about, 17
republican constitutions, see democracy
Rhine Commission, 160, 176
Rhineland, 94, 118
Ricardo, David, 128, 138, 277, 279
Romania, 118, 121, 291
Russia,
  Chinese alliance with, 283–89
  cultural shift in, 251n
  democracy in, 15, 45, 52, 272–73, 283,
    284, 291
  disputes with, 121
  distance computations for, 101n
  ethnic minorities in, 289
  as great power, 101–2, 282
  isolation of, 285
  in Kantian peace, 273, 282–92
  limitations on trade with, 135, 137, 220
  and nuclear power, 284, 285, 304
  options of, 285–86
  political instability of, 290–91
  private investment in, 291
  territory of, 88
  and Thirty Years War, 19

and trust, 289–90
and United Nations, 297
and World War I, 24, 92, 104, 152, 175–76
see also Soviet Union
Rwanda, 164

Sarajevo, assassination in, 177
SATISFIED measure, 186–87, 188, 189
Scandinavia, 31, 45, 196
Schuman, Robert, 24, 25, 228
science, cooperative, 313
scientific methods, in epidemiology, 82–85
scientific progress, and peace, 59
Scotland, 28
security communities,
    alliances and, 89, 163*n*, 173, 214, 225, 229–30
    conflict reduction in, 90
    democratic peace and, 74–76, 231
    economic interdependence and, 277–78
    international organizations in, 158, 163, 297
    legitimacy of, 77
    mutual responsiveness in, 58
    networks in, 75
    regional, 193
    social values of, 77
security dilemma, vicious circle of, 22–23, 179–80
self-interest, 269
separation of government powers, 29, 53
Serbia, 118, 121, 136, 190, 237, 240, 295, 299, 300*n*
Singapore, 144, 193
Sinic civilization, 244, 246, 251, 256, 257, 259, 260, 261
Slavic-Orthodox civilization, 246, 251, 256, 257, 259, 260, 261, 265
Slovakia, 118, 121
Slovenia, 121
Smith, Adam, 29, 36, 128
social capital, 75
social community, models of, 77
socialism, 129, 132, 298
social psychology, 242–43
social welfare, 78–79
soft power, 192
Somalia, 303
South Africa, 232*n*, 252*n*, 260–61
South America, *see* Latin America
Southeast Asia, *see* Asia
South Korea, 222*n*, 232*n*, 296
South Vietnam, 180*n*, 296
sovereignty,
    challenges to, 22, 81
    in conflict reduction, 90, 274
    popular, 18–19
    principle of, 17–19, 21, 23, 28, 75, 180, 303*n*, 310

UN and, 20, 21
    violations of, 64
Soviet Union,
    autarky in, 37, 110, 257
    and cold war, *see* cold war
    and Cuba, 132
    democratization of, 15, 31–32, 51–52, 118, 282
    dissolved (1991), 92, 291
    economic collapse of, 31, 92, 167, 186, 299, 302
    economic isolation of, 25, 144
    as "evil empire," 262
    former, ethnic disputes in, 248, 289
    glasnost and perestroika in, 32
    as great power, 101–2, 260, 261
    and international organizations, 32–33, 167, 214
    and international trade, 227–28
    Marxist-Leninist doctrine in, 293
    in post–cold war era, *see* Russia
    and United Nations, 20, 32–33
    in Warsaw Pact, 104
    in World War II, 298
Spain, 50, 61, 222, 290
Spengler, Oswald, 242
spillover, use of term, 27
SPLIT variable, 250–51, 253–55, 258, 262, 264–66
Sri Lanka, 252*n*
Stalin, Joseph, 70, 262
standard deviation, 108*n*
START treaty delays, 284
Statesman's Yearbook, The, 140
states,
    anarchic, 18, 22–23
    characteristics of, 97
    citizens' empowerment in, 204, 209–11, 274
    citizens' multiple loyalties within, 28
    citizens' rights in, 29
    civil society in, 73, 204, 209
    collective security of, 19
    competition between, 18
    core, 245, 249, 260–61
    extinction of, 180*n*
    great powers, *see* great powers
    interstate systems, 17, 19–21, 29–33, 34
    Kantian subsystem of, 180
    MIDs of, 94–96
    military rivalries of, 37
    minor powers, 195
    modern system of, 16–22
    in multilevel systems, 34
    national interest of, 60, 136
    neighboring, 50, 52, 57, 86, 102, 108, 121, 171, 176, 214, 226, 252, 255*n*, 265, 309
    noncontiguous, 223
    pairs of, *see* dyads

states (*continued*)
  peace between, *see* peace
  postwar national economies of, 24–26
  power ratio of, 103, 185
  preferences of, 230–36
  relative importance of, 17, 18
  satisfaction with status quo of, 186–87, 190
  security interests of, 74, 136
  social responsiveness of, 73
  sovereignty of, 17–19, 20, 21, 23, 28, 75, 180, 303*n*, 310
  strategic thinking in, 52, 54–57
  territorial boundaries of, 57, 86
  and UN authority, 20, 194
  use of term, 17
  violence within, 247–48
statistical analyses,
  adjustments in, 105
  AFFINITY variable in, 231–36
  ALLIES variable in, 104, 109, 173, 189, 214, 216, 225, 226, 236*n*, 252, 253, 256
  autoregressive process AR1 in, 311
  AUT-to-DEM variable in, 119
  AVGDEMOC variable in, 181–83, 189
  AVGDEPEND variable in, 181–83, 189
  AVGIGO variable in, 181–83, 189
  bell-shaped ("normal") curve in, 108*n*
  causality considered in, 97
  for cold war years (1950–85), 232–37
  COW data used in, 94–96, 185, 310–11
  database for, 93
  delimitations of, 106
  DEMOC measure in, 98–100, 109–10, 114–16, 138, 170–73, 213, 215–16, 223, 224–25, 252–53, 256, 265–66
  DEM-to-AUT variable in, 119
  DEPEND variable in, 141, 143, 145–47, 149*n*, 170–73, 214, 216–17, 236*n*, 252–53, 256, 259, 265–66
  for different periods, 111–14
  DISPUTE variable in, 213, 215–16, 224–25, 233–35, 250
  dyads used in, 93–95, 102–3, 250–51, 308–9, 310
  dyad-year as unit in, 105
  empirical, 152
  in epidemiology, 83, 91–94, 105
  fixed-effects model in, 106*n*, 107*n*, 312
  GDPPerCap variable in, 215–17, 223, 226
  GEE used in, 106*n*, 311
  Granger model in, 226*n*, 312–13
  GROWTH variable in, 153
  HEGDEFENSE variable in, 187–88, 189, 190
  HEGPOWER indicator in, 185–86, 188, 189
  of Huntington's theories, 247, 248–69
  IGO variable in, 169–74, 213–18, 225, 232–35, 253, 256

  independent effect in, 105
  least squares regression analysis in, 217*n*
  logistic regression in, 105, 138, 311
  methodology in, 307–13
  model formulated in, 106
  multiple regression analysis, 105
  noncontiguity measure in, 101
  OPEN measure in, 144, 148–49, 223, 224, 225, 227
  peace-years method in, 106*n*
  for period 1885–1992, 92, 98, 102–3, 111, 177, 185, 255, 272
  Polity III data in, 97–99
  POPULATION variable in, 223, 225, 226
  for post-World War II years (1950–92), 249–60, 267
  POWER RATIO variable in, 103, 109, 149*n*, 189, 236*n*, 252, 253, 256
  probability in, 85
  rejecting true hypothesis in, 311
  RELATIVEDEMOC variable in, 181–83, 189
  RELATIVEDEPEND variable, 181–83, 189
  RELATIVEIGO variable, 181–83, 189
  SATISFIED measure in, 186–87, 188, 189
  simultaneous effects in, 235*n*
  SPLIT variable in, 250–51, 253–55, 258, 262, 264
  standard deviation, 108*n*
  Stata package for, 105*n*
  statistical significance computed in, 110–11
  tables, 314–29
  temporal dependence in, 311
  theoretical influences in, 106
  TRADE variable, 222, 224–25, 226*n*
  variance in, 39*n*, 52
  vector autoregression (VAR) in, 312–13
  years excluded from, 93, 309–11
  YEAR variable in, 262*n*
statistical significance, one-tailed tests of, 111*n*
strategy, innovations in, 103
Sudan, 68
suffrage,
  changes in status of, 98–99
  in democracy, 44
  limits on, 176
  property ownership and, 34
Sweden, 222*n*
Switzerland, 81, 87, 99, 161, 222*n*, 232*n*
Syria, 81, 189*n*
system,
  component parts of, 17
  use of term, 16

Taisho democracy, 31, 41, 150
Taiwan, 137, 144, 294, 296

technology,
   English language used in, 299
   in global economy, 20, 21
   military, 22, 298
   and power ratio, 103, 298
   trade and, 134
territorial issues, 86
Thailand, 193, 260
third world, 273
Thirty Years War, 17, 18, 19
Thucydides, 85, 88
Tlateloco, Treaty of, 40
totalitarianism,
   imperfect, 98
   and world wars, 24
Toynbee, Arnold, 242
trade,
   free, 29, 36, 38, 71–72, 126, 129, 137, 144,
      148, 198, 199, 278, 302
   gravity model of, 222–23
   international, *see* international trade
   mutual benefits of, 129, 148
   openness and, 199
   rational self-interest in, 76
   as source of conflict, 132, 134–38
   total, 136–37, 144, 149
trade-to-GDP ratio, 137, 141, 142, 143, 145,
   147, 154, 179, 183n, 214, 253
TRADE variable, 222, 224–25, 226n
transparency, of democracies, 54, 64, 65, 79,
   168, 201
Truman, Harry S., 307
Turgot, Anne Robert, 128
Turkey, 61, 103, 164, 247, 251n, 260–61,
   265, 290, 291

Uganda, 48
Ukraine, democracy in, 15
UN, *see* United Nations
UNDP (United Nations Development Programme), 30, 207, 209, 210–11
UNICEF, 206, 210
unilateralists, 305
Union of International Associations, 160–61
unipolar system, 93, 305
United Fruit, 142
United Kingdom, *see* Great Britain
United Nations (UN),
   and adversarial states, 38
   authority of, 20, 194
   and collective security, 163
   and decolonization, 21
   and democracy, 33, 38, 167–68, 200–
      206
   and elections, 167–68, 201, 204, 210–11
   founding of, 20, 30, 177, 297
   in Gulf War, 303
   and human rights, 30, 33, 202, 204, 210

as IGO, 16, 161, 168
   in Mozambique, 203, 205, 206–11
   and multilateralism, 304
   peacekeeping activities of, 202–6
   secretary general of, 30
   Security Council of, 20, 30, 163, 201, 232n,
      297, 304
   and states' sovereignty, 20, 180n
   structure of, 30–31
   universal nature of, 297
   voting patterns in, 61, 229–36
United States,
   Britain's relationship with, 81, 196, 220,
      288
   and Canada, 16, 196, 212
   Civil War of, 70–71
   and cold war, *see* cold war
   cultural influence of, 299
   defense spending of, 249, 262–64, 299
   distance computations for, 101n
   economic leverage of, 299
   and European integration, 28, 185, 212
   GDP of, 144
   geography of, 88, 185
   as great power, 102, 185, 288, 299
   hegemony of, 58, 93, 185, 186, 189–90,
      297–304
   IGOs and, 31, 289
   interventions by, 62–64, 142–43
   and Iraq, 68, 136, 190, 240
   isolationism in, 185
   and Japan, 196, 212, 231, 294
   and League of Nations, 19–20, 41
   military capability of, 299
   and Mozambique, 208
   and NAFTA, 16, 199, 212, 299
   and NATO, 89, 261
   open economy of, 144
   trade embargoes of, 135–36
   and United Nations, 20, 33, 297, 304
   in Vietnam War, 63, 67, 86, 190
   women suffrage in, 98–99
   in world wars, 176
Universal Declaration of Human Rights
   (1948), 30
Universal Postal Union, 176
UNOCHA (UN Office for Coordination of
   Humanitarian Activities), 210
Uruguay, 40
USSR, *see* Soviet Union

vector autoregression (VAR), 312–13
Versailles Treaty, 118
vicious circle,
   anarchy as, 22–23
   Hobbesian system and, 42
   of military threats, 41, 179–80
   of political differences, 228

Vietnam,
    communism in, 34
    in security community, 193
    sovereignty of, 180*n*
    U.S. troops in, 63, 67, 86, 190
Vietnam War, 67, 86, 139*n*, 190, 262, 263,
    274
virtuous circles, 24–33, 197–237
    feedback loops and, 38
    IGOs in, 212–18
    interruption of, 41
    Kantian triangle in, 29–33, 38, 40, 228
    as self-reinforcing, 35
voting rights, 34, 44, 98–99, 176

war,
    anarchy and, 90, 230
    battlefield operations in, 67
    between autocracies, 49, 50, 180, 275
    between democracies, 47–48
    casualties in, 67
    constant danger of, 85
    cost-benefit analysis of, 56, 58, 66–67, 79,
        151
    defined as deaths in battle, 95
    and democratization process, 51–52
    disruption caused by, 185, 278
    diversionary theory of, 117, 151–52
    domestic political costs of, 54
    economic irrationality of, 26
    escalation to, 94, 96
    events leading to, 52
    Geneva Convention and, 67
    imperialism and, 151, 152
    and MIDs, 94–96
    multiple influences in, 50–51, 53, 69
    necessity of, 81, 303*n*
    nuclear threat of, *see* nuclear war
    and principle of sovereignty, 23, 303*n*
    security dilemma and, 23
    state extinction in, 180*n*
    trade deterred by, 37
    see also conflict; *specific wars*
War Powers Act (1973), 274
Warsaw Pact,
    autocracies in, 111
    coercive actions of, 163
    in cold war, 220, 293, 300
    conflicts in, 104
    disbanded (1991), 92
    as military alliance, 173, 265
Waterloo, Battle of, 118
Wealth of Nations, The (Smith), 29
West,
    and cold war, *see* cold war
    economic growth in, 287
    and future peace, *see* Kantian peace
    and human rights, 244, 294

    in Huntington's civilization grouping, 246,
        251, 252*n*, 256–61, 265
    vs. "others," 241, 243, 244, 249, 258–60,
        263, 267–69
    postmodernism in, 303
    Russia-China alliance and, 283–89
    warming relations between China and, 16,
        147, 223, 272–73, 285, 293–97
Western Europe,
    cooperation in, 196
    on democracy scale, 110
    Kantian factors in, 193
Western European Union, 28
Westphalia, Treaty of,
    and Concert of Europe, 19
    as European construction, 33, 34
    and principle of sovereignty, 17, 18, 21, 28
    and vicious circles, 23
WHO (World Health Organization), 206
Wilson, Woodrow, 228
    Fourteen Points of, 30
    and League of Nations, 19–20, 30, 41
World Bank, 21, 30, 168, 201, 299
World Food Programme, 210
World Health Organization (WHO), 206
World Trade Organization (WTO), 21, 30, 38,
    165, 168, 194, 297, 299
World War I, 174–77
    alliances in, 19–20, 92, 104, 173, 176, 236
    crisis leading to, 23, 176–77
    death rate in, 300
    dyadic relationships in, 175
    Germany and, 19, 24, 92, 104, 152, 175, 278
    global economy and, 20–21, 150, 174–76,
        278–80
    hegemony and, 184–85, 188
    information gap in, 93
    international organizations and, 160, 174–
        75, 176
    international trade and, 183*n*
    and League of Nations, 19–20, 30
    liberalism and, 278–79
    Versailles Treaty of, 118
World War II,
    combatants in, 310
    death rate in, 300
    events leading to, 52, 94
    Germany and, 19–20, 22, 24, 25, 31, 94,
        288, 298, 310
    global economy and, 20–21
    Great Depression and, 20, 24–25, 41
    hegemony and, 184–85, 188, 298
    information gap in, 93
    postwar conflicts, 161, 174
    postwar democratization, 179
    postwar Europe, 24–33, 40, 193
    postwar networks, 26–29, 113, 160, 161,
        173, 195, 216, 231

postwar peace, 112, 194, 228, 229–37
postwar prosperity, 25, 132, 179, 237, 298
sovereignty and, 23
totalitarianism vs. democracy in, 24, 232n, 236
and UN, 20, 21
WTO, *see* World Trade Organization

Yearbook of International Organizations, 169–70
YEAR variable, 262n
Yeltsin, Boris, 286, 292n
Yugoslavia, 252n

Zemin, Jiang, 286